A GUIDE TO SAFE AND RESPONSIBLE BOATING

Boat Smart Chronicles

LAKE MICHIGAN DEVOURS ITS WOUNDED

Tom Rau

- *The Lake of the Sinking Waters*
- *Accessibility*
- *Close Quarter Arena*
- *Congested Waters*
- *Seasonal Dangers*
- *Wanton Ignorance*
- *Life Jacket Denial*
- *Naive Assumptions*
- *Rescue Responders Capabilities and Limitations*
- *Sensible Boating, Key to Search and Rescue*
- *A Historical View of Recreational Boating*

Seaworthy
PUBLICATIONS

Seaworthy Publications, Inc. • PORT WASHINGTON, WISCONSIN

The Boat Smart Chronicles, Lake Michigan Devours Its Wounded
by Tom Rau

Copyright ©2006 Tom Rau

ISBN 1-892399-23-7

Published in the USA by: Seaworthy Publications, Inc.
626 W. Pierre
Port Washington, WI 53074
PHONE: 262-268-9250
FAX: 262-268-9208
E-MAIL: orders@seaworthy.com
WEB: www.seaworthy.com

PHOTOS: Todd & Brad Reed Photography, LLC
Marge Beaver, Photography Plus
Tom Rau, Boat Smart
Jeff Kiessel Ludington Daily News, girls on Ludington breakwater
Rod Burdick, motor vessel Columbia Star, Mackinac Bridge
Jim Kransberger, boat fire

ILLUSTRATIONS: Amanda Thomas
Jill Minidis
Daniel Wrzesinski

EDITS: Richard Hubbard
Richard Brown
Betsy Reed

COVER DESIGN: Ken Quant, Broad Reach Marketing & Design, Mequon, Wisconsin

Library of Congress Cataloging-in-Publication Data

Rau, Tom.
   The Boat Smart Chronicles : Lake Michigan devours its wounded : a guide to safe and responsible boating / Tom Rau.
      p. cm.
   ISBN 1-892399-23-7 (alk. paper)
 1. Boats and boating--Michigan, Lake--Safety measures 2. Boating accidents--Michigan, Lake--Safety measures. 3. Navigation--Michigan, Lake--Safety measures. I. Title.

GV777.55.R38 2006
797.1'09774--dc22

2006042232

DEDICATION

To America's professional rescue responders land, sea and air and to citizen rescue volunteers you are indeed a joy to behold. With resounding respect, I salute you all.

More of what others are saying...

"Excellent, a must read for anyone who goes to sea and should be a required read for beginning boaters. Great Lakes Maritime Academy will use this book in conjunction with our survival training classes."

Rear Admiral, John Tanner
Superintendent, Great Lakes Maritime Academy

"As former Coast Guard Ninth District and Atlantic Area Commander, I often received reports of recreational boating deaths and injuries—most were absolutely avoidable. I urge that anyone young or old, experienced or novice who lives or plays on or near the water to take this book to heart. It's offers an invaluable ounce of prevention that could well save your life."

Vice Admiral Jim Hull, U.S. Coast Guard (ret)

"I am extremely pleased to see that Tom Rau has taken the time to put forward a lasting collection of his fabulous 'Boat Smart' stories. Boaters who have enjoyed his weekly column for years now stand to benefit by having his timeless words of wisdom at their finger tips on a lasting basis."

Anthony Popiel, Commander, U.S. Coast Guard

"Their folksy tone bolstered by fascinating detail and eyewitness accounts, Tom Rau's stories of inland sea survival – and disaster – have thrilled me for years. Rau's cautionary tales are a must-read for any would-be boater – and a captivating read for anyone, even a non-boater like me."

Ben Beversluis
Lakeshore Editor, the Grand Rapids Press

"I strongly urge all boaters, fisherman, snowmobilers and anyone else that spends time on the water or ice to read this book. Senior Chief Tom Rau has put a collective lifetime of boating lessons learned 'the hard way' by boaters into this book. This must-read tells it all!"

George Miller, Director of Flight Operations, County Rescue Services, Green Bay Wisconsin/former United States Marine Corp Combat Pilot, recipient Distinguished Flying Cross

"Historically, most of those who 'went down to the sea in boats' were skilled mariners. Today all it takes is money and few if any skills. Tom Rau's 'Boat Smart Chronicles' reveals that this is often a hard way and even fatal way to approach boating. For certain, it's ways that mariners of old would find incomprehensible."

Steve Herald
President, Association for Great Lakes Maritime History

"As I read 'Boat Smart Chronicles,' I found myself shaking my head knowing it's a true miracle that far more boaters haven't died. Hopefully this remarkable exposé on recreational boating will lead to educational measures that have safe-guarded scuba divers for years."

Vickie M. Annis
Master Scuba Diver Trainer, Professional Association of Diving Instructors

ACKNOWLEDGEMENTS

During the 2001 Coast Guard festival in Grand Haven, Michigan, Coast Guard Commandant, James M. Loy presented me with the 2000 Alex Haley award for the Boat Smart column. Alex Haley, the famed author of *Roots*, served twenty years in the Coast Guard, retiring as a Chief Petty Officer. After the award presentation, the Commandant approached me and thanked me for spreading the Boat Smart message while noting that the Coast Guard has implemented Operation "BoatSmart" nationwide. "You have created a process that is taking on a life of its own," he said.

I pointed up to the second floor of the Group Grand Haven building located across the street from where we were standing and said, "Admiral, those guys and gals up there in the search and rescue operation's center also deserve a lion's share of the credit. Without them, I simply would not have available first-hand accounts of search and rescue cases so vital to the Boat Smart column."

These same sources so close to the search and rescue process still feed the column as I continue to pound out Boat Smart copy; these sources also have proven to be invaluable regarding the book. There have been so many contributors, in fact, I elected not to name individuals but rather the organizations they serve. These good folks are team players serving a common good, and recognizing their collective efforts will do. In fact, to name one contributor and not another would offend them all.

Let me begin with my fellow chiefs, many of whom I served with along the eastern shore of Lake Michigan along with their top-gun crews, who have provided me hands-on accounts of search and rescue cases. More importantly, they have provided me Boat Smart stories because they firmly stand by the safety messages these stories impart. A will to spread the Boat Smart message extends up the Coast Guard chain of command: Group Grand Haven command has edited Boat Smart copy and provided valuable feedback, the folks in the Ninth District headquarters, which oversees the Great Lakes, have been terrific in supporting the Boat Smart cause, and more than once the air folks at Coast Guard Traverse Air have shared their rescue experiences and keen insights regarding the challenges they face as rescue responders. Lastly, the Coast Guard Auxiliary: these citizen patriots have performed countless recreational boating Vessel Safety Checks and have amassed a wealth of dockside information that I have tapped into over the years and passed onto boaters. In all, what a search and rescue asset these Coast Guard folks are. There is none better.

The desire, however, to disseminate safety information to recreational boaters is also shared by a greater collective voice outside the Coast Guard. Sheriff marine deputies, conservation officers, and safe boating advocates all champion the cause. They and so many others have provided me invaluable feedback that I have recorded in nearly 200 interviews gathered between 2003 and 2005 during my journeys around Lake Michigan. You know who you are, and I can't thank you enough.

Just as one might expect feedback from professionals committed to spreading the Boat Smart message came as well from the commercial fleet: from captains of large motor vessels to captains of small passenger-carrying vessels, all have expressed a common desire to educate the recreational boating fleet. I thank the dozens of captains I rode with for inviting me onto their bridges and allowing me to witness firsthand the ordeals and tribulations imposed upon them by recreational boaters—transgressions they must so often bear in silent indignation. You good fellows know who you are, and I think the world of you all: truly the Great Lakes' consummate maritime professionals.

This collective effort to shape the Boat Smart message, though, would be of little value if it lacked a forum in which to be voiced. Providing that forum are the many newspapers and magazines that have carried the Boat Smart column over the years. You good folks also know who you are, and I hail your invaluable commitment as you gave up precious space in your publications to spread the Boat Smart message.

Then there are the radio and TV folks who have joined league in spreading the Boat Smart message. One particular radio station in southern Michigan helped me record twenty-one 60-second Boat Smart radio spots that reached millions of listeners over the airways throughout the Midwest, and across the globe via the Internet. Also, let me give my appreciation to the web sites that link to the Boat Smart site. I extend a huge thanks to you all!

Then there are the boaters who have shared their stories with me or my mates, often revealing their less than Boat Smart behavior, knowing that it would find its way into print. That they divulged their boating foibles so others might learn speaks well of them, and should they read their story in the book, they will know that it's still serving a greater good. Also, I want to thank those many souls for offering encouragement through e-mails, letters to editors, and in person. These words often provided me the incentive to continue to write the Boat Smart column. You know who you are, and your thoughtfulness touched me so.

Lastly, I salute the gifted folks who helped edit the book. Not just the grammar, but the content. As professional mariners no one was more qualified to edit the material than these intuitive maritime minds, and for darn sure you know who you are. Remember, I owe you a beverage or two of your choice as I do my publisher at Seaworthy Publications, a long-time Lake Michigan rag sailor in his own right, and a staunch advocate of the Boat Smart message.

So, was this massive collection of real-time recreational boating data that I collected and published over two decades worth it? You bet! I'm absolutely convinced that whoever reads the *Boat Smart Chronicles* regardless of his or her level of experience can't help but be a more alert and far safer person on the water. I know I am, Coast Guard background or not, and I promise you will be too.

Tom Rau

Contents

AUTHOR BIO   245

A GUIDE TO SAFE AND RESPONSIBLE BOATING

Boat Smart Chronicles

Lake Michigan Devours Its Wounded

Mission Brief

Before Coast Guard boat and air crews embark on a mission, it's standard operating procedure for the person in command to deliver a brief to the crew. So I thought, why not follow this pre-mission procedure. Instead of an introduction I will provide a mission brief on the book's objectives mixed with a slice of background information to provide overview. That said, let's get on with the brief.

The Coast Guard enjoys a rich tradition as Guardian of the Inland Seas, a stewardship that dates back to the heralded U.S. Lifesaving Service and its hardy crews that nineteenth century newsmen and many of their contemporaries often venerated as "Storm Warriors" and "Heroes of the Surf." Although as glamorous as this noble maritime tradition might seem, there is an ugly and often heartbreaking downside to assisting mariners in distress, especially now in this modern era of recreational boating.

So often the Coast Guard, along with other marine rescue agencies, must deal with the painful aftermath of an ill-fated rescue. This task is made ever more painful by the fact that most recreational boating accidents can be prevented if the boaters are aware of, or prepared to deal with, unexpected emergencies. Such emergencies, when they occur, are often the byproduct of boater shortcomings. It seems a great deal more sensible to prevent boating calamities in the first place by educating boaters rather than dealing with the sour aftermath of boater miscues. Thus, the *Boat Smart Chronicles* were born.

This book addresses these recreational boating shortcomings. What more effective way than to use the follies of others to instruct boaters and water enthusiasts in the ways to avoid the unfortunate and sometimes fatal mistakes others have made. When I began developing the material for this book I didn't ask what do people need to know to keep safe, I let the hundreds of stories I wrote over the years do that. This wide array of boating information has resulted in a collective learning curve that promises to benefit all boaters whether novice or old salt.

The *Chronicles* capture these stories in two formats: "On Watch" cases involve the Coast Guard and are told from the viewpoint of the rescue responder and the survivors. "Case Files" are cases processed by other marine rescue agencies, cases reported in newspapers, or cases reported from boater's firsthand accounts.

Both formats—"On Watch" and "Case Files"— are followed by a "Boat Smart Brief" which highlights the lessons learned from the case and how boaters can avoid ill fortunes. In all, this book documents over 200 real-life stories and anecdotes rich with water-wise lessons and enhanced by photos, illustrations and side bars.

Most of the stories in this book occurred between 1986 and 2005. In that span of nearly twenty years, the prevalence of boating misbehavior promises a continuum that shows little promise of improvement. My publisher and I went back and forth about his concern that by placing dates on stories I would outdate the material. Not a concern, I advised him, for if current trends in recreational boating continue—all signs indicate they will—yesterday's follies will surely be tomorrow's repeats.

So, while the book strives to enlighten boaters, the stories cast light on the often "dark side" of recreational boating, revealing time and again why thousands of recreational boaters and water enthusiasts have needlessly died or been seriously injured, and will continue to die and be seriously injured unless countermeasures are adopted in particular legislation mandating boating education for all ages. Hopefully too the *Chronicles* will encourage stiffer laws for those who operate vessels under the influence of alcohol and drugs, and harsher penalties for those who make false Maydays. If the following stories fail to arouse public outcry on these issues, I beg to know what it will take to arouse an effect.

I can't imagine a more suitable stage than Lake Michigan to enact the *Boat Smart Chronicles*. On one hand it possesses qualities analogous to a great ocean, while on the other hand it offers a multitude of safe havens in the form of bays, river-channel outlets, and connecting inland lakes. To access Lake Michigan's vast reaches via its many outlets is as effortless as climbing aboard a boat. I know of no other body of water that is so ocean-like and yet so accessible as Lake Michigan.

Lake Michigan also features ocean-like cargo ships and smaller commercial vessels, including cruise ships, that weave through the marine tapestry and create conflict and drama with recreational players. And the *Chronicles* have drawn from a huge cast of players: the State of Michigan alone has led the nation in registered recreational boats for a decade, finally yielding to second place in 2004, falling short by a mere 1,272 boats to Florida's 946,072 recreational boats. It's not only recreational boaters, however, that fall prey to the lake's precarious moods. Other water enthusiasts, mainly beach goers and pier and breakwater strollers, have also died in scores. These issues are addressed in the book as well.

In short, Lake Michigan features it all. I'm sure the undesirable traits boaters have displayed on the Inland Sea are reflected by recreational boaters and water enthusiasts nationwide, whether it be San Francisco Bay, Great Salt Lake, the Colorado River, or Lake Okeechobee. In the *Chronicles*, I often reference the Coast Guard's annual *Boating Statistics*, a computation of recreational boating data provided by the 50 States and the U.S. territories. This insightful report provides details such as the time of day, size and type of boat involved in accidents, the weather conditions, accident causes, and even the age groups of those involved in recreational boating mishaps. True to form, Lake Michigan boating mishaps mirror national statistics, proving that careless boating can happen anywhere. To that effect, the *Chronicles* venture into the greater Lake Michigan basin including inland lakes and streams, and beyond to Lake Huron and Lake Erie, and even as far as the U.S. coastal waters to show that in any waters, recreational boaters share universal challenges and failings, deadly as they may be.

The *Chronicles* also pay tribute to the nineteenth century mariners and the ugly toll Lake Michigan inflicted on their commercial fleet. Lake Michigan finds no equal in our nation's maritime annals for the sheer number of shipwrecks that lie beneath her waters. Thank God, because of the carnage that befell these men of iron and ships of wood and their will to overcome adversities through invention we now find few, if any, commercial mariners falling prey to the lake's unruly will.

As for recreational boaters, now that's another story. They have suffered far more casualties than all the Great Lakes' shipwreck victims of old. So, batten down the hatches for a turbulent voyage ahead into uncharted, unregulated waters churned up by a "do as you please" mentality so reminiscent of San Francisco's old Barbary Coast. If you believe this analogy is off course, I urge you to read the following stories and then tell me that recreational boating isn't in need of being re-righted.

That said, let's haul in the lines and get underway for a sure voyage to safe and responsible boating.

The Lake of the Sinking Waters

HISTORY TELLS US THAT THE FIRST EUROPEAN TO VENTURE ONTO LAKE MICHIGAN was a Frenchman named Jean Nicolet who in 1634, while canoeing from east to west across Lake Huron, stopped at Mackinac Island. From there, his westerly bound journey carried him across upper Lake Michigan to Wisconsin near Green Bay where he hoped to encounter Chinese that would lead him westward to the illusive gateway to Peking. Instead, skin-clad natives greeted him, referring to the lake he had just crossed as "The Lake of the Stinking Waters." For Nicolet it turned out to be a stinking disappointment, as he soon discovered that to the west lay a vast uncharted wilderness.

OMINOUS BEGINNINGS

The origin of the phrase "Stinking Waters" is unclear. However, today Lake Michigan might more appropriately be called "The Lake of the Sinking Waters." Plenty of maritime disasters have occurred to claim the name "Sinking Waters," beginning with the 45-ton *Griffin*, the first sailing vessel to ply Lake Michigan. It went down with the loss of all hands on September 18, 1679. According to Steve Harold, Director of Manistee County Historical Museum and noted maritime historian, after the loss of the *Griffin*, nearly 5,000 commercial ships have sunk on Lake Michigan, carrying hundreds of sailors to watery graves.

As to be expected, historians dispute the exact number of commercial shipwrecks, but most agree that Lake Michigan, by far, has claimed the most victims across the Inland Seas and that includes Lake Superior, which indisputably holds the title as the fiercest of the Great Lakes. Yet as "superior" as she may be, Lake Michigan has proven, by far, to be more deadly.

EASY PREY

Two conditions allowed Lake Michigan to prey on nineteenth century mariners: heavy commercial vessel traffic, and her narrowness, which left little room for mariners to escape her wrath. Lake Michigan centers on a north-south axis that runs nearly 333 miles, comprising the line of demarcation between the states of Wisconsin and Michigan. Land lies within a short reach of either side of that axis, and for yesteryear's ship captains, attempting to outrun heavy weather with land so close to leeward often found themselves being driven aground. The close quarters drew tighter in the lake's northern regions, as sailing ships funneled through Manitou passage, bordered by North and South Manitou Islands to the west and nearby Sleeping Bear and Pyramid Points to the east.

Squeezing through Manitou passage, known as the "narrows," vessels sailing north skirted along a series of islands above the Manitou (South Fox, North Fox, Beaver, Garden and Hog Islands), and then through Grays Reef Passage, a narrow, rocky

This is a view of the Manitou Passage known as the "Narrows." In the foreground is Sleeping Bear Dunes National Park and on the horizon the Manitou Islands. Many nineteenth century sailors were driven aground within the Narrows.

corridor leading to the Straits of Mackinac. During mild weather, captains faced little danger, but the entire 333-mile length of Lake Michigan lay broadside to the prevailing westerly winds that often, with little notice, bore down on nineteenth century sailing ships. Fog and collisions with other boats and objects also claimed a deadly toll within her narrow span.

Another danger that mariners faced was transporting resources and perishables from land to boat. Few man-made pier systems and river channels existed along Lake Michigan's 300-mile long shorelines during the early nineteenth century. Kenosha, Wisconsin, introduced the first extended pier on Lake Michigan in 1842. Before the introduction of piers, local townsfolk transported goods to shore aboard "lighters" from sailing vessels anchored off shore. One Kenosha resident describes ferrying goods to shore in December of 1842 in

wet garments that he had to change out of eight to ten times a day to shield against the freezing rain.

On the lake, captains faced exposed moorings and often took deadly gambles as their ships and crews sat offshore while lighters and barges transported lumber, fruit and other resources to and from seaward-waiting craft. Often high seas driven by gale force winds swooped down on helpless mariners.

Even long after local lake front communities developed harbor systems, the lake continued to assault vessels, especially sailboats. By 1860 there were on all of the lakes an estimated 1,500 ships, of which over 1,100 were sailing vessels. The winter of 1870–1871 proved especially harsh; more than 214 people died in maritime-related accidents across the Great Lakes. Many of these occurred on Lake Michigan.

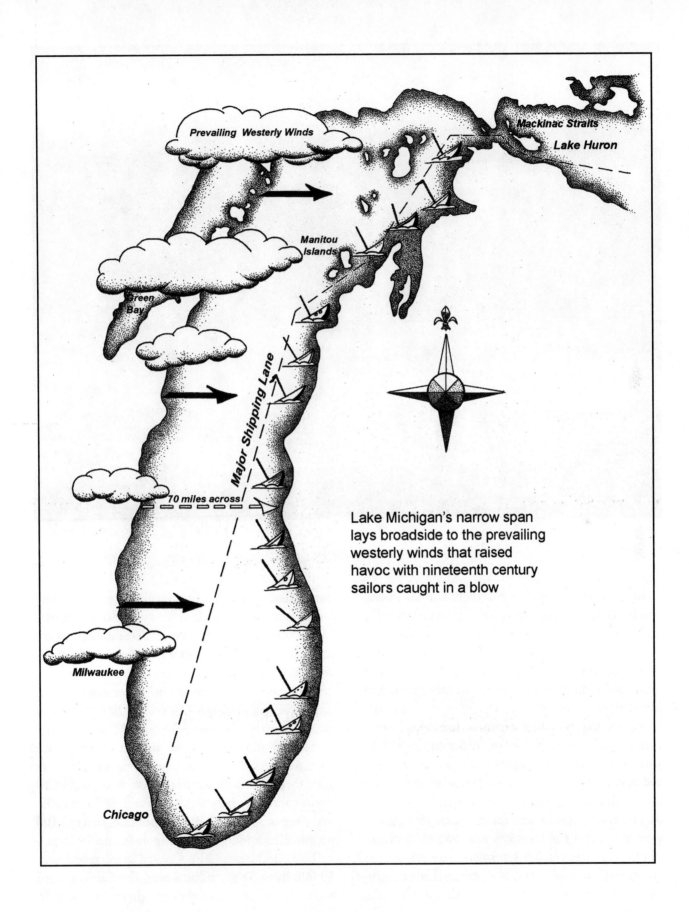

Prevailing Westerly Winds

Mackinac Straits

Lake Huron

Manitou Islands

Green Bay

Major Shipping Lane

70 miles across

Milwaukee

Chicago

Lake Michigan's narrow span lays broadside to the prevailing westerly winds that raised havoc with nineteenth century sailors caught in a blow

Lake Michigan unleashes its furor on the Ludington Lighthouse. Woe be it for nineteenth century mariners who found themselves under siege from the lake's unruly will.

Enough was enough – mariners and lakefront communities fought back with human resources and invention. The first steam-driven tugs appeared on Lake Michigan in the mid 1850s, providing sail boat captains some relief by offering a means of being towed to safety. Tugs also provided the first motored search and rescue resource on Lake Michigan. Most rescues, however, were conducted by the U.S. Lifesaving Service (USLSS) with oared life boats, mostly near shore or from the beach. By 1879, the service began earnestly deploying lifesaving stations around Lake Michigan. By the end of the nineteenth century, 25 stations existed around the lake, representing 40 percent of USLSS Great Lakes stations.

With the introduction of steam, and later gasoline and diesel powered motor vessels constructed of iron and steel coupled with advanced electronic navigation systems, commercial vessels became far less vulnerable to the lake's voracious appetite. Large well-built motor vessels could out-muscle the lake. The pay off is that today commercial accidents seldom occur.

MODERN DAY PREY

Lake Michigan and its sister lakes have long since changed diets. They now have recreational boaters and other water enthusiasts to feast on. Coast Guard figures certainly bare this out. From 1986 to 2005, in those cases in which they responded, nearly 2,100 people died and many were recreational boaters.

The good news—the Coast Guard saved over 10,000 lives. What if, however, the Coast Guard had not reached in time the ones that were saved? In that event, over 12,000 recreational water-related

On October 20, 1905, one of the worst storms recorded to date on Lake Michigan drove the schooner *Lydia* aground around 500 feet from the south pier at Manistee. The three-man crew was rescued by the members of the United States Lifesaving Service at Manistee.

fatalities would have transpired across the Great Lakes during that 20-year period. Those figures do not include lives saved by local rescue agencies and private parties, especially "Good Samaritans" that according to my research, number in the thousands.

What's more, most recreational fatalities on the Great Lakes transpire during a short boating season. I dread to think what the count would be if boaters had access to the Great Lakes year round. During 2005 alone, I know of 76 recreational water-related fatalities that occurred within the western region of the Great Lakes; most of those occurred during a short boating season. Seventy-six lives lost you would think would raise eyebrows, but apparently not, for no public outcry has been heard. Why? Out of sight, out of mind: Great Lakes seasons come and go and soon fade

into the mists of time, as do the memories of those departed.

Also mitigating public reaction to recreational boating deaths is a popular mindset that links boating disasters to boats and foul weather. This beguiling link between foul weather and boating mishaps is dangerously misleading because it assumes that boating accidents occur only during foul weather. This widely held perspective is understandable considering all the ado that has been made over Lake Michigan's shipwreck history. Yet, over the second half of the twentieth century far more recreational boaters have died within the Lake Michigan marine environment than have merchant sailors, and most of the recreational fatalities occurred not in foul weather but during fair weather.

The last major Lake Michigan commercial shipwreck fatality struck nearly a half century ago.

The 623-foot lake freighter *Carl D. Bradley* sank on November 18, 1958, near Beaver Island, breaking up in 30-foot seas with the loss of 33 men. The disaster drew national media coverage. Yet what attention have hundreds of Lake Michigan recreational boating fatalities drawn? None.

Not only do Lake Michigan shipwrecks overshadow recreational boating fatalities, the most celebrated shipwreck of the twentieth century, *Titanic*, with the loss of 1,522 lives, pales in comparison to recreational boating fatalities. Over a recent 43-year period 47,273 recreational boaters nationwide have died. These fatalities do not include non-registered boats or other recreational water-related fatalities. If the U.S. commercial fleet generated these numbers it would cause "60-Minutes-like" spectaculars while elevating finger-pointing to new heights. Sadly, however, since there is no one but the boater to blame, the "finger-pointers" show little interest.

By the way, were you aware that 47,273 recreational boaters died? If so you are amongst a great minority.

Economics is another factor that diminishes public concern regarding recreational fatalities. Other than the direct economic impact a fatality may inflict on loved ones, residual cost to the public is minimal. On the other hand should a commercial maritime enterprise experience fatalities the economic repercussions, legal woes, and regulatory penalties could result in serious financial repercussions. Enough economic pain, in fact, that companies go to great efforts to avoid such loses through preventive measures. Conversely, few if any, economic repercussions exist regarding recreational boating that would prompt preventive measures in the manner that safeguards the commercial fleet. After all, what does a boater have to lose other than his or her life.

Another factor that is very insidious and distracts public awareness regarding recreational fatalities is weather. Unless a recreational boating fatality is foul-weather related, it draws little attention. I believe that the foul-weather "shipwreck syndrome" has so permeated the public mindset that it's difficult for many people to escape its influence. While discussing recreational mishaps with boaters, I find many readily assume that the boating casualty stemmed from a boater's failure to pay heed to weather forecasts, which then leads into a dissertation on boater's lack of respect for the lake's prowess. I point out that in a few cases foul weather plays a part; however, I further note that nearly 83 percent of recreational boating mishaps nationwide occur in calm to moderate weather. Of the total rescue cases conducted by the Coast Guard across the Great Lakes in 2004, only one percent of the cases were beset by foul weather. When I point this out to people they look at me as if I dumped Lake Michigan's shipwreck history up-side down like an over-turned turtle.

This foul-weather misconception, I believe, places recreational boaters in far greater peril than heavy weather did with commercial mariners a century ago. Yesteryear's mariners understood heavy weather risks, and although they possessed the skills to deal with those risks, they simply lacked the tools to overcome the storm. Today's recreational boaters possess the tools but lack the skills. Worse yet, many simply fail to even see a need for boating skills. After all, what harm could a "nice boating day" generate? Answer: Most recreational boating accidents, personal injuries and fatalities occur on "nice days." And so I stress, when you feel you want to let down your guard around water, that is when you should be foremost on guard. The many Boat Smart stories to follow bear this out.

And in all due respect to nineteenth century mariners, most were driven by economic necessity and personal survival, struggling the best they could with limited means to etch out a living. In my heart, they hold a special place, for without these men of iron and ships of wood the economic advancement of this great nation and its Midwest, and many of the advantages that we now enjoy, simply would not exist.

I would be less than forthright, however, if I claimed to hold the same respect for many recreational boaters and water sports enthusiasts. As you read the less-than-Boat-Smart stories to follow, I believe you will share my viewpoint, which is bolstered by many years of performing search and rescue on Lake Michigan at seven different

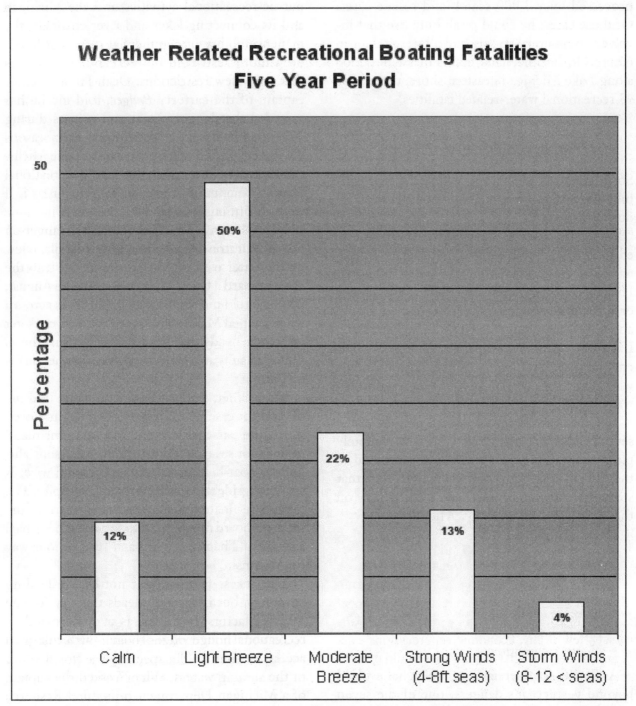

Weather Related Recreational Boating Fatalities
Five Year Period

Percentage

50

50%

22%

13%

12%

4%

Calm | Light Breeze | Moderate Breeze | Strong Winds (4-8ft seas) | Storm Winds (8-12 < seas)

Coast Guard *Boating Statistics* between 1999 and 2003 reported 3,194 recreational boating fatalities in which weather at the time of the fatality could be determined: 83 percent of those fatalities occurred in calm to moderate weather.

search and rescue facilities, including the Coast Guard rescue coordination center at Group Grand Haven. Note, that during it all, I've been involved in only one commercial rescue.

I asked Commander Anthony Popiel just before he completed his three-year tour of duty as

Commander Group Grand Haven how many rescues his station crews executed during his tenure (May 2001 to July 2004). Group Grand Haven's eight stations provide search and rescue coverage along the eastern shore of Lake Michigan and 25 miles out into the Lake. Under his watch, crews processed over 3,000 search and rescue cases. Of those cases, he could recall only five that involved commercial vessels, and all were minor in nature. On the other hand, during that same period along Lake Michigan's eastern shore, there were 43 recreational water-related fatalities.

SEVEN DANGEROUS FACTORS

So what allows the marine environment to willfully aim at the recreational community, especially during fair weather? I read and reread years of "Boat Smart" columns. Many of the stories repeated themselves while weaving familiar patterns. I narrowed these patterns down to seven factors that I believe draw recreational boaters and other water enthusiasts into harm's way. Although these factors apply to most waters, the Great Lakes, including Lake Michigan, possess dangers unique to their environment. Still, the real-life stories to follow will strike a common chord wherever recreational water-related activities abound.

Let me stress again: Weather is not one of the seven factors that lead boaters astray. It definitely plays a role, but only a minor one, compared to the real villains. Who are these culprits then that spare the commercial fleet, but willfully prey on the recreational community? They are:

- Accessibility
- Close Quarters
- Congested Waters
- Short Season
- Ignorance
- Life Jacket Denial
- Naive Assumptions

As for the commercial fleet, which has evolved beyond yesteryear's dangers, one of the seven factors imposes a threat that captains and crews can't avoid, can't outrun, can't wait out, can't even predict—the accessibility factor. As a greater cross-mix of recreational boaters and water enthusiasts pursue recreational activities on Lake Michigan and its connecting lakes and river channels, the maneuverability of commercial vessels becomes even more restricted by recreational activities that enjoy few restrictions. Dean Hobbs, senior captain of the carferry *Badger*, told me he has sounded the danger signal more times during 2003 than he has over the previous eight seasons combined. Captain Hobbs, a veteran Lake Michigan captain believes many within the recreational boating community treat Lake Michigan as if it were a giant unsupervised water park.

Nate Mazurek, a United States park ranger on South Manitou Island, expressed a similar view on the water park theme. During my visit to the island aboard a Coast Guard vessel in late August, 2003, he told me while sweeping his eyes across a white capped Manitou passage: "Boaters can't get into their heads that it's a wilderness out there. Unfortunately anyone can access it, whether qualified or not."

His partner, Ranger Rachael Deque, told me of a recent case where a father and son motored across the passage from the Michigan mainland in five foot seas aboard a 10-foot make-shift aluminum boat held together by pipes and wire. It sank alongside the South Manitou Island pier. The rangers re-floated the boat and after starting the small outboard motor, the father turned to Rachael and said: "Thanks, my son and I are on our way to Wisconsin."

The access factor might not be the leading adversary, but it certainly leads the way for the other six factors to take aim as an ever-expanding recreational hodgepodge of boaters with unlimited access, but limited "boat smarts," access the lake of the sinking waters. When I asked the captain of a Michigan Department of Natural Resource research vessel if he's noticed an increase in recreational boating he replied: "Yes, I see more and more boaters but with less and less smarts." Read on....

Accessibility

BETWEEN 2003 AND 2005, I MADE SEVERAL TRIPS AROUND LAKE MICHIGAN conducting research for the book. I marveled at how access to the lake seemed effortless, even in remote areas like Big Bay de Noc, tucked away in a northwest corner of the lake above Green Bay. At Big Bay de Noc and around the lake, the challenge wasn't finding access roads but rather choosing which one to take. But it hasn't always been like that.

REMOTE TO ROBUST

After Jean Nicolet's first-time visit to the 'Lake of the Stinking Waters' in 1634, only a handful of explorers, traders and men of the cloth traversed Lake Michigan over the next one-hundred-and-fifty years. Even by 1810 the population of the entire Michigan territory held a mere 4,762 inhabitants. However, with the opening of the Erie Canal in 1825, Lake Michigan access began in earnest. By 1837 the 205-foot long *Illinois* was steaming from Buffalo to Chicago, completing the 1,054-mile run in five days, a journey that took earlier explorers months of hardship. By 1845, several steamboats made regularly-scheduled trips between Buffalo and Chicago, and in 1846 the first railroad rolled into Michigan. By the end of the decade, Michigan's population had expanded to 212, 267.

Michigan's main resources—agricultural products, timber, and minerals—found huge markets both in the Atlantic States and Midwest. By the end of the Civil War, Michigan was supplying enough salt to satisfy the needs of the entire Midwest and Mississippi valley. Michigan's fruit crops had reached national prominence by the 1860s. Much of the fruit was grown along the sandy, hilly eastern

shore of Lake Michigan and the adjoining lands that run from South Haven to the Traverse City area, a 200 mile stretch called the "Fruit Strip." So lucrative were these fruit crops that many within the industry referred to them as "green gold." Even far outpacing the demand for fruit, was the demand for Michigan lumber, the total value of which far exceeded all the gold extracted from the California gold fields during the great gold rush.

Regional and later national demand for Michigan resources required access and a means to transport product to market. A series of coastal river systems that fed Lake Michigan were dredged, channeled, and reinforced with stone, wood, and iron to allow access to the resources. These port systems also provided refuge from an ill-tempered lake that was often provoked by sudden weather variances.

Chicago, the hub of commerce for the Midwest and points beyond, provided the terminus for Michigan's products, products from the eastern seaboard, and products arriving from distant lands.

By the turn of the twentieth century Chicago had expanded into the nation's second largest city,

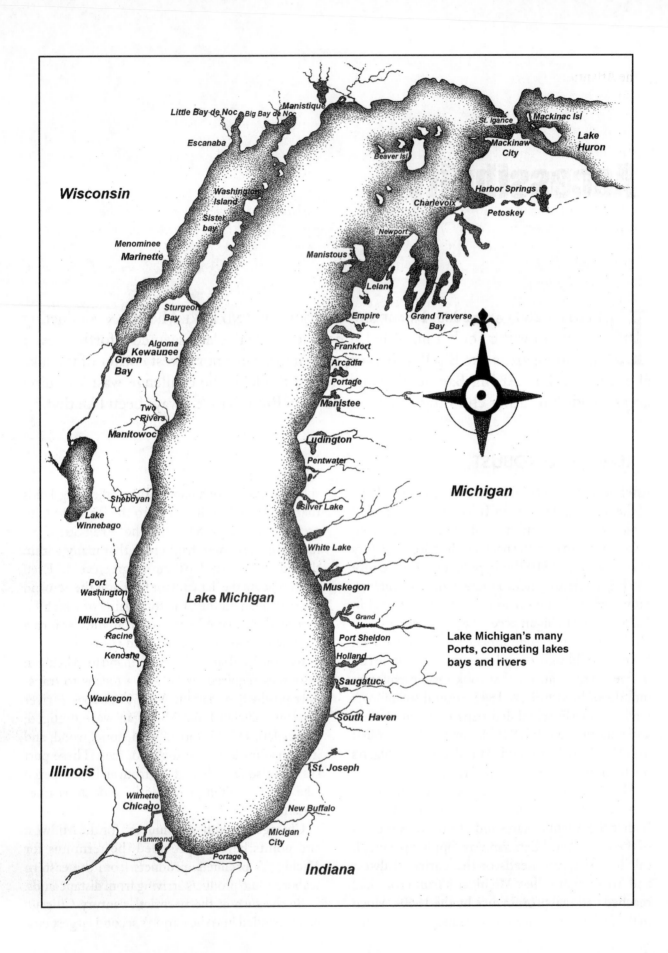

Lake Michigan's many
Ports, connecting lakes
bays and rivers

surpassed only by New York, which with the rest of the Atlantic Seaboard enjoyed an abundance of Michigan products.

Indiana, Illinois and Wisconsin also border Lake Michigan, and they too vigorously competed for the lion's share and like Michigan resources, reached eastern markets via the Great Lakes.

The demand for Midwest products surged into the twentieth century, expanding the marine transportation system across the Great Lakes into a network of commercial shipping that today transports annually over 200 million tons of commerce valued in the billions.

The explosive economic boom that echoed across the Great Lakes produced immense wealth while elevating wages to levels that allowed workers to enjoy discretionary spending. These choices often translated into boats and other water-related toys, which were made even more alluring by unlimited access to water. And not only did Michigan boaters enjoy easy access to Lake Michigan, but to Lake Huron, Erie and Superior, which like Lake Michigan offered myriad streams, bays, rivers and inland lakes interwoven within an inviting complex marine infrastructure. A perfect set up for "stooge"-like boating behavior played out by a cast of countless characters. With easy access to water by so many it is no wonder the State of Michigan has led the nation with registered recreational water craft for decades. That is until 2004 when Florida skirted ahead by a mere 1,272 boats.

Indiana, Illinois, and Wisconsin share Lake Michigan, and these states also enjoy easy access to her waters. In all, the four states that border Lake Michigan boast 2.2 million recreational watercraft, accounting for nearly one half of the registered boats in all the Great Lakes states, which in turn account for one third of all registered boats nationwide. Of course, not all these watercraft reach Lake Michigan. But, on an inviting summer weekend, when the lake buzzes with boats, it can seem so.

Especially off Chicago, the nation's third largest city. Then, just 65 miles north of Chicago, sits Milwaukee. When the summer sun bakes the cities and cool lake breezes fan the shores, city folks flock to the beaches while countless boaters seek relief in the Lake's open waters—whether qualified to operate a boat or not.

AN INVITATION FOR MISHAPS

Not only is the lake readily accessible by millions, but it also can be easily accessed by the most uninformed. Remarkably, the only qualification required of a power boater is the ability to turn a key or pull a starter cord, or with human-powered watercraft the strength to dip an oar. An 85-year-old man can purchase a giant yacht if it's under 200-gross tons.

And he doesn't need a certificate to operate the boat. Federal law requires a "Certificate of Competency" for vessels greater that 200 gross tons: a law that dates back to 1936. So grandpa may load family members down to great grand children aboard a 199-ton yacht and steam out into Lake Michigan, having never operated a boat before. If that sounds absurd, it's no more absurd than the loophole in the law that fails to prevent grandpa's maiden voyage.

Do boaters actually buy and operate large power boats with little or no experience? Apparently so. Sergeant Bill Halliday, director of Racine, Wisconsin's County Sheriff's Water Patrol, said that after assisting a 56-foot Bayliner that had run aground 100 yards offshore near Racine, he had to instruct the operator how to work the engine's throttles while the operator moored the boat.

A Coast Guard buddy of mine, Ron Hubbard, witnessed a similar mishandling while assigned to the Coast Guard buoy tender, *Sundew*. But the inept boater wasn't as lucky as the Racine rookie. The boater had recently bought a large, brand new yacht, and on the maiden voyage ran the vessel full speed between two buoys in Northport harbor, Michigan, mistaking them for channel buoys. They were not. The buoys marked the ends of a rocky shoal extending between the buoys. Had the skipper checked the local chart of the area—presuming he could read it—he could have avoided the disaster. He left his propellers, struts, shafts, and most of the bottom of his new boat, in that order, on the boulders. The Coast Guard took his wife to the hospital. The boat was a total loss.

Beaver Island's harbor master, Glen Felixson, nicknamed the local municipal marina "Bumper City" after years of watching neophyte boaters struggling to make dock. A man told me that while visiting Mackinac Island in August of 2003, he watched a 35-foot long Sea Ray powerboat attempt to moor at a dock slip at Mackinac Island State Dock. Boaters in nearby slips hurriedly manned fender buoys to protect their boats as they watched the fumble bum attempt to enter a 45-foot long slip. After an hour, he gave up and motored off. There were seven people aboard, including kids.

I'm not deliberately picking on power boaters, but merely illustrating a cavalier attitude shared amongst most recreational boaters—a carefree, "what me worry" attitude. On South Manitou Island, Park Ranger Rachael Deque told me about eight people crammed aboard a 12-foot boat, piled with camping gear, preparing to head across the Manitou Passage in five-foot seas. "There was less than a foot of freeboard from water's edge to the boat's gunwale," said Deque. "They had life jackets aboard but were not wearing them." She stopped the voyage under a federal law that authorizes Federal Park Rangers to terminate a voyage if it's deemed to be an especially hazardous situation.

Did the incident raise my eyebrows? You bet, the voyage was not only unsafe, it was insane. Hold on, it gets even more insane. John Watson a 26-year veteran with Michigan's Department of Natural Resources told me a story that even shocked me. While on patrol on Lake Michigan off Glen Harbor, Michigan, he spotted a couple sailing along in a 18-foot catamaran dragging an object between the pontoons. As he neared the sailing boat, which was gliding along at five knots, he couldn't believe his eyes. "A woman was straddling one pontoon a man the other; between them they were holding an infant by the arms dipping him into the on-coming lake. What blew me away, the infant was not wearing a life jacket," said Watson, who went on to say. "A boat wake, a gust of wind, a number of other things could have separated the infant from their hold and the toddler would have sank like a rock." What Watson found to be most disturbing the couple couldn't understand his concerns. But what gives me real concern, I now hear

such stories more often than ever. This increase in boating baboonery correlates to an increase in recreational boats and easy access to the lake and its surround waters. In 1980 the State of Michigan reported 617, 723 registered water craft. By 2004, the count had climbed to just under one million, and the numbers will surely increase as more folks pursue the Lake Michigan marine environment.

GROWTH SIGNS ABOUND

Beach-front housing and vacation condominium development have exploded along Lake Michigan as well as connecting lakes and bays. When I first arrived at Coast Guard Station Manistee in 1983, few condominiums stood near the harbor mouth. Now hundreds of townhouses, condo units, and cottages parade north and south of the harbor mouth, and developers vigorously pursue opportunities to build units as much as water-front space will allow. Once-ignored water-front property now features sprawling beach-front homes. Developers have even filled swamp lands to build houses and condos.

The demand for waterfront property runs the entire length of Lake Michigan from Michigan City to Mackinaw City. In South Haven developers have leveled turn-of-the-century beach-front Victorian homes and replaced them with layers of condos. Freeway systems have crawled northward on both sides of the lake, allowing easy access from the big cities to northern waters and coveted fishing grounds.

According to the 2000 Census, the populations of coastal and near-coastal counties that border Lake Michigan's eastern shore have witnessed a 14.8 percent increase since 1990, compared to a 5.5 percent increase for other state-wide counties. In some areas growth signs are obvious, in others they blend into the terrain amongst the foliage. From the air, however, the sprawl can be more readily seen. In March 2003, while flying at night aboard a commuter aircraft along the coast between Muskegon and Manistee, I expected the lights of White Lake, Pentwater, Ludington and Manistee to beam skyward amongst a dark rolling terrain that separates the lakeside villages and towns. But instead of dark terrain, lighted road grids checkered the 90-mile coastal stretch and the towns lying somewhere amongst the glitter eluded my eye.

Oddly, the coastal boom has not affected boat ramp fees. The average boat launch fee around Lake Michigan is five dollars or less. Many launch ramps offer seasonal passes for as little as twenty-five dollars. In many locations, including Chicago, there's no charge at all. That's a heck of a deal compared to other regions. A friend in Sausalito, California reported a daily launch fee of fifteen dollars at a bay-side marina.

Not only is the lake accessible to millions at little or no cost, it is readily accessible from numerous river channels, connecting lakes, bays and a number of private, local, state and federal parks. On Lake Michigan's eastern shore between Mackinac City and Michigan City, Indiana, 23 coastal ports offer safe refuge. That averages out to a port every 14 miles. Although the distance between ports may be greater or lesser, this clearly illustrates the lake's accessibility to its heavily populated eastern shore.

Then there's Chicago, which hosts the largest municipal marine system in the nation, offering 10 public marinas with 5,600 boat slips. Seventy-four miles north of Chicago, Milwaukee's harbor and river bustle with recreational boating, and ports running northward along the Wisconsin coastline, including Green Bay up to the Upper Peninsula and over to St. Ignace, claim their bountiful share of recreational boaters. The entire lake boasts 67 sheltered harbors and nearly 3,200 miles of shoreline access, including major bays.

That's a heck of a lot of ports with access to an ocean-like body of water. I've delivered yachts and conducted a number of patrols aboard Coast Guard cutters between Long Beach and San Francisco, and I recall seven available ports of call along the 450-mile coast.

Few areas around Lake Michigan have escaped the hoards of boaters, even in the less visited

Grand Haven is but one of the many river systems that feed into Lake Michigan.

Access roads to Lake Michigan abound, and on a nice summer day they can draw thousands of motorists to lakeside beaches.

northern waters near St. Ignace and the Straits of Mackinac. During my travels around the Lake, I interviewed several Shepler's Mackinac Island Ferry captains who make the run between Mackinaw City, St. Ignace and Mackinac Island. While departing Shepler's St. Ignace dock aboard the passenger ferry *Hope*, Richard Weaver, a senior 15-year captain with the company, pointed towards a new public boating ramp built two years ago. "Recreational boating has proliferated," he said. "It definitely offers a challenge to our captains."

He told me when Shepler began running the St. Ignace route 15 years ago it was the first ferry boat to operate out of St Ignace. Now three lines, including Shepler, make the trip on a regular schedule. Once-barren beaches north of St. Ignace now feature numerous hotels. Although most of the visitors are tourists, the area undoubtedly leaves lasting impressions that someday will draw some back for good. I understand the magic lure all too

well. When I traveled from Southern California to Manistee, Michigan, in 1983, the beauty of the region with its natural splendor and the grandeur of Lake Michigan hooked me. When yearnings for Southern California stir within, even in winter when my California bones chatter from the cold, the discomfort quickly ebbs when I recall L.A.'s 24-7 grid-locked freeways and foul air. If a California transplant willing to bear the winters calls it home, you can imagine the lure for those accustomed to winter arriving from large, congested Midwest cities.

Several days after my visit with captain Weaver, I interviewed George Miller, Director of Operations for Eagle III Brown County Air Rescue Services in Green Bay. He said, "I've seen a horrendous increase in recreational water-related activity as a helicopter pilot and recreational boater." He described a nearby lake he once fished: "Now the lake is overrun with all kinds of boaters." He no

Chicago boasts the largest municipal marina systems in the country offering over 5,600 boat slips.

longer fishes there. Chief Huph, Officer in Charge at Coast Guard Station Sturgeon Bay, told me there has been a notable increase in residential development along Sturgeon Bay's seven and a half mile long channel. "With the growing influx of people and boats, I foresee boaters' demands for rescue assistance exceeding rescuers' resources. Over the last four summers we've had 14 recreational water-related fatalities in the area," said Huph.

Notice that my interviews addressed boating proliferation in the lake's less accessible areas. Lake Michigan's boating surge in its more southern waters, surrounded by huge population centers, is far more intense. Huge public access numbers could explain the seven drownings at Warren Dunes on the 4th of July, 2003. According to Mike Terell, the park manager at Warren State Park,

approximately 20,000 visitors entered the park that day. Half appeared to be in the water, despite 15 minute warnings over loud hailers and posted red flags proclaiming dangerous swimming conditions. Unlike federal statutes authorizing federal agents like Coast Guard personnel and park rangers to terminate unsafe voyages, state officials have little enforcement power to prevent beach-goers from accessing Lake Michigan in spite of dangerous conditions or to prevent boaters whose impulses lead them into her domain despite the season. One such ill-advised late season adventure cost two fishermen their lives.

ON WATCH: Coast Guard auxiliarists at Escanaba responded to a case in late November, 2002, in which two fishermen died in Escanaba Bay during foul weather. Coast Guard auxiliarist Dave

Schwalback recalls driving up Highway 2 along Little Bay De Noc, looking out into a snow swept bay and saying, "Thank God there are no fools out there." Several hours later he was pounding across the bay with three auxiliary members under Coast Guard orders to search for three walleye fisherman whose 19-foot open boat had capsized and was reportedly drifting across the bay. "It was so miserable that sea spray crusted my beard and eyebrows with ice. The sleeve of my foul weather coat froze to the cabin hatch," said Schwalback.

The sole survivor stayed with the capsized boat and drifted into shallow water where Delta County Sheriff Sergeant Ed Oswald, volunteer search and rescue member Dale Shirely, and Coast Guard auxilarist Paul Smith rescued the near-dead fisherman. A Coast Guard helicopter crew plucked his two dead buddies from the Arctic-like bay. Was alcohol involved? No. Madness? Yes.

Although the access factor might not cause mishaps, it does provide myriad avenues for boaters to access Lake Michigan's marine environment. Easy access coupled with an expanding recreational boating fleet promise to increase the odds for mishaps as more boaters bustle and tussle about upon the waters. So maintain a sharp lookout and pay close attention as we ease into the next area of concern and a frequent source of mishaps— the Close Quarter Arena.

Close Quarter Arena

HEAVY WEATHER OFTEN DROVE NINETEENTH CENTURY MARINERS and their vessels onto shore, onto shoals, and onto piers and breakwaters. These close-quarter encounters often proved fatal. Fog also took its toll within the close quarter arena, leading to collisions between boats, with man-made structures, and groundings upon shoals and rocks. Then there was the fire threat aboard wooden sailing vessels, which were often set ablaze by wood burning stoves and boilers dislodged in a collision. Those brutal days of close-quarter disasters seldom visit today's commercial fleet; however, a new form of close-quarter calamity has emerged: recreational boating. These modern players seem to have a fondness for seawalls and piers.

BOATS, SEAWALLS AND PIERS A DANGEROUS MIX

It was one thing for sailors of old to get tossed onto breakwaters, seawalls, and piers by roaring winds and high seas, but it's another thing for modern day boaters to toss themselves upon these structures. And for many boaters, it has nothing to do with high seas, but rather a high blood alcohol count.

I know of 36 Coast Guard-reported seawall collisions along the eastern shore of Lake Michigan between the years 2000 and 2005. In addition Chicago marine authorities reported 21 seawall collisions between 1996 and 2005. All 57 collisions involved excessive speed, operator error, and/or alcohol. I suspect many more occurred, especially if the operator, after striking a seawall or pier, maintained control of the craft and fled.

In short, I suspect seawall and pier collisions occur frequently, and unless the collision disables the boat, the incident will escape public notice.

Alcohol plays a significant role in seawall collisions. What is it about drunk drivers that spares them mayhem when, by all accounts, the "accident" should have inflicted serious injury? The following Boat Smart story, "Breakwaters, boats and alcohol—a dangerous and costly affair," illustrates this paradox.

ON WATCH: U.S. Coast Guard Station Manistee, May 04, 2002. The ringing telephone jarred Coast Guardsman Chris Bouchard awake. His eyes slowly focused on a nearby clock. It was 1:30 a.m. "A fisherman calling for the weather," he thought.

A moment later he was running for the motor lifeboat. The telephone call had come from

Manistee

a boater claiming that his boat had slammed into the Manistee South Breakwater.

Within minutes, the 47-foot motor lifeboat was standing off the Manistee Breakwater Light. The 22-foot boat, however, was not on the seaward side of the breakwater as first reported, but on the inside. "The man was standing on the breakwater holding a cell phone in one hand and in the other a bow line to the boat, which was rapidly taking on water. The boat rolled over before we could take action," said Bouchard.

Manistee police and paramedics soon arrived and attended to the 36-year-old male on the breakwater. According to them, the man thought his boat was on the south side of the breakwater. The fact that he blew a 0.16 on the Breathalyzer helped explain his muddled state.

Soon after first light the Coast Guard understood why the boater seemed confused. "Early that morning I went out with a couple of guys to check the capsized boat to make sure it was still tied off to the breakwater. A man fishing near the boat asked me if the guy survived 'the jump," said Bouchard, who looked at the fisherman, then his mates, in disbelief. The fisherman pointed to an oil and fiberglass trail that streaked right across the cement breakwater, revealing the path the 22-foot boat had taken. "We were in shock and awe regarding this impossible feat," said Bouchard.

Disbelief was my reaction as well when Bouchard told me the story that morning. I had to see for myself and sure enough, I found it mind-boggling. The speeding boat struck a two-foot wide piece of rock riprap with a slight incline that acted like a ramp, propelling it completely over the entire 75-foot seawall. Had the boat hit a foot or two right or left of that small flat rock it might have proved fatal. Of the thousands of squared riprap stones that lace the 1700-foot long seawall, the boat operator hit one with a gentle upward slope.

In my years of conducting search and rescue on Lake Michigan, I've responded to and read reports of dozens of seawall collisions, but never

one that found a boat jumping the entire seawall. The odds of that happening would defy Las Vegas. Unbelievably, not only did it happen again, it happened on Manistee's South Breakwater a month later, with a 22-foot boat, and within yards of the previous collision.

ON WATCH: On June 21, 2002, a Coast Guard crew aboard a 21-foot rescue boat, while conducting training with a Coast Guard helicopter off Manistee Harbor around 11 p.m., heard a collision-like sound. Within moments, they were alongside a 22-foot cabin cruiser rapidly taking on water near the South Breakwater Light. They transported the two occupants, a husband and wife, to a nearby boat ramp where emergency personnel waited. Both refused medical treatment.

The Manistee police took the 42-year-old male into custody for operating a boat while intoxicated. His blood alcohol count was 0.14. The Coast Guard returned to the foundering boat and towed it to the boat ramp.

The boat had struck a wedge-shaped rock that propelled it up and over the seawall. That v-shaped piece of riprap lay on the other side of the seawall almost in line with the one that the inebriated boater had struck a month earlier. Drunk luck, however, can run out for some, as seen in the following Coast Guard On Watch files.

ON WATCH: That same night our water borne Evil Knievel rocketed over the Manistee breakwater, a 22-foot boat collided with Muskegon's North Breakwater. The people aboard were less fortunate. Although the 21-year-old male operator escaped injury, his 19-year-old female passenger suffered facial injuries. "When I arrived on scene I could see her lower teeth had been knocked out, and she was complaining of shoulder pain," said Coast Guardsman Allan Hasford. The crew raced the victims to Coast Guard Station Muskegon where paramedics transported the injured woman to Hackley Hospital in Muskegon. Authorities took the boater into custody for operating a boat while intoxicated. His blood alcohol count was 0.138. When the Coast Gurad crew returned for the boat, it had sunk.

A Coast Guard Auxiliary 22-foot boat approaches the spot where a 22-foot powerboat rocketed over Manistee's South Break-water. The airborne boater traveled 75 feet before crashing into the inner basin. A month later another boater repeated the Evil Knievel stunt. The average alcohol count of the operators was 1.5, almost twice the legal limit.

Muskegon

On June 18, 2004, while operating a 16-foot jet boat at a high rate of speed, a 20-year-old male slammed into the Saugatuck North Pier. The accident happened at 5:30 a.m. and in fog. His alcohol count was .156. He died on impact.

And on August 7, 2004, just before midnight, an 18-foot Crownline run-about, with five people aboard, slammed into the Muskegon breakwater at 20 mph. The 52-year-old operator suffered neck injuries, his wife fractured ribs and a passenger broke a leg. The impact severed off the pedestal seats where two teen-age girls were sitting at bow; they too sustained injuries. Alcohol was involved.

However, it's not just boozed-up boaters contributing to nighttime seawall and pier collisions. Many boaters abruptly end their voyage by failing to properly read lighted aids atop breakwaters and piers. I once intercepted a 33-foot motor boat

before it ran aground on a public beach adjacent to Manistee's north pier. The befuddled boater had passed the North Pier head's white 6-second isophase white light to starboard rather than port. Across from the 6-second isophase white light sat a 4-second red-flashing light on the end of the south breakwater, that provided a safe gateway into the harbor between the two lighted aids. That he missed running between the white and red lights came as no surprise, just another unenlightened boater wandering into port.

At that same harbor one night, a sailboat did safely pass between Manistee's outer pier head and south breakwater lights, but then ran aground after failing to keep the harbor's red inner pier head lighted aid to starboard. The captain's misread landed the 26-foot Pearson sailboat onto the south breakwater where running 6-foot seas pounded the sailboat. The two people aboard were rescued from shore by fire department personnel. The boat was totaled. I nearly ran a Coast Guard 41-foot rescue boat aground attempting to reach the sailboat.

Another close-quarters situation that leads boats onto breakwaters is boaters confusing breakwater lights with pier head lights. Many of the harbor systems along Lake Michigan feature extended breakwaters that protect river channel outlets from the elements. Most of these channel entrances at one time were river mouths that have been dredged and lined with steel seawalls, ending in finger piers that protrude into the lake. Navigation aids are placed at the seaward end of these short piers to guide boaters into the channel. The seaward ends of the outer breakwaters also carry lighted aids that guide mariners into the harbor mouth from the lake. However, the inner pier head lights and outer breakwater lights transmit different light characteristics.

Ludington

Confusing? Absolutely not. Confusion enters the picture when boaters fail to properly read the light characteristics at the harbor mouth, as in the case of a 21-foot power boat with four persons aboard that slammed into Ludington harbor's south breakwater on September 14, 2004. The operator told Coast Guardsman Larry Hall, coxswain aboard the 30-foot rescue boat that responded to the emergency, that he was not familiar with the area and that he had confused the inner pier head lighted aid with the outer breakwater lighted aid.

Manistee's south breakwater experienced two boat collisions over a week's span during 2005. The operators told Coast Guard officials that they had mistaken the outer breakwater red light for the inner red pier head light. If the boater had "Red Right Returning" in mind he would've noticed that he also had a red light off the portside when approaching the harbor. What's wrong with this picture he may of thought. He discovered soon enough—a breakwater.

Over the years, while teaching aids to navigation to Coast Guard personnel and public boating safety classes for the Coast Guard Auxiliary, I've used a simple training aid that you can perform at home. I take a flash light, cover the lens with a red transparent plastic film, turn off the overhead light and play "lighted aid." An example: for a 6-second isophase light, I turn on the flash light, count to three, turn it off while continuing to count to six. Then I begin the cycle again—light on for three seconds off for three. Then I exhibit the characteristics of a 4-second flashing light: one second on and three seconds off—total cycle, 4 seconds. The defining characteristic of a 'flashing light' is that it is off longer than it is on. Students can readily see the difference between the light characteristics. I then recommend they drive to the harbor mouth at night and time the lights with a watch. Presto—an abstract concept now becomes a useful tool, and it's stress free learning the concept from landward in a user-friendly mode. It sure beats learning it the hard way as two sailors did in the following story

ON WATCH: Manistee, Michigan, July 20, 1994, 4:49 a.m.. Station Manistee received a call of a sailboat pounding against the South Breakwater. At 4:52 a.m. the Coast Guard boat reached the 35-foot sailboat. The coxswain, Scott Mcquire said: "I steadied the rescue boat into white-capped seas and backed down as my crew passed over a tow line. The sailboat pounding on the rocks gnawed on my nerves as did eye-blinding lightning and the possibility of a bolt striking the sailboat's tall mast, or my crew."

Scott Gregorwicz and Dave Thompson, hooked up the sailboat as seas drove the rescue boat towards the breakwater. The sailboat's rudder snapped off as Mcquire pulled the floundering sailboat off the rocks. He towed the sailboat to safe water on the leeward side of the seawall.

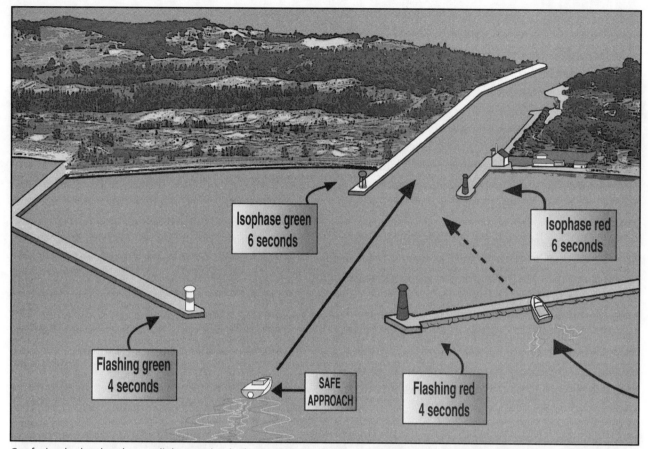

Confusing harbor breakwater lights can lead a boater into the breakwater. Remember "Red right returning": keep the red light to starboard when entering a port at night and approach the port well to seaward of the seawalls

The 16-year-old male aboard told Thompson that his grandfather was below sleeping with a string tied to his toe; he was to yank it if he needed help. The lad had failed to pass between Manistee's north pier head white light and the red 4-second breakwater light. Instead, he passed the harbor mouth and approached the harbor between two red navigation lights. No, I do not make up these stories, but how I wish less than smart boaters would attach a string to their brains and give it a tug.

Mindless boaters have also struck the seawall while outbound.

ON WATCH: On August 14, 2004 a 17-foot Ranger boat struck Manistee's South Breakwater while outbound into the Lake. Coast Guardsman Clark Bates, while conducting boat checks around 5 a.m., heard an engine roar. "It sounded like a personal water craft accelerating, and then I heard a loud bang followed by someone hollering for help," said Bates. A stream of outbound fishermen

ignored the boater's cries for help. A fisherman did, however, out of the goodness of his heart, call 911. But by then Bates and his crew were already underway to assist.

Ironically, a week or so after the collision, I happened to be on the Manistee's South pier walk snapping photos for the Boat Smart column. By happenstance, I ran into a fisherman on the pier who happened to be standing on the breakwater that morning within yards of the crash.

The fisherman, Scott Valle, told me he heard a boat engine accelerate: "I couldn't believe this boat was roaring towards me with its bow up. I could clearly see the operator in the glow of the boat's console lights." Valle reached for a flash light to ward off the boat, while hollering out to the operator, but to no avail. "It sounded like a gun exploding when it slammed into the breakwater. I ran over to the boat, and a woman was sitting on the rocks holding her wrist, and there was blood on the rocks. The male operator kept crying out to her I'm sorry I did this to your boat. I didn't mean to"

Valle told me the crash shook him up so that later when he returned to fishing, he could not steady his hands to set bait on his lures. "It wrecked my day," he said.

"Fortunately, the boat had struck the breakwater rocks with its bow pointing upward, which spared the couple aboard serious injury," said Coast Guardsman Jeremy Morris, who coordinated the rescue. The impact fractured the boat's fiberglass hull.

Some boaters apparently ignore lighted navigation aids and rely on their GPS systems to guide them safely into port at night, a useful method—unless it leads them into a seawall or pier. Laugh not; I know of several seawall collisions that occurred where boaters reportedly programmed GPS coordinates inside the harbor mouth. GPS signals can't laser-cut through seawalls as the boat pursues the GPS waypoint. Several boaters literally learned the hard way this concrete axiom. Let's review their hard-earned lessons.

ON WATCH: Ludington Harbor, Friday July 18, 2004, 10:45 p.m. To those on shore, the light configuration on the Ludington North breakwater looked like an adjunct to the many lighted attractions highlighting the annual Ludington Carferry festival that was being staged at a nearby beach. For Erin Marion, wife of the Station Ludington's executive officer, the peculiar lights told another story. She called her husband on a cell phone and within minutes a ready boat crew launched Station Ludington's 30-foot rescue boat. Approximately 50 yards east of the Ludington's north breakwater light, lay a 27-foot Baja power boat atop the wall.

Coastguardsman Joe Marion had reached by foot the high and dry vessel moments after the 30-foot rescue boat. There he found four people on the boat; two complaining of injuries that included facial injuries to a female. The operator told Marion that he was adjusting his trim device

red 6-sec. isophase light

red 4-sec. flashing light

Manistee Harbor; boaters have also been known to strike the breakwaters while heading outbound into the lake.

when the boat struck the breakwater. His GPS waypoint indicated he had 1,600 yards to travel to reach the designated waypoint into the harbor. This suggested that he had set the waypoint inside the harbor. Even had the waypoint been programmed for the breakwater, his approaching speed to the harbor was far too excessive. And too, the breakwater light atop a 55-foot tower clearly marked the seawall. I suspect light from his cabin console diminished his night vision, which is more reason than ever to bring back the throttles when approaching a harbor at night.

During the 2005 boating season Ludington Harbor saw two more breakwater collisions where the boat operator had programmed his waypoint inside the harbor basin.

Another case involving a misguided GPS boater cost him his boat and nearly his life.

ON WATCH: On October 15, 2004, a 34-foot cabin cruiser with one person aboard slammed

into Muskegon's north breakwater about 11 p.m. According to Muskegon County marine deputy Sgt. Gary Berdinski, the operator drove into the breakwater at about 14 knots while steering on a GPS waypoint between the breakwaters.

The 48-year-old operator fired off a Mayday over VHF-FM Channel 16 and then managed to climb onto the sea wall as his boat slid into the lake and sank. Coast Guard Group Grand Haven intercepted the Mayday and launched Muskegon's 21-foot rigid hull inflatable.

At Station Muskegon, Coast Guardsman Jay Douglas reported NOAA weather gauges were registering wind speeds up to 33 knots. "When I reached the man on the seawall, eight-to ten-foot seas were breaking over the wall with five footers surging down the channel," said Douglas. A cluster of rip rap rocks awash with channel surge at the base of the breakwater prevented the rescue boat from nearing the seawall. A crewman tossed

A 27-foot powerboat sits atop the Ludington Breakwater. According to authorities, the operator may have been steering on a GPS way point located inside the harbor. Authorities estimate the powerboat was traveling around 35 knots when it struck the breakwater after dark. Alcohol was not involved.

a rescue heaving line to the stranded captain and pulled him to safety.

The CG crew whisked the man back to the station to awaiting paramedics. He suffered multiple bruises and hypothermia. According to Douglas, the man wore a life jacket.

BOAT SMART BRIEF: Most GPS devices offer a handy function called "auto-waypoint" that allows operators to record their geographical position (GP) simply by pressing the auto-waypoint key. Some operators elect to record a waypoint inside a harbor before venturing out into open water, a procedure most professional mariners would frown upon. I prefer programming waypoints several hundred yards to seaward of pier heads and breakwaters; there I can set my approach to the harbor using lighted aids as my guide. That isn't to suggest one shouldn't program waypoints for pier and breakwater lights. Not at all. Knowing your location, range and bearing to these structures is critical, especially in fog and at night. However, I depend on my seaward waypoint as my primary waypoint for entering a harbor at night. For as much as I appreciate GPS input, I appreciate even more real features I can see with my eyes. And I dread surprises, especially concrete ones.

BOAT SMART BRIEF: Seawall collisions are becoming so frequent that several Lake Michigan communities are considering stringing lights along breakwaters to ward off boat strikes. On face value this approach seems prudent; however, it is ostensively misleading and what seems apparent could result in not fewer boating mishaps but more. Let me explain.

Although seawall or breakwater collisions occasionally occur, it's important to ask: how many do not? Countless boaters have safely entered harbor systems at night without incident. That tells me that the current aids to navigation on these structures serve their intended purpose: safely guiding boaters into port at night. I believe that most boaters are aware of the location of harbor structures and that most approach them at night with caution. However, during daylight that is not the case. Take Muskegon harbor. I have stood at the end of Muskegon's South Breakwater and have watched numerous boaters race towards the harbor, round the breakwater light, and roar down the boat basin, only to bring back the throttles as they near the inner pier heads.

At night do they roar into the harbor in similar fashion? I doubt it, but what if they now have a lighted breakwater as a reference point. I believe

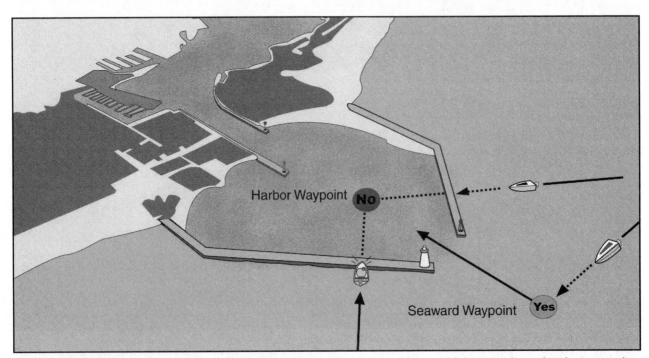

Programming a GPS waypoint to seaward off a harbor entrance is a prudent way to avoid slamming into a breakwater or pier.

it would encourage throttle jockeys to turn daytime behavior into a nighttime hazard. What about boaters or people in the water that could be readily seen in daylight that are now shrouded in darkness? Harbor officials and commercial captains from the Straits of Mackinac to Chicago report a noticeable increase in man-powered craft on the water at night particularly kayaks. Rather than hitting the seawall and inflicting self-imposed mayhem, they will inflict mayhem on others who for what ever reason might be near the structures. And if you light these structures up, you will undoubtedly draw more people out into the lake at night.

Not only will lighted structures draw more watercraft out into the lake, but lights will also draw breakwater strollers. I discussed foot traffic with Chief Warrant Officer Brad Hinken, Aids to Navigation manager at Coast Guard Sector Milwaukee and former officer in charge of Station Muskegon. He raised an interesting point in the form of a question: "How many boat collisions have resulted in fatalities and how many people have died off breakwaters and piers?"

I told him that over my 23 years of Coast Guarding on Lake Michigan, I know of three fatalities resulting from seawall collisions, and all involved alcohol. One, which I addressed earlier, involved a 20-year old male who slammed into the Saugatuck pier at a high rate of speed, in early morning and in fog, so the light issue is irrelevant in this case. On the other hand, I know of 14 fatalities occurring off Lake Michigan seawalls and breakwaters between 2003 and 2005. Ironically, one of these fatalities that occurred on November 30, 2003, took place off Grand Haven's South pier when a 10-foot wave snatched a 19-year-old male off the pier late at night. And wouldn't you know, the catwalk on the pier is lined with lights, and it's a short pier compared to Muskegon's north and south breakwaters that extend 2,300 feet out into Lake Michigan. The breakwater offers a walkway that sits much closer to the water than the Grand Haven pier, and when the breakwater becomes awash with running seas it poses a threat to foot traffic.

The foot traffic concern is not an issue in Chicago where officials are considering placing lights

Chicago

on the breakwater off the Navy Pier since access to the breakwater is not accessible by foot. Thank God! Chicago also must deal with city background lights that compete with lighted aids to navigation, as does Calumet Harbor. I discussed the background light issue with Captain Dean Hobbs, Car Ferry *Badger*, who in addition has operated tug boats out of Chicago. Captain Hobbs voiced concern that boaters might confuse a lighted breakwater with background lights and slam into a breakwater. I have made countless approaches to harbors at night and background lights can play havoc with night vision, which is all the more reason to bring back the throttles.

Notwithstanding the pros and cons of lighting up breakwaters, there is a common deterrent regarding all breakwater and pier collisions that totally lies in the hands of boaters—bring back the throttles. Throttle jockeys can be restrained in two ways: by the boat operator or by law. Yes, law and Indiana has one on the books that offers a pliable alternative to stringing lights along breakwaters. During a discussion with Chief Paul Decker, Officer in Charge, Michigan City, Indiana, I discovered that Indiana has a state law that prohibits motorized boats from exceeding 10 mph when operating on Lake Michigan within the state border and inland bodies of water under Indiana jurisdiction.

This could explain why Indiana has few seawall and breakwater collisions, especially at Michigan City where a 1,300 foot-long detached breakwater

Michigan City

with lighted aids at opposite ends marks its location some 2,000 feet off shore. This open-water structure invites mishaps, yet they seldom occur. I spoke with Lieutenant Shepherd of the Indiana Department of Natural Resources. He told me that in his 27 years of dealing with Lake Michigan boating he can recall only four boat collisions with

Lighting up breakwaters would draw people out onto these structures at night. Breakwaters sit close to water's edge and can be awash with running seas.

seaward structures. The law was in effect when he began with the department.

Indiana has clearly placed the burden of responsibility on the boater, where it appropriately belongs. And a smart boater would have it no other way.

Now, let's look at our next close-quarter player: the Grounder.

THE GROUNDER

In the old days of sailing when wooden boats ran aground in heavy surf, they would often break up with lives lost, or they were holed so badly they couldn't be salvaged. Today, however, fiberglass, steel, and aluminum hull boats can often withstand most groundings.

I can't recall a recreational boater dying as result of running aground. I know of grounding cases where fatalities occurred after people separated from the boat. Or I know of cases where rocks, piers or breakwaters inflicted fatal injuries; however, I know of no fatality that resulted from a person staying with the boat, except in the case of a heart attack.

And the heart attach might not have anything to due with the grounding, but rather later when the boater receives the salvage bill. Lake Michigan groundings can be a great deal more costly than inland lake groundings due to the access factor. The following Boat Smart story, illustrates the hazards Lake Michigan offers, especially when water depths reach all-time lows.

ON WATCH: Lake Michigan's eastern shore, June 19, 2000. Coast Guard policy directs all boat crews assigned to search and rescue stations to conduct one night and day patrol through their entire area of operation every six months. The directive's primary purpose is to keep boat crews up to speed on hazards to navigation, especially unsafe water. As Lake Michigan water levels near historical lows, area familiarization patrols are more important than ever.

A rash of recent groundings along Lake Michigan's eastern shoreline and connecting lakes indicates that boaters would do well to follow the Commandant's guidelines regarding area familiarization. During one recent weekend, Coast Guard personnel along Lake Michigan's eastern shoreline responded to six groundings. Of those six cases, I was involved in four.

One of these groundings involved a powerboat, the other three sailboats. One sailboat ran aground late Friday afternoon on the north shore of Muskegon Lake, an area known for its shallow waters. The water was too shallow to allow my 25-foot inflatable rescue boat to reach the grounded boat.

Fortunately, a Coast Guard auxiliary boat was nearby and was able to reach it with a small dingy. After some effort, the 26-foot sailboat was liberated. A crew member aboard the sailboat told me later that there should be buoys marking the shallow area. "Nonsense, try using a chart," was my response.

If she had consulted a nautical chart, she could have clearly seen that the entire northern part of Muskegon Lake lies in shallow water. The captain advised me that she was unfamiliar with that part of the lake! So in effect she was suggesting that the Coast Guard, rather than the boater, should bear responsibility for poor seamanship even when appropriate tools are available to assure safe navigation.

ON WATCH: The day after assisting the wayward Muskegon sail boater, I was called out on another grounding. A father, mother and their infant had run aground aboard a sailboat on the east end of Muskegon Lake late at night in driving rain. As I stood off in the rescue boat, I watched lightning flash across the lake and billowing dark clouds churning eastward. Gary Berdinski, a veteran Muskegon marine sheriff, in a 24-foot single screw boat, made a gutsy maneuver in the shallows that only a 25-year veteran of Muskegon Lake would dare. On his first pass, he heaved a tow line to the captain of the 24-foot sailboat, who attached it to a forward cleat. The deputy pulled the sailboat to safety. Gary Berdinski said: "It was really sparkly: a lightning bolt exploded within 100 yards of the grounded boat." The operator later told Berdinski that he was unfamiliar with the lake. The fact that he was out there at night with his family under those conditions suggests that he was just as unfamiliar with the realities of boating or perhaps reality itself.

Earlier that same day a 40-foot power boat ran aground on White Lake near buoy Number 9, which marks a shoal area were water depths suddenly shift from twenty feet to two feet. Commercial tower Dan McCormick of Great Lakes Assist told me it took four hours to free the boat. McCormick figures the operator cut inside the green buoy, which he should've passed off his left or port side returning from seaward. During 2003 a large power boat repeated the stunt near buoy Number 9, resulting in a substantial salvage fee.

Strong winds played a part in most of the groundings, along with near-record low water depths. When I wrote that Boat Smart story, 'Know Your Waters,' in June 2000, the lake water level was within two feet of its all time 1964 recorded low of 576.44 feet. As of November 2003, the U.S. Corps of Engineer's Monthly Bulletin reported Lake Michigan's water levels had dropped another foot. Len Vandernack, auxiliary flotilla commander, lower Green Bay, reported nine groundings in one month in 2003.

Low water levels can spell financial grief for boat operators. I spoke with several commercial towing services and marine salvagers; their charges range from $135 to $160 an hour to liberate a grounded boat. One marine salvage operator told me the bill could go up considerably if the boat needs to be towed, or repaired on scene, or if additional salvage vessels have to be deployed. He quoted a recent salvage bill for a 24-foot powerboat that ran aground onto rocks on a breakwater: the bill came to over $3,000. I told him I hope the boat owner's insurance policy covered the cost. "If they don't carry insurance, I demand money up front, or I will not assist," he said.

While visiting Warren Dunes State Park located near St. Joseph, Michigan, I spoke with several

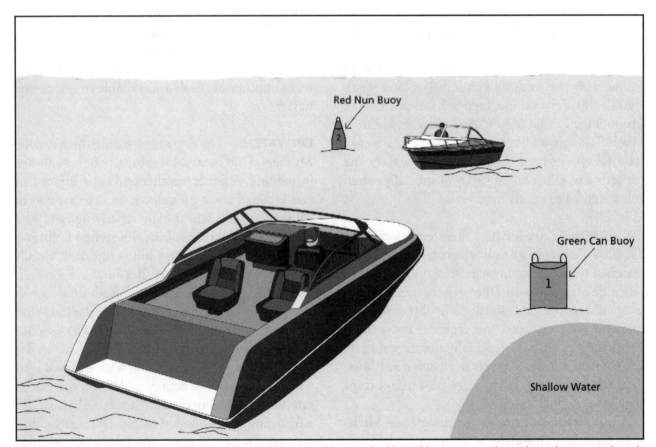

Red Nun Buoy

Green Can Buoy

Shallow Water

"Red right returning" is a sure guide to avoid running aground in a marked lateral buoy system: keep the red even-numbered nun buoys to starboard when arriving from seaward, and the green odd-numbered can buoys to starboard when heading out.

DNR officers regarding sand bars that parallel the Lake Michigan shoreline. DNR officer Rex Hubb said that during the 2004 boating season in separate incidences, two power boaters, 24 and 26 feet in length had entered a sand bar area. The operators dropped their anchors off the stern after striking a sandbar that tore off the boats' props. Lake waves rolled over the transoms and swamped the boats. According to the DNR officer, commercial salvage charged the captains $100 a foot to remove the boats and an additional $150 an hour for time underway. The dollar meter started ticking from the moment the salvage boat departed its moorings to the moment it returned. And salvage cost can be even greater, read on.

Washington Isl.

ON WATCH: Washington Island, Wisconsin, Summer 2003. Compared to the cost of some salvage operations, that could be considered pocket change. Chief John Poker at the Coast Guard's search and rescue facility on Washington Island, Wisconsin, told me about a 37-foot powerboat with a father and mother, three kids and two dogs aboard, running onto Horseshoe reef, Green Bay. The grounding occurred just west of Sister Bay on July 4th, 2003.

The operator had passed a red buoy to port rather than starboard (remember, red-right-returning) while approaching the harbor. Two kids below in the cabin were playing video games and another was napping. "The five-year-old told me she was sleeping and woke up to see water in the boat. They all were wearing life jackets," said Poker. The boat had an electronic chart plotter aboard that can automatically mark a boat's position on an LCD screen. It is unclear why the operator failed to follow the electronic chart that marks the boats position on the water. The boat incurred over $52,000 in damage.

Several months later Chief Poker and his crew responded to a 25-foot sailboat that ran onto a shoal near Rawley Bay, which is located at the north end of Door Peninsula, Wisconsin. The sailboat had two adults and a young girl aboard, along with a pet ferret. Chief Poker said: "They had sold their home to purchase the boat, and everything they owned was aboard. They were not familiar with the area; they failed to take the red nun buoy to starboard while approaching the bay." It took a salvage firm two days to remove the sailboat, which suffered a separated keel.

BOAT SMART BRIEF: So, why didn't the Coast Guard remove the boat? Under law, the Coast Guard must allow commercial salvagers the opportunity. Should commercial assistance not be unavailable or should the operator of the grounded boat refuse commercial help, the Coast Guard will consider the following before de-grounding a boat: if Coast Guard personnel and boats are not put in jeopardy, if the Coast Guard boat is capable of safely undertaking the operation, if the owner agrees to the arrangement, and if it can be assessed that no further damage to the boat will occur during the de-grounding.

Unquestionably, the safest policy against running aground is area familiarization, beginning with a review of navigation charts of the area. Also, call ahead to marinas, harbor masters, or fellow boaters to determine safe water, especially when sailing into unfamiliar waters. But even in familiar waters one has to be keenly aware of hazardous waters, especially near boat ramps. Coast Guard crews carry an expandable skiff hook onboard rescue boats; when nearing questionable waters, especially near boat ramps, a crewman will test the water's depth with the hook. It could save you some bucks. One distributor of marine supplies told me that due to low water levels the demand for props has never been greater.

Of all the advice I could pass regarding groundings, however, none could be more important than to wear a life jacket. The following Boat Story, "A fatal grounding," mournfully drives home the point.

ON WATCH: South Haven, Michigan, June 9, 2001. When I first heard the "Pan-Pan" late Saturday afternoon my ears perked up. The Coast Guard issues a Pan Pans over Channel 16, the international and distress frequency, when there exist a threat to life or property. A Pan-Pan request that boaters in the area of a reported distress maintain a lookout and report all sightings to the Coast Guard.

White Lake

The Pan-Pan at hand was reporting a person in the water off buoy Number 9, in White Lake, Michigan. I turned to the Coast Guard Auxiliary person manning the radio in the operation's shack at the South Haven Marina and told him a fatality had occurred. I had spent four seasons patrolling White Lake and knew the exact location of buoy Number 9.

If someone ended up in the water in that location, he or she would be quickly located. When Coast Guard Group Grand Haven continued issuing the Pan-Pan call, I knew for certain something dreadful had occurred. I reached for the phone to call our Operations Center in Grand Haven, but decided not to. They had enough on their hands. I would learn soon enough the details from the marine sheriff deputy who took the fatality report from the victim's wife.

Marine deputy Eric Anderson e-mailed me on Sunday with this account:

I stayed on the land with the wife, while the sheriff and divers looked for the body. The victim, a 41-year-old-male, was operating a 25-foot power boat, westbound on White Lake in a slight chop with a steady breeze from the south. The air temperature lingered in the low 80s, conditions ideal for boating.

Heading out for the channel, he passed Number Nine buoy to port. Taking the buoy on the wrong side he ran onto a sandy point, which then set off a series of events that claimed his life. He climbed out of the boat without wearing a life jacket and attempted to push the boat off the shallows near buoy Number 9 where the depth of water drops from 4 to 30 feet. He freed the boat; however, a stiff breeze carried the boat out into deep water.

He scrambled after the boat and began struggling. His 32-year-old wife tossed a life jacket, but the wind carried it off. As the wind carried the boat further out into the lake she threw out a type IV flotation cushion, which also missed the mark. Desperate, she donned a life jacket, leaped into the water, and swam towards him. No luck again.

Sometime during the ordeal she grabbed the marine radio and started frantically calling Mayday. People on shore heard the wife's screams and called 911. Our White Lake patrol boat was on scene within minutes, but couldn't immediately determine a location where the victim was last seen from witnesses on shore.

Somehow, and I'm not sure how, the wife made it to shore. I suspect she paddled or a boater picked her up and carried her there. You know how confusing it can be during a life-and-death struggle on the water, especially when the victim disappears below the surface. Even though we located the wife on shore and she provided an approximate location it was vague and precious deadly minutes had passed.

The Coast Guard, White Lake Fire Authority, the Montague Fire Department, and the Muskegon County Sheriff Department Volunteer Dive Team all took part in the search. Divers found his body at 7:35 p.m. in a sitting position in eight feet of water, about two hours after he disappeared.

I inspected the victim's boat while search efforts were underway. There appeared to be no alcohol in their cooler, just picnic items. How could they have ever imagined, while packing the cooler, that it would be a meal they would never share because of a simple boating mistake? But what a stark reminder it is that a couple of small mistakes on the water can add up to a fatality. The sea, no matter the size, is an inherently dangerous environment, made even more dangerous if a person fails to wear a life jacket.

BOAT SMART BRIEF: Inland lakes or river channel groundings mainly result from poor navigation, failure to properly read aids to navigation or failure to consult navigation charts. Alcohol also plays a heavy hand. The Grand River Channel in Grand

Haven routinely finds boaters misreading aids or shortcutting buoys and running aground.

Lake Michigan groundings occur when strong onshore winds and high seas drive crippled boats onto shore or onto pier heads or breakwaters. Boaters also run aground because they misread or don't understand aids to navigation. Lieutenant Earl Zuelke, Commanding Officer, Chicago Police Marine Unit, told me about Morgan Shoals, which lies east of the entrance to the Chicago River, Lake Michigan. The hazardous near-shore waters are marked by a lighted buoy, yet boaters still find their way onto the shoals. "Boaters don't understand Morgan Shoals' lighted buoy marks unsafe waters. They're drawn to the light like a moth to the flame" said Zuelke. I told him, it could be some boaters actually perceive the Morgan Shoal buoy as user-friendly and steer for it rather than away.

For boaters running aground, it's usually advisable to stay with the boat and avoid entering the water. It doesn't take a great deal of wave action to toss a boat about in shallow water. Entering the water near a heaving boat could inflict serious injuries. The jarring and pounding may seem like the boat is breaking up, but modern boat construction and materials most likely will pull the boater through the ordeal; staying with the boat most often offers far better odds of avoiding injury than entering the water.

The following Boat Smart story is about a boater who was driven aground north of South Haven, Michigan, and it offers several valuable lessons.

ON WATCH: South Haven, Michigan, Sunday, May 20, 2001, 12:05 p.m. As the 50-foot tug *Whilhelm Baum* neared the South Haven Channel leading into Lake Michigan, its captain, Coast Guard aux-

South Haven

iliarist Jim Bradley, reported seas breaking over the pier head. The veteran rescue responder advised the radio operator at the Coast Guard Auxiliary South Haven radio shack that the seas exceeded the search and rescue limits of his 20-ton tug and he would not be able to respond to the Mayday. I listened to the transmission and agreed with the captain's risk assessment.

A tether line attached to the boat with a flotation ball at the line's end is a must for anyone entering the water to deground a boat. Should the boat drift off the person in the water (PIW) can pull it back rather than swimming for it which could lead to a PIW removing his or her life jacket, a sure set up for a drowning.

Meanwhile, 20 miles to the south, a St. Joseph Coast Guard 47-foot motor lifeboat pounded north into heavy seas to assist. Based on its reported position three miles off shore, winds and seas would soon drive the 21-foot aluminum boat and its two-man crew ashore.

As the seas drove them towards shore, the captain attempted to set the anchor, but he failed to secure it to the boat, and the anchor line's bitter end slipped through his hands. Without an anchor, the best he could do was to steer the bow towards shore and prevent the light aluminum craft from turning broadside and capsizing in the eight-foot seas. They did the right thing by staying with the boat and wearing life jackets. The water temperature was 49-degrees. "I was terrorized; the seas were spilling over us," said Mr. Smith, the owner. "It was a nightmare."

BOAT SMART BRIEF: I reached the grounded boat after descending a 114-foot staircase from atop a nearby bluff. The captain was clearly shaken and with good cause, I thought, as I watched white-capped seas thundering towards shore, driven by a chilly 30-knot northwesterly wind that needled my ears.

Smith, 31, told me that he suspected contaminated gas from winter storage may have damaged his fuel pump, which led to engine failure. He did fire off two flares, but they went unnoticed, which I could understand, since the foul weather that whipped up that morning had driven boaters into port. I asked him about future boating plans, and he said, "Park it in my driveway and slap a 'For Sale' sign on it." This experienced boater was definitely shaken by his ordeal.

The boat ran aground north of South Haven Michigan after 30-knot winds and 8-foot seas drove it ashore after it had experienced an engine causality. The Coast Guard Auxiliary 50-foot tug, *Whilhelm Baum,* stands by offshore to tow the beached boat to open water.

Running aground onto a seawall or pier with seas running high could severely damage a boat, but again, modern boat construction favors the boater. The jarring and pounding that a boat experiences and the grinding racket can terrify boaters; however, getting off a boat being battered on rocks can be extremely dangerous. Slimy riprap rocks and crashing waves can undercut footing. It might sound like a world-ending event but the boat probably won't sink, not as long as it stays on the rocks. Besides, I would rather have the boat take the beating than my body. Whatever you do—*wear a life jacket*!

As for shallow water grounding in river channels or connecting lakes, boaters have a tendency to enter the water to free the boat. Make sure you kill the engine to avoid propeller strike, also trail a line off the boat to hold it at bay should it be set by wind or current. Again, let me stress—*wear a life jacket*!

Now let's look at our next close-quarters player and a deadly one at that—The Inviter.

THE INVITER

When warm winds blow and seas run high the Inviter lures folks out onto Lake Michigan's many seawalls and piers. Southerly summer winds carry warm air that can drive air temperatures into the nineties that in turn warm the waters. Seas, driven by strong southerly winds, can pound into pier heads and seawalls, creating rip tide-like currents. For swimmers or those washed off seawalls and piers and caught in the turbulence, the turbulence can prove fatal. Along Lake Michigan's eastern shore between the years 2000 and 2005, piers and nearby beaches claimed 38 lives. Grand Haven's south pier and nearby state beach, alone, claimed three teenage males during the 2003 season. One of those occurred in late November.

Muskegon South Breakwater. Boaters should use extreme caution while exiting a boat when aground. If the boat isn't sinking, it's advisable to stay aboard until assistance arrives.

ON WATCH: Grand Haven Pier, November 30, 2003. Chief Albert, Officer In Charge, Coast Guard Station Grand Haven, received a call at 12:24 a.m. from his officer of the day, stating that a young lad had been swept off the South Pier. "At first, I thought I was dreaming, no way could this happen, not this late in the year," said Albert, who already had dealt with two other teen drownings off the same pier just a few months earlier.

Grand Haven

The victim's friends reported looking up as a wave carried him away. The weather in the Coast Guard Situation Report read: "30 knot winds from 220 degrees true, seas: 10 feet, visibility five nautical miles, air temperature 42-degrees, water temperate 47 degrees." The Coast Guard, along with the Ottawa County Sheriff's Marine Division, Grand Haven Department of Public Safety and Michigan State police personnel, conducted a massive air and surface search with negative results. The victim remains missing.

Unfortunately, those for whom the bell tolled are unable to revisit the living and tell their life-ending struggle so others may be spared. Fortunately some swimmers have survived close-quarters near-death experiences. Their stories beg to be heard.

ON WATCH: Grand Haven, Michigan, September, 1999. A recent lifesaving rescue of two men floundering in heavy surf just off the Grand Haven's south pier sends an urgent message: Use extreme caution when around Lake Michigan piers and breakwaters, especially when fall approaches and water temperatures plunge.

The two men that were rescued can thank their lucky stars for Sara Overholt, 19, and her three friends: Michael McRae, 19, Katie Froberg, 18, and Randy McClain 14. Early in the evening, while walking on Grand Haven's South Pier, they noticed a man struggling in the Lake Michigan surf, hollering for help. Just moments before they had seen him windsurfing, and now there he was without his board, screaming for help.

They rushed to a nearby emergency 911 call box only to find it out of order. Fortunately the bright warning light atop the box caught a crewman's eye aboard a Coast Guard Motor Life Boat (MLB) inbound Grand Haven channel. The coxswain, Senior Chief Joe Vernier, nosed the MLB up to the channel side of the pier; a crewman passed a rescue heaving line to the girls. Heavy surf on the seaward side of the pier prevented the Coast Guard vessel from approaching the surfer.

The girls raced over to assist the man but now had to deal with a second person in the water. A Good Samaritan, responding to the frantic teens' urgent calls for help, had leaped into the water to assist the surfer and soon found himself overwhelmed by heavy surf. After several tosses, the life line found its mark, and the girls pulled the "Good Sam," with help from his wife, onto the pier. The teens then struggled to haul the windsurfer to safety. Ms. Sara Overholt, said: "The man yelled out, I cannot do this anymore! I'm already dead!"

These men couldn't have been luckier. If not for the teens' quick actions, chalk up another Lake Michigan pier fatality.

Holland

The next Boat Smart story involved 12 players in a life-saving rescue that included Coast Guard personnel, "Good Sams," and the victims who teamed up to deny Lake Michigan from devouring more easy prey.

ON WATCH: Holland State Park, Michigan, Friday, July 19, 2002. As I pulled into the parking lot at Coast Guard Station Holland, the 25-foot inflatable rescue craft was approaching the boat slip. Chief Reed, the boat coxswain, told me they were returning from a life-saving rescue that involved several Good Samaritans. Had I arrived earlier, as I had planned, I could have witnessed the joint rescue first-hand. But then on the other hand, had I arrived earlier, we would have been underway elsewhere as planned, far from the harbor mouth and the life-saving rescue.

How sweet it is to believe that I played a part in this life-saving rescue, perhaps in some cosmic

Breaking surf near brearkwaters and piers can be extremely dangerous, yet it seems to draw swimmers nonetheless.

manner. Be what may, one thing is for certain: if not for some good folks willing to place their lives on the line, two terrestrial souls would be elsewhere in the great domain. Now the story.

The 90-degree mid-afternoon heat found Meghann Oudman, 19, swimming in the warm waters off Holland State Park in a designated swim area marked by a line of buoys that ran north about 300 feet out from the Holland channel seawall.

Meghann, a self-acclaimed good swimmer, said, "I was so hot I hit the water." She joined other swimmers frolicking in the four to six foot surf. After swimming awhile, she decided to return to shore. "I started going back to shore, but I kept getting pulled under and sucked out further. A moment before, I had been thinking these waves are so cool; I want to move to California to be a surfer."

Meghann found herself drifting towards the seawall. "I was treading water about 20 minutes, then my legs went numb; I grew tired from treading

water. I ended up over my head. The waves were bigger in deeper water. I was getting close to the rocks, so I hollered," said Meghann.

Her cries drew the attention of Larry Nassar, 43, and his son Lawrence, 14. Ironically, twenty minutes earlier Larry had warned her of the under tow. He could see she was outside the swim zone and drifting towards the rocks. "My son swam out to her when he heard her calls for help," Larry said.

A man walking on the nearby pier also heard the girl hollering for help. He yelled to a nearby jet skier. Meanwhile, the boy had reached the girl and was holding her head above the water.

"I swam out to help my son, but was overcome by the waves. I felt the water sucking me under like a whirlpool," said the father. "I thought I was at the end of my string."

Marcus Gardiner, 29, also responded. "I saw her drifting towards the rocks with her head tilted back. When I reached her, she was in shock and couldn't comprehend what was going on. She was deadly quiet," said Gardiner. Now there were three people in the water attending to the girl. "There was no way we could get back to shore," said Gardiner, a British citizen who was visiting family in Holland.

A personal watercraft with three people aboard also responded to the girl's cries. Its operator, Troy Barsemeyer, 17, realized that he was dangerously near the rocks. "I made several sweeps around them but feared if I shut down the motor it might not start and I would drift into the rocks." His passenger, Erick Dozema, 17, jumped into the water, removed his life jacket and passed it to Meghann. Troy and his other passenger, Danae Koolenga, 17, tossed their life jackets to Meghann and the others. Koolenga then spun around in the saddle seat and dragged her feet in the water as Barsemeyer made another pass. "As we neared the girl in the water I grabbed her hand, but it slipped away," said Koolenga.

Mehgann then grabbed Koolenga's foot. "I could feel she was losing her grip, so I twisted around and grabbed her hand. We pulled her away from the breakwater." Barsemeyer then shut off the motor in order to pull her aboard. "When we scooped her aboard she had no strength. We were only ten feet from the seawall. I was getting scared." said Koolenga. "The jet ski fired up. She lay limp cradled against my shoulder as we headed for shore."

Meanwhile, the Coast Guard crew on a 25-foot inflatable elected to execute a rescue from inside the seawall, away from the rocks and pounding waves. Two crewmen with rescue heaving lines leaped onto the pier. "When I saw the line coming from above, I thought it was a line from God. If not for that line, I would be dead," said, Larry Nassar, the father.

Coast Guardsman Jay Douglas and Auxiliarist David Gaylord pulled the three swimmers towards the rocks. "A wave knocked me off one rock onto another," said Douglas, who weighs over 200 pounds. "The father was a big man and weighed around 275 pounds. I hauled the son out, placed a knee on his back to keep him from slipping away and hauled the father onto the rocks with help from my crewman." Gardiner and Dozema climbed out on their own.

Coast Guardsman Chad Everhart, an EMT, administered first aid to the survivors who had suffered leg and arm abrasions.

Moments later Douglas again tossed the rescue line to 11-year-old Sean O'Hara, floundering near the rocks, and pulled him to safety.

Later Nassar said: "I was really proud of my son. He's autistic and all his life I've cared for him. Now he cared for me and helped save my life and the girl's."

Gardiner told me that during his recent visit to Australia, he had struggled with riptides. "The lake reminded me of that experience, except the wave action on Lake Michigan keeps pounding on you in rapid succession, rapidly wearing you down."

Chief Reed, coxswain of the rescue boat, spoke with Meghann regarding the rescue and the autistic boy. "The boy was the first one to help me," she said. Asked if he was a hero, she replied: "I think everyone was a hero that day."

On August 10, 2005, a nine-year-old boy drowned off Holland's north breakwater near where Meghann was saved. An adult male jumped in to assist but failed to retrieve the boy who slipped beneath the surface.

Sadly, heroes can die while attempting to save another. On July 4, 2003, seven swimmers were lost along a three-mile stretch of beach along Lake Michigan's eastern shore near St. Joseph, Michigan. The victims included two swimmers at Warren State Dunes struggling to save a 12-year-old boy.

CASE FILE: Warren State Dunes, Lake Michigan, July 4, 2003. A special marine warning statement issued by the National Weather Service, Grand Rapids, Michigan at 9:15 a.m. eastern daylight time, July 4, 2003, read: "Doppler radar indicated a line of severe thunderstorms near mid lake...moving east at 35 knots. These storms could produce winds in excess of 50 knots...high waves...heavy rain...large hail...and dangerous lightning. Boaters should seek safe harbor immediately or

Warren Dunes
State Park

remain in port until the storm has passed. Keep away from piers…breakwaters and beaches. A severe thunderstorm watch remains in effect."

At 9:39 a.m. EDT, National Weather Service radar indicated that the line of thunderstorms that prompted the special marine warning was moving onshore.

Thus the warning had been allowed to expire.

According to officials, the drownings occurred in mid-afternoon long after the storm had rumbled through the area where the victims had drowned. Melisa Pese, the duty coxswain that day at Coast Guard Station St. Joseph, told me that by mid-day she noted three-four foot swells but no breakers near shore off St. Joseph. "The beaches were packed, I couldn't see an open spot on the beach," said Pese.

Mike Terrel, manager of Warren Dunes State Park, estimated 20,000 park visitors that day, and half appeared to be in the lake. "The drowning at the park occurred around 3:30 p.m.," said Terrel. "Water conditions were such that we continued to fly the red warning flag and announce warnings over loud hailers every fifteen minutes."

After word reached me regarding the drownings I read the National Weather Service message calling for severe weather, I concluded that heavy surf overpowered the victims. Not so. The drownings occurred in three-four foot swells, not heavy surf.

What's more, thousands of swimmers entered the water that day between New Buffalo and Manistee, Michigan, the north and south boundaries that the National Weather service set for the 9:15 a.m. severe marine warning. Yet, oddly, along that 200 mile span with thousands of swimmers in the lake, seven people drowned within a three mile stretch.

Arguably, more people accessed the lake near Warren State Dunes park than did people from beaches to the north. With Chicago a short two-hour drive away, thousands could readily reach the pristine beaches near Warren State Dunes Park, apparently a popular destination for city folks. Five of the seven people that drowned hailed from the windy city.

So what happened? The following Water-Wise Brief, I believe, holds the answers, but more importantly it offers a sure way for beach-goers to

Warren Dunes State Park located on the south-eastern shore of Lake Michigan, draws thousands to its beaches during the warm months of summer. On July 4, 2003, seven swimmers drowned off nearby beaches. Park officials estimate there were over 20,000 visitors to the park that day.

survive when they find themselves over their heads in deep water.

WATER-WISE BRIEF: So why did seven people drown along a short span of beach? Was it city folks unaccustomed to rip-tides and currents that swept the lake that morning, stirred up by truculent weather? Although sheer numbers and inexperienced swimmers may have certainly played a part, these factors alone fail to tell the complete story.

To comprehend what happened that day, I traveled to Warren State Park and entered the water where three of the victims drowned, hoping to discover more clues. One clue jumped out at me—sand bars. I waded through thigh-deep water to reach the first of two sand bars that lay off shore. At 150 feet out I stood in ankle deep water atop the first bar. I then waded through waist-deep water towards the second sand bar, which lay 150 feet beyond the first. Beyond that sand bar lay deep water. Violating my own life jacket creed, I entered into deep water without a life jacket; however, I often swim in the lake and felt fit for the challenge. Still I was gambling, especially alone without a life jacket.

Dropping below the surface in a vertical position, an eerie stillness embraced me. Underwater, the lake bottom appeared tombstone grey embalmed in lime-green fluid. "Was that how the doomed victims saw it during their final struggle," I thought? I felt as if I had unearthed a grave.

So what sealed their fate? Did wave backlash sweep them off a sand bar into deep water, or did rip tides, or did currents? Most likely. The last sand bar that dropped off into deep water explained how their predicament befell them, but not why. That final clue—the why—I felt held the answer to the drownings. That clue would came to me several weeks later in a most unexpected fashion, and it would solve the mystery.

Two weeks after visiting Warren Dunes State Park, I received a tip that Jim Dreyer had stopped at Orchard State Park during his quest to swim the length of Lake Michigan. The park overlooks Lake Michigan and is located within a mile of my home. I figured if anyone might provide insight into the seven drownings it would be Dreyer, who

has swum across four of the Great Lakes and partially swam Lake Superior, a swim he had to abort due to cold-induced leg cramps.

I tracked him down in the park. He graciously invited me into his home on wheels, an RV manned by a husband and wife team overseeing his odyssey. Three days earlier, while swimming between Little and Big Sable points, he told me he confronted the worst conditions he had ever encountered, including at Lake Superior. "This lake can drown anyone at any time," he said.

At one point during the swim he spotted a large freighter between him and the shore. That from atop a 20-foot swell it was like looking out a second floor window. He told me that lake currents near the Manistee River outlet spun him around, negating his sense of direction. He swam to a nearby beach and fired off a flare to beckon his support team.

I explained my reason for the visit. Aware of the drowning, he said, "If you're not familiar with water, the tendency for humans when experiencing panic is to flee by standing vertical and running away. Unless conditioned otherwise, a person in the water will do what comes naturally and go vertical to flee. You must think horizontal when caught in a rip tide or current and swim or float on the surface to reduce current affect. And don't panic."

"Don't panic" may sound glib coming from a swimmer in Dreyer's class, but if anyone understood panic, it's Dreyer, who nearly drowned at age three after stumbling off a pier into a lake near his parents' cottage in Byron Center, Michigan. His near-death experience occurred in early spring; an older sister snatched him from the frigid water. The experience caused such a phobia of water that washing his hair would spark panic attacks. He didn't begin swimming until 1996, at age 32. Eight years later, on October 7, 2003, he completed the 340-mile Lake Michigan swim at the base of the Mackinac Bridge in Mackinaw City.

For Dreyer, Great Lakes marathon swimming offers an opportunity to promote a heart-felt crusade—raising money for the Big Brothers and Big Sisters of America mentoring program. Jim Dreyer can be considered a mentor in his own right.

Sandbars run the entire length of the eastern shore of Lake Michigan. Swimmers beware: sandbars can suddenly drop off into deep water.

His wise advice regarding open water survival in rip currents and wave backlash can be summed up in two words: "think horizontal."

CASE FILE: Two male swimmers, ages 20 and 23, unfortunately failed to pay heed to Dreyer's advice while swimming in Lake Michigan off Washington Park, Michigan City, Indiana. The drownings occurred on July 16, 2004, seventeen miles south of Warren Dunes State Park where the seven swimmers perished in one afternoon a year earlier. The park had posted warning signs and red flags advising people not to swim in the lake festered up by a stiff northwesterly that sent waves racing to shore.

Witnesses told authorities the men appeared to have stepped off a sand bar into deep water and were overwhelmed by the rapid wave action. An inexperienced swimmer can easily panic while struggling to regain footing as waves tumble over his or her head, forcing a rapid intake of water and subsequent choking.

Those drownings were soon followed by two more in nearby waters. On August 11, 2004, a young man drowned in Lake Michigan off Covert Park, South Haven, Michigan. On September 12, 2004, another man lost his life in a drowning in Lake Michigan off Wells Beach, Indiana Dunes.

With the 2005 beach season barely underway a pier fatality occurred along the eastern shore of Lake Michigan. On April 9, 2005 the lake snatched a 19-year old male off the St. Joseph's South Pier late at night. Rescue divers discovered his body in 18-feet of water along side the pier. The water temperature was 51 degrees. Alcohol was not involved. He was last seen my friends walking along the pier with a cell phone to his ear. By the end of August 2005 the waters along the eastern shore of Lake Michigan had claimed seven more swimmers. I know of two other drownings in a nearby inland lake. One victim was only three years old. These rash of accidents prompted me to write a special Boat Smart Labor Day weekend advisory.

Advisory

Coast Guard Group Grand Haven, Michigan, August 27, 2005. I had requested from Lieutenant Commander Tracy Wannamaker, Commander Coast Guard Group Grand Haven, safety points regarding kids and water. A rash of recent drownings have involved youths. One in particular involved a nine-year-old boy who drowned on August 11, 2005 in Lake Michigan near Holland's north pier. Commander Wannamaker had the woeful task of consulting in person with the parents who lost their son.

What makes it especially difficult for the Commander, she has a son the same age with many of the same interests and habits as the deceased nine year old. In fact, their birth days were a week apart. The Commander e-mailed me that afternoon: "If I ever have to do that again it will be too soon—it's been an awful year for that. The child did not know how to swim and was pulled out over his head by the current."

I responded to her e-mail by suggesting she write water safety instructions regarding kids and water, not necessarily as a veteran Coast Guard rescue responder, but as a mother of three. She more than willingly provided these Water-Wise Anchor Points:

COMMANDER TRACY WANNAMAKER: Two weeks ago I was in the heartbreaking position of telling a Mom and Dad that their nine year old son had drowned in Lake Michigan. This is the part of my job that keeps me awake at night, the part that I could do without. As I read through the search paperwork, I noted that this child was only one week younger than my own son. Immediately I was thrust into the "what if" self-questioning that all parents do, and I came up with a few items that all parents or caregivers need to know:

- **You are in charge: respect the water.** Our beautiful lakes are also very unforgiving at times. *You* need to understand how the water moves, how deep it is and what is on the bottom. *You* also need to understand rip currents and explain them to children that are old enough to understand. I make my kids recite what they would do if caught in a rip current every time we go to the lake. The Beach and Pier Safety Task Force, based in Grand Haven, has a useful website that

When being set out from shore by currents a person should float horizontally on the surface in order to reduce the current effect of water returning to seaward from shore. Shore-bound surface waves and winds will carry a person towards shore. Remember think HORIZONTAL

A mother tosses a Rescue Heaving Line Bag to her 12-year-old son. Mother and son were practicing open water rescue techniques in Lake Michigan. The bag contains a 70-foot line and floatation ball, which will float.

discusses rip currents and other hazards: www.respectthepower.org

- **Invest in swim lessons for the whole family**. Non-swimming parents can't help when the children are in trouble in the water, and often get into trouble as well while attempting to help. I can think of nothing worse than watching your child drown because you are not equipped to help him or her. Swim lessons not only teach children how to keep their head above water, but also promote safety and confidence in the water.

- **If you or your children cannot swim a proper-fitting life jacket is a must for both of you**. On more than one occasion my kids have fought me on this, but it's not open for discussion: "put it on or you are sitting on the beach." Many drownings occur when non-swimmers suddenly find themselves in water over their head. In addition, many

"good swimmers" drown because of fatigue, panic or medical issues.

Unfortunately, rescuers don't get called until someone goes under, and there are only a few precious minutes to save a life. Often it's too late. Pride is never a good excuse for drowning. Wear a life jacket.

- **Be vigilant**. Don't take your eyes off of them—we all know how fast the little ones can move, in or out of the water! Know how to respond in case of emergency and run these scenarios through your mind—you may be the one that saves the unsuspecting swimmer. I strongly suggest having available a flotation device like a rescue heaving line with a flotation ball that you can toss to a person struggling in the water. Also, carry a whistle to draw attention to an emergency.

- **Avoid Dangerous Waters**. Stay within designated swim areas. Do not swim near breakwaters or piers. Turbulent water and wave backlash can overcome the best swimmer and jagged rocks that line breakwaters and piers can inflict lacerations, broken bones, and head injuries. Pay heed to red warning flags or pennants that warn of dangerous surf conditions.

- **A myth**. There's a wide-spread belief that an underwater force "sucks" or "tows" a swimmer under. The fact is there is no such thing as an undertow in Lake Michigan. The force that most waders feel pulling at their legs in shallow water is wave backlash resulting from waves that have washed up onto the beach. A sandbar can act like a dam, building up water that can break down a section of sand bar, thus creating an opening through which the dammed-up water escapes. This force can carry a person away from the sandbar and into deep water. Do not panic you are not being sucked under. Float on your back or stomach to negate current effects.

- **Do not allow kids to float out into deep water on rubber rafts or inner tubes**. Should they separate from the flotation device, they could find themselves in deep water. During August 2003, a mother nearly lost her 11-year-old daughter after she separated from a three-man raft off a Ludington beach. If not for the heroic actions of a 16-year-old lad who fought through four-foot seas to reach the floundering youth, the child would have drowned.

- **Beware**. When you put your guard down around water, that is when you should be foremost on guard.

Thanks Commander for the safety brief and I'm sure a lot of mother's will be thankful as well. I know one in particular who is. She approached me after reading the Labor Day advisory in the local newspaper and thanked me and the Commander. She told me she considered herself lucky because while raising her kids she was unaware of many of the Commander's safety points. "Looking back it's scary that I didn't consider these safety issues," she said.

Thus far we have covered two factors that provide Lake Michigan the opportunity to devour its wounded: unlimited access by millions and the hazards a close-quarter arena offers. Let's move on now to the next adversary: Congested Waters.

Congested Waters

THE SHEER NUMBER OF RECREATIONAL BOATERS operating within Lake Michigan's close-quarter arena invites disorder. The four states that border Lake Michigan boast 2.2 million registered recreational water craft; within the mix has evolved a whole new breed of boaters: jet skiers, jet boats, bowriders, wind surfers, and wind boards, to name a few. And one can only imagine what new form of watercraft yet unborn will appear. If current trends continue most boaters now and in the future will display a common trait: no formal boating education coupled with limited experience. Add to this enormous hodgepodge of untrained boaters a growing commercial fleet, including cruise ships and high-speed ferries, all jockeying for space within Lake Michigan's close quarter arena, and the ingredients for mishaps abound upon these congested waters.

This chapter will address boating congestion within the close quarter arena and its players who often present a threat to recreational boaters, commercial vessels and even non-boaters. The chapter will also address how water buffs can defend themselves against close-quarter congestion. I'm absolutely convinced that the points I stress will help recreational boaters operate safely within the close quarter arena, so stay with me through the sleepy classroom stuff.

I promise there will be only a few ho-hum segments; however, I promise to spice them up with real-life cases. Several of the ho-hum issues will address the Inland Navigation Rules, and although there are 35 rules and five annexes, I will address only a handful that I believe are absolutely essential to safe close-quarter boating. These are the same rules and procedures that I have stressed while training Coast Guard boat crews over the years.

In some cases, I will repeat the rules as they apply to different circumstances; I do this in order to stress the importance of the rule, and by repeating it, hopefully I impart a lasting impression.

As far as telling the woeful stories of boaters, by no means do the true stories intend to belittle the misfortunes of those involved. Instead they serve to enlighten, so others may avoid mishaps while enjoying the Lake Michigan marine environment in a safe and responsible manner. For certain, the Lake Michigan marine environment can only devour its wounded if provided the opportunity. Now, let me introduce one of the formable dangers in congested waters—collisions.

COLLISIONS WITH OTHER BOATS AND OBJECTS

Wayne Comstock of Wolverine Mutual, whose company insures a large number of recreational

On a busy summer weekend, hoards of boats can be seen swarming around Lake Michigan harbor river channels.

watercraft in Michigan and Indiana, told me that the majority of the company's claims involve collisions with floating objects or other boats. According to the Coast Guard's annual recreational boating statistics, over a five-year period between 2000 and 2004 collisions with vessels and floating objects, which includes swimmers and divers, accounted for 36 percent of boating accidents and 33 percent of injuries.

Those figures, however, depict only a small slice of the pie according to the latest Coast Guard *Boating Statistics* on recreational boating. The report states that only a small fraction of all non-fatal boating accidents occurring in the United States are reported to the Coast Guard, state or local law enforcement agencies.

I believe this reporting shortfall holds especially true for recreational boating collisions. Unlike automobile collisions that often draw a great deal of attention, that often cripple a vehicle, and often spark calls to 911, boating collisions often go unreported. When automobiles collide, fenders bend, tires explode, radiators rupture, and nearby objects, including other automobiles, may join the fray, inflicting additional damage and personal injuries.

But when boats collide it takes considerable force to render the boat inoperative. Especially damage to power boats, with engines located at the stern. Unless a boat is struck from behind where impact cripples the propeller, shaft or rudder, the vessel can continue on. In most boat collisions, the shock is transferred to the water, or the boat glances off on impact. And unlike car wrecks, residual damage to other boats or objects is rare. So, unless a personal injury occurs requiring medial response, boaters can go their way with little attention drawn to the ordeal.

Looking back over my years in search and rescue, I cannot recall one official Coast Guard report of a hit and run collision. I did, however, receive an e-mail from a woman reporting that her nephew was killed in a hit-and-run boating accident. The case sparked a campaign that led to stiffer penalties for a hit-and-run boating accident involving a fatality. That and the case to follow hopefully raises a red flag for those who speed boat and drink.

CASE FILE: Wixon Lake, Gladwin County, Michigan, September 1, 2002. According to the aunt's e-mail, her nephew and his wife were returning to the family cottage when a boat traveling at a high rate of speed slammed into the couple's boat, knocking the man into the lake and leaving his wife circling in a sinking boat. The operator of the other boat raced off. Divers recovered her nephew's body 33 hours later. Authorities apprehended the offending operator the following day. Although authorities suspected alcohol and drugs were involved, the passage of time precluded testing the operator for alcohol.

Prior to that incident, the penalty for leaving the scene of a water-related fatality in Michigan carried a 90-day misdemeanor sentence. Due to the diligent lobbying efforts by the family of the deceased, on December 3, 2003, the Michigan Senate passed legislation decreeing hit-and-run water-related fatalities on par with automobile hit-and-run fatalities, a felony that caries a maximum five-year jail sentence.

The following Boat Smart story, "Boat collision leading cause of injuries," reveals how suddenly and unexpectedly a collision can occur. The incident also constitutes a valid argument regarding mandatory boating education.

CASE FILE: Portage Lake, Onekama, Michigan, July 24, 2003. The balmy mid-summer day found Douglas Kalis patrolling the southern rim of Portage Lake. At age 49, he had recently retired and now spent his days fishing. An avid fisherman, he had reached his zenith: a pristine lake well-stocked with fish, a waterfront home with his own dock, a wife with a gourmet touch, and a faithful golden retriever. Life couldn't have been finer, but it nearly ended in the genesis of his retirement.

"I first saw the boat approaching at a high rate of speed around a hundred yards off my port beam. I knew he was going to hit me, and there was nothing I could do," said Kalis. Trolling at one knot aboard his 14-foot aluminum boat with one hand on the tiller and the other on a fishing rod, he threw the rod onto the deck and grabbed a beach towel, stood up, and waved it over his head. The towel and the bright yellow shirt he wore failed to attract the attention of the boater bearing down on him.

According to Mr. Kalis, several youngsters sitting in the open bow of the approaching 17-foot powerboat turned and screamed at the operator. A female passenger sitting alongside the driver pounded on his shoulder to draw his attention. "His head suddenly appeared above the dashboard. He looked at me. I hollered at him to veer but he froze, his eyes dilated like a deer in headlights," said Mr. Kalis.

Mr. Kalis leaped over the starboard side. The bow of the oncoming boat plowed over the port gunwale, driving the starboard side of the boat skyward, catching Mr. Kalis in the back, tearing off an oar lock riveted to the port railing. "I felt an excruciating pain in my back," he said. The impact killed the motor. He dog-paddled over to his boat and draped his arms over the gunwale.

"The boat operator while circling my boat kept crying out he didn't know what to do and that he was new at this. I directed him to come alongside my boat and grab the hand rail, and pull me and the boat to shore." Writhing in pain, Kalis could not stand in the shallow water near shore. An ambulance soon arrived and transported him to a nearby hospital.

Several shore side witnesses told Steve Block, a Manistee County marine deputy, that the boat was traveling at a high rate of speed when it struck the smaller craft. The operator later told Block that he had less than 20 hours of boating experience.

For Mr. Kalis, it proved to be a painful experience, physically and emotionally. A day later, after being released from the hospital, he collapsed from back spasms and ended up back in the hospital. X-rays revealed three broken ribs and a fractured vertebra.

Although roiling from physical pain, he apparently suffered foremost from the damage to his boat. He bemoans that the damage might not be repairable. "My dad bought that boat in 1962 new, and I've fished all the Great Lakes, as well as the Atlantic and Gulf with her. She's made of high grade aluminum with a reinforced deck that

Douglas Kalis points to where a 17-foot power boat slammed into his aluminum fishing boat on Portage Lake. He sustained three broken ribs and a fractured vertebra. The operator of the boat that struck him later told authorities he had less than 20 hours of boating experience.

provides a stable fishing platform." He talked about her as one might a cherished family member. And well he should, for the boat absorbed a crushing blow, but he admits had he not leaped overboard he would be dead. Alcohol was not involved.

Unlike Mr. Kalis, the boat operator in the following story had no forewarning before impact. The collision inflicted serious physical injury.

ON WATCH: Muskegon, Michigan, July 25, 2001. On Monday morning, the Coast Guard Station Muskegon crew responded to a boat collision on Lake Michigan that sent a boater to the hospital in critical condition. Two 18-foot Lund fishing boats were racing outbound in tandem from Muskegon Harbor when the lead boat suddenly slowed down. The trailing boat climbed up the stern of the lead boat at 30 knots, driving the lead boat's operator into the boat's console. Fortunately a Muskegon Fire Department boat with a paramedic aboard was nearby to assist the victim. They transported him to a local hospital in critical condition with facial and neck fractures and heavy blood loss. Alcohol was not involved.

The victim in the next story faired far worse than the previous two collision victims—she died.

CASE FILE: Green Lake, Michigan. In July, 2003, a 22-year-old swimmer died after she was srtuck by a 20-foot power boat while swimming in Green Lake, located 25 miles east of Holland, Michigan. Allegan County marine deputy, Kevin Giles, told me the operator was towing several of her kids behind the boat on tubes while one of her children, a 9-year-old, maintained lookout aboard the boat. Michigan law requires a spotter when towing people. Reportedly, neither she nor her son ever saw the swimmer. The fatal accident occurred in early afternoon, in calm conditions with air temperatures in the mid eighties. An ideal set up that can find boaters distracted by the euphoria of the moment

BOAT SMART BRIEF: In all but one of these accidents, "operator inattention" was listed as the leading cause, and according to Coast Guard *Boating Statistics*, it is the leading cause of preventable boating accidents nationwide. It's possible that the accident involving the hit-and-run fatality could also fall under "inattention." But what about the collisions that finds two boats heading on a collision course, clearly in sight of each other? I suspect two factors could be at play: ignorance of the Navigation Rules or alcohol, or both as the following case reveals.

CASE FILE: Saugatuck, Michigan, July 2000. Duels bring to mind combat between two persons, fought with deadly weapons under prescribed rules. I can't think of anything more deadly than two powerboat captains engaged in such a duel while ignoring all rules of engagement.

Such a duel recently took place on Lake Michigan when two large powerboats collided, nearly splitting one vessel in half. According to Coast Guard reports, the two boats collided one nautical mile southwest of Saugatuck, Michigan, around 7:25 p.m. Weather conditions at the time were one-foot seas with eight miles visibility.

The larger boat, a 58-foot SeaRay, struck a smaller 42-foot Wellcraft broadside. Two people aboard the Wellcraft were seriously injured; four others were transported to the hospital with lesser injuries. In all, 15 people were involved in the two-boat collision. The Wellcraft later sank when it was separated from the larger SeaRay. Although the cause of the accident is under investigation, it's safe to assume that one of vessels was in serious violation of the Navigation Rules. Later it was determined alcohol did play a part. It is apparent that since the SeaRay hit the Wellcraft broadside, both boats encountered a crossing situation.

BOAT SMART BRIEF: A crossing situation exists when a boat approaches another boat on a course perpendicular to the other boat's course line. When two boats approach each other during a crossing situation, one must give way if it appears a collision seems certain. So who gives way? According to the Navigation Rules the vessel to port (left) is the give-way vessel, and the vessel to starboard (right) is the stand-on boat. The give-way vessel must do whatever it can to avoid collision. The rule is similar to the rules governing automobiles at a four-way stop: a driver must give the right-of-way to the automobile to its right when both approach an intersection at the same time.

We'll further discuss the crossing rule in just a moment with illustrations, but for now let's focus on another critical rule at play in the four previously mentioned collisions and a leading cause of boating accidents and injuries. This often violated rule is Navigation Rule 6, which address safe speed. The rule reads: "Every vessel shall at all times proceed at a safe speed so that she can take proper and effective action to avoid collision and be stopped with a distance appropriate to the prevailing circumstances and conditions." These conditions include visibility, vessel traffic density, background lights at night such as shore lights, weather conditions, and depth of water.

Safe speed applies especially at night and in restricted visibility. It has been my experience that entrances to harbor mouths along Lake Michigan and channels leading into inland lakes often appear as dark voids at night, made worse by background lights that distract the eye. Under these conditions fishermen in small boats take great risks when they turn off their navigation lights in order to save their battery. Often during patrols I would come across these phantom boaters who instantly turned on their navigation lights when I lit them up with the flashing blue law enforcement light.

The fact that one boater is in violation of the law does not exonerate the boater who runs into a darkened boat at night. It brings us back to Rule 6 and safe speed for prevailing conditions. If that rule doesn't hold up in court, Rule 5 will definitely find attorneys flipping pages. Rule 5 reads: "Every vessel shall at all times maintain a proper lookout by sight and hearing as well as by all available means appropriate to the prevailing circumstances and conditions so as to make a full appraisal of the situation and of the risk of collision." Oh, how a boat captain in the following story wishes he had followed Rule 5 and 6.

CASE FILE: Grand Traverse Bay, Michigan, July 14, 2001. Following a fireworks show on Grand Traverse West Bay, Michigan a 28-foot powerboat with two people aboard (POB) slammed into the stern of a 21-foot pontoon boat with six POB. Reportedly the stern light on the pontoon boat was out when the accident occurred. The stern

light outage, however, could not be confirmed due to severe damage to the boat's stern. Deputy Paul Pierce of the Traverse County Marine Sheriff's department was the first official on the scene and he told me the victim had sustained serious injuries. Alcohol was not involved.

So who was at fault, the boater who failed to display a stern light or the boater who apparently failed to stop in accordance with Rule 6, which addresses safe speed? The rule is worth repeating: "Every vessel shall at all times proceed at a safe speed so that she can take proper and effective action to avoid collision and be stopped within a distance appropriate to the prevailing circumstances and conditions."

I spoke with Michigan Department of Natural Resource officer Sean Kehoe the investigating officer on the pontoon boat accident. According to Officer Kehoe both boats were in the lower bay heading on a westerly course towards a nearby shore where a major shoreline road rims the lower bay. That night the road was packed with post fireworks traffic that looked like a string of white and red Christmas tree lights moving along the shore. Back ground lights in this case certainly would quality as a prevailing circumstance that a prudent operator should consider regarding boat speed and background light.

I've conducted dozens of Coast Guard security patrols for firework events and another prevailing circumstance that loomed ever present after firework's event was the possibility of a disabled boat adrift without lights. Rule 6, states: "In determining a safe speed traffic density shall be taken into account" Hundreds of boats would turn out for the fireworks and without fail a handful or more would break down and become adrift, some without lights. For that reason, I posted extra lookouts and operated at slow bells.

The next case shows the deadly aftermath of a boat operator who failed to adhere to Rule 5, which requires a boater to maintain a proper lookout at all times.

CASE FILE: Mona Lake, Michigan, June 8, 2002. An 18-year-old girl drowned after the 24-foot boat she was aboard was struck from behind by a 26-foot power boat. The accident happened at night. According to Muskegon Marine Deputy Gary Berdinski, the operator of the boat she was aboard flicked his boat's lights a number of times as he lay dead in the water. The speeding boat slammed into the stern, throwing the victim and several others into the dark lake.

Deputy Berdinski said, "I determined the impact speed was about 25 miles an hour. The two boat operators—cousins—shared many hours underway. They were not inexperienced boaters, nor was alcohol involved. A motorist wouldn't race along a dark country road at night without head lights. Well, it's no different for boaters, and they don't carry headlights. If you can't see beyond your bow, bring back the throttles, especially in dark confined waters and near structures."

What happened to the young driver could happen to anyone operating a boat on dark waters with an elevated bow obstructing forward vision. What a lesson the young lad learned—the hard way.

As a Coast Guard coxswain, Rule 6 used to occupy my thoughts at night when I operated near shore, around harbor mouths, in river channels, and upon inland lakes. In these dark, close-quarter waters, I often felt as if I were walking on eggshells even with radar on. My concerns: boaters disabled and adrift, kayakers and canoeists, people in the water who may have separated from a water craft, boats failing to display anchor lights, or boaters failing to display navigation lights or displaying improper navigation lights. Lots of things to consider. Let's move on to to our next discussion: the "unenlightened."

THE UNENLIGHTENED

Another hazardous game played at nighttime in congested waters features recreational boaters who fail to display proper navigation lights. Boats under 40-foot in length appear to be the main participants in this after dark light charade. According to "Inland Navigation Rules" a power driven vessel less than 12 meters (39 feet) in length must display a white masthead light visible for two nautical miles, separate or combined side lights visible for one nautical mile, and a white stern

light visible for two miles. It's important that the lights can be seen from a distance so boaters can take appropriate action in time to avoid a collision. The lights also provide a means for other boaters to determine the aspect of a boat.

During daylight, one can readily determine a boat's starboard and port sides, bow or stern aspect. After dark what appears obvious in daylight appears as colored dots darting across a black backdrop. To the trained eyes of professional mariners, these points of light tell a lot about another boat and its relative movement to their own. It's a simple, time-proven concept that has allowed mariners for centuries to safely operate at night to avoid collisions, especially in restricted or congested waters. The following illustrations will help illuminate the concept.

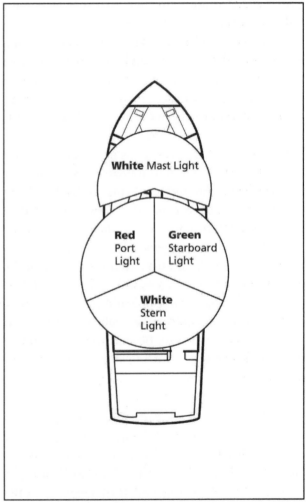

The basic light configuration on boats allows one to determine a boat's aspect at night.

A useful memory aid is to view the boat that has a red side light to starboard as a red stop light and thus take appropriate action, if risk of collision exists. But beware—some things aren't as they appear in the often capricious world of recreational boating. I once spotted a pleasure boat displaying a green side light on the port side. The red and green side lights were reversed—it could have spelled disaster. This condition is not uncommon.

You can imagine my confusion when I spotted the boat with the reversed side lights. A green light to starboard meant I was good to go, however, I opted to use the rule of experience, and Inland Navigation Rule 8, "If necessary to avoid collision or allow more time to assess the situation, a vessel shall slacken her speed or take all way off by stopping or reversing her means of propulsion." In other words, take preventative action regardless of whether you're the stand-on vessel or not. What's more, Rule 2 came into play: "You may make a departure from these rules necessary to avoid immediate danger." If you fail to take action, stand-on vessel or not, you may find yourself standing before a judge in the event of a mishap. And I might further note that maritime attorneys are scarce and costly. But then, what attorney isn't?

Over the years I've learned that assuming recreational boaters know the rules can be risky business. Perhaps Rule 2 should read: "Due regard shall be had to all dangers of navigation and collision and to special circumstances, including the limitations of the vessels, and knowledge limitations of recreational boaters." Regarding the approaching boat off my starboard side, I opted to follow Rule 8. I slackened my speed and assessed the situation. How could a boat approaching from starboard in a crossing situation display a green light. It should be red (boat's port side), and if it were green, it would be heading away from me, not approaching.

As the boat neared, I took evasive action, lit up the "blues" and hailed it over. I discovered that the captain had removed the red and green lenses to clean them, but reversed the lenses when he reinstalled them. I told the operator he should perhaps consider daytime boating only.

I believe a number of boaters should keep to daytime boating. A number of fellow rescue responder agree. Many report that it's not uncommon to come across boats with their side lights reversed. Commander Anthony Popiel, Commander Group Grand Haven, told me that while conducting night-time "Ready for Operations" drills with the Muskegon boat crew in the spring of 2004, the coxswain hailed over a boat on Lake Michigan whose side lights were reversed. On smaller boats, a combination side light slides into a socket located on the bow. Apparently some boaters, after removing the combo light, place it back in backwards. Boaters that carry red-and-green clamp-on lights, found on smaller boats, have been known to clamp the lights on backwards.

These miscues might not be of concern to the unenlightened, but they do concern those who depend on proper light displays to safely navigate at night. The following story addresses a boater who finally saw the light and cursed himself for operating in the darkness for so long.

ON WATCH: Several years ago I boarded a 46-foot long speedboat in Muskegon lake. During the inspection, the captain told me he had been a fast boat dealer for over 10 years and that he recently completed a Coast Guard Auxiliary 13-week Boating Safety course. "I thought I knew about boating, but the course revealed just how stupid I was. I no longer operate on the water at night—too many stupid and cocky types like myself are out there without a clue," said the captain. I told the captain I understood his concerns.

Oh, how well I do. I stopped a boat that, instead of red and green side lights, displayed generator-powered white light bulbs dangling from extension cords draped across the cabin roof. In another case, I hailed over a boat displaying a strobe light for a stern light. In yet another case, a neon light illuminated the stern of a boat. Was I approaching a bar or a café? Chuckle you may, but there's little humor in the mind of a boater, especially a trained commercial captain, attempting to figure out these crazy light configurations in congested waters.

A common light discrepancy I often encountered: fishermen that cover their stern light with a fish cooler or down-rigger boards. Solution: an all-round white light on an extendable pole would

At night, if you see the green light of an approaching boat off your port side, your boat is the stand-on vessel in a crossing situation. The other boat must take action to avoid crossing in front of your boat. Treat the other boat's green light as if it were a green traffic light.

At night, if you see the red light of an approaching boat off your starboard side you're the give-way vessel in a crossing situation. You must take action to avoid crossing in front of the boat. Treat the other boat's red light as if it were a red traffic light.

be in order, and it would keep other boaters at a safe distance astern.

Early one morning while heading outbound to Lake Michigan along the Portage Lake channel, I spotted a boat without a stern light. As we approached the boat, I noticed an ice cooler blocking the stern light. I walked to the bow of the 41-foot patrol boat and hollered to the captain to display his stern light. He responded with "f— you," apparently unaware that I was with the Coast Guard. I signaled the pilothouse to light up: The flashing blue law enforcement light instantly drew the Dr. Jekyll out of Mr. Hyde. He graciously removed the cooler, and I bid him farewell with a chuckle.

ON WATCH: Some boaters, however, are apparently unmoved by "officer presence." I was running a rescue operation in Muskegon Lake one dark night, and I mean dark like a black hole, a night-time characteristic common to the many connecting lakes and river channels along Lake Michigan. Muskegon Lake, however, is one of the darkest lakes I've ever operated on. I was towing a disabled 22-foot boat alongside on the port hip of our 25-foot inflatable rescue boat. I was operating at "one bell," slowly picking through a series of mooring buoys to reach a boat slip located at a nearby marina at the southwest corner of the lake.

Without warning, out of the dark loomed a 19-foot boat off my starboard side, whose operator I suspect was playing "light peek-a-boo." The boat operator suddenly energized his navigation lights to announce that he would be crossing ahead of me. My blue law enforcement light was flashing; my mate, Big John was beaming a safe passage through the anchor buoys with a search light. There wasn't a boater within miles who could not see us.

As the bozo crossed within feet of my bow, a twanging sound plucked the air, followed by the shrill wail of a female voice bellowing that we had snagged their fishing lines and poles. She demanded that we stop and retrieve the fishing rods. If not for the boat on my hip, I would have hailed them over and cited them for negligent operation, and I suspect for operating a boat under the influence. What else could explain such disregard for

the rules, especially while law enforcement officers were engaged in a rescue.

You can bet too, after I safely moored the 22-foot boat, Big John and I went looking. It's probably a good thing we didn't track them down. Oh, was Big John's hair up!

Then there are the sail boaters who display a white anchor and white masthead light at the same time. This oversight occurs when the operator inadvertently energizes both lights, or forgets to turn off the anchor light after weighing anchor, or switches on the anchor or spreader lights to read the sails. Two vertical white lights on a mast may appear harmless, but to a knowledgeable boater it signals "power-driven vessel towing astern."

Sailors that run with all-around white masthead light atop the main, or with an anchor light, announce to other boaters they are a power boat even though they are under sail. Inland Rule 25 states: "a sailing vessel underway shall exhibit: side lights and a stern light [only]." Sailing boats not under auxiliary power and under sail only enjoy certain rule privileges over power boats, and different rules apply. According to Rule 3, the term "sailing vessel" means any vessel under sail "provided that propelled machinery, if fitted, is not being used." The one who has the most to lose could be the sailboat operator, who believes, since he's under sail only, he's the stand-on vessel even though he's announcing to other vessels he's under power by displaying a white mast light. A situation that should a mishap occur as a result would negate his stand-on privileges in a court of law.

ON WATCH: Of all the nonconforming light configurations I've encountered, the car-boat hybrid stands out foremost. While standing at the Coast Guard moorings at Station Manistee late at night, I noticed what appeared to be a car's headlights heading outbound into Lake Michigan. As the lights approached, a small boat-like car emerged from the darkness. It looked like a 1954 Nash convertible. I piped my crew to the ready rescue boat. By the time the crew cast off lines, the car-boat had reached Manistee's north pier head light. Within moments, we reached the lighthouse. A crewman pointed to the nearby shore where the car-boat rolled up onto the shore and drove away. Very clever, I thought, at least until next time.

Don't take me wrong; there are a lot of enlightened boaters out there, but unfortunately, there are enough unenlightened boaters operating on the dark side to make nighttime boating a hazardous and challenging affair—including boaters who play nighttime peek-a-boo.

NIGHT TIME PEEK-A-BOO

One of the most hazardous close-quarter games played by fishermen at night is light peek-a-boo. Anglers fishing from small boats sometimes troll without navigation lights. I suspect they do it to preserve their battery or enjoy the lightless solitude of night or to avoid alerting fish to their presence. And some do it to avoid attracting insects. This foolish nighttime game involves many players. Coast Guard boat crews and marine sheriff deputies around Lake Michigan tell me it's the most common infraction they encounter on the water at night. Crewmen at Coast Guard Station Frankfort tell me that at night when they fire up the patrol boat, lights on small fishing boats twinkle on across nearby Lake Betsie. Marine sheriffs also report that when they light up the boat's blue law enforcement light at night, boat lights begin blinking on around them. The light peek-a-boo game can get really dicey around harbor mouths and river channel outlets.

Many Lake Michigan harbor mouths lead to river channels. Some channel systems are short; others can run for several miles to inland waters and many are shrouded in darkness. Most of these channels fall under a no-wake ordinance that requires boaters to operate at minimum, no-wake speeds. However, many harbor mouths and inland lake outlets do not fall under no-wake ordinance. In these headwaters, throttle jockeys take the risk of mowing down a powerboat or a man-powered watercraft failing to display navigation lights. Two teens in the following story nearly lost their lives because of a throttle jockey.

CASE FILE: Grand Haven, Michigan, Spring 2003. Two teenage males, while canoeing after dark on Spring Lake, Grand Haven, Michigan, barely escaped with their lives when a powerboat plowed into their hapless craft. "A twenty-five foot-long powerboat t-boned the canoe. The lads leaped overboard just before impact," said Sergeant Kevin Allman, an Ottawa marine deputy. The power boat operator retrieved the teens from the water unharmed. The canoe was mangled.

Although these youngsters failed to carry a flashlight or other illumination device to announce their presence, that did not exonerate the powerboat operator according to Rule 6, which we discussed earlier and is worth repeating. Boaters shall operate at a safe speed commensurate to prevailing conditions, not the least of which is state of visibility in restrictive waters.

But even operating at a safe speed, a boat operator must maintain a lookout in accordance with Rule 5 of the Inland Rules. During the summer of 2001, a recreational boat with another boat in tow struck two young adult males floating upon a beach raft at dusk off the entrance to Leland Harbor, Michigan. For whatever reason, the boat operator didn't see the raft. Perhaps he was distracted while towing a boat into a small restricted harbor with a nearby shoal extending out from a beach just a few yards off his starboard side. One victim received a slight prop-strike injury to the leg; the other however, suffered severe injuries. Reportedly, a Good Samaritan on shore held the victim's entrails in place by compressing a towel against his lower abdomen. Although the court exonerated the operator under criminal proceedings, he wasn't as fortunate regarding civil litigation, and the case remains mired in legal wrangling.

BOAT SMART BRIEF: In the event a boater should run down a fisherman that failed to energize navigation lights in time, chances are Rule 5 of the Navigation Rules would be their legal Achilles' tendon. That is unless they were "maintaining a proper look-out by sight and hearing as well as by all available means." A married couple told me they used their dog Buddy, a Shih Tzu, as an "available means." While sailing their 39-foot sloop, Buddy would jump onto the helm seat and cower against them when he heard a powerboat approaching.

Sure enough, over the horizon or from around a bend, a power boat would soon appear. Buddy never failed.

While operating a 25-foot inflatable rescue boat on Muskegon Lake at night, I adhered to Rule 5 almost to a fault. The boat has a center console with an overhead canopy. Protective glass shields the console, which houses radar, GPS, a radio, depth finder and engine gauges. These devices emit light that degraded my night vision. I would step aside from the center console to avoid the glare meanwhile a crewman focused on the radar while I peered into the darkness and steered the boat. I wore protective eye gear to prevent eye-strike from insects. And when I neared the channel mouth where the peek-a-boo crowd clustered, I brought back the throttles and activated the blue law enforcement light (rule 5, "all available means") and then watched as white all-round lights blinked on across the channel mouth. Rules 5 and 6 faithfully guided me, which I also believe would have safely guided me through court in the event of a mishap.

I believe what spares peek-a-boo fishermen from collisions is that most of them troll in no-wake areas or near shore away from the open water where boats whiz to and fro. But all it takes is one time and one can only guess how many near misses there have been. What about you, do you know someone with a near miss story to tell? I bet you do.

It's now time to introduce the next congested water player: Lake Michigan's ubiquitous fish-crazed anglers.

FISHING FRENZY

A human induced ecological event occurred on Lake Michigan in the mid 1960s that spawned a billion-dollar industry. It began with an overabundance of alewives, a small fish that resembles an oversized sardine, had entered the Great Lakes through the Welland Canal. It eventually found its way onto Lake Michigan's pristine beaches. Hundreds of miles of shoreline lay blanketed in rotting fish, creating a miasmic mist that invaded the homes of lakeside residents and repelled beach goers. Since the alewives have no natural predator

besides their own natural demise in the spring, they proliferated unchecked.

Some ingenious folks suggested the import of Coho Salmon from the Pacific Northwest to prey on the alewives. Some, however, claim economic incentives motivated the ingenious Coho scheme, which seems more likely. Whatever the reasons were for the Coho introduction, Lake Michigan would now have new bait to draw fishermen into her drowning fields. In the spring of 1966, the first Coho were planted in Lake Michigan: 264,000 in the Platte River, and 395,000 in Bear Creek, a tributary of the Manistee River. By 1967, the Coho fishing boom began in earnest as did Lake Michigan's feeding frenzy of fishermen.

CASE FILES: During the infamous Coho storm that ripped across upper Lake Michigan on September 23, 1967, eight fishermen died in one afternoon in the waters off Point Betsie and the Platte River outlet. "The wind storm caught about 1,000 boats, nearly all of them small craft manned by amateurs, in 25 foot waves Saturday.... More than a 100 boats were hurled onto the beach," reported the *Manistee News Advocate*. Twenty-five foot seas? Perhaps an exaggeration; however, reportedly many of the small boats capsized near shore in the shallows where wave backlash accentuated wave heights.

Apparently the fish-crazed anglers seemed undaunted by the carnage. A day later the *News Advocate* reported that according to authorities at least 700 sport fishermen were out again in small boats in five-to-seven foot seas fishing for Coho Salmon in spite of warnings from local officials and the Coast Guard.

Even remote Beaver Island, with its small year-round population of 540 inhabitants, has witnessed Lake Michigan's propensity to devour fishermen. During a visit to the island in 2003, Phil Gregg, a long-time resident, told me the story of charter boat captain, Floyd Potts. The captain along with three fishermen on Labor Day 1962, set out from Petoskey, Michigan for Hog Island (located near Beaver Island) aboard a 26-foot Chris Craft towing a small dinghy. Near Hog Island they anchored the boat 1500 yards off shore. Three of the fishermen climbed aboard the dinghy and rowed towards shallow water. A wave swamped the dingy, sending two of the fishermen on a non-refundable trip to the bottom. The surviving fisherman swam to shore and was later rescued by the Coast Guard.

The 26-foot Chris Craft must of carried a curse. The deceased captain's son Floyd Pott's inherited his father's fishing charter business, and two years later almost to the date of his father's tragic demise set out from Petoskey, Michigan for Hog Island with three fishermen aboard his father's 26-foot fishing boat, but they never returned. A Coast Guard crew from the Beaver Island Station located wreckage near Hog Island where they recovered three bodies. The forth body, Lake Michigan consumed. In all, the fishermen left a total of 12 children: the oldest 12, the youngest three.

Bill Cashman, curator of the Beaver Island historical museum and owner of the *Beaver Beacon*, an island monthly, told the story of three local teenage brothers who went out to set fishing nets a few hundred yards seaward of St. James Harbor. In spite of their mother's pleas to stay ashore, they launched even with heavy seas brewing. The small fishing boat capsized, and all three perished. The incident occurred in 1982, yet it remains a vivid memory in the islanders' collective heart. In all, nine fishermen have died in the waters off remote Beaver Island.

For years I've watched the lake consume a fisherman here, a fisherman there, although not in such dramatic fashion as the Coho storm or the Beaver Island tragedies. It's not just the lake but the entire Lake Michigan marine environment that willfully devours fishermen. During the early stages of the 2004 boating season, six fishermen drowned in Michigan waters between March 22 and May 5, 2004. In each case, the fishermen were separated from their boats. The average boat length was 16-feet and the water temperatures ranged between 33 and 45 degrees Fahrenheit. None of the victims wore *life jackets*.

The spring of 2005 began with more fishermen fatalities. On April 24, 2005, at the mouth of Sturgeon Bay canal, Green Bay, a 15-foot Nissan boat capsized with three fishermen aboard. Two

males, ages 46 and 18, drowned. At the time of the accident the air temperature was 33 degrees, water temperature 44 degrees, with running four-foot seas. On April 15, 2005 in nearby Oshkosh, Wisconsin, two brothers ages 23 and 16, drowned after their small duck hunting skiff capsized in a small Winnebago County park pond. Neither of the fishermen were wearing life jackets and reportedly one of them could not swim.

The lake will continue to feast on fishermen that enter her domain unprepared and unarmed. Boat Smart don't provide her the opportunity, wear a life jacket.

Notwithstanding the dark side of recreational fishing, it can be a royal pain in the stern for other boaters, including the commercial fleet operating in close-quarters. The following Boat Smart story, "Manistee channel or L.A. freeway?" appeared in the *Manistee News Advocate* many years ago, yet it reads like today's news regarding fish-crazed anglers' relentless pursuit of Coho Salmon.

ON WATCH: Manistee River Channel, August 31, 1987. Late Sunday morning the Manistee channel resembled the L.A. freeway system: congestion, confusion, festering tempers, disregard for the safety of others, everything but gunplay prevailed, at least from what I know. Those were my thoughts as I looked out Station Manistee's radio watch room at the river channel.

I ordered the crew to saddle up, and within minutes we were underway to establish traffic control in the Manistee river channel buzzing with fish-crazed anglers pursuing a lee from gusty winds and high seas. The running of the Coho had drawn hundreds of fishermen to the harbor mouth.

A solo fisherman, determined to land his catch, nearly ran his 16-foot boat into several other boats. He hooked a fish near the South Pier Head Light, then began zigzagging across the 300-foot wide Manistee channel while steering the boat with one hand and battling the fish with the other. Approaching the seawall, he turned away from the helm and faced the stern to reel in the fish. I watched in disbelief as the boat bounced off the wall. Ignoring the collision, he continued to battle the fish. A 25-knot wind pinned the boat against the pier wall; two gentlemen fishing off the pier leaped onto the boat to assist as he fought the Coho.

This account may sound humorous, but not to the many boaters forced to change course to avoid a collision with our possessed angler. A situation made even more hazardous by gusty southwesterly winds that threatened to set boaters onto the north seawall while attempting to avoid Captain Zigzag, who in the end lost the fish.

Unfortunately due to more pressing matters I couldn't cite the boater for hazardous operation. I flipped on the blue law enforcement light and steamed down the center of the channel, acting as a center highway line in order to keep outbound boats on the right side of the channel and those inbound on the left, and fishermen from zigzagging to and fro. This certainly wasn't the first time nor would it be the last I had to perform traffic cop duties to enforce proper vessel traffic flow in a channel in accordance with Inland Navigation Rules.

The captain got his due coming in the form of poetic justice. After the piece appeared in the *Manistee News Advocate*, several of his fishing chums connected him to the incident, and hence forth he was known about town as Captain Zigzag.

Soon after that fiasco, several fishermen drew me into another fish-frenzy episode. A fisherman casting off the seawall near the Coast Guard Station snagged the stern of an outbound boat with a lure. They exchanged foul words. The boater pulled his 16-foot boat alongside the seawall, scrabbled up a seawall ladder, grabbed a piece of driftwood and knocked the dockside fisherman to the ground. I watched this Laurel and Hardy stunt unfold from the radio watch room. I sprang out the window and leaped amongst the fray before the ill-tempered boater could land another blow. In the end, Stanley went off to the hospital, Ollie to the city jail.

In another fish frenzy episode that season, a throng of disgruntled fishermen threatened to run cable across Manistee Lake to snag charter boat down-rigger lines. The narrow two mile long

Manistee's 1st Street public boat launch draws hundreds of boaters from near and far when the Coho are running during August and September. Other ports around Lake Michigan also experience a surge in fishing activity as fishermen flock to the open waters of Lake Michigan, where freshwater sport fishing knows few equals.

lake runs north-south and narrows to about 150 yards at the south end, where the salmon converge during their return to the Little Manistee River, their home of origin. When weather drives the larger boats off Lake Michigan, they join the smaller boats in pursuit of the catch. Lots of boats, limited space, and fish-crazed anglers. Watch the testosterone explode, especially when the big guys trail down-rigger lines off the stern with cannon balls to keep the lures below the surface—a nasty set-up that snags fishing lures trailing off the stern of smaller boats.

My response to the ill-tempered fishermen who shared with me their cable-snag scheme was I didn't hear it. I suspect they shared their sinister plan in hopes the Coast Guard would take action, which we did. That afternoon again found me playing traffic cop and mediator, this time at Manistee Lake's south end.

I spoke with a Muskegon resident who told me for live entertainment he and his buddies would set up chairs along the Muskegon's River Channel walkway on a Friday evening and watch fishermen go at it like Popeye and Bluto.

Apparently, time has changed little. While visiting the crew at Station Frankfort in 2003, the crew told me for entertainment they tune in the VHF-FM channel 10, a common working frequency used by the local fishermen, for an update on what they call Lake Michigan combat fishing. "You should hear these guys go at each other threatening to cut lines, ram boats, inflict bodily harm," said Coast Guardsman Kevin Cook. He then told me about the fisherman on the Frankfort pier in late fall, who was casting off with his right arm while the other arm was rapped around a seawall ladder as waves crashed over the pier. After a fishing tournament in Manistee in 2003 a, disgruntled fisherman attacked another fisherman with a knife at a fish-cleaning station. Fortunately a bystander stepped in and thwarted the knife-wielding angler. The incident found its way to the county prosecutor's office.

Fortunately such malicious outbursts are more the exception than the rule; however, there are other rule violations fishermen often commit. One rule violation in particular that often plays out upon the water—a misguided belief that recreational fishermen enjoy stand-on privileges over other vessels because they're engaged in fishing.

BOAT SMART BRIEF: Nothing could be further from the truth. The rules apply to fishing boats that due to the nature of their *work* are restricted in their ability to maneuver. A vessel engaged in trawling, which according to Navigation Rule 26 means: "the dragging through the water of a dredge net or other apparatus," has the right-of-way over power and sail boats. These fishing boats with extended nets trailing far off the stern, or off the beam, or trailing cable with ice-hook like barbs (line fishing), are working fishing boats according to the rules and enjoy certain privileges.

The nature of their work clearly restricts their ability to maneuver, so power and sailboats must give way. These boats also display distinct day shapes: a black cone pointing upward if fishing nets extend more than 150 meters horizontally from the vessel, and two vertical cones with their apexes together or a basket that can readily be seen by other boaters. At night, they display a vertical green over white light on the mast to announce they are engaged in fishing and, if trawling, a red over white light.

A recreational sport fisherman, and that includes licensed recreational charter boat captains, do *not* have the right-of-way over power or sailboats while engaged in sport fishing, unless they are operating in open water where they enjoy certain privileges as a boat under power. Most of the fishing lines that sport fishermen troll with could be cut with a finger nail clipper. Granted, some sport fishing boats trail down-rigger devices with lead canon balls attached to wire cable that extend off the stern. The lead balls with line and lures attached allow fishermen to troll beneath the surface at desired depths where the fish are running at.

These apparatuses, which extend directly off the stern, do not significantly impede a boat's ability to maneuver. Should fisherman need to put on speed, the balls and rigging will rise to the surface. Inconvenient? You bet. Impede maneuverability? Hardly. Remember: sport fishermen troll, working fishermen trawl. Many recreational fishermen, however, conveniently confuse the words or interpret them as alike.

A Lake Michigan fisherman slices into a Chinook (King) salmon. The largest Chinook salmon caught in Lake Michigan waters measured 43.5 inches in length and weighed 46 pounds.

A sportfishing boat displays a typical downrigger system at the stern. These fishing boats troll not trawl and thus are not privileged under the Navigation Rules as a vessel restricted in its ability to maneuver. The rules treat them as a powerboat only.

Navigation Rules addressing fishing apply to harbors and channels as well. In fact, according to the rules, even working fishing boats "shall not impede the passage of any other vessel navigating within a *narrow channel or fairway*."

While many fishermen attempt to lord over Lake Michigan's river channels, harbor mouths and bays, they do so while in violation of the rules that are in place to maintain order and safety upon the waters. So what's more important: fishing or safety? Those who Boat Smart needn't answer.

Now brace yourself as we steam into turbulent waters churned up by boat wakes the ubiquitous by product of congested waters. So, hold on.

BOATERS NEED TO WAKE UP

Addressing boat wakes requires me to use enormous restraint to curb my sailor's tongue. Sure,

I have created my own share of boat wakes, but mostly when an urgent rescue case demanded a greater precedence. But even then I had to consider: was racing to the rescue creating a greater threat to nearby boaters than the dangers facing those requesting assistance? Never an easy call, but at least I was aware of the dangers wakes posed to other boaters. However, for the many boaters who disregard the rolling menaces pealing off their stern, they need to wake up and look around. The following Boat Smart cases reveal just how blatant and naïve recreational boaters can be when it comes to their boat wakes.

ON WATCH: Muskegon Harbor, August 20, 2001. The 24-foot boat lay dangerously close to the sea wall, its captain trying his best to prevent his stern from pounding against nearby rocks that fronted the wall. Mild sea conditions were in his favor, but wakes from passing boats favored him not.

I switched on the blue law enforcement light aboard the Coast Guard 25-foot rescue boat and steamed over to assist. Even with the blue light flashing, boats continued to enter Muskegon Harbor, throwing their wake towards the disabled vessel, which precariously tugged on its anchor line, its stern brushing the rocks.

What could I do to stop boats from kicking up a wake? Not much! The emergency forced us to focus on hooking up the boat and towing it into safe water, which we did in spite of wakes. No sooner did we have the boat safely moored at a nearby marina when our Operations Command Center directed us to assist another boat with seven people aboard that reportedly was sinking near the NOAA station, located near the harbor mouth. With blue lights flashing, we raced towards the NOAA station.

ON WATCH: When we arrived on scene, a 21-foot pleasure boat lay alongside a seawall, its entire stern submerged in water. We moored the rescue boat alongside the seawall and transferred a pump up onto the seawall.

From our 49-foot aids to navigation boat we snatched another pump; the NOAA research boat next door to the Coast Guard station supplied its own. Within moments, the chatter from three pumps hummed across the channel. Aboard the sinking boat, a Coast Guardsman probed around the submerged engine space looking for the source of the leak, while pump discharge hoses shot streams into the channel. The North Muskegon 22-foot fireboat joined the trio of pumps with its fire pump.

Meanwhile, a Muskegon marine sheriff deputy aboard his 24-foot boat controlled vessel traffic. His blue law enforcement light, the Coast Guard's blue law enforcement light, and the red flashing light from the Muskegon fireboat lit up the channel. Still, some boats kicked up wakes as they steamed past the rescue scene. It took an aggressive sheriff with a loud hailer to finally impose no-wake order in the channel. Even then a few sailors ignored their warnings, including a large sloop under full sail churning up a huge wake, which crashed into the disabled boat and slammed a coast guardsman against the sea wall.

As with the previous case, the emergency took precedence over the wake throwers, but had we had a free unit, that sailboat might well have been cited for negligent operation, which carries a $1,000 fine. Incidentally, that the sailboat was under sail and not power did not exonerate it from the no-wake rules. But regardless of the rules, you would think especially with emergency lights flashing on three vessels, a gathering of people on the seawall above the disabled vessel, the chattering pumps, and a Muskegon fire truck now on scene with its lights flashing that the captain would use the most basic of rules—common sense.

In spite of his and other wake throwers counter-contributions to our rescue efforts, we were able to secure the leak. The sheriff's boat towed the disabled boat to a safe mooring while we steamed alongside, pump at the ready.

BOAT SMART BRIEF: After the boat was safely moored, the captain told us that he had ventured out three miles into Lake Michigan, and that fortunately the leak did not spring until he re-entered Muskegon harbor. The leak stemmed from a broken seal around the boat's out drive unit. With seven people aboard, all the ingredients were there to make headline news. Wisely, the captain had enough life jackets aboard. Now, whether his crew could have donned them in time, well that's another story.

The story provided a subtle and often ignored lesson: boaters are connected by a common element—water. In close quarter situations, as with channels and harbor mouths, that connection can be closer than we might like, especially if we're at the receiving end of an unwelcome wake. Understandably, boaters can easily develop tunnel vision as they focus on the course ahead. I see it often with Coast Guard coxswains under instruction as they focus on staying on course, often ignoring traffic around them.

On the other hand, I can quickly spot veteran coxswains by their bird-like head movements and rotating eyes that miss little around them. This is a prudent and thoughtful way to handle a boat and one that reveals the difference between a skilled boater and one who merely steers a boat.

I recall a case where a wake capsized a 16-foot boat on Manistee Lake. Two middle-aged brothers died: one drowned; the other died of a heart attack shortly after being rescued. Eyewitnesses reported that a boat wake from a large power boat caused the capsizing. But, how many boat-wake related deaths go unnoticed? Understand boat wakes can strike long after the wake source has motored off, often leaving behind uncorrelated evidence as to the wake's origin. This leads me to wonder, just how many uncorrelated wake-related deaths and injuries occur on our waters? I suspect many, and Coast Guard statistics addressing recreational boating seem to corroborate my suspicions.

Coast Guard nationwide *Boating Statistics* reveal that annually over 55 percent of boating fatalities and injuries occur off small boats such as open motorboats, rowboats, canoes and kayaks, and that nearly 76 percent of recreational boating fatalities are caused by boats capsizing, boats being swamped

or flooded, and people falling overboard off boats. How many of these fatalities are due to wakes is difficult to determine. However, when you consider that nearly 83 percent of boating fatalities occur in moderate weather, it's not unreasonable to assume that boat wakes were the cause?

On July 11, 2005, I happened to be at Station Manistee when a boater voiced a wake complaint with the officer of the day. Moments earlier he had been fishing near the Manistee River Channel where it flows into Manistee Lake. A large power boat's wake slammed into his 14-foot boat, sending him overboard. He managed to climb back aboard. He told me he had been sitting at the time of the overboard ejection.

Boat wakes are contagious. One boater kicks up a wake in a no-wake zone, then another, then another, setting off a chain reaction that soon finds the area boiling in wakes, which greatly enhances the chance of a boater being pitched overboard as with the Manistee fisherman.

Capsizing and falls overboard are two of the leading contributors to boating fatalities. Since most boating fatalities occur during calm to moderate weather, wakes could be the leading cause.

Why boaters ignore or seem oblivious to the damage wakes inflict has baffled me for years, although I suspect wake shortsightedness stems from a blind exuberance to reach a destination. Or as the following boat wake case suggests, it could be just good old wanton ignorance

CASE FILE: Muskegon Lake, September 2003. John Wetterhold, captains the *Port City Princess*, a 79-ton cruise boat, homeport, Muskegon. He told me while transiting Muskegon Lake aboard the *Port City Princess* a large power boat flew past, throwing out a giant wake that forced him to make an urgent public announcement warning of the approaching tide. A private party aboard celebrating a couple's marriage renewal vows braced themselves as the wake slammed into the Princess; dishes flew off kitchen counters and shattered across the galley floor. Captain Wetterhold said, "What made it worse? The boater came about and roared by again, the operator waving and cheering as another wake slammed into the hull, again sending dishes flying and passengers bracing themselves."

Many fellow marine rescue responders also have voiced great displeasure with wake-makers, and much of it is not fit for print. Ottawa County marine deputy Kelly Brandfield, who patrols Lake Macatawa in Holland, Michigan, told me that even with blue law enforcement lights flashing and with a disabled boat strapped alongside, boaters still threw out wakes. How would wake-makers respond if their boat was alongside the sheriff's boat, heaving and pitching as tow lines yanked on cleats? I can assure you, their response would never pass edit. In the following On Watch story, a wake sank a 26-foot Sea Tow boat.

ON WATCH: Lake Macatawa, Holland, July 4, 2004. Coast Guardsman Jason Bernard, duty coxswain aboard Station Holland's 25-foot inflatable rescue boat, stood by as he watched Sea Tow, a commercial salvage operation, free a boat that had run aground off Drake Point Light on Lake Macatawa. Sea Tow had just liberated the 50-foot cabin cruiser with five people aboard and was alongside the larger boat taking in lines.

"I saw a large 34-foot power boat approaching the area, throwing off a massive roaster tail-like

wake," said Bernard. "We had our blue law enforcement light flashing. Several crewmen hollered out to the boat to slow down." With the boat's bow reaching skyward and stern squatted low in the water, the Coast Guard crew's attempts to hail down the approaching boat went unnoticed. "He was close enough that we could hear a boy aboard calling out to his father to slow down."

The first wake slammed into the helpless Sea Tow boat, rolling lake water over the gunnels. A second wake swamped the boat, sending the 26-foot-long boat beneath the surface. The Sea Tow operator scrambled onto the cabin cruiser as the second wake rolled over his boat.

The Holland crew tracked down the wake thrower and cited him for negligent operation, a misdemeanor that carries a $1,000 fine or one year in jail. The operator confessed to Bernard that he never saw the Sea Tow or Coast Guard boat.

As for the operator of the 50-foot boat that ran aground, they too confessed that they had no charts aboard nor did they understand the purpose of the navigation buoys that mark safe water.

I nearly lost my life aboard a Coast Guard rescue boat when a wake's aftermath yanked a cleat off the deck of a sailboat. The nylon line attached to the cleat stretched out like a rubber slingshot line, and when it parted, it sounded like a bullet as it whizzed pass my ear. Scary? You bet.

Boat wakes not only pose a threat to boaters in confined waters, but in open water as well. There boat wakes and sea waves often join forces forming a deadly alliance that wake jumpers apparently can't resist in spite of the risks.

CASE FILES: New Buffalo, Lake Michigan, August 2002. Two males ages 43 and 44, were thrown into Lake Michigan near New Buffalo when the operator of a 24-foot Baja made a hard high speed turn into a boat wake. One person drowned, the other ended up in the hospital. Rescuers found a 13-year-old boy aboard, unharmed. Neither of the adult males were wearing life jackets.

In 2003, a wake fatality occurred just outside Chicago's Calumet Harbor when a Baja power boat flew airborne off a wake, ejecting a father and daughter into the lake. The father broke his neck. The daughter kept him afloat while waiting for help to arrive.

ON WATCH FILES: Muskegon Michigan, August 23, 2003. A 24-foot powerboat rocketed over a boat wake near Muskegon and crashed into the lake. The family of four were returning from an offshore powerboat race in Grand Haven. A nine-year-old girl received facial cuts from flying glass, the wife a broken leg, and the husband cracked ribs. The impact separated the deck from the hull. "When I arrived on scene, I could see through the hull to the other side of the boat," said Coast Guardsman Travis Jones, coxswain aboard the 27-foot rescue boat.

In September 2003, in Lake Macatawa, Holland, Michigan, a run-about with five people aboard jumped the boat wake of a 34-foot power boat. The wake jumper's bow dug into a second wake, swamping the boat. A mother and father and three children escaped injury—all were wearing life jackets. "When I arrived on scene, only the bow was visible," said Chief Stein, who responded to the call.

The 2004 boating season on Lake Michigan saw a continuation of wake and wave jumping incidents. In July, a 36-foot fast boat while wave jumping in two to four foot seas rocketed off a wave at 65 mph, spun over and crashed into the lake upside down. The boat sank. A nearby boater rescued the two people aboard; both were wearing life jackets. The operator told the Coast Guard coxswain who responded to the incident, "Without life jackets, we would have died." A female passenger aboard was hospitalized.

In early August, in the waters off Ludington, Michigan an 18-foot fast boat powered by a 350 horsepower engine flew over a wave, landed lopsided into two-foot seas, throwing the 20-year-old male operator into the lake. The operator who was wearing a life jacket escaped injury.

In another 2004 wave jump case a boater's failure to wear a life jacket cost her life. In June, three adults were testing a 16-foot tri-haul boat in the lower waters of Green Bay in early evening. The boat jumped a wave, slammed down into another wave, ejecting the people aboard into the bay. Two adult males aboard survived the ejection; however, a female passenger in her 50s drowned along with her Scotch Terrier. According to Chief Chris Wissen of Coast Guard Station Green Bay, none of the people aboard were wearing life jackets.

Wake jumping can prove fatal. On September 11, 2005, a 32-year-old male was killed in the waters off Sheboygan, Wisconsin. The personal watercraft he was driving jumped a wake and crashed into the lake. The crash knocked him out. A female companion riding with him attempted to keep him afloat. He drowned before rescuers could respond. There was only one life jacket between them.

I've nearly been ejected off Coast Guard rescue boats while battling Lake Michigan's short wave action; to wake jump on top of it is inviting disaster. Lake Michigan's prevailing westerly winds generate a short wave fetch that due to the lake's narrowness lacks the distance and energy required to form giant ocean-like waves. An ocean fetch can run hundreds of miles and as waves build up energy and grow in size the distance between them increases. Eight to ten second intervals between wave sets on the ocean is common.

Lake Michigan's short wave fetch, however, produces far shorter intervals with two to four seconds between wave sets. These short waves form steep backsides, but still pack enough energy to deliver a knockout punch to heedless wave jumpers. I liken ocean waves to a heavy weight fighter who with one blow can score a knockout. Lake Michigan is more like a middle weight fighter who can deck you with a series of rapid punches delivered from all directions and with considerable power.

One thing is for certain regarding wakes, whether they be launching pads for wake jumpers or rolling menaces that rock other boats, both can be prevented by those who Boat Smart.

Boat Smart Anchor Points

Wake up advice

↬ "Slow—No Wake" is defined as the slowest speed at which it is still possible to maintain steering and does not create a wake.

↬ When operating a boat in wake infested waters, keep people off the bow where they are more likely to be tossed into the air or slammed into the deck.

↬ Sound off if you see an approaching wake, especially if people are below decks.

↬ If time allows, steer into a wake with the bow at a slight angle to the wake and keep way on at 3-5 knots, and keep the power on until the wake passes. If possible, do not take a wake broadside or off the stern, especially in a small boat for it could swamp.

↬ Many no-wake river channels lead into open lake waters with wake free zones. Here boaters should be on the alert for menacing wakes and wear a life jacket, please.

SHOW TIME

A warm, inviting Lake Michigan day will find the marine environment in the close-quarter arena bustling with boating activity. Perhaps swarming would better describe the stir. One finds boaters transiting the wrong side of the channel, some going too fast and others not going at all, sail boaters tacking back and forth in confined waters, personal water craft darting here and there, huge recreational gunboats kicking up wakes, fishing boats trailing downriggers going wherever the catch lures them. Yet, for some miraculous reason they seemingly avoid contact. At least until Show Time.

Chief Albert, Officer in Charge, Coast Guard Station Grand Haven, referred to the annual Coast Guard Festival fireworks extravaganza that draws thousands of boaters into Grand Haven river channel as nothing short of "controlled chaos." The event attracts over 200,000 spectators in what some say is the most spectacular fireworks display of the season along Lake Michigan's eastern shore.

Needless to say, maritime officials have their hands full.

And in spite of efforts to keep boaters out of harm's way, serious mishaps occur. Several years ago an aerial canister exploded on a barge during a fireworks display in Charlevoix, Michigan. A chunk of scrap metal struck a 41-year-old male in the head, instantly killing him. It goes without saying, that keeping people safe during fireworks or other waterfront events offers an enormous challenge to maritime authorities. Let's review some common challenges authorities face and how boaters can help them tame the "controlled chaos" while assuring their own safety during marine events.

ON WATCH: Lake Muskegon, August 2000. During a major high-speed powerboat race I watched a recreational boater penetrate the safety spectator line and head towards the race course. I was patrolling the western end of the safety zone aboard a Coast Guard 25-foot high-speed inflatable when my crewman drew my attention to blue lights flashing and sirens wailing on several law enforcement boats. I jammed down the throttles and joined the chase. We cut off the stray

A cadre of law enforcement officials enforce security around the fireworks safety zone on the Grand River during the Coast Guard festival in Grand Haven, Michigan. Besides maintaining the security zone, they perform rescue operations and law enforcement, in particular removing impaired boaters from the water.

boater within yards of the race course. A hail of water rained down on us as the race boats roared by at 90 mph.

Amid the race boats' giant rooster tails, I doubt the raceboat drivers could spot the family of five on the stray boat. Why the boat operator slipped past a spectator security zone clearly marked by a line of spectator boats might baffle some; however, it would not surprise those who regularly police these events. That's why the Coast Guard, along with fellow marine law enforcement agencies, create security zones, and why they aggressively enforce them.

What may appear to some as too much regulation may appear to others as too little. Marine authorities in Chicagoland seem to have reached a common ground with boaters through creative enforcement methods that bode well with the boating community, a remarkable achievement in itself.

Jim Harmon, Commanding Officer, Coast Guard Calumet Harbor, proposed establishing a no-wake zone around the security parameters for major marine events like fireworks and air shows. The no-wake zone would extend one-half mile out into Lake Michigan from the outer edge of

the security zone and inward to shore, including marinas and harbors.

At first, Earl Zuelke, Commanding Officer, Chicago Police Marine Unit, doubted the plan. Over the years he had witnessed serious mishaps after marine events as boaters raced for their moorings in an attempt to outrun the throng in spite of the presence of law enforcement officials and their aggressive tactics to prevent mayhem.

Lieutenant Zuelke couldn't have been more pleased when the plan worked.

The Coast Guard and Chicago marine police launched an aggressive public outreach program, distributing fliers around local marinas, airing public safety messages through radio stations and soliciting the help from marina officials and local yacht clubs to promote the plan. And during the marine event, Coast Guard crews frequently announced the no-wake provision over the VHF-FM marine radio. "Boaters were actually clapping and cheering our boat crews in response to the no-wake ordinance," said CWO Jim Harmon.

For me, the no-wake campaign reinforced a belief I strongly harbor—most boaters are squared away and, if properly informed and educated, will bare forth the fruits necessary to nourish safe boating. Moreover, most boaters understand they share the marine environment with others, and it's not an exclusive playground for a few self-serving egos that fail to understand that the waterways are not their exclusive domain.

Now let's move on to our next congested close-quarter arena subject the commercial players. So let's go aboard and see firsthand the challenges they face as they gingerly muscle their way through the recreational swarm.

Boat Smart Anchor Points

A Safe Ticket to Marine Events

The following guide lines will make for a safe and enjoyable marine event.

↦ Boaters should keep within safety buoys and avoid transiting across buffer zones.

↦ Fireworks zones require up to a 1000-foot distance between spectator boats and the fireworks platform. Authorities will delay the fireworks until all boaters are in compliance. In those cases where a river channel is temporarily shut down due to fireworks, such as when the fireworks platform is located near a harbor mouth, boaters will be notified in advance on marine radio (VHF-FM Channel 22) and Local Notice to Mariners of the channel closure and times. For those occasional late-comers, channel-closing times will be strictly enforced so the show may begin on time.

↦ Boaters attending events after dusk are required to display proper running lights, and if anchored, the proper anchor light. Marine officials will send boaters back to their moorings if they fail to display proper navigation lights. Boaters should remember to fully charge batteries; a low battery may prevent engine start, which could find the boater adrift in the dark amongst heavy boating traffic.

↦ Over the years, I've often seen boaters transiting a congested channel at night with their stern light covered with gear. This is a good way to get run down from behind. Keep that stern light clear and keep extra bulbs aboard.

↦ Near channel mouths and in dark river channels, post a forward lookout. You just might come upon a boater with a dead battery. Keep a flash light nearby, which can also be handy for disabled and adrift boaters to flash their presence.

↦ Always operate at a safe speed. After larger events, Lake Michigan harbor mouths, river channels, and nearby lakes can swarm with boaters. I've patrolled many of these waters and know that dark waters can make navigation treacherous. Operate at a safe speed, and to repeat: post a forward lookout.

↦ Of utmost importance: Enjoy the event and be assured the safest way home is the Boat Smart way.

LARGE BOATS SMALL MINDS

I hold the highest regard for Great Lakes commercial captains, and now ever more so after experiencing first-hand the trials and tribulations they must endure while dealing with recreational boaters. Commercial captains lack the intimidating advantages marine law enforcement agencies wield. Not even vessel size seems to move recreational boaters. In fact, often the one most intimidated is the commercial captain who must gingerly maneuver the vessel's bulk through a willy-nilly recreational fleet.

As a captain of a research vessel told me: "recreational boaters place professional captains at a huge disadvantage." Oh, how true that is, for commercial captains are expected to know the rules and can face career-ending repercussions should they fail to abide by them. Worse, they may abide by the rules but still be held accountable in the event of a mishap, since they are the "professional." It's terribly inequitable: it would be like holding commercial aviation pilots to the highest safety standards while allowing general aviation that is private pilots to fly to and fro as they please. Or to expect commercial truck carriers on the nation's highways to follow prescribed rules while the rest of us drive as we please. It would be absurd, yet commercial captains deal with such absurdity without the slightest ado from the public or authorities, except for public awareness programs like Boat Smart columns, or the Coast Guard's Detroit River freighter-tag program intended to dissuade recreational boaters from "playing games" like touch and run shenanigans with deep draft vessels.

By the way, if freighter tag sounds preposterous, what about close-up freighter photo shoot. Captain Herald Person, master of the 635-foot-long motor vessel *Sam Laud*, told me that while departing Holland Harbor outbound into Lake Michigan at night, his forward lookout reported an 18-foot power boat approaching from starboard. Captain Person pilots the ship from the aft pilothouse and is unable to see 300 feet ahead of the bow, therefore he must depend on forward lookouts. "Johnson, my lookout, reported that the boater stopped right in front of the bow. I ordered the helm hard left and the small boat passed down my starboard side. I saw the flash from his camera just before giving the helm command. He probably got a great shot of Johnson gawking at him," said Captain Person who added. "Large boats attract recreational boaters as might curiosity seekers flock to a zoo featuring large dinosaurs."

And you wonder why commercial captains pack an attitude regarding recreational boaters. The disgruntlement spans the entire commercial fleet from captains of large motor vessels to skippers of 30-foot long Army Corps of Engineers survey boats. I asked a Corps surveyor his feelings regarding recreational boating. "It's a pain in the butt," he replied.

Notwithstanding the photo and freighter tag mischief, most pain-in-the stern engagements the commercial fleet encounter stem from misguided or uninformed boaters, except in some cases where willful arrogance boils up in the form of fishermen and sail boaters pompously lording their misinformed, often self-serving right-of-way privileges over the commercial fleet. Then there are those boaters who are just downright nasty as one captain in particular will attest.

Captain Dennis Donahue, Marine Superintendent at NOAA's Great Lakes Environmental Research Laboratory, Muskegon, Michigan told me that while inbound Pentwater Channel from Lake Michigan aboard the research vessel *Laurentian* he encountered a small power boat heading outbound.

Rule 9 of the Inland Rules states: "A vessel proceeding along the course of a narrow channel or fairway shall keep as near to the outer limit of the channel or fairway which lies on her starboard side as is safe and practicable." Pentwater channel is definitely narrow, measuring just over a hundred feet in width; still it was plenty of room for the small boat to safely pass the 80-foot long, 129-ton *Laurentian* with a beam of 21.8 feet. You would think.

Captain Donahue in accordance with the "Inland Rules" eased over to starboard to allow the small power boat to safely pass on his port side, while also adhering to Rule 14, of the Inland Rules: "When two power-driven vessels are meeting on reciprocal or nearly reciprocal course so as to involve risk of collision each shall alter her course to starboard so that each shall pass on the port side of the other." Sounds pretty simple that is unless you are dealing with a bafoon. The small boat continued to advance dead on *Laurentian's* bow even after Captain Donahue moved to starboard. Captain Donahue said, "I stepped out on the bridge wing and gestured for the boat to move over toward the left side of the channel. The guy wouldn't bulge." Facing an extreme head-on situation, Captain Donahue had no choice but to back hard down to avoid a collision, the prop kicking up a maelstrom off the stern and within feet of the channel seawall.

The small boater then moved over and passed along the *Lauentian's* portside. "I stepped out onto the port bridge wing and this guy hollers up: 'What do you think, you own the channel?'" said Captain Donahue, who reported that in addition to the male operator there was an adult female and kids aboard. Just swell! This adult role model was spawning the next generation of grief for the commercial fleet.

Notwithstanding these miscreants, for most recreational boaters, it's ignorance, not arrogance, that influences their behavior regarding commercial vessels, a thought process which fortunately can be altered if intelligently redirected. What

The 640-foot-long motor vessel *Algoway* in a meeting situation, Manistee River Channel. Size and strength do have sway, but when it comes to large commercial motor vessels and small recreational boats, the one most often intimidated is the large motor vessel.

better way of educating the recreational fleet than through the eyes of commercial captains. So, let's go aboard and experience firsthand the unique challenges commercial captains face regarding recreational boats. Let's begin our fleet excursion atop the pecking order.

LARGE MOTOR VESSELS: Recreational boaters would do large motor vessels well if they followed a rule of thumb I learned while patrolling Long Beach Harbor aboard a Coast Guard patrol boat: "give way to gray." I served aboard an 82-foot cutter and being a small mobile cutter, we could

easily maneuver around large naval vessels. We often gave way to the large naval vessels even if we enjoyed stand-on privileges. I couldn't imagine hailing the 887-foot-long battle ship *New Jersey* and asking them what were their intentions in a close quarter encounter. I might, however, if I wanted to hear a roar of laughter explode from the bows of the enormous battleship.

Ridiculous? Hardly. Norm Nelson, chief engineer aboard the 875-foot long composite unit *Great Lakes Trader* barge and tug *VanEnkevort*, told me that while approaching a harbor on Lake Michigan, a sail boater hailed them on Channel 16 and asked the *VanEnkwvort's* captain, "What are your intentions?" That's like the pilot of a small private aircraft standing by on a runway cutout radioing the pilot of a 747 just before touch down and asking him what his intentions are.

On the Great Lakes the "give way to gray" rule is commonly know as the "rule of gross tonnage." The gross-tonnage implications seem obvious, you would think, however.

Coast Guardsman coxswain Jay Douglas described an incident in the spring of 2004 on Muskegon Lake that lends further credence to the small mind assertion. The motor vessel *Joseph L. Block*, a 728-foot long, 78-foot wide "lake carrier" was transiting three-mile-long Muskegon Lake in early evening. At the time, a sailboat regatta was underway. "I couldn't believe it, this 30-foot sail boat comes about directly in front of the *Block* and loses it wind," said Douglas.

Captain Sheldon of the *Block* said, "The sailboat disappeared underneath my bow. All I could do is sound the danger singnal [five short blast]," What could any captain do traveling at five knots, while drawing 23.6 feet. Not even the bow and stern thrusters were effective at that speed.

"He missed hitting the sailboat by feet, "said Douglas, who approached the sailboat captain after the *Block* had passed. "I stood down the captain for such a bone-head maneuver and his response: 'I'm a sailboat I have the right-of-way.'" With that mentality, he had no right being on the water. If this sailboat arrogance was a one time write-off I wouldn't be writing about it at all, but I often hear similar sailboat right-of-way concerns from other commercial captains and even Coast Guardsmen.

Chief Reed told me that while transiting a narrow channel in Lake Macatawa, Holland with a vessel in tow with the Coast Guard boat's blue light flashing he encountered a sailboat tacking back and forth in the narrow channel. The sailboat captain insisted that Chief Reed stop and give way. Chief Reed in accordance with the Navigation Rules maintained course and speed. When the sailboater drew near he hollered out: "Don't you know the rules, sailboats have the right-of-way."

I've heard similar stories from other Coasties. My old boss, Commander Roger Dubuc told me

that while he was outbound aboard the Coast Guard cutter, *Sherman*, in San Diego, Harbor a sailboat ran into the 378-foot long cutter's bow just aft of the anchor pocket. "We were steaming along at one knot, if that, due to heavy vessel traffic in the restricted channel. The sailboat lay along side our cutter and it's captain starts yelling up at our captain that as a sailboat he had the right-of-way," said Dubuc.

Unbelievable or maybe totally believable—read on.

Mackinac Isl.

Captain Paul Allers skippers for Arnold Transit Company, a Mackinac Island ferry and freight service that has been operating in the Straits of Mackinac for over a hundred years. Captain Allers himself has been working on boats for over fifty years. "I've gone from coal steam driven boats to jet driven boats," said Captain Allers, who hails from a long line of family mariners that date backs over 150 years, a maritime history that includes nineteenth century Great Lakes sailors.

Captain Allers described an incident he witnessed in the Round Island passage, which borders Mackinac Island, Lake Huron. The incident would make the most devout sailboat advocate wince. According to Captain Allers, the motor vessel *Indiana Harbor*, a 1000-foot ore carrier encountered a sailboat in a meeting situation while steaming along on a westerly course through the narrow passage. The operator of the 36-foot sailboat hailed the *Indiana Harbor* on Channel 16 insisting that the captain move over to the right side of the channel. The sailboater was demanding right-of-way privileges over the giant vessel while crowing over the marine radio his sailboat status. The captain of the *Indiana Harbor*, which at the time was drawing 28 feet in a 35 feet-foot deep channel, faced two options: either muscle past the nincompoop or comply.

After a heated exchange over the marine radio, the *Indiana Harbor* captain acquiesced even though according to the rules he was the stand-on vessel. Navigation Inland Rule 9 clearly reads: "A sailing vessel shall not impede the passage of a vessel that can safely navigate only within a narrow channel or fairway." The 60,000 ton leviathan with a beam of 105 feet—nearly three times the length of the sailboat—eased over to the right side of the 400-yard wide channel precariously close to shallow water. Captain Allers said, "The *Indiana Harbor* was kicking up mud. I had to hand it to the Captain, he displayed remarkable seamanship skills. It was a very close call."

While the motor vessel captain displayed remarkable skills, the sailboat captain displayed remarkable ignorance and a total lack of respect for proper decorum so honored by professional sailors. He also displayed a sailboat right-of-way carte blanche mentality so often seen on the water. "In my many years on the water, I've seen far too many incidents with pleasure craft, mostly sail, that fail to abide by the rules of seamanship and courtesy," said Captain Allers.

Other captains agree. During an interview with Captain Larry Spenser of Star Lines, a Mackinac Island ferry service, he told me he watched a sailboat captain stand down the 1000-foot motor vessel *Burns Harbor* near buoys number 5 and 6 in the Straits of Mackinac. "The sailboat captain chewed out the *Burns Harbor* captain over the marine radio insisting that as a sailboat he was the stand-on privileged vessel," said Captain Spenser. Again this is a case of a large motor vessel operating in restricted waters following prescribed track lines. "Stand-on vessel," someone should have stood that sailboat captain on his head.

Don't take me wrong, many sail boaters use extreme caution when operating near large boats and those that do, no doubt, are appalled. Who wouldn't be offended, boater or not.

I don't mean to be bitter, mean, or sarcastic but I must set the record straight regarding these wayward sailors. The commercial ranks run deep with experience far deeper than the shallow egos of those self acclaimed rag sailors who lord themselves over commercial captains. I've done some sailing myself. I had the good fortune of making a 13-day run from Suva Fiji to the Bay of Islands, New Zeeland aboard the 50-foot schooner, *Lady Sterling*, homeport Auckland, New Zealand. Also I have made numerous yacht deliverers along the California coast. The sailboaters I know are squared-away and they hold the highest regard for the commercial fleet and would be appalled as anyone regarding these buffoons.

Commercial captains are the quintessence of first-class seamanship. Moreover, the cargos they transport are vital to the economic well-being of the Great Lakes and the nation. To have a recreational boater toy with them would be like someone entering the workplace of a commercial enterprise and raising mischief. I'm hard-pressed to think of another profession that must deal with workplace intrusions as do commercial captains regarding recreational boaters. Worse yet, captains have no means to prevent recreational boaters from invading their space besides the Navigation Rules. But what value are the rules if recreational boaters don't know them, nor are they obligated to.

That's why I marvel at how captains work through workplace intrusions even when the intruders are in violation of the Navigation Rules that are intended to facilitate order and safe operation between vessels. The fact that mishaps between commercial and recreational boats seldom occur gives testimony to the skills of commercial captains.

I had the good fortune to interview Captain Grahm Grattan master of the Canadian motor vessel *Algorail* and discuss the challenges he faces in dealing with recreational boaters. I met up with the good captain after the *Algorail* ported at Manistee shortly after dawn.

The *Algorail's* small boat picked me up at Seng's loading dock on Manistee Lake and whisked me out to the motor vessel. Arriving at mid ship along the starboard side, I climbed up a side ladder that carried more rungs than a fire truck's hook and ladder. There would be no need that day to visit the local fitness center.

Once aboard, I headed for the forward pilothouse, which seemed a football field away and stood higher than a goal post. The self-unloading bulk carrier is considered a medium-sized motor vessel at 640 feet in length, 360 feet shorter than the 1,000-foot giants that plow the lakes.

Captain Grattan greeted me on the bridge, and I immediately thanked him for granting the interview. He had made port that morning around

3 a.m. and making time for me that early morning amidst a hurried in-and-out schedule spoke well for the captain's desire to help spread the Boat Smart message. From the pilot house, the enormity of the vessel captures the eye. Looking towards the stern a string of athwart ships' deck hatches run aft and look like elongated shoe boxes. The seventeen deck hatches and three holds can receive up to 23,750 tons of bulk material. At the moment, slag—a material used in concrete projects—poured off the end of a 250-foot discharge boom extending off the portside. It would take approximately four hours to download the 15,000-ton order.

As the slag piled up, forming a pyramid-like mound, Captain Grattan shared with me challenges he encounters with small boats. He told me the stern of a large motor vessel offers a threat to small boats due to stern suction created by water flowing down the hull and flowing into a low area near the stern curvature. For vessels with forward pilothouses, the superstructure can obscure the stern area, especially motor vessels like the *Algorail* with an A-frame that supports the boom device.

The frame is stationed directly behind the pilot-house windows. Captain Grattan told me he must walk from one side of the bridge to the other to see aft around the A-frame. Recreational boaters should stay well clear of the stern because a captain may not see them when maneuvering the vessel. Other captains have expressed similar concerns including those with stern pilot houses.

Admiral John Tanner, Superintendent, Great Lakes Maritime Academy, told me he has seen stern suction grab sailboats and suck them into the aft hull of large motor vessels. It can also happen to motor vessels.

On October 23, 2001, the pilot vessel *J.W. West-cott II* capsized and sank in the Detroit River while along side the stern of the tank ship *Sidsel Knutsen*. The pilot vessel approached the 533-foot tanker off the stern rather that forward near amidships. At the time of the accident the *Sidsel Knutsen* was making speed at about nine knots. Water flowing down the tanker's hull sucked the *Westcott* starboard side up into the hull forcing the portside hard over. The boat capsized.

Boaters should stay well clear of the stern and bow of large motor vessels. Blind spots or danger zones on large motor vessel can extend out to a 1000 feet.

PHOTO BY RON BURDICK

According to the Coast Guard report the wheel was found in the "hard port" position. The throttle in the "full" position indicating the captain attempted to power out. The captain and engineer went down with the vessel. The two pilots aboard floated away from the stern and were rescued. Both were wearing life jackets. The captain and engineer who died were not.

Another concern Captain Grattan addressed regarded unexpected course changes small boats make in restricted waters that force him to alter course: "If a small boat in restricted waters forces me to make a course change, I could have but one move to make and in so doing I could create a much greater threat to nearby boaters," said Captain Grattan.

Recreational boaters who demand stand-on privileges in open waters near harbor mouths or in congested recreational fishing areas near shipping lanes should consider this: not only could they be jeopardizing their own safety, but that of other boaters if they force a motor vessel to abruptly change course.

Apparently some recreational boaters could give a hoot even when the motor vessel enjoys stand-on

privileges. Captain Grattan said, "I can be transmitting a narrow channel or fairway, and small fishing boats will wave me off as if I were in the way. Some boaters even drop anchor in designate turning basins for large motor vessels that strictly prohibit anchoring and then insist the motor vessel maneuver around them," Both incidences are in violation of the Navigation Rules.

Captain Grattan has served as a Great Lakes captain for over 24 years, and I marvel at his patience. He will be the first to tell you that far more recreational boaters abide by the rules than those that don't. It's just that the ones that don't make it very uncomfortable for the many who abide by the rules and who exercise good-old fashion common sense.

Several weeks after my interview with Captain Grattan, I rode aboard the steamer *Wilfred Sykes*, a 671-foot long bulk carrier capable of carrying 21,550 tons of cargo in her six compartments below decks. I picked the boat up in Muskegon and rode her down to Grand Haven. We departed Muskegon at sunrise. The *Sykes* had dumped a load in the early hours at the VerPlank dock located at the east end of Muskegon Lake and was now on

The flow of water down hull of a large motor vessel accelerates near the stern. Boat should stay well clear of the stern especially deep keeled sailboats.

her way to the VerPlank docks in Spring Lake. A two port visit across 24 hours would call for an 18-hour workday for the crew.

The departure from Muskegon Harbor carried us out into a placid Lake Michigan. By the time we reached the waters off the Grand Haven harbor mouth, the morning sun sat 15 degrees about the eastern horizon, casting eye-squinting rays across a glimmering surface.

Despite the fact the *Sykes* carried electronic charts that interfaced with GPS input to pinpoint a vessels position on an LCD screen, the captain, for the most part, relied on time-proven methods—reading nature's telltale signs.

Captain Ron Brezinski, pointed to the harbor mouth: "If you look closely you can see darker water around the harbor mouth. That's river sediment. Notice it's setting towards the south. That means a surface current that will set us south," said Captain Brezinski

The captain then pointed out wave movement from the northwest and a slight breeze that brushed surface waters indicating wind direction. At the moment, a calm Lake Michigan hardly announced these subtle movements, but to the veteran captain they seemed apparent, however slight they might be. All can influence the large bulk carrier, often in opposing directions. Imagine the challenge dealing with these elemental influences while maneuvering through a sea of boats.

While riding aboard the car ferry *Emerald Isle* that runs between Beaver Island and Charlevoix, Michigan, Captain Kevin McDonough told me when approaching the Charlevoix harbor mouth he can experience river currents, lake currents and wind—all working in opposite directions. At 130-feet long and weighting 380 gross tons fully loaded, boat handling in a close-quarter environment can be challenging. Throw in a bunch of recreational boaters into the mix and watch the sweat flow.

That morning the *Sykes'* captain set up an approach to the Grand Haven harbor mouth three quarters of a mile out. Captain Brezinski said, "If I start my final approach too soon I could find myself making unwanted maneuvers to stay on course as the elements play on my vessel. If I make it too late I could miss the mouth." One can understand, then, why small boats can raise havoc once the large boat commences its final approach. The last thing the captain needs is to make unnecessary course maneuvers. Fortunately, most recreational boaters follow the common sense rule—the rule of gross tonnage.

Entering the Grand Haven channel the size of the motor vessel became apparent as we passed the lighthouse on the South Pier. I've passed the light structure numerous times aboard Coast Guard small boats and always looked upward at the 51-foot high cylindrical light that loomed over the Coast Guard small boat. Now, I was looking down onto the top of the lighthouse.

Entering the Grand River, the captain piloted through a series of lateral buoys marking safe passage through the shoal-ridden waters. He used landmarks on shore as reference points for the helmsman to steer on while making slight compass changes when needed. Like any experienced boat handler, the captain was a boat length or so ahead of his position. The maneuver he made now could moments later raise havoc should he miscalculate even a subtle course change, especially in a narrow channel. He certainly doesn't need recreational boaters throwing unexpected surprises onto his tenuous path.

The *Sykes* does carry a bow thruster a rotating propeller device located beneath the bow that allows the captain to pivot the bow left and right. However, the thruster is of little use at speeds above three knots, or in winds exceeding twenty-five knots.

Watching the veteran captain focus on the task at hand, one would conclude that it was his first channel transit as a master. Even though he has

Captain Brezinski pilots the *Wilfred Sykes* into Grand Haven Harbor.

made countless passages in his 12 years as master, he focused on the task at hand as if it the experience were anew.

Most boaters would be utterly impressed, as I was, by the professional skills displayed by Captain Brezinski and his crew. Smart boaters can show their respect by staying well out of the captain's workspace, and I believe most do except for a few loggerheads. Remember, "give way to gray." Only the ignorant or arrogant wouldn't.

Let's sign aboard on some other commercial boats and experience the challenges they face regarding recreational boats.

CROSS LAKE FERRIES: Two cross-lake ferry services operate on Lake Michigan: the *Lake Express* offers passenger and vehicle transport between Muskegon, Michigan and Milwaukee, Wisconsin, and The Carferry *S.S.Badger* offers like services between Ludington, and Manitowoc,

Wisconsin. Let's first go aboard the Carferry *S.S. Badger* for some first-hand accounts of the challenges its captains deal with regarding recreational boating.

In October 2003, I rode with Coast Guard Marine Safety Officers during their fall safety inspection of the Carferry *S.S. Badger*. During the summer months the *Badger* makes two daily round-trip runs between Ludington, Michigan, and Manitowoc, Wisconsin. The sixty-mile run takes four hours one way. And yes, she does steam, being the only remaining coal-fired steam-driven vessel, in the entire U.S. commercial fleet.

The *Badger's* Second Mate, Mike Stewart, said: "I'm concerned about boaters' apparent lack of knowledge regarding the rules of the road." His point is well taken. Commercial ships are restricted in their ability to maneuver in harbor mouths and narrow channels, and the rules clearly state recreational boats, including sail, must give way.

The car ferry *S.S. Badger* offers cross-lake service between Ludington, Michigan and Manitowoc, Wisconsin. The *Badger* is 410 feet long and carries up to 620 passengers and 180 vehicles. The *Badger* is the only remaining coal-fired steam-driven vessel in the entire U.S. commercial fleet.

Captain Fitch said he was making port at Ludington one morning around 6 a.m. when the forward lookout spotted a 16-foot catamaran anchored in mid channel without an anchor light. If the forward lookout had not spotted the catamaran with binoculars in the early dawn light, the *Badger* may have run down the boat. The small craft pulled anchor and fled after the *Badger* blasted the danger signal.

In another incident, Captain Fitch was approaching Manitowoc harbor when he spotted a small fishing boat at the harbor entrance. The operator of the small boat hailed the *Badger* on the marine radio and requested that the car ferry come dead in the water while he reeled in a fish. The *Badger* is a 410-foot-long vessel, carries up to 620 passengers and 180 vehicles, and makes port at a minimum speed of around 10 knots. At that speed, the *Badger* was committed to entering the pier heads. The small fishing craft gave way, but not until its captain flipped off Captain Fitch after losing his fish.

And in another case, Second Mate, Mike Stewart, told of time the *Badger* was approaching its moorings in Ludington. A maneuver that involves swinging the boat and dropping a three-ton anchor to steady the bow while backing the *Badger* into its slip. During the maneuver an adult male with two youngsters in a small wooden boat approached the *Badger*. They rowed up to the forward part of the bow near the anchor and touched the boat. Had the crew let go the anchor, it might have smashed the small boat or capsized it with the anchor wake. No one in the small boat was wearing a life jacket.

In another *Badger episode*, Chief Mann was standing near the Coast Guard Station Ludington moorings when he heard the *Badger* blast the danger signal. The danger signal carries five short and rapid blasts on the ship's whistle. His eyes traveled to the harbor mouth to see a small fishing boat disappear under the badger's bow. He and a crewman leaped onto the station's 22-foot rescue boat and raced out to the harbor mouth. The *Badger* had barely missed the small boat, which had slid down the starboard side and was now bobbing in the giant car ferry's wake.

Chief Mann motored up to the small craft and hailed over the captain, who ignored the order. Coming alongside, chief could readily see why the fisherman had failed to hear the *Badger's* danger signal: headphones covered the boat operator's ears.

Senior *Badger* Captain Dean Hobbs told me that small boats operating near the stern are unnerving. Water pressure differentials boiling around the stern could suck a small boat into the *Badger's* 14-foot high prop. From the forward bridge it's difficult to see the stern area. Captain Hobbs also explained how difficult it can be to view the movement of a small boat relative to his own: "In order for me to determine the *Badger's* forward movement, I must look to the side to judge movement through the water. The superstructure of large boats influences one's ability to judge the movement of a small boat. It's far easier for the operator of a small boat to make accurate speed and distant judgments to a large boat."

Captain Hobbs told me that if a boater while approaching a large motor vessel in a crossing situation should decide to change course he or she make the course change readily apparent. This holds true especially for sailboats. Slight course changes do little to abate the captain's concerns and could even elevate them. The ideal situation is for the small boat operator to pass astern of the larger vessel. A smart boater would.

Challenging as it is in clear weather to determine a recreational boater's intentions, it can be daunting in fog. "Boaters call me up on the marine radio in fog and ask for course recommendations to avoid the *Badger*. I advise them: get radar, and I continue to tell them to get radar when they come back seeking further instructions," said Captain Hobbs, who went on to say, "few recreational boaters sound the proper sound signal one prolonged blast in intervals not to exceed two minutes and those that do often have it wrong. I encountered a boat sounding two short and one prolonged blast, which is a vessel restricted in its ability to maneuver, and when it appeared out of the fog it was a sailboat, bare poled, and under power." Other captains have told me they have come across sailboats proclaiming their right-of-way privileges under sail, yet

The carferry SS *Badger*, while outbound Ludington harbor to Manitowoc, Wisconsin steams past a fishing boat. Lake Michigan harbor mouths can draw out hundreds of anglers aboard small fishing boats pursuing salmon.

engine exhaust steam can clearly be seen misting from the engine's stern exhaust port.

On Saturday September 4, 2005, the *Badger* while inbound Ludington Harbor at 6:15 a.m. with its searchlight scanning the outer harbor entrance was forced to take evasive action and sound the danger signal. A recreational fishing boat adrift at the mouth of the harbor lay in the path of the *Badger*, which was steaming in at ten knots. The operator of the small boat hailed Coast Guard Group Grand Haven and complained the *Badger* was trying to "run" him down. Did the boater broadcast over Channel 16 his predicament to alert the *Badger* or other boats in the area? No, and It probably never crossed his mind.

"When I passed alongside the small powerboat I could see its trolling motor raised up. The boat apparently had its main engine available, but apparently the captain elected not to use it. He had one hand on the helm and in the other hand a coffee mug," said Dean Hobbs, the *Badger's* captain.

No sooner did the *Badger* maneuver around the fisherman than another small boat challenge surfaced. While mooring at its dock the *Badger's* search light picked up a small rubber watercraft directly under the anchor. The watercraft carried no lights and if not for the search light and a vigilant lookout its occupants could well have become mush.

I also interviewed the *Badger's* competitor, *Lake Express* out of Muskegon. The cross-lake service transports passengers and vehicles between Milwaukee, WI and Muskegon, MI. During a cross-lake trip to Milwaukee, I interviewed with Captain Rick Hopper and First Mate, Jeff Waldman. They expressed the same concerns voiced by Captain Hobbs. Captain Hopper did, however, raise an interesting point. He believes that a commercial vessel assuming stand-on vessel privileges could be more vulnerable than if it were the give-way vessel. "While attempting to maintain course and speed as the stand-on vessel, you could be inviting a mishap because the recreational boater might not know the rules, and there's a good chance they don't, and so by doing the right thing you could in fact be sailing into a collision," said Hopper.

Many commercial captains of large vessels tell me they would rather maintain course and speed than change course in compliance with the rules, and, in many cases, close-quarter conditions often preclude compliance with the Navigation Rules. Unbelievable as it is a 16-foot boat in open waters can demand stand-on privileges, and a large vessel must take appropriate action to avoid a collision even though such a maneuver could raise havoc with nearby vessels and even man-made structures. Talk about a rock and a hard spot predicament.

Captain Hopper admits the *Lake Express*'s maneuverability has reduced some of the tension that comes with dealing with smaller boats. The *Lake Express* can come to a full stop in a distance equal to one and a half times the length of vessel. But he went on to say that is not the case when driving tug boats that are pushing or towing barges. That

The *Lake Express* runs between Muskegon, Michigan and Milwaukee, Wisconsin. The 192 foot-long vessel, which can reach a speed of 40 miles per hour, makes the run in two and one-half hours.

brings us to our next disadvantaged player in the recreational free-for-all: tug boats.

First, however, let me salute Captain Hopper on a lifesaving rescue he performed on August 21, 2005. The *Lake Express* had departed Milwaukee at 6 a.m. Sunday morning on its run to Muskegon. Around 20 miles east of Milwaukee, Captain Hopper spotted an object in the water that drew his attention. A closer look with binoculars revealed a man clinging to debris. The *Lake Express* crew rescued the man, and returned to Milwaukee.

Reportedly the man, age 44, had departed that morning from Milwaukee on a 22-foot Sea Ray powerboat. His boat capsized after taking a wave over the stern; the boat rapidly sank before he could call for help on the marine radio. He was not wearing a life jacket. For me, the rescue once again illustrates the contributions commercial captains make to assisting mariners including recreational boaters and it is not without cost. Because the *Lake Express* returned to Milwaukee it had to cancel its midday round trip from Milwaukee to Muskegon. That said, let's tug ahead.

TUG BOATS: Tug boats, as with large motor vessels and cross-lake ferries, face challenges in kind regarding recreational boaters; however, it could be argued that a tug's ability to maneuver in some ways is even more prohibited than that of a large motor vessel.

When a tug is muscling along pulling a barge with 600 feet of cable or pushing a barge ahead, maneuvering the duet can be a challenge, especially with currents at play. Throw recreational boats into the picture and it's enough to turn knuckles white. Captain Hopper, who also drives tugs boats, told me that while he was towing a barge down the Milwaukee River, he grew so frustrated dealing with recreational boats that he kicked a hand rail and broke his foot. He once worked with an old tug boat captain who would boil to a flash point, rip off his hat, and stomp up and down on it while machine-gunning nearby recreational boaters with a salvo of sailor slang.

Captain Jan Sickterman of Great Lakes Dock and Materials, Muskegon, Michigan, told me that

while outbound the Grand Haven channel aboard a tug pushing a barge, an elderly couple aboard a power boat passed the tug's starboard side then cut in front of the barge. The small boat lost its engine power and stalled. It required every skill he possessed and then some to avoid hitting the boat. Fortunately, the abrupt maneuver missed other boats transiting the area.

In another incident, Tug boat captain Mike Oleary, told me that while pushing ahead a barge along the Saginaw river channel at night a recreational powerboat passed him on his starboard side. The boater, after clearing the tug's bow, turned the boat hard to starboard and ran into the barge. The tug was displaying the proper towing lights—two yellow towing lights in a vertical line along with two white masthead lights in a vertical line, indicating he was pushing a barge. The barge also carried proper lights: green and red side lights at the bow along with a special flashing light. The vessels might just as well have been displaying a lighted Christmas tree.

It didn't help either that the clueless boater was under the influence of alcohol, leaving the besotted boater with little financial recourse. Not all commercial captains get off the financial hook that easily even when the violator is intoxicated and in violation of the Inland Rules.

Robert Cross, a project engineer for M.C.M Marine, Inc, told me that while engaged in dredging operations in Grand Haven Channel, a 45-foot long fast boat ran up onto the dredge pipe, inflicting extensive damage to the boat. The operator backed down and fled. The dredge operator reported the boat operator showed signs of being intoxicated; however, he fled before the operator could summons authorities.

Later on, the company received a lawsuit from the fast boat operator's lawyer. On July 29, 2004, a judge ruled in favor of the fast boat operator and awarded the plaintiff $25,000 in retributions. "The guy got himself a slick attorney and we ended up footing the bill even though our dredge pipes were properly marked in accordance with Navigation Rules and that a no-wake zone was in effect within 500 feet of our construction zone," said Cross. What a sad commentary but in this age of depraved litigation, commercial enterprises make lucrative targets for lawsuit hungry jackals. Be damned with what's right or wrong.

Cross believes that many boaters simply don't understand what they are encountering on the water. One evening near twilight the sound of a power boater revving its engine caught his attention. He looked out into Lake Michigan and watched in disbelief as the power boat raced towards a dredge pipe floating above the surface. "The 25-foot boat slammed into the pipe, tearing off its lower unit. The operator mistook it as a wave he could jump," said Cross.

No, I don't make up all these big boat small mind stories for they are all-so true and as abundant as there are commercial captains to tell them. Now, let's go aboard some passenger carrying vessels and experience the bouts their captains must deal with daily regarding recreational boating.

TOUR BOATS: Recreational boaters tend to view medium sized tour boats as agile watercraft that can easily maneuver if need be. That's a fair assumption; however, the passengers they carry are also maneuverable and can find themselves unexpectedly flying into bulkheads or whatever during an abrupt vessel maneuver. Captain Dean Hobbs, of the car ferry *Badger*, told me that although the large motor vessels are accountable for the bulk cargo, the human cargo carried by passenger vessels imposes a greater burden of responsibility on captains. Valid point.

I spoke with Captain John Weatherholt regarding his concerns about passenger safety and unexpected maneuvers. Captain Weatherhold skippers the *Port City Princess*, homeport Muskegon Lake. The popular cruise ship tours Muskegon Lake and Lake Michigan waters near the harbor mouth. The 79-ton vessel carries up to 150 passengers. The good captain invited me aboard for a cruise.

During the cruise he shared experiences dealing with the recreational fleet. Captain Weatherhold said, "One night I was approaching the headwaters where Muskegon Channel meets Muskegon Lake. I spotted off the port beam a 35-foot powerboat approaching at a high rate of speed. The boat was maintaining a constant bearing and decreasing range a sure collision course. I jerked the throttles into reverse sending passengers sprawling about. The boat whizzed by right under the bow. I had no time to even sound the danger signal or warn passengers. Fortunately no one was injured."

Captain Weatherholt is a standup guy as with so many other captains he earned my immediate respect. I feel honored to share the bridge with these captains. My heart reaches out to these captains who are forced to deal with a recreational boating mentality that often does as it pleases unfair as it might be.

Captain Weatherholt said, "One night I was approaching the channel mouth from Lake Muskegon and counted fifty-eight fishing boats at the mouth. Twenty-eight of them were anchored. I advised my lookouts to point out the ones that were underway because that's where I was headed. I prayed may the 'rule of gross tonnage' prevail." Muskegon channel can become overrun with boats. I used to tell people on a busy boating day I could walk across the channel from boat to boat. I understood all to well Captain Weatherholts frustrations, but, at least, I could draw respect from boaters by lighting up the Coast Guard boat's flashing blue law enforcement light.

Captain Weatherholt continued: "I worked my way through the boating hodgepodge, maintaining minimum steerageway through the channel to avoid collisions. I had no idea what the fools were going to do. These aren't the rules of the road but rather the rules of convenience for those boaters who chose to do as they please. After all what do they have to lose, certainly not a career. Nor do they make lucrative financial legal targets. Not like us commercial folks."

Captain Weatherholt told me there are times after coming off a late-night cruise he will linger awake for hours waning from an adrenalin overload. He said, "It brought to mind my combat days in Korea during night attacks. My stomach lay in knots anticipating an enemy attack. But from where?"

For sure, Captain Weatherholt is not alone when it comes to anxiety attacks induced by recreational boaters. Let's go aboard and visit with the captains

Muskegon Lake and connecting channel to Lake Michigan can become congested with recreational boaters that can challenge captains of commercial vessels as they maneuver amongst the mix.

who skipper the ferry boats to and from Mackinac Island. Although I found them to be not as assertive with their opinions as Captain Weatherholt, I still detected a sharp edge to their words.

Now, let's haul in the lines and get underway and experience firsthand the trials and tribulations ferry boat captains often must endure regarding recreational boating. It's a trial for some captains that begins the moment they don the captain's hat.

FERRY BOATS: When Captain Jason Jewell of Shepler Line made his first solo run as captain while outbound Mackinac Island, he soon learned that the Navigation Rules he had so diligently learned in pursuit of his master license held little water amongst the recreational fishing fleet. Jewell

said, "Right outside the harbor I encountered a fleet of fishing boats which I had to maneuver around. A 35-foot fishing boat trailing fishing lines forced me to bring back the throttles and pass it astern even though I was the stand-on vessel." The incident taught the young captain a lesson experienced commercial captains know all to well: don't expect recreational boaters to know the rules. For the young captain it would be a lesson often repeated.

Captain Jewell said, "One night while approaching Island Harbor, Mackinac Island, a 25-foot power boat approached my vessel from my port side and cut right across my bow, forcing me to bring back the throttles even though I was the stand-on vessel. The guy then flipped me off." Captain

Jewell is responsible for the 80-foot, 100-ton boat that carries a maximum of 265 passengers. He is also held accountable as a professional captain and so is his parent company. What is the culprit that cut across his bow accountable too—himself. It gets worse.

Captain Jewell said boaters call on the marine radio in fog and ask can you see me on radar. "The radar screen is dotted with targets and this naïve boater believes I can see him amongst the clutter. What does he think, the name of his boat appears on the radar screen? Then these same wayward boaters insist I lead them into port though fog," said Jewell.

Once again let me use the commercial aviation analogy. Allowing clueless recreational boaters to operate in fog in the Straits of Mackinac is like allowing private aircraft pilots without an instrument rating to fly as they please in fog. Worse yet allow them to fly near major airports. Even worse still hold commercial pilots accountable in the event of a collision.

Absurd! Hardly, welcome to the come-what-may, do-as-you-please world of recreational boating. As for the young captain, he can expect little relief from the recreational fleet as its numbers swell.

Shepler captain Richard Weaver, told me he has seen a noticeable growth in recreational boating in recent years and for certain more misbehavior. The 17-year veteran of the Mackinac Island run also reports a noticeable increase in fast powerboats like "Bow Riders" that whiz to and fro like ill-tempered wasps. Some of these smaller watercraft—operated by anyone who can turn an ignition key—can reach speeds in excess of 55 mph. Then there are the personal water craft (PWC) to deal with.

Captain Weaver said, "One day while outbound from Mackinac Island I watched a PWC operator jumping boat wakes. One guy hit a wake and went vertical around 100 yards off my bow. He crashed into the lake, and I had to veer hard over to avoid him. I could see the terror in his eyes as I passed him within yards."

Captain Weaver also addressed the fog issue. "After years of running the Straits, I can picture in my mind's eye the position of fellow ferry boats and other commercial traffic as they report their position in fog over Channel 16." Captain Weaver finds this mental discipline useful in avoiding collisions and near misses. However, fishermen trolling to and fro in fog can force boat captains to execute various courses and speed changes.

These unanticipated boat maneuvers disrupt the synchronic flow of commercial traffic, sending Captain Weaver's and other captains' mind maps into disarray. "What makes it tough is that it can be nice one moment and the next moment the waters can be blanketed in fog, leaving many recreational boaters operating in blind ignorance in a sea of commercial traffic." During peak periods there can be up to 20 ferryboats, including freight carriers, transiting to and from the Mackinac Island between St. Ignace and Mackinaw City.

The Mackinaw City run takes ferry boats across major shipping lanes in the Straits of Mackinac. Throw in large motor vessels and tug boats towing or pushing barges, and the Straits when shrouded in fog can challenge the most experienced captain. Then on top of that throw in a pack of inexperienced recreational boaters, and the tension on commercial bridges can become as thick as pea-soup fog.

Captain Weaver suggested the possibility of a Vessel Traffic Service system (VTS) in the Straits. These are the same traffic control systems found in major U.S. ports to control the flow of commercial traffic. Such a system manned by the Coast Guard is similar to the traffic control systems found in commercial aviation. None of the captains I spoke with favor VTS, but as the waters become more congested with recreational boaters, a VTS might be the only solution in a situation apparently beyond the capacity of recreational boaters to solve. Unless, of course, they learn to boat smart—if only.

This large boat, small mind segment has been difficult to write since there are so many tales of woe I hear from commercial captains. Other than expressing their frustrations they simply have little recourse other than their own vigilance, and even then vigilance is not enough as the following case reveals.

CASE FILE: Detroit River, Lake Huron, October 23, 2004. The 432-foot tanker, *Gemini*,

Several ferry boats departing Mackinac Island encounter a sailboat.

collided with a 35-foot pleasure craft on the Detroit River. The collision happened around 3:35 p.m. The Coast Guard reported the weather as: visibility 4 nautical miles; wind speed: 10 knots; wave height: 1 foot.

Coast Guard Station Belle Isle launched a 25-foot rescue boat at 3:36 p.m. and arrived on scene at 3:56 p.m. A Good Samaritan had retrieved four people from the water with bruises and cuts. The Coast Guard crew treated the small-boat operator for hypothermia and shock.

Although the incident was still under investigation when the book went to press, a reliable source, who wished to remain anonymous, told me that the 35-foot power boat had overtaken the *Gemini* on the tanker's port side, then drifted across the motor vessel's bow to starboard, then drifted back to port where it was struck by the *Gemini's* bow. What could the Captain do besides sound the danger signal which he did? Rule 13, of the Inland Navigation Rules states: "Any vessel overtaking any other shall keep out of the way of the vessel being overtaken." The rules goes on to read: "Any subsequent alteration of the

bearing between the two vessels shall not make the overtaking vessel a crossing vessel within the meaning of these Rules or relieve her of the duty of keeping clear of the overtaken vessel until she is finally past and clear." That the 35-foot power boat crossed in front of the *Gemini's* bow places her in a crossing situation.

The *Gemini* also has Rule 5 in her favor, which states: "Every vessel shall at all times maintain a proper look-out by sight and hearing as well as by all available means appropriate in the prevailing circumstances and conditions so as to make a full appraisal of the situation and of the risk of collision." That the 35-foot powerboat drifted in front of the *Gemini* suggests that those aboard the powerboat were not maintaining a vigilant lookout. How will all this sort out in court? In this era of run-away civil litigation money often trumps what's right. I would have to place my bet on the powerboat.

One parting note regarding the *Gemini* and a very reliable source close to the investigation. He told me what he found totaly inequitable: the entire on-watch crew of the *Gemini* was tested for drugs

The 1000-foot motor vessel Columbia Star passes under the Mackinac Bridge. The Mackinac Straits mark one of the busiest shipping lanes on the Great Lakes. The five-mile-long bridge, which connects lower and upper Michigan, is the longest suspension bridge in the western hemisphere.   PHOTO BY RON BURDICK

and alcohol. Yet no one aboard the recreational boat was tested.

Notwithstanding the *Gemini* "damned if you are and damned if you're not" scenario, commercial vessels and the ever expanding recreational fleet to coexist in harmony, it may require appropriate authorities to revisit the Navigation Rules. Following the 1972 Convention on the International Regulations of Preventing Collisions at Sea, a new effort was made to unify and update the various Inland Navigation rules. This effort culminated in the enactment of the Inland Navigational Rules Act of 1980.

Many of the old navigation rules were originally enacted in the last century, and it appears several were carried over to the Inland Navigation Rules Act of 1980. In particular, the rule that addresses sailing vessels; the rule states: "sailing vessels not propelled by machinery shall have certain privileges over power vessels." The rule specifically

reads: "A power-driven vessel underway shall keep out of the way of a sailing vessel, however, a sailing vessel shall not impede the passage of a vessel that can safely navigate only within a narrow channel or fairway, or if a sailing vessel is overtaking a power vessel."

So open waters are fair game, meaning a 21-foot sailboat under sail can stand down a 1000-foot motor vessel on Lake Michigan. Ludicrous but sadly true, an inequity many commercial captains deal with on a daily basis—sail boaters lording their way over large motor vessels."

A commercial captain pointed out to me that the Navigation Rules for sailboats were effective a century ago when large commercial sailboats plied the Great Lakes. Some still do, like passenger-carrying sailing ships commonly know as "tall ships." Indeed, these large sailing vessels do merit certain privileges over power vessels, and captains of large motor vessels understand the challenges these large sailing vessels face and are more than willing to oblige. And they understand too, that "tall ships" are manned by licensed captains.

On the other hand, a day sailor, with little experience operating a 23-foot sail boat, can stand as tall as a tall ship while enjoying stand-on privileges. I don't believe rule makers had small sailboats in mind when they drafted the rules. If they did, did they not take into account that a small sailboat and even larger ones can quickly change a point of sail, power up, or both. For recreational sailboats, it's often not a case of maneuverability but more so a case of inconvenience. What's more, since the Inland Navigation rules were developed back in the 1970s, recreational boating has nearly doubled. The Great Lake states boast one third of the nearly 13-million registered recreational boats nationwide. Many of these watercraft are sailboats.

Another rule that applies only to International Rules could well merit application on the Great Lakes: a vessel constrained by her draft. The international rule reads: "Any vessel other than a vessel not under command or a vessel restricted in her ability to maneuver shall, if the circumstances of the case admit, avoid impeding the safe passage of a vessel constrained by her draft." Draft refers to the depth to which a vessel hull is submerged below the water. I believe the draft rule should apply to large motor vessels on the Great Lakes when approaching ports. Some large motor vessels like the 1000-foot *Indiana Harbor* can draw 34-feet.

Large motor vessels approaching the many ports around the Great Lakes, are often restricted in their ability to maneuver when transiting through a sea of recreational boats that cluster near harbor mouths. The waters off the entrance to Michigan ports—I know this to be a fact—can be swarming with recreational boats. The constrained by draft should take effect three miles out into the lake near ports trafficked by large motor vessels and along major shipping routes. The huge increase in recreational boating since the rules were formed in the 1970s begs review. Or, rather than change the rules, could it be more convenient to continue to subject commercial captains to sweating their way through a recreational boating free-for-all?

Thus far we have covered three factors that lead to recreational boating mishaps: unlimited access, into a close-quarter arena, where congested waters bustle with boating traffic. Now let's move on to the next contributing factor that leads to mishaps—seasonal pressures that offer their own array of challenges.

Seasonal Dangers

IMAGINE IF BOATERS AND WATER ENTHUSIASTS ENJOYED ACCESS TO THE GREAT LAKES YEAR ROUND. I would rather not. For I believe, year round access would generate alarming numbers of fatalities and accidents, enough to stir a public outcry. But as it goes, water-related fatalities come and go along with a short boating season and soon become old news, swept away with the passage of time and seasons.

On January 6, 2004, I attended a public safety meeting with local officials at Coast Guard Station Grand Haven regarding the recent fatalities of three young men off Grand Haven's South Pier and nearby beach during the 2003 summer season. Sitting at a table in the mess deck, my eyes occasionally glanced out the windows at the harbor channel, where a stiff westerly wind drove snow horizontally across grey and white-capped water. Coast Guardsman Michael White described retrieving a victim that a "Good Sam" had kept afloat with aid of a life ring supplied by a nearby boater. The Coast Guard crew pulled the pulse-less victim aboard the rescue craft and administered CPR while rushing the victim to awaiting paramedics. Unfortunately, he died two days later while on life support.

This incident occurred in late August, and it seemed surreal against the winter backdrop. If the discussion at hand seemed a season removed, what thoughts then occupy the general boating population when Lake Michigan hibernates.

Except for a few hardy fishermen, commercial vessels, and a handful of odd-ball boaters, the lake lies dormant, free of recreational activities, for around eight months each year. Some might proclaim this a blessing, yet blessed as it might seem, the short season offers its own shortcomings. This chapter will address the short-season factor and its challenges and dangers. Such as anxious, ill-prepared boaters, cold water, and boaters and water enthusiasts with a now-or-never mentality that often overrides good sense. Let's begin with the spring-time surge and the impetuous boater.

THE SPRING-TIME SURGE

Lake Michigan's limited window of opportunity in which to comfortably enjoy the marine environment creates a sense of urgency that finds boaters and beach goers itching to hit the water when the warm weather arrives. Boaters paying winter storage fees and monthly boat payments jump at

The Grand Haven Pier draws thrill-seeking youngsters by the scores. Although local and federal ordinances prohibit pier jumping into a navigable channel, there are no laws in place to restrict unabated pier jumping into Lake Michigan's open waters.

the opportunity to launch when spring flowers bloom.

This springtime exuberance often finds anxious boaters overlooking details, which can lead to mishaps and vessel breakdowns. During the 2003 and 2004 season, 51 percent of the Coast Guard's case load around the Great Lakes involved disabled vessels. A figure that has remained consistent over

the years. Many of the disabled cases were the result of simple maintenance oversights that lead to needless breakdowns. Also, in their haste to hit the water, boaters often overlook safety items.

Coast Guard boarding officers at Station Muskegon reported that one third of the vessels they inspected during the spring of 2004 failed to carry the appropriate number of life jackets or fire ex-

The ice-breaking tug, *Evan Mckeil*, stands a lone winter stay at the Manistee, Michigan Municipal Marina. Come summer the marina bustles with activity as boaters take advantage of a few months of short-sleeve weather.

tinguishers. Failing to carry these items will result in a vessel termination. As of mid-June, of the 191 vessels Muskegon crews boarded, they sent back 31 boaters to their moorings because they failed to carry either life jackets or fire extinguishers.

Across the Great Lakes during 2004 Coast Guard crews inspected 13,623 boats, of those 34 percent failed to meet federal safety requirements.

My Coast Guard cohorts at the Group Grand Haven and Milwaukee Rescue Coordination Centers advise me that, usually in mid-to-late spring, they witness a surge in boat breakdowns and requests for assistance. Most of these calls for assistance result from boaters failing to properly prepare their boats after winter storage.

Some, however, can't even wait until winter ends. Chief Jim Ellison, Officer In Charge, Coast Guard Station Kenosha, told me about a canoeist in mid-March 2003, struggling to work his canoe through the ice in the harbor while outbound to the lake. "He was jabbing at the ice with a pole and rocking back and forth to make headway. People standing in the parking lot at a nearby Holiday Inn were hollering at him to turn back," said Chief Ellison. What perplexed the chief was that their rescue boat wasn't in the water and this ice-breaking buffoon's only destination, should he have capsized, would have been a frozen grave.

I recall in spring of 2002 talking with the coxswain of a 47-foot motor lifeboat about a rescue he performed in mid-May off Grand Haven. The rescue involved a 37-foot power boat. According to the coxswain, the captain had run out of fuel and couldn't understand why, since he had fuel in the tanks when he stowed the boat in fall.

ON WATCH: Muskegon, Lake Michigan, Spring 2000. The boater's failure to check his fuel level in spring before launching, which brought to mind a rescue I performed on Lake Michigan off Muskegon harbor a year earlier in the spring. A thirty-nine foot sloop went aground in mild seas just north of Muskegon Harbor in heavy fog. I located the boat with my radar just off the beach. I approach the sailboat in shallow water and hooked it up and towed it to

its moorings in Muskegon Harbor. My crewman and I conducted a boat inspection for safety gear, which is routine procedure after a search and rescue case. There were nine people aboard, including an infant, but not one life jacket. The owner had sailed over from Wisconsin and in his haste had failed to re-stow life jackets that he removed from the boat in the fall. Needless to say he was ashamed, and I don't know whether it was the early morning sun's rays or embarrassment that tinted his face bright red.

I cited him for failure to carry life jackets and in the comments section of the boarding form noted his cross-lake trip without life jackets. I have no idea what the Coast Guard hearing officer did with that information, or how much he fined the skipper. I do know, however, that when the spring-time boating urge strikes, far too many boaters *strikeout* when it comes to preparation and maintenance.

Boaters bent on hitting the water after a long winter lay-up might learn from how Coast Guard boat crews prepare for the boating season. Preparation for the season takes on a two-fold approach: one, the boat and its equipment; two, the crew that runs the equipment. Already I can hear the lazy boaters saying, "That's their job. They're professionals." I couldn't agree with them more, but when was the last time a Coast Guardsman lost his life on Lake Michigan? In my twenty-three years associated with search and rescue on Lake Michigan, I can recall only one Coast Guard fatality. Now, as for recreational water related fatalities—hundreds.

The first line of defense for warding off mishaps on the water begins at the dock. A quick pre-underway boat check can prevent a possible prolonged underway ordeal. Coast Guardsman Mitch Muehlhausen, a veteran search and rescue coordinator at Group Grand Haven, Michigan has processed hundreds of search and rescue cases. Muehlhausen was also aboard Coast Guard cutter *Tamaroa* during the "Perfect Storm" when its crew snatched four Air National Guard airmen from 90-foot seas after their Jayhawk helicopter ditched off the Massachusetts's coast, 70 miles south of Long Island, New York.

Mitch offers the following pre-underway advice to boaters. This ol' seadog's advice is more than seaworthy.

The window of opportunity for water-related recreational activities opens on Memorial Day and closes in early September, just after Labor Day. That period may be even shorter, depending on the warm weather factor; however, the longer the season, the greater the opportunity for mishaps.

Coast Guard personnel at the District Nine Headquarters in Cleveland, Ohio, track "Boatable Days." Boatable Days are based on feedback from fourteen weather NOAA buoys across the Great Lakes that provide wave heights and wind speeds. Winds greater than 20 knots, seas greater than three feet, and visibility less than five nautical miles must all be present to constitute a non-boatable day. Surprisingly, air temperature is not included.

Boatable day figures reveal a troubling perplexity. A normal short boating season as it is, can be made even shorter by adverse weather, which can further reduce the limited time boaters spend on the water, and thus opportunities to gain experience. Between 2001 and 2004 the average number of "Boatable Days" on the Great Lakes equated to four months. That recreational boaters remain idle for eight months further diminishes whatever limited skills they may have acquired during a short boating season.

On top of limited boating experience and long periods of down time, we find a large number of boaters operating small watercraft. In fact, watercraft less than 26 feet in length are by far the largest class of registered boats on the water, making up over 95 percent of all registered watercraft nationwide. Smaller boats cost less, they can be towed by vehicles on boat trailers, they can be readily

"Federal Requirements and Safety Tips for Recreational Boats" is a hand-sized brochure filled with useful information along with illustrations. It also contains safety standards for recreational vessels and associated equipment required by federal law. Call the Coast Guard at 800-368-5647 to order one free.

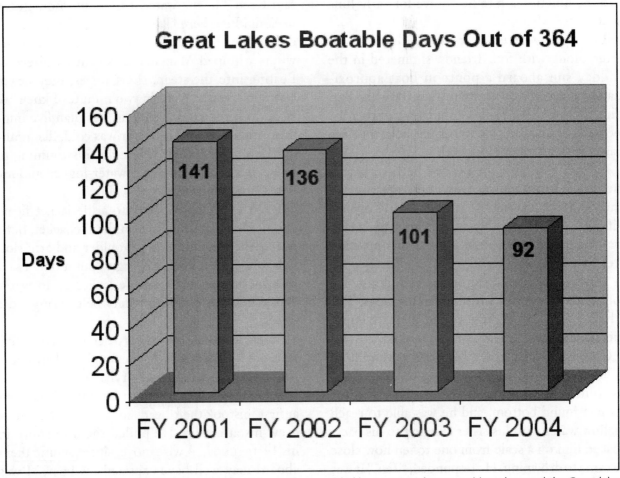

Great Lakes Boatable Days Out of 364

Days

141 FY 2001
136 FY 2002
101 FY 2003
92 FY 2004

The Coast Guard bases Boatable Days on weather information provided by 14 NOAA buoys positioned around the Great lakes.

launched, they can be fuel-friendly, and they can be unstable in adverse weather. Small unstable boats make for an ideal setup for cold water mishaps.

Lake Michigan's seasonal weapon of choice is cold water. Fog, downburst, lightening, and boater impetuousness all take their toll, but their damage pales in comparison to the human suffering that cold water inflicts.

During 2004, twenty-two percent of the fatalities in Coast Guard-related cases occurred during spring. This figure coincides with national figures that reveal the risk is far greater for a fatality to occur in spring and fall. Why? Well, one, there are fewer boaters on the water to assist fellow boaters, and two, there are fewer emergency responders patrolling in spring and fall. Three and this is the coup de grace—cold water. Cold water is an insidious danger that can be even

more treacherous when warm winds blow and cold water flows.

WARM AIR/COLD WATER SUCKER PUNCH

During springtime and early summer when warm winds blow, boaters are lured out onto the water, as one might be lured by warmth of a beguiling lover with a stone cold heart. I prefer to call it a warm-air/cold-water sucker punch that can often strike when you least expect it as illustrated in the case to follow.

CASE FILE: Grand Traverse Bay, Lake Michigan, Spring 1999. Corbin Buttleman and his sister couldn't have wished for a nicer boating day on Grand Traverse Bay, or a warmer one. Exceptionally warm weather lifted temperatures into the nineties, a rare heat wave for early June in northern Michigan.

The twenty-seven-year-old Corbin and his sister, along with four friends, simmered in the midday sun aboard a pontoon boat approximately 150 yards off shore in East Traverse Bay. The farthest thing from Corbin's mind when he foolishly pushed his sister off the boat into the water was that it could be fatal.

In fact, even after he pushed her overboard, the crew continued on with their merriment. She couldn't cry out. It wasn't until Corbin's wife saw life-threatening fear in his sister's eyes that it became readily apparent that something dreadful was unfolding. Corbin impulsively dove in and instantly realized his sister's plight. Ice cold water ripped the breath from his lungs. The others aboard, including a state police trooper friend, appeared oblivious to the trauma.

Corbin's sister clasped her arms around him, pulling him under. Floundering to stay afloat, Corbin struggled towards shore. Fortunately his feet found bottom, and he was able to reach shallow water with his sister clinging to his back. I asked him on a scale from one to ten how close he came to drowning. He responded, "Ten." It was that close; the cold water nearly broke his will. I asked him why he didn't throw his sister a flotation device. It never occurred to him; he dove in because that's what they do in the movies.

He told me that he had lived near water all this life and kept physically fit; yet a seemingly benign environment nearly claimed his life. Corbin told me his story during an airplane flight from California to Michigan in late March. I remember the date because when I arrived home in Manistee, Michigan, I was greeted by headlines in the local paper about three young men who were rescued from Manistee Lake after their 14-foot boat capsized. Later, I spoke with Leland Reed, one of the young men involved. His recollection of events sounded much like Corbin's story.

CASE FILE: Manistee Lake, March 28, 2000. A nice day, an inland lake, only yards from shore. "I never thought I would be swimming that day,

said Reed. "In the water, I thought, 'how in the heck did I get here?'"

Reed and his friend's ordeal began when strong winds whipped Manistee Lake into whitecaps. Beating into the steep, short waves, they began taking on water. "Within two minutes I knew we were going down. We sank in less than five minutes," said Reed. "The water was cold, like nothing I ever felt before. I thought of swimming to shore, but my clothing was water-logged and my boots prevented me from kicking."

Reed struggled to slip into a life jacket floating nearby. "I tried to put on the life jacket, but I put my head through the shoulder and arm slot. I almost choked myself trying to put it on." I said to him, "trying to put a life jacket on in water is like trying to put on a safety belt during a car wreck."

"Heck, the lake wasn't very deep, about twelve feet, but I guess it was deep enough to drown me. And it nearly did," he said dryly.

A boater on shore who spotted the three men at first mistook their heads for buoys. Their cries drew his attention. He pulled them to shore in his 14-foot boat. A wise move, since hauling them aboard may well have capsized his boat. "I was really weak. Sitting on some rocks near shore, I couldn't stand up. I needed assistance," said Reed, a big man at six feet, four inches and 290 pounds.

"It never occurred to me that this could happen in friendly and familiar waters," said Reed. The fact is, that is exactly where many boating mishaps do occur—in familiar waters.

The comfort-level familiar waters offer can lure boaters into a sense of false security. Apparently this was the case in the Spring of 2004 regarding 300 or more small fishing boats milling about on a warm spring day near the Fox River outlet in Lower Green Bay. Their occupants were apparently oblivious to the arctic-like waters. "These guys were fishing for walleye wearing tee shirts, no life jackets, and the water temperature was 30-degrees," said Len Vandenack, Coast Guard flotilla commander, Green Bay.

These fishermen did enjoy a safety net as fragile as it was: numbers. Hopefully a fellow

The Fox River outlet into lower Green Bay draws hundreds of fishermen to these waters in spring. Water temperatures can linger in the 30s and low 40s. I plead with fishermen to wear life jackets.

fisherman would reach a person in the water before the cold snuffed him out. Cold water immersions involve a desperate race against time that can crunch survival minutes down to seconds if the person is not wearing a life jacket.

Boaters are not the only victims of cold water. The following story, "St. Joe Snatches Boys from Grim Reaper" finds two teenage boys nearly drowning after warm winds lured them into the frigid waters of the St. Joseph river channel.

ON WATCH: Motor Lifeboat Station St. Joseph, Michigan, June 19, 2001. For Seaman Gribbins, the radio watch lingered on through the warm June afternoon. The radio watch room offered a sweeping view of the St. Joseph harbor, piers and Lake Michigan. Three youths caught his eye just as they leaped off a nearby seawall into the river channel.

Seaman Gribbins called out to his Officer in Charge, Chief Ahlin, in a nearby office. The alerted chief, binoculars in hand, watched as one of the teens struggled against the river channel's current. The veteran Coast Guard surfman threw down the binoculars, ran to the station's front lawn and yelled across to the floundering boys.

One of the kids, clinging to the steel seawall, yelled back that his friend was drowning. The Chief's instincts told him that the Grim Reaper's blade would soon fall. A surge of adrenaline propelled him to the station moorings where he fired up the 21-foot inflatable rescue boat. He barked out orders to his crew to launch the 47-foot motor lifeboat. Precious moments ticked by.

To worsen matters, one of the 21-footer's twin engines stalled and died. Chief Ahlin's executive officer, Robert Lemon, struggled to restart the engine. With only one engine, Lemon battled the stiff river current. A feeling of dread filled the Chief as he envisioned picking up a couple of drowned kids. The smallest boy weighting 90 lbs hugged the steel seawall like a monkey, his head dipping into the current, bubbles streamed from his mouth. His eyes told the real story; they registered primal fear, unlike anything the Chief had ever seen.

Chief Ahlin urged them to hang on as Lemon fought the current with one engine. For the chief, the seconds passed like minutes. He had a throw line and life ring at hand but feared the boys lacked the strength to grasp it. He knew that if he didn't get his hands on the kids *now* they were done. Lemon drove the inflatable up-current of the youths then spun the bow around. The chief snagged one kid and rolled him into the boat, nearly falling overboard in the struggle.

Then he snagged the other kid who had a tenuous fingertip hold on an 1/8 inch piece of steel protruding from the seawall. According to Chief, the first boy sat in the boat, his eyes looking as if he had just encountered Freddie Kruger. From the time Chief first spotted the struggling youths to the time he hauled them aboard, six minutes had elapsed. For Chief and his executive officer, it seemed like six years.

WATERWISE BRIEF: I later spoke with two of the survivors, Josh Cottingrim, 13, and Alex Stuard, 14. Alex actually had made it across the channel where he managed to climb a ladder to safety. He had commandeered a cane from an elderly man and attempted to reach Josh, but to no avail.

Josh told me while clinging to the side of the seawall, his arms felt like lead. Seawall slime had threatened his grip, and the steel wall's ragged edges had cut at his feet and hands. A swift current broke his grip. With his hands and legs, he had straddled another vertical facing, exhausting what little energy his 90-pound body could muster. He was about to slip under when the chief yanked him aboard.

I asked why they jumped into the channel. They told me they had walked around from the South Beach, which took around 45 minutes, and decided why not jump into the channel and swim across, rather than trudge all the way back around. The 250-foot-wide channel might as well have been wider than Lake Michigan itself.

I asked what they would tell a group of kids about their experience. Alex told me he had no idea that the current was that strong or the water that cold, but the air temperature was so warm. Being a good swimmer, he thought he could easily swim across the narrow channel. Josh willfully followed his lead and jumped in, as did Tony Medina, age 14. I asked Alex if he would do it again. "It was stupid," he said. "I would never do it again."

I will give these kids the benefit of the doubt. How could I not? As a teen surfing the waters of Southern California, I thought no wave was large enough. But never have I experienced a body of water as treacherous as Lake Michigan and its connecting waters. In California's surf, I knew the foe, and learned to deal with it. Lake Michigan and connecting waters often appear serene until you enter her domain. Then she attacks, as she did with young Josh, Tony, and Alex. Once she pulls you into her cold embrace, you're done.

Had Josh and Tony slipped under the murky water, their fate would have been sealed.

In 2000, four youths, ages 12-19, died swimming off piers and breakwaters between Frankfort and Michigan City. Thanks to Chief Alhin, BM1 Lemon, and the vigilant eye of Seaman Gribbins, the count wasn't six. Josh and his buddies were very lucky as were the lads in the following story.

Kenosha

ON WATCH: Kenosha, Wisconsin, April 17th, 2004. Coast Guard Station Kenosha responded to a capsized canoe with two people in the water reportedly three-quarters of a mile north of the Kenosha pier head light in Lake Michigan. The air temperature was 75 degrees and the water temp 50 degrees with one to two foot seas. It took four minutes from the time a Good Samaritan on shore reported the capsizing to the time a Coast Guard crew reached the capsized canoe.

Coast Guardsmen George Amon grabbed the extended finger of a young male as the teen slipped below the surface. If the boat had arrived seconds later, the lad would have drowned.

Neither of the teens, ages 14 and 16, were wearing life jackets. Personnel from the Kenosha fire department rescued the other teen.

In the next story, we find a Coast Guardsman decked by a warm air/cold water sucker punch. The blow nearly cost him his life.

ON WATCH: Straits of Mackinac, April 2002. Near record-high temperatures in mid-April drew 22 year-old Coast Guardsman Allan Grundhoffer out onto Lake Michigan. After launching his 14-foot sailboat, he set sail from Coast Guard Station St. Ignace and headed out towards the Straits of Mackinac. Moments after launching, he realized that the stiff summer-like breeze offered more challenge than his limited sailing experience could handle. He prepared to come about and head back for shore. A sudden wind gust caught his sail, knocking the small rig over, pitching him into the icy lake.

"It was as if someone slapped me in the face," said Grundhoffer, remembering what it felt like after he hit the 35-degree water wearing only a tank top and shorts. He struggled to re-right the sail boat in the stiff breeze, but to no avail. His portable marine radio had spilled overboard during the knockdown, and there were no other boats in the area. Removing his red tank top, he began waving it over his head to draw attention. He had the presence of mind to stay with the boat; however, he was not wearing a life jacket.

Fortunately for him, the Coast Guard Cutter *Acacia*, a 180-foot buoy tender, was just backing down as it prepared to moor at St. Ignace Station. A seaman standing in the *Acacia's* pilot house spotted the sailboat and sounded the alarm. Within moments, those on *Acacia's* bridge watched St. Ignace's 23-foot rescue boat kicking up spray as it pounded through choppy seas towards the sailboat.

Unbeknownst to the boat crew, they were about to save one of their own. From the time Grundhoffer hit the water to the time his mates pulled him aboard, 15 minutes had elapsed. During that short time span, his core body temperature had plummeted to 92 degrees, dangerously near a comatose condition.

Some reading this may wonder how this could happen to a trained Coast Guardsman, especially one schooled aboard Coast Guard rescue craft, where safety is stressed and drilled almost to a fault. In all fairness to Grundhoffer, I view this mistake not as an indictment against the training nor him, but more so an indictment against Lake Michigan and its beguiling lure when warm winds blow and cold water flows. Hey, he's a young lad who is the first to admit that the lake snookered him. Speaking from personal experience, I can say he's certainly not the first to be hoodwinked by Lake Michigan.

Nor will he unfortunately be the last.

I have my own story to tell of dealing with the warm-air/cold-water sucker punch, and I was dressed to defend myself. My cold water encounter occurred on a Saturday in mid-September of 1993.

For coasties to maintain their annual boat qualifications, Coast Guard regulations require them to perform an open water survival swim. The Coast Guard boat crew had dropped me off in the water near Blood Creek, which is located around four miles south of Portage Lake, Onekama, Michigan. My intent was to swim ashore and walk to my home located a short distance from the beach. I had swum in the Lake on Friday night and the water temperature was more than comfortable. Unbeknownst to me, and despite the fact it was sunny and warm on Saturday, the lake had dropped at least 10 degrees from the previous evening. To put it mildly, the lake jolted me when I hit the water.

I swim regularly in Lake Michigan, often up to a mile. Over the years I've performed many open water survival swims, some in six-foot seas, others at night, and even some in frigid water, although properly dressed in a cold water survival suit. I have little fear of water. Respect, yes. Yet, in spite of my many experiences, the cold water off Blood Creek gnawed on my confidence. I drew on prior experiences to stay in control. Yes, the water was that cold, and the full-body mustang suit I wore kept me afloat, but it did not keep the cold water from seeping in and slowly, relentlessly, draining my energy.

That I had committed to backstroke to shore prevented the 41-foot rescue boat from reaching me in the shallow water. I was on my own on the 300-yard stretch to the beach. The recommended swim stroke while wearing a full body exposure suit is to float on your back and make sweeping side strokes. It's very slow going, made even slower by the air-bloated full-body suit. The cold water registered foremost in my feet and hands, especially my feet. I likened it to walking in snow with bare feet. I could only imagine what such an ordeal would be for someone who ended up in the water alone in open water and without benefit of a life jacket or a full body survival suit.

Fear? Yes! Panic? For certain.

I felt apprehensive as I stroked toward the beach even thought the outside air temperatures hovered in the mid-70s with a bright sun shining overhead. The 41-boat had headed south, and the nearby beach offered not a soul in sight. Had I developed cramps, I don't know what I would have done. I've experienced those before during cold-water

survival swims; one time it took several days before my leg muscle healed. Cramps are painful enough but in water they can be excruciating, and you can't stand up to relieve the spasm.

Thank God the cramps didn't attack me! By the time I reached shore, my fingers looked like shriveled up raisins, and my feet had numbed to the point I could barely feel the pebbles underfoot as I stumbled towards the beach. I slipped out of the mustang suit and walked to my home nearby. There I spent two hours stretched out on the couch, covered in blankets waiting for the shivering to abate.

Boy, did Lake Michigan fool me. During the night, an easterly wind had driven the warm water, which I had enjoyed the night before, well offshore. Over a 12-hour period, offshore winds and a cool mid-September night had turned bath water into ice water. Twelve hours!

Should I have known better? You bet, but I'm not the only professional sucked in by the warm/air cold-water punch. Bob Dukeshere is a senior weather forecaster at NOAA's Grand Rapid's weather center; he's the guy who calls the near shore weather for Lake Michigan. Dukeshere told me that while sailing with friends aboard a 31-foot sloop off Frankfort, Michigan, in the summer of 2002, he leaped into Lake Michigan. Dukeshere said, "The cold water ripped the air out of my lungs. I couldn't breathe for 10 seconds. I should have known better." The air temperature was in the low 80s, the water temperature in the low 50s. A northeasterly had blown the warm water offshore, and cold water, which seldom warms, welled up from below. Bob gets credit, at least, for wearing a life jacket; it probably saved his life.

During the first week of August, 2003, I swam daily in the lake across the street from my Manistee home. During that period, the water temperature ranged between 65 to 67 degrees. One day it felt like bath water. Then a cold front swept through the region, and by August 11th, the water temperatures, according to NOAA, had plunged into the low 50s. I waded into shallow water off the beach; it felt like I had stepped into crushed ice.

A friend, Muskegon County marine deputy Eric Anderson told me on August 9, 2003, while fishing with his dad off Muskegon, the reported water temperatures was in the mid 40s. And Chief Dan Haney, Officer in Charge, Station Milwaukee told me that he has seen Lake Michigan water temperatures drop from 67 to 47 degrees within a ten mile area.

The folks who have survived cold water sucker punches can consider themselves lucky. The following cases tell a much grimmer story. These cold water stories appeared in my final column of the 2002 boating season, entitled "A Fatality Ridden Season."

CASE FILES: Lake Michigan, spring 2002. The tragic loss of three fishermen off a 16-foot boat in Calumet Harbor on March 30, 2002, marked the beginning of what would be a fatality-ridden season on Lake Michigan and nearby lakes and streams. At least 41 people lost their lives in water-related incidents around Lake Michigan and adjoining lakes and rivers during 2002.

The first incident occurred on Sunday, March 31, 2002. Coast Guard Group Grand Haven received a telephone call from a woman in Chicago reporting that her two sons and a friend had failed to show up for Easter dinner. The three men, between ages 28 and 31, had departed Hammond Harbor Marina in Chicago the previous day aboard a 16-foot fiberglass boat, to Coho fish a mile offshore. The weather on Saturday offered sunshine, calm seas, five-knot winds, and a water temperature of 35 degrees. The missing fishermen sparked a massive Easter-day hunt.

The Coast Guard, along with other rescue agencies, launched an aggressive search covering the entire south end of Lake Michigan. On Tuesday, the Coast Guarded called off the search after finding several life jackets. A family member identified one of them as belonging to one of the victims. On April 4, the boat was discovered at the bottom of the Calumet Harbor shipping channel with no apparent damage to the boat, nor were there any apparent malfunctions with the trolling motor and outboard engine. The 31-year-old boat did lack built-in flotation material required of newer boats, which would have prevented it from sinking, hopefully.

A month later, on May 2, the first body was discovered on shore; the other two bodies were found by a tug boat crew on May 11, less than a quarter of a mile from where the boat sank. Some officials suspect that a wake from a large vessel may have swamped the boat. One thing is for certain: the supposedly experienced boaters were not wearing life jackets, and in the frigid water their efforts to stay afloat would have consumed precious body energy, quickly resulting in advanced hypothermia.

The next cold-water fatality occurred on May 19, when a 51-year-old male drowned while fishing on the St. Joseph River. The man's wife called authorities after he failed to return from a fishing trip near Berrien Springs dam. Two days later, rescuers found his body. Reportedly, at the time of the incident, six of the dam's flood gates were open, with river currents exceeding 10 knots near where the man drowned. He was aboard a 14-foot bass boat. The water temperature was 49 degrees and the air 43. He was not wearing a life jacket.

On June 6, a 52-year-old man drowned in Glovers Lake, Manistee County. According to Manistee County Sheriff Dale Kowalkowski, the bolts attaching the seat to the wood frame of his pontoon boat separated. "The bolts were new, but the wood they were attached to was punky," said Kowalkowski. A witness said the man fell backwards, yelled out, hit the water, and didn't come up. His body was discovered in six feet of water about 50 feet offshore. The water temperature was in the mid 50s, the weather calm, with air temperatures in the low 60s. He was wearing a medium-heavy wool blend jacket, heavy boots and trousers, but no life jacket. "He would have had a much better chance of surviving had he worn one," said Kowalkowski "The cold water certainly didn't help and may have induced severe shock."

On Friday, September 13th, off Waugoshance Point, near the Straits of Mackinac, a 40-year-old male's kayak capsized in two-foot seas near an abandoned lighthouse. After a three-hour struggle within three-quarters of a mile of shore, fatigue took its toll, and he slipped into advanced hypothermia. Rescuers discovered his body the following morning.

BOAT SMART BRIEF: In all four cases, cold water played a part in the fatalities, and in four of these fatalities, it was the leading cause. It's fair to ask: Would the six men who perished have survived had the water and air temperatures been at summer levels? I believe so. Also, except for the kayaker, I believe the other victims' survival odds would have skyrocketed had they worn life jackets.

Chief Jim Ellison, Officer In Charge, Coast Guard Station Kenosha, Michigan, told me about a small power boat that was swamped by three to four foot seas off Kenosha during the spring of 2003. The three males aboard were wearing life jackets. "If we had not rescued those fellows as quickly as we did, they would have died. Without life jackets they would have died before we reached them," said Chief Ellison.

That's the killer regarding early season mishaps, for whereas there is safety in numbers in the summer, it is often the lack of numbers in fall and spring that decreases the odds for cold-water victims. During colder weather there are few boaters and patrol officers available to rescue boaters in distress.

That certainly was the case with the three victims who capsized in Calumet Harbor off their 16-foot boat in spring of 2001, as well as a kayaker near the Straits of Mackinac. And on April 8, 2001, a 30-year-old male perished in cold water while windsurfing alone off Little Sable Point, Lake Michigan. The Coast Guard and Oceana County rescue teams launched an extensive search after family members reported him overdue. A yellow board was located on the beach bearing the name of the missing man. Shortly thereafter a Coast Guard crew located the subject's body in the nets off the Ludington Pumped Storage water intake. The weather according to the Coast Guard SITREP read: wind: south/15 knots, seas: 2-3 feet, visibility 10 nautical miles, air temperature: 42f, water temperature: 39f.

The 2004 season began with a rash of cold-water related fatalities. Between March 22, and May 19, 2004, seven boaters lost their lives in Michigan.

Little Point Sable is one of many Lighthouses that grace the shores of Lake Michigan.

The average size of the six boats involved was 14 feet in length. All involved males, none were wearing life jackets, the weather was calm, but the average water temperature in which they drowned was 45 degrees.

Coast Guardsman Allan Grundhoffer, who took the mid-April plunge off his sailboat into the frigid waters near the Mackinac Straits, will be the first to tell you to wear a life jacket, and he feels darned lucky to be alive to do so. Boat Smart—follow his hard-earned, bone-chilling advice.

No sooner does the spring-time surge and cold-water threat pass than does a new form of impetuosity take hold. I call it the seasonal Now-or-Never Syndrome.

Boat Smart Anchor Points

Chilling cold water facts

These cold hard facts regarding cold water immersion will send chills up your spine

↪ Body heat loss in cold water can occur 25 times faster than in cold air. If your boat is overturned, attempt to get up onto the overturned boat. According to Coast Guard studies, even in high winds, wind chill is not found to be a factor as long as the victim is clothed.

↪ Initial contact with cold water will rip the breath from your lungs causing "Torso Reflex," which is an immediate and involuntary gasp for air in response to being immersed in cold water. If your mouth is underwater when gasping occurs, drowning is the most probable outcome, unless you're wearing a life jacket. If you know you are about to fall into cold water, cover your face with your hands. This helps you to avoid sucking water into your lungs. Expect muscles to tighten and shivering to increase in an automatic reflex to produce more body heat. Some people liken it to a total full-body muscle cramp or spasm with no relief.

↪ Those people with a positive attitude will most likely survive longer if, and I stress if, they are wearing a life jacket.

↪ Wear a life jacket at all times. Mark these words. This advice comes from seasoned chiefs who have too often dealt with the gruesome aftermath of victims that have drowned.

↪ At the first sign of trouble, radio for help or fire off a flare. Don't wait until the lake has you by the ice cubes

↪ Wear several layers of clothing to reduce body heat loss. Protect your groin, neck, torso, and especially your head.

↪ If you must enter the water, do so slowly to reduce respiratory/cardiac shock and to avoid swallowing water. That's easier said than done. During drills, even though I had prepared to deal with the pain, it still jolted me. I can't imagine the shock of unexpectedly landing in frigid water.

↪ Do not attempt to swim except to reach a nearby craft. Beware: the drift rate of small boats can exhaust even good-swimmers. More than once, I've hopelessly searched for the bodies of so-called good swimmers, much too often to no avail. Studies have shown that a strong swimmer has only about a 50/50 chance of reaching shore one-half mile away in 50-degree water.

↪ If more than one unfortunate soul finds themselves in cold water, huddle together and pull legs up toward chest with arms tight against sides. Of course, this maneuver is only possible if you're wearing a life jacket.

IT'S NOW OR NEVER

Unlike springtime urge that finds boaters anxious to hit the water after a long winter lay-up, a Now-or-Never Syndrome finds boaters and beach goers motivated to hit the water before the short window of opportunity slams shut. I recall when I first reported to Coast Guard duty on Lake Michigan in 1983, Chief Moose, a Michigan native, told me in late July to enjoy the next three weeks because that will be the extent of the Lake Michigan summer.

From a California native's viewpoint, the Chief's short-selling of a Lake Michigan summer seemed far-fetched. Over the years, however, Chief Moose's observation proved to be true time and again as I have experienced the warm, hot, and cold cycles of Lake Michigan summers. Boaters anxious to take advantage of these warm spells and precious vacation time can develop now-or-never-jitters that send them venturing out onto the Lake in uncertain weather, at night, and particularly in fog. Foul weather and the uncertainty of night, however, can dampen a boater's adventurous spirit, but apparently not fog. It could be boaters perceive it as nothing more than a nuisance, or at least that's what they rationalize in their zest to go boating. These boaters need to get their head out of the fog and stop allowing now-or-never impulse to fog their judgment.

Most Coasties and professional mariners would rather deal with almost any other type of weather than fog, particularly in close quarters amongst heavy boating traffic.

I suspect many boaters drive from afar to go boating on Lake Michigan and will not be denied. After all, when the opportunity presents itself and time is of the essence, especially during the few precious weekends available within a limited window of opportunity, boaters are going to go for it fog or not.

The following Boat Smart story, "Fog Could Liven Up a Corpse," illustrates how boaters seem oblivious to the dangers fog offers.

ON WATCH: Muskegon, Michigan. Saturday August 8, 1998. Understandably, boaters can get caught in a sudden and unpredictable fog bank. This happened to me in August 2002 while steaming down from Muskegon to the Mona Lake entrance to rendezvous with Station Grand Haven's 47-foot motor lifeboat. During the trip down, the visibility was about a mile, but on the return leg visibility had closed to within feet. I could barely see the bow of the 21-foot inflatable boat.

It brought to mind Tristan Jones, holder of the most single-handed sailing records in seagoing history, in his book "Outward Leg" accurately described sailing in fog: "There's nothing in the world better for sharpening the senses—all of them—than a couple of days stuck in the middle of the English Channel, or Long Island Sound, in a thick pea-soup fog. It would liven up a corpse."

Apparently, not all boaters agree. If you observe the habits of many here along Lake Michigan's eastern shore during heavy fog, you would think professional sailors like Jones were either misguided or over-reacting, or just plain paranoid.

During my sudden and unexpected bout with fog during my return to Muskegon Harbor, thank God for GPS and radar.

The radar screen aboard was splattered with small, intimidating dots that grew into large blotches as fishing boats loomed out of the fog, passing within feet, many trailing fishing lines. I anxiously picked my way through the dots and at last entered the Muskegon harbor mouth.

There, dozens of boaters greeted me, blindly heading out onto the lake. Were these folks insane? There are no written laws preventing boaters from operating in restricted visibility. There are, however, laws governing how one operates a boat in restricted visibility. As I approached the Muskegon south pier head, I spotted a boat that was definitely in violation of the Inland Rules. In fact, it was not even a boat, but a 9-foot motorized rubber dingy with an adult male and three kids aboard, heading out into the lake. It carried no lights, no sound signals, and no flares. In short, it had no business being out there.

I hailed the boat over and directed the operator to follow me as I guided him through the fog into the light of day and while doing so enlightened him in no uncertain terms on his less-than bright voyage.

In another Boat Smart story, "Mid Season Concerns," which I wrote several years later, I pointed out that not only do boaters willfully venture out onto Lake Michigan in fog, but many do so lacking basic boating skills.

ON WATCH: South Haven, Michigan, Saturday, August 4, 2001. Thick fog rolled across Lake Michigan's eastern shore, yet many boaters still ventured out onto the lake. It didn't take long before Channel 16, the VHF radio hailing and distress frequency, carried the cries of lost boaters. I heard a boater south of Saugatuck asking the Coast Guard at Group Grand Haven if they would plot his GPS coordinates and provide a course to Saugatuck Harbor. Then he requested the water depth at Saugatuck's pier head. Obviously, he didn't carry charts, lacked basic GPS knowledge, and didn't have a clue to his whereabouts, yet he didn't hesitate to request Coast Guard assistance. But what could the Coast Guard do?

BOAT SMART BRIEF: For the Coast Guard to provide courses over the marine radio based on a boater's input would not only be foolish, it would be an open invitation for a lawsuit should the boater encounter a mishap as a result of that information. The Coast Guard can provide hardcopy information off charts and nautical publications, but not courses based on a boater's reported position on the water. A position that could be inaccurate and thus the course provided could be also.

I salute the boaters who exercised caution regarding the fog off South Haven. A boater asked me if he should get underway for Chicago without radar, but with a GPS. I can't provide such advice, but I did share with him a Coast Guard standing order regarding Coast Guard boats and fog: no radar, stay moored. Wisely, he stayed moored until the fog lifted the following day, as did many other prudent boaters in South Haven.

It should be pointed out that most fog horns along Lake Michigan's eastern shore have a range of only one-half mile. Why? Because many shoreline residents complain about the intrusive sound. Moreover, many fog horns have baffles, which deflect the sound out into the lake and away from shore. Boaters behind the horn may not hear it, or they may not hear it if more than one-half mile seaward of the horn.

Boaters can easily venture beyond the one-half mile range of a foghorn, and without the help of the horn to guide them back, they freak out and begin hollering for assistance over the marine radio like a child crying out in the dark. Boat

Smart: stay moored until the fog lifts, or better yet, take up RV-ing.

CASE FILE: Captain Tony Fiore, Fleet Captain for the Annis Water Resources Institute, Grand Valley State University, often encounters fogless boaters. He told me when underway on Lake Michigan aboard the Institute's research vessels, he encounters numerous recreational boats during fog. Captain Fiore said, "I will be underway, not making way, sounding the appropriate two prolonged blasts. I watch boats on radar closing in on my vessel as if I was a fog horn. When I get underway, they follow me into the harbor as if I was mother goose leading her goslings safely home."

What troubles Captain Fiore is this: what would boaters do if they experienced an emergency? How could they direct help to their location? They couldn't; worse yet, he doubts that those who operate blindly in fog even consider potential emergencies, or if they do they brush off the thought. And as a former Coast Guard search and rescue responder, he becomes livid about how often emergency resources were needlessly drawn out into the lake to assist astray boaters in fog. I share his sentiments.

I suspect that the Coast Guard and other marine rescue responders actually reinforce boaters' now-or-never impulses because recreational boaters take chances, believing help is but a radio call away. In some cases help is readily available. But in others it is not, which could prove fatal to boaters assuming they will be rescued. Let's review several cases involving boaters who were lucky, despite their now-or-never impulses, to have benefited from a rapid rescue response. Then we will review several cases in which boaters died before help could arrive.

Lets begin with lucky ones. The following story is based on an e-mail Patrick Weaver of Coast Guard Station Michigan City shared with me. The e-mail describes a sailboat race from Michigan City to Chicago that took place on Labor Day, 2000. The return leg of the race was postponed the night before due to heavy seas, yet in spite of conditions worsening overnight and unbeknownst to the Coast Guard, race officials launched the race at dawn.

I asked Jeff Bradbury, Commanding Officer, motor lifeboat station Michigan City, what happened. He advised me that the race committee failed to advise him because they feared he would cancel the race. I asked him if he would have done so. "You bet," said Mister Bradbury.

After reviewing Weaver's account, it's apparent Mister Bradbury had more than good cause to shut down the race. I'm surprised he didn't bring action against the race committee for allowing their now-or-never impulses to endanger the sailing fleet and Coast Guard crews attempting to rescue them. Right from the very get go of the race all hell broke loose.

ON WATCH: Michigan City, Indiana, Labor Day, 2000. When the sailboats departed Michigan City harbor around 6:30 a.m., 10 to 15 foot breaking seas greeted them at the harbor mouth. Right off the bat, one boat lost its rudder. Seas carried it towards a familiar nearby shoal being pounded by heavy surf. Weaver positioned the

44-foot motor lifeboat MLB near the 40-foot sailboat while holding the MLB's bow into the seas. Lake water rained down on the crew. The crew passed a double bridle over to the sail boat. A crewman aboard the sailboat placed the bridle eyes over two bow cleats. Once in tow, Weaver had to travel a quarter of a mile abeam to the surf in order to avoid nearby shoals.

Overhead a Coast Guard helicopter maintained station, directing Weaver through the surf zone. A monstrous wave slammed into the MLB, rolling it hard over. Seconds later it hit the sailboat and Weaver thought it was all over. Weaver wrote, "All I could see was a red keel as it heaved skyward. I wheeled the bow into the seas and slammed down on the engine throttles." The sailboat's bow spun into the seas, sending a hail of water skyward. The tow line held despite the fact the sailboat was lurching 30 to 40 yards from starboard to port. Heavy seas prevented passing a sea drogue to reduce yawing.

No sooner did the crew safely moor the sailboat than the station SAR alarm sounded again. Another sailboat had lost it rudder just north of

Michigan City Harbor and detached seawall.

the harbor entrance near a detached 200-yard long breakwater lined with jagged rocks. This rescue turned out to be even more intense than the last one, since the winds had increased and the sailboat was so close to the breakwater. The waves held no set pattern. They raced at the MLB from the north, then northeast attacking the MLB in rapid order. The sailboat had no radio, so it forced Weaver to maneuver dangerously close to the crippled boat in order to communicate towing instructions.

When Weaver drew near enough to communicate he discovered the sailboat had no forward cleats or bow post to hook the tow line onto. He couldn't believe it. What was he going to do? Weaver wrote, "What the heck was I doing out here I thought as I watched the crew vomit onto the decks." Rational thinking turned to desperation. "I radioed the station and threw up while talking to them."

Easing the MLB away from the sailboat he reassessed the situation, which really helped calm his nerves and the crews. After briefly discussing a game plan with the crew, Weaver again approached the sailboat. A crewman passed over a tow line with a bridle and shackle. A crewman on the sailboat hooked together the bridle eyes after placing them around the mast. The MLB then towed the sailboat into port.

"No sooner had had the MLB crew moored than the SAR alarm sounded. The captain of a 65-foot sailboat had issued a Mayday after the boat lost its rudder. Fortunately, the sailboat's position placed it well off shore and in open water. That hookup in open water was a breeze compared to the other two. Weaver said, "I never towed such a large sailboat. It was huge. We got it safely moored and finally around 5 p.m. we stood down." But not for long. At 6:30 p.m. the SAR alarm again sounded. Reportedly high seas had washed a 12-year-old boy off the lighthouse pier. The Coast Guard along with the local marine sheriff found nothing and suspended the search at 11:30 p.m. A week later, Weaver and his crew recovered the boy's body near the lighthouse break wall. "I hope no one ever has to see anything like that, ever," wrote Weaver.

Not all impetuous boaters fare so well. A friend of mine, Sheral Bradley, the first female 44-foot motor lifeboat coxswain in the Coast Guard, told me of the case of four young men who departed Chicago on September 25, 1980, to deliver a yacht to Holland, Michigan. At the time, Sheral was stationed at Coast Guard Station Michigan City. The reportedly-experienced boaters set out from Chicago in spite of the National Weather Service's warnings for lower Lake Michigan. Two of the young men aboard the 32-foot cabin cruiser, *Sea Mar III*, had served in the Coast Guard.

According to Sheral, nightfall found the northwesterly winds shrieking across the lake and the waves high enough to shake the ground when they crashed on shore near South Haven. Coast Guard Station South Haven received a radio transmission over Channel 16 from the vessel *Sea Mar III* stating its call sign. That was all. End of transmission. That was the last radio call *Sea Mar III* made. The four young men and the boat disappeared. Searchers located debris on shore eight miles northwest of South Haven. The only vestige ever found of the ill-fated voyage.

Sheral shared the story of another fatal voyage that occurred the year before on Friday, October 12, 1979. Robert Burns, 47, of Arlington Heights, Illinois, and two companions departed Monroe Harbor, Chicago, for Holland, Michigan, aboard the 27-foot sailboat, *Jenny Too*. They launched despite the forecast for gale warnings. Later that day they encountered 16-foot seas and 50-knot winds. Midnight found the *Jenny Too* wrecked on the beach three miles south of South Haven. Burns survived; his two mates had perished.

BOAT SMART BRIEF: Sheral believes both accidents occurred because the skippers pushed their boats and crews beyond their limitations. Sheral said, "The tragedy of all this is that each of these accidents could have been avoided if these skippers had taken the time to learn the operating limits of their boats, made a realistic appraisal of their own seamanship abilities, and stayed within those limits."

True, but I believe there were more insidious influences at play, mainly the Seasonal Factor.

In the first incident, the run from Chicago to Holland, Michigan, was only 80 nautical miles, a four-hour trip at most when cruising at 20 knots. I bet they had a boatyard removal schedule to meet and so they went for it.

As for the 27-foot sailboat, the skipper was foolish venturing out with gale warnings in effect, especially aboard a 27-foot sail boat with a 7-horse power outboard engine puttering the boat along a track line that placed it broadside to a leeward shore. Foolish? Nuts is more like it.

This story brings to mind a seawall collision I addressed earlier in the book regarding the 48-year-old male who slammed into the Muskegon breakwater on October 15, 2004, while attempting to make port at Muskegon aboard a 34-foot powerboat. According to the Coast Guard boat coxswain Jay Douglas, eight to ten foot seas were crashing over the seawall.

The operator had departed White Lake Harbor for the Mart Docks in Muskegon to stow the boat for the winter. With White Lake only 10 miles north of Muskegon and eight to-ten foot seas running at the time of the crash, it's reasonable to assume that when the operator departed White Lake seas were running high there also. Douglas reported that at the time of the accident wind speeds up to 33 mph, according to NOAA weather gauges.

Why the operator elected to make the run under those conditions, I suspect, stemmed from an urgency to meet a boatyard schedule. The fact that he had traveled from Indianapolis could well have found him yielding to the now-or-never syndrome.

Boatyard schedules explain why marinas around the Great Lakes begin thinning out after Labor Day. I once believed vacant slips stemmed from a physiological transition from summer into fall and that boaters followed suit, leaving behind the things of summer, which I found puzzling since September weather patterns are the most predictable on Lake Michigan offering ideal boating conditions even in October.

Finally, it dawned on me that boatyard schedules had something to do with vacant boat slips.

Boatyards can only handle so many boat removals a day for winter storage. So when they schedule a haul-out date boaters acquiesce. If not, face foul weather later on or no haul out at all. View it from another vantage; imagine if boaters all elected to pull their boats on October 15th. Tell me how a marina that hauls out 600 boats a season can do this if they average eight per day on a good day. They can't.

One marina owner told me she's considering increasing removal boat lift fees after October 15th, since lousy weather can make withdrawing boats hazardous. The same schedule time crunch holds true for spring, when anxious boaters must wait their turn to hit the water. Hopefully, the event isn't delayed by poor weather. Great Lakes weather can be as fickle as a politician, and there's not a damn thing you can do about it, except yearn for "good days."

Even when a boater enjoys a mild weather window of opportunity, it can close rapidly. I've spent years operating in Southern California waters where weather patterns are consistent and remain stable for days. So consistent and predictable are patterns that boaters can plan voyages far in advance, and they can make voyages year round. On Lake Michigan and her sister lakes, weather systems rapidly pass through; predictable weather can be anyone's guess; forget making a week-long prediction months ahead. An April day can be summer-like and an August day frigid and cold. On August 6, 2004, the thermometer in my backyard in Manistee read 47 degrees; on August 6, 2005 it read 89 degrees. Planning an extended boating trip on Lake Michigan involves a roll of the weather dice. You can only hope the outcome doesn't get too dicey.

It can get dicey enough that some boat haul out services insist boaters file a float plan. A good friend of mine, Wendy Seng, told me while managing the winter haul out schedule at Harbor Isle Marina in Saint Joseph, Michigan, that boaters traveling from afar had to file a float plan as stipulated in the contract, or else the marine would not pull the boat in fall or release it in spring.

Harbor Isle drew a number of sail boaters from the Chicago area, a 50-mile run to St. Joe.

Across the Great Lakes during fall, boats are removed from the water and placed in winter storage.

"I recall a couple who were sailing from Chicago in mid October and failed to arrive at the marina mid day as scheduled," Said Wendy. "When they failed to show up by early afternoon, I called the Coast Guard." Good call! A Coast Guard boat crew found the 35-foot sailboat with its two occupants hard aground south of St. Joe. Although they were unharmed, one can only imagine the harm the grounding inflicted on their wallets after commercial salvage removed the beached stray.

There is one more seasonal danger boaters must consider and that is thunderstorms and lightning. Boats who set out on long voyages across Lake Michigan should keep a close eye on weather forecasts calling for thunderstorms. I spoke with Jan Miles, captain of one of America's premiere sailing ships *Pride of Baltimore* regarding

Great Lakes weather. The veteran captain was attending the "Tall Ship" gathering in Muskegon in the summer or 2003 when we spoke. He said, "I noticed that on the Great Lakes that severe weather systems can rapidly move through the region." Boaters who take the chance of running before heavy weather charged with lightning should read closely the following Boat Smart story.

ON WATCH: Lake Huron, Summer 1988. The lightning bolt danced across the five Coast Guardsmen, entering the head of the first and blowing the boots off the last in line. They lay scattered about like bowling pins, some as far as 20 feet from the point of impact. Chief Tim Monck of Station Ludington witnessed this nightmarish scene; he was just five yards from shore when lightning stuck his mates as they stood at water's edge. One "coastie" still remains in a coma.

The strike occurred in 1988 near the Fort Gratiot Light, Port Huron, during the Huron to Mackinac race. More than 3,000 boats had set sail, only to be recalled moments later as foul weather rolled in. Monck said, "The skies were clear overhead when lightning struck; then gray clouds rumbled in."

Clear skies and lightning are not an unusual combination. Once the leading edge of the thunderstorm approached to within 10 miles, Monck and his crew were at immediate risk. Towering anvil shaped clouds can release lightning bolts from afar, which explains why many lightning bolts occur with clear skies overhead.

"I learned one valuable lesson from that strike," Monck said. "As soon as there is a hint of lightning, race for cover."

Racing for cover is excellent advice, but it's not always easy advice to follow. A boat usually is the tallest feature on open water offering lightning an inviting target.

Since air is an insulator, lightning will attempt to cover the shortest distance between surfaces. This is why trees and other tall objects draw lightning. The "tall ships" of years past were especially vulnerable. In Peter E. Viemeister's book, "The Lightning Book," he reports that lightning so plagued the Royal Navy that in 1847 they conducted a survey of 220 ships that had been struck by lightning. In most cases, heavy damage was incurred: fires, splintered masts, holes in the hull, and death to beast and man. The survey found 90 seamen had been killed and nearly 200 wounded.

The study led to the introduction of continuous conductors, mainly metal lightning rods extending above the mast with metallic cables running to grounding components below decks. With the introduction of metal ships in 1860, a composite lightning rod was born, and today modern ships are rarely damaged by lightning.

Lightning over Lake Michigan

Small boats, however, remain easy prey for lightning. Suitable lightning protection can be provided by installing a continuous conductor from a point at least six inches above the highest part of the vessel down to a submerged metal "ground" plate. This route should be as short and straight as possible. A continuous mast, if properly grounded would work.

Also, isolated metal objects such as motors, winches and railings should be connected by a conductor wire and tied into the grounding system. On sailboats, shrouds and stays should be grounded in similar fashion. All radio antennas should be protected by lightning arresters.

Should a boater get caught in a storm, heading toward the nearest shore may provide a distraction for lightning since it seeks the highest objects such as rocks, trees and other objects that occupy overhead bluffs.

Whether or not you have a lightning protection system, it is critical to take additional precautions to protect yourself. You should consider these Boat Smart Anchor Points:

- Stay in the center of the cabin. If there is no cabin, stay low in the boat—avoid becoming a human lightning rod.
- Keep arms and legs in the boat, don't dangle them overboard.
- Halt fishing or other water activities.
- Don't operate major electronic equipment, including the radio; disconnect if possible.

- Lower, remove, or tie down the radio antenna and other protruding devices if they are not part of the lightning protection system.
- Do not make yourself a conductor between two components connected to the lightning ground system such as between gear levels and a metal handrail. Should you have a hand on each when lightning strikes "adios."

Perhaps the best advice of all is first check out the weather forecast before it later checks you out.

Now it's time to leave the seasons behind and make ready to steam into turbulent waters and the injurious dark side of recreational boating- boater ignorance.

Wanton Ignorance

I BELIEVE CERTAIN FORMS OF BOATING IGNORANCE, even if you want to call it that, stem from inexperience, and considering Lake Michigan's short boating season, the opportunity to acquire experience is rather limited. Thus boaters do less than smart things. Case in hand—three fellows pulled up to the fueling dock in South Haven in a small boat after coming off the "big lake." The fuel dock attendant saw the boat filling with water. He asked the operator if he had installed the boat plug. "What's that?" replied the operator.

Here's another less than smart boating mishap. A Coast Guard chief told me he responded to an oil spill at a marina in Hilton Head, South Carolina. The owner of a new 55-foot Hatteras powerboat dumped 600 gallons of diesel fuel into a marina bay when he walked away after placing a fuel nozzle into a recessed fishing rod holder on the stern of the boat. The fuel flowed onto the deck, into the engine space, and out through the bilge pump's discharge ports. He mistook the rod holder for the fuel fill spout. The bloke was a retired army general.

These snafus may seem far-fetched, yet such foibles often play out upon the waters like the mischief generated by youthful innocence on a playground. After all, it's only recreational boating.

There prevails, however, a pure form of wanton ignorance festering upon the waters that transcends individual boater foibles: a willful ignorance that inflicts malady upon the entire maritime community. This chapter will address these ignorant transgressions such as alcohol debauchery, false maydays, VHF-FM Channel 16 abuse, and other transgressions that endanger boaters and affect the safety and well-being of others. Let's take a look at these culprits and the mayhem they inflict.

ALCOHOL AND BOATING: A DEADLY MIX

Coast Guard recreational *Boating Statistics* reported that alcohol-related fatal accidents accounted for 39 percent of all recreational boating fatalities during 2002. The alcohol fatality figure has been steadily climbing since 1999, when alcohol accounted for 26 percent of all boating fatalities. This alarming increased called for aggressive measures to curb the growing tide of alcoholic activity in the Great Lakes region. During 2004, alcohol contributed to 37 percent of the 150 Great Lakes recreational boating fatalities. Alcoholic related fatalities may have been higher that year if not for Coast Guard Group Milwaukee's Operation Midnight Badger.

In 2004, Group Milwaukee unleashed Operation Midnight Badger with the sole purpose of removing impaired boaters from the water. Badger boat crews roamed Lake Michigan's western shore like midnight marauders determined to pounce on drunk boaters. Within two seasons, Coast Guard boarding officers had tallied up 336 boating under the influence (BUI) citations between Chicago and Door County, Wisconsin. In Chicago during 2004, Station Wilmette Boarding officers, alone, scored 72 BUI citations, the most for any Coast Guard unit in the nation.

Operation Midnight Badger had a sequential effect: the news of BUI busts spread through marinas and harbors like the beat of bongo drums but with IBM efficiency. The bongo drums beat grew even louder when word spread of BUI citations drawing thousands in federal fines. The maximum penalty for a federal Boating Under the Influence conviction is $5,500.

Those who may decry Operation Midnight Badger should consider the following: of the 306 BUI citations Coast Guard crews issued across the Great Lakes during 2004, the average blood alcohol concentration (BAC) was 0.152. A Coast Guard study revealed that boat operators with a BAC above 0.10 percent are estimated to be over 10 times more likely to be killed in a boating accident that boat operators with zero blood-alcohol concentration. The following Boat Smart story, "Boozers and boats: a deadly mix," unearths the gruesome effects of operating a boat under the influence of alcohol.

CASE FILE: St. Croix River, Minnesota, July 3, 1999. The booze-driven carnage occurred on the St. Croix River near Bayport, Minnesota, at 1:24 a.m. Five adult males died: three from drowning, two from blunt force trauma. The average blood alcohol concentration (BAC) of the five victims was 0.197, more than twice the limits set by most states. Worse yet, the owners and operators of the two boats involved average BAC was 0.235. Now the story:

The accident occurred near Bayport, Minnesota. According to the NTSB accident report, the owner of an Advantage Victory—a 27-foot cuddy-cabin motorboat—spent the day with guests drinking on board the boat, starting about 4 p.m. on July 3. The Advantage operator shifted from one marina berth to another around 6.30 p.m. According to witnesses, there were parties on both the Advantage and the boat to which the Advantage was moored, and the people on both boats were seriously consuming beer and mixed drinks.

Around 1 a.m. the Advantage operator got underway and stopped briefly at a marina. There a boater in the marina complained about the Advantage entering the marina at an "excessive speed" which stirred up a wake. Someone at the marina called out to the Advantage operator to watch his speed. The Advantage operator hollered back: "You're talking to the wrong guy, buddy," and then sped out of the marina heading downriver, leaving boats in the marina rocking at their moorings. Moments later big-time-Charlie arrived at the accident site about 1:25 a.m.

Meanwhile the owner of the second boat, a Bayliner, had indulged in a similar intake of "devil juice." According to a witness, he had joined a friend in a bar, and they swigged down shots until the bar closed.

The Bayliner's skipper promised to meet his bar buddy later in the town of Hudson. An idle promise, indeed. It wouldn't be the first booze-broken promise, but for certain the last for the Bayliner crew.

How the boozers actually collided, only they and the booze demons really know. A witness stated that he got his boat underway shortly before the collision occurred and proceeded downriver along the Minnesota side of the river. As he shined a spotlight on the water to see and avoid floating debris he sighted the capsized Advantage. He and his passenger stopped to render assistance. He said that the Advantage engine was not running, and he could not see any sign of the vessel's occupants. He recognized the Advantage as being the boat that had entered the municipal marina at an excessive speed a few minutes earlier. Moments later the witness noticed the Bayliner about 100 yards upriver. Upon approaching the Bayliner, the witness observed that it was extremely damaged and that two occupants were severely mangled and appeared to be dead.

Later that day, divers recovered the Advantage: A body was found on the bottom of the river during the next afternoon. A second body was found floating on the Wisconsin side of the river the following day. The third body was found on the river bottom not far from the first body. Divers found the Advantage's throttle was in the full speed position. Authorities estimate that the combined speed of the boats on impact may have been 105 mph.

Both boat operators reportedly were known to be experienced boaters. But studies have shown that even highly qualified boat operators begin suffering measurable impairment at BAC levels of 0.035 percent. It takes longer to process information, such as recognizing whether a potentially dangerous situation is developing with another vessel, and then deciding how to avoid an accident. At such BAC levels, a person's nocturnal vision will be more affected by glare from lights, including boat navigation lights, shore lights, and even moonlight.

That's at a BAC of 0.035, which equates to around two beers. The average BAC of the boat operators in this case was 0.2345, three times the legal limit. A factor that makes alcohol so deadly is that liquid courage significantly increases self-confidence while severely debilitating the body's defense mechanisms—a deadly set up. Boat Smart. Don't be set up: boat sober.

I didn't realize the extent of alcohol consumption upon the waters until I began snooping around the waterfront in search of boat smart material for the column and book. In my travels around Lake Michigan, I heard numerous stories of alcohol-related accidents, it brought to mind a comment I once heard regarding Dodger Stadium—someone called it the largest outdoor bar in the world. Could it instead be Lake Michigan?

CASE FILES: Lake Michigan at Large. During the fall of 2003 Glen Felixson, the harbor master of Beaver Island, told me he witnesses a great deal of drinking on the water. He told me about a recent case where two adult males rumbled into the harbor aboard a 40-foot Donzi. After docking the boat, they headed for the nearby Shamrock Bar, trailing the poignant odor of alcohol. When they returned to the dock, they were more aglow than before. "They asked for the course to Charlevoix. I told them 161 degrees," said Felixson. In a roar, they sped across the bay, following the course provided. Failing to realize they were within an enclosed bay, they ran full speed onto a beach and right on into the woods, miraculously unscathed.

The following day during the return trip to Charlevoix aboard the car ferry *Emerald Isle*, I spoke with Captain Kevin McDonough about the speed boat that attempted to reach Charlevoix via land. He said: "Our local salvager, Robert Gillespie, traveled to the site the following morning and returned disgruntled because there was no boat. He thought they were playing a gag on him. He failed to see the speed boat because the woods had swallowed it."

Beyond James Harbor sits Garden and Hog Island. Beaver island is the most remote inhabited Island on the Great Lakes. The island sports a year-round population of 550 inhabitants and is a popular destination for boaters.

In another Beaver Island boat booze story, Felixson told about the captain who drove his 37-foot power boat aground near Looney Point, located near the mouth of St. James Harbor. He stumbled up to the roadway, leaving his drinking companions behind on the boat. A motorist pulled over to assist. The captain's first words came in the form of a question: "How to get to the Shamrock bar?" In another case, a besotted boater called me on the marine radio and rather than ask for the Beaver Island Harbor Master he slurred out: "Harbor Island Beaver Master."

These stories, although humorous, could have led to tragic results. And the booze stories flowed on like a beer tap in an old Milwaukee brewery. Coast Guard Auxiliary flotilla commander Len Van Denack of Green Bay said he approached a boater sitting on the side of a small boat. "I advised him that sitting on the side of the boat was unsafe and that a wake might knock him into the water," said Van Denack. The man raised a beer can above his head and said, "Don't worry. I won't get the beer wet."

Van Denack pointed towards a shallow area in the bay. "Hundreds of small boats gather there to drink and party. I watch them load up at the docks, piling one, two, three... six packs of beer into coolers."

A harbor master in the southern part of the lake told me he sees a lot of alcohol on boats. "One guy who we call Thirty-Pack Pete seldom gets underway with any amount less than," said the harbor master, who wished to remain anonymous.

And the museum curator in Kenosha told me when she visits family members at a local marina she notices a lot of drinking. I told her from what I've been hearing around the lake regarding alcohol it reminds me of the old wild-west towns of Abilene and Tombstone. But instead of hell-raising, cattle-driving cowboys, we now find beer-can-toting, boat-driving good-old-boys.

My trip around the lake confirmed what I already knew about boaters and booze, but there's nothing like seeing it firsthand. On a Sunday afternoon in August, 2003, I was on patrol with Manistee's marine deputy Steve Block when he stopped a boater who cut in front of his bow in the Manistee River

Channel. He hailed the male operator over and was immediately greeted with blood-shot eyes, slurred speech and a strong odor of alcohol. On shore the rummy blew 0.22, more than twice the legal limit. It was mid-afternoon.

Sergeant Bill Halliday, Racine County Sheriff Water Patrol director, believes many boaters approach boating citations, including alcohol, as if they were nothing more than a parking citation: "I've had jet-boat operators offer to pay off the citation on the spot as if it were a mere inconvenience," said Halliday.

Halliday described an incident that occurred in a no-wake zone where a jet-boat's wake rolled into a sailboat, knocking a three-year-old child off the boat. Fortunately, she was wearing a life jacket. The sailboat operator pressed charges that led to serious repercussions for the jet-boat operator. "After that incident the high-rolling fast-boat operators cooled their jets," said Halliday.

"What, me worry?" mentality regarding operating a boat under the influence of alcohol or drugs also seems to be a popular notion. Nothing could be further from the truth. Besides the ordeal of being removed from the water, booked and jailed, a boater could also suffer boat damage, lost equipment, salvage fees, court fines, federal fines and insurance rate hikes. It can be costly enough to sway any sensible boater to cork the bottle. In the following story, two boaters wished they had.

ON WATCH: Pentwater, Michigan, August 2004. Two male boaters, ages 37 and 43, recently cited by a Coast Guard Ludington boat crew for operating a watercraft under the influence of alcohol could be facing hefty local and federal fines. Coast Guard officials from the Ludington Station, along with local police, recently removed several boaters off Pentwater Lake, Michigan, after a Coast Guard boat crew observed them ramming their 12-foot boats together as if they were floating bumper cars. The police hauled them off to jail after they registered a BAC of 0.173 and 0.263. "The support we receive from the Pentwater police was outstanding," said Coast Guard boarding officer Larry Hall, who initiated the arrest.

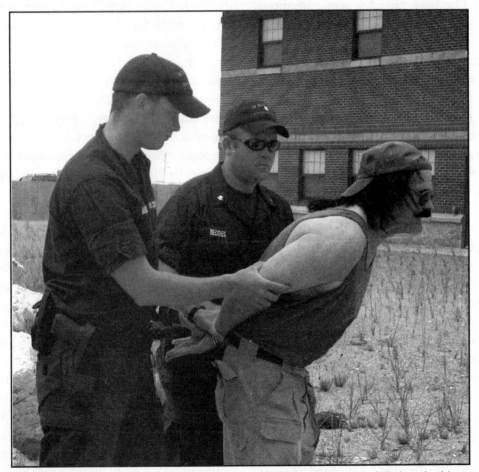

A boater with a BAC of 0.08 and higher will be removed from the water, jailed, and subject to local and federal fines.

BOAT SMART BRIEF: Hopefully, the two men appeared in court to pay their citation. If they fail to, it could invite additional woes: Local municipal courts will levy bench warrants for offenders who fail to appear on a boating appearance citation. In the event a motorist is later pulled over by a road unit, the officer will check the computer for liens and warrants. That person is headed for jail if a boating-related bench warrant flashes on the patrol car's computer. Many boaters, however, mistakenly believe that water-related citations carry little weight. Nothing could be further from the truth.

The state of Indiana tags alcoholic boating citations to motor vehicle records, treating them as the same. Other states need to follow suit. Read on and understand why.

Coast Guardsman Jonathan Picket of Motor Lifeboat Station, Michigan City, during the summer of 2004 cited two different boaters on the same day for operating under the influence. "Between the eleven people aboard the two boats there was not one life jacket," said Picket.

While on patrol in early June 2005, another Coast Guard boarding team from Station Michigan City, spotted a boat with two kids aboard under the age of six not wearing life jackets. During the course of the boarding the operator displayed signs of intoxication. Coast Guardsman, Justin Klitch, performed a Breathalyzer test on the operator. He blew 0.20, which is more than twice Michigan's legal limit. That's bad enough but worse yet, there were not enough life jackets aboard for the kids. Klitch told me the operator become belligerent. "I cuffed the guy and turned him over to local authorities," said Klitch. If that story doesn't raise the eyebrows of law makers, what then will it take?

State legislators should seriously consider applying boating citations to a boat operator's driving record. Until boating under the influence penalties hookup with motor vehicle codes that have so successfully cracked down on drunken carnage on our highways, the Coast Guard, along with the dedicated efforts of local law enforcement agencies, will continue to team up to keep our waters safe. Join the team. Boat sober.

Thus far we have discussed civil penalties and fines for operating a boat under the influence; however there is another negative consequence boaters often overlook—insurance. Wayne Comstock of Wolverine Mutual, whose company insures a large number of recreational watercraft in Michigan and Indiana, told me that if a boater is found guilty of operating a boat while intoxicated and is involved in an accident, Wolverine will cancel his insurance.

I asked Wayne what a new premium would cost a boater. He told me if the boater can find an insurer, the policy coverage will be limited and his *monthly* premium cost will be around what he was paying *annually* before. And that's not all—if a boater fails to find an insurer, and the boat is financed through a lender, the lender can demand the loan be paid in full unless proof of insurance is provided.

As much as I loathe drunk boaters, as do fellow marine law enforcement agents, there exists a maritime scourge worthy of much greater wrath—the brainless fools who make false distress calls, more commonly know as hoax calls.

Boat Smart Anchor Points

↔ Alcohol affects your ability to operate a boat in the same manner that it affects your ability to operate a car, but certain factors can make the effects even more debilitating. Exposure to sun, glare, wind, noise, vibration and motion on the water can lead to "boater's hypnosis" or fatigue, which can reduce reaction time. Believe me, I can vouch for these environmental effects, having spent many a prolonged period on the water. There were times when my brain felt like mush. I took pride in keeping in top physical condition in order to maintain the stamina and confidence to execute prolonged search and rescue cases, yet there was little I could do to reduce brain overload, or "boater's hypnosis."

To add alcohol to the condition only intensifies its effects. Studies show that an amount of alcohol that has little effect on land can seriously impair your performance on the water.

According to a National Transportation Safety Board study, it takes one-third as much alcohol to affect a boater's balance, coordination and judgment as it does to affect the same person on land. Booze or not, it's difficult enough at night to navigate, especially with night vision being compromised by instruments lights, and illuminated electronic screens like radar, GPS, radio and depth finders. The human eye under the best of conditions adapts poorly to darkness. We need all the help with night vision we can muster, and alcohol certainly doesn't help an already disadvantaged situation.

Let me sum it up by saying this: you're estupido if you drink and operate a boat—night or day. Be cool and hand the wheel over to a sober mate while you attend to cooler affairs.

HOAX CALLS A NEEDLESS CURSE

I'll give boaters who drink the benefit of the doubt in that their pickled brain diminishes their judgment. Although some might argue that when a sober person chooses to drink they are at the time in full control of their facilities and thus responsible for the consequences of that choice. That could well be; however I still believe people who suffer from a drinking problem do deserve some benefit of the doubt.

But for those who make false distress calls, they deserve no benefit of the doubt, no considerations, no concessions, nothing. When they pick up a marine radio and knowingly broadcast a false request for assistance, they disenfranchise themselves from humanity. The following Boat Smart story describes a miraculous rescue that was almost soured by a false Mayday that almost cost the life of a father and son after their small aircraft crashed into Lake Michigan.

ON WATCH: Station Grand Haven, Saturday, 15 April 2000. At 2:42 p.m., the Officer of the Day at Station Grand Haven, Boatswain Mate First Class John Hersrud, received a telephone call from Telecommunications Specialist Debra Ball at the Group Grand Haven communications center regarding a possible downed aircraft in Lake Michigan. Doctor Charles Rousch, the reporting party, whose home overlooks Lake Michigan, later said: "I had the feeling he [the pilot] was feeling his way down in the fog. So I ran to the bluff to try and see it, but didn't see anything. Then I heard a loud bang, and the engine noise stopped." Rousch, a pilot himself, immediately called the Coast Guard and 911 with his portable phone.

Within minutes of Rousch's call, a Station Grand Haven boat crew aboard a 25-foot ridged hull inflatable boat (RHIB) broke the pier heads at Grand Haven en route to the reported crash site approximately seven miles north of Grand Haven. A heavy fog greeted the boat crew. "It was spooky," said Chief John Anten. "The water, sky, and nearby shore took on an eerie silver-gray likeness. It was difficult telling one from the other."

The crew sped north through the fog; the coxswain's eyes shifted from the radar screen to the bow where tears trickled from crewmen's eyes as they peered into the thick soup. "It was cold," said Coast Guardsman Hosford.

Approximately seven miles north, the boat crew encountered a lone kayaker near the Mona Lake entrance; on shore a gathering of people suggested that the crew was near the crash site. This was confirmed by the kayaker, who told the crew he heard an airplane, then a splash, then nothing.

Following the kayaker's lead, the boat crew headed off into the fog toward the northwest. Approximately two miles out, Boatswain Mate Second Class Roland Ashby throttled down. The crew leaned their ears into the fog—nothing. Back up to speed, a couple of minutes later they throttled down again. The Group radio operator's voice along with the sputtering Johnson outboards echoed across the foggy lake. Chief Anten suggested that they shut down the engines and tune out the radio. They did but heard nothing. "I was turning to tell Ashby to fire up the engines when I heard a faint cry," said Chief Anten. Ashby and Hosford heard nothing. Firing up the engines, they continued northwest.

A minute or so later, Ashby stopped and again shut down the engines and radio. "This time we all heard a kid-like cry. It sounded like the distant shrill of kids at play," said Hosford.

Continuing northwest for a moment or two, Ashby again shut down the engines for the third time. The hollering grew louder. The boat crew shouted instructions into the fog to keep hollering. Picking their way through the fog, they found a small clearing where an amazing sight greeted them. Off the bow, a dark head-like object loomed upon the still water. As they drew nearer, they saw a man and boy clinging to an airplane tire. "It was as if fingers from above placed them there," said Hosford. "There was no wreckage, no gas or oil on the water, nothing, just this man and a boy clinging to a small tire. It was like a scene from the Twilight Zone."

Above the fog clattered a Coast Guard helicopter. From Grand Haven raced the station's 47-foot Motor Life Boat; a nearby North Muskegon County fire boat with paramedics aboard zoomed toward the Coast Guard boat.

The crew hauled the victims aboard. "The father could barely speak or move. He couldn't hold his head straight, his lips were blue, his body rigid. We had a heck of a time getting a life jacket on him," said Ashby. The father, age 50, was wearing blue jeans, a polo shirt, and boat shoes. His boy wore the same except he had no shoes or socks.

"This rescue was definitely divinely influenced," said Hosford. "It was only a matter of minutes before they would've slipped way."

"I thought we were going to die," said 12-year-old Charlie Lawrence. "My fingers were getting so cold it was hard to hang onto the tire. When the Coast Guard got to us, I figured I could last another 10 minutes."

Charlie and his dad were lucky they even survived the impact. "I couldn't push the door open because of the water pressure, so I had to swim out the window as the plane went down," said Bernie Lawrence.

According to Charlie, his dad had to bust out a window to get him out; by then the cockpit was under water. "It seemed within a minute the plane filled with water," said Charlie. "My hands and legs were numb by the time the Coast Guard arrived."

When the Muskegon fire boat arrived on scene, they transferred a paramedic over to the RHIB, and the crew raced toward Muskegon. Moments later they moored at Station Muskegon where an ambulance greeted the father and son. At the hospital, the father's core body temperature read 89 degrees, up from an estimated 85 degrees in the water. The elapsed time from the moment the boat crew launched to when they plucked the father and son from the water was 18 minutes.

Bernie Lawrence and his son Charlie were later released from Muskegon's Hackley hospital. "I guess it just wasn't their time," said Chief Anten.

Well, Chief, it could well have been their time. Shortly after the rescue, Group Grand Haven radio received a Mayday, which turned out to be a hoax. The hoax call drew the RHIB crew back out into the Lake. Had the hoax call been made an hour earlier, the RHIB crew may not have been available to assist Charlie and his son. Charlie told me later: "If they were out on that hoax call an hour earlier, I would be dead."

The following Boat Smart story, "Hoax Calls Made to The Coast Guard a Deadly and Costly Game," not only reveals the costs of hoax calls, but the just retribution delivered to the foul scoundrels who needlessly cry "wolf" on the water.

Rear Admiral McGowen, commander of the Coast Guard's Ninth District in Cleveland, said of hoax callers: "If you call the Coast Guard out, we will respond, and if you call in a hoax, we will prosecute."

Broadcasting a false distress call is a felony punishable with a fine up to $250,000 and six-and-a-half years in prison. The caller could also be liable for all search costs, and that includes any death or injury which may occur during the Coast Guard's efforts. Certainly, the most onerous aspect of hoax calls is the waste of costly resources that might be needed elsewhere. "Our biggest concern isn't necessarily catching these people. The most threatening thing is trying to weed out the hoaxes from the real thing," said Admiral McGowen.

The Admiral was alluding to hoax case where a 14-year-old Lorain, Ohio, boy drowned in Lorain Harbor within view of the Lorain Coast Guard

A crane from a marine salvage company lifts up a Cesna 172 that crashed in Lake Michigan in heavy fog. A Coast Guard crew rescued a father and son before 39-degree water took its deadly toll—that, and a hoax call.

station while rescuers were 18 miles away responding to a hoax.

The most notorious and vile hoaxer raised his sinister voice in Fairport Harbor, Lake Erie. Gary Goodmanson, 43, of Mentor, Ohio, pled guilty to making ten false distress calls to Coast Guard Station Fairport Harbor, Ohio, between May 1 and July 2, 1997.

The Coast Guard spent nearly $140,000 on 10 needles searches. Worse yet, several of these hoax calls were made during heavy weather. It was during one of these calls, on May 2, 1997, that a Coast Guard crew nearly perished in high seas.

It began with a Mayday call to the Coast Guard Fairport Station, Lake Erie, Ohio regarding a 45-foot boat with 21 people on board taking on water four miles north of Perry Nuclear Power Plant. Searchers faced 14-foot seas and winds up to 50 miles per hour. In all, there were two Coast Guard HH65 helicopters, a Canadian C-130 and Labrador helicopter, two civilian aircraft, a merchant ship, a CG 41-foot utility boat and 44-foot Motor Life Boat chasing the Mayday. After searchers covered 200 square miles, it was determined a hoax. "Our people put their lives at risk, and anyone who increases the risk should be held accountable," said Admiral McGowen.

Others agree. Norm Schultz, executive vice president of the Cleveland-based Lake Erie Marine Trades Association, said this about the Goodmanson case: "Actions such as Goodmanson's not only put at risk the lives of dedicated Coast Guard personnel, but in a very real way also jeopardize the lives of boaters who might truly be in need of Coast Guard assistance."

Ironically, the sentence handed down to Goodmanson was on Halloween, and it was no treat: the trickster was ordered to spend 15 months in federal prison and make restitution to the Coast Guard for $139,245 in expenses. He's to pay off the debt at 15 percent per month of whatever gross monthly income he makes. The payments will be garnished from his wages.

And for those who recklessly make distress calls, the cost may go up. Legislators are considering stiffer fines, stiffer jail time, and stiffer sentencing guidelines for those found guilty of transmitting false Maydays.

In a recent case in Texas, a 37-year-old male pled guilty to making one false distress call and was sentenced to ten years in prison, three years supervised probation, and restitution to the Coast Guard in the amount of $229,925.

Recently in Charleston, South Carolina, a 40-year-old male, his wife and his 70-year-old father were indicted in Federal court for making a false distress call to the Coast Guard. In February 2005, a Tennessee woman was sentenced to two years in federal prison and ordered to pay over $56,000 in restitution. That same year, a San Diego-based Coast Guard seaman apprentice made hoax calls while serving in Alaska. The reprobate was sent to a naval brig for six months and dishonorable discharged from the Coast Guard.

Between 2000 and 2005 the Coast Guard responded to 1,244 uncorrelated distress calls across the Great Lakes, 119 of which were confirmed hoax calls. An "uncorrelated" distress call means that the caller requested help but failed to identify himself or failed to respond after the Coast Guard responded to the call.

What sense does that make calling for help then hanging up? On one hand the marine radio has proven to be tremendous lifesaving tool, but on the other hand it can bring a great deal of grief as hoax calls have proven. One can't help but wonder who these miscreants are and what drives their depravity. Who knows perhaps only the devil does.

There exists, however, another form of grief that plagues the marine radio and it is as abundant as there are boaters and one of them could be as near as one boat slip over. Unlike hoax pranksters these radio infidels are driven by good old ignorance and they number in the hundreds of thousands. Who are they? They are the everyday abusers of Channel 16, the International Distress and Hailing frequency.

CHANNEL 16 ABUSE

Operating a boat while intoxicated and broadcasting hoax calls knows no equal as far as ignorant behavior in the maritime environment. Although not as sinister as these villains, there exists another form of boating ignorance that by its sheer magnitude breeds widespread agitation upon the waters and that is VHF-FM Channel 16 abuse.

Over the years, I have witnessed widespread radio misuse of VHF-FM Channel 16 on Lake Michigan and simply cannot understand why recreational boaters can abuse such a life-saving device. Are boaters that ignorant or that brash? Could be both, but I suspect it's more ignorance than attitude.

I've probably written as many columns regarding marine radio ignorance as about boating and alcohol. One of my favorite columns about Channel 16 abuse addressed the colossal shipwreck of the ages, the *Titanic*. It's ironic that Channel 16 was born of the *Titanic* disaster and that radio misuse that cold bitter night on April 15, 1912 led to the loss of so many. Had *Titanic's* radio calls for help reached the nearby Leland Liner *California*, 1,522 souls might have escaped a miserable death. Sadly, time erases history's hard-earned lessons. The story and its message are worth repeating.

CASE FILE: North Atlantic, 14 April 1912, 11:05 p.m. local mean time. Cecil Evans, radio operator on the Leland Liner *California*, which lay dead in the water, had just fired off a radio message to *Titanic*: "Say, Old Man, we are stopped and surrounded by ice."

Harold Philips, chief radio operator aboard *Titanic* fired back: "Shut up shut up, I am busy, I am working Cape Race and you are jamming me."

International radio procedure in 1912 required that shipboard radio operators formally address radio traffic to ship command. Since Evans had sent an informal message from radio operator to radio operator the iceberg warning never reached Titanic's bridge. A stack of Marconigrams had Philips and his assistant swamped as they tapped out radio traffic to Cape Race. Most of the commercial messages dealt with the first class passengers, requesting personal arrangements on their arrival in New York the following day.

Apparently the personal needs of the affluent out weighted Philips's concern for icebergs. His nasty response apparently discouraged any further warnings from Cecil Evans. At 11:35, *California's* only radio operator shut down, having sent no further iceberg warnings to *Titanic*. Five minutes later, at 11:40, Titanic struck the iceberg and for over an hour Philips and his radio assistant's desperate calls for help searched the dark North Atlantic night until silenced by the sea. Only a few miles from *Titanic, California's* radio sat silent and unattended.

On top of that miscue, the *California's* bridge crew told the U.S. Senate *Titanic* Hearings Committee of sighting eight white rockets above the horizon in the direction of a row of lights of which one officer said, "She looks very queer out of the water—her lights look queer." *California's* Captain, Standley Lord, responded evasively to inquires about the white rockets and his bridge officer's sworn testimony of spotting eight white distress rockets. That the rocket sightings failed to appear in the *California's* log suggested a cover-up. When the lights "disappeared," it was assumed the "mystery" ship had passed over the horizon, but, in fact, it was *Titanic* descending to her grave two miles below.

The distress rockets and radio miscues rank as one of maritime history's most profound errors in judgment. Is there any wonder why Captain Lord attempted to cover it up? According to author Craig Wade, in his insightful book, *The Titanic, End of a Dream*, when the research vessel *Knorr* discovered the wreck of the *Titanic* in September 1985, the head of the expedition, Dr. Robert Ballard, make an astonishing discovery. The *California* sat much closer to *Titanic* than 19 miles, which was originally reported by Captain Lord during the Senate hearings. Ballard, who pinpointed the *Titanic's* latitude and longitude, revealed *California* lay close enough to *Titanic* to have seen her distress rockets and rescue her passengers. Ballard insisted, "He was a lot closer. Inside of ten miles, perhaps as close as five miles.... The passengers could have been rescued. No one needed to die."

Why Captain Lord, after being notified three times by his bridge officers of the rockets, failed to awaken his radio operator, Cecil Evans, remains a mystery locked in time. From the bitter soil of experience grew strict maritime radio procedures that legislators chiseled into law. Never again would a commercial vessel's radio go unmanned, around-the-clock manned radio watches became law.

BOAT SMART BRIEF: I would like to believe the *Titanic* story persuaded boaters to respect Channel 16, but I know better and in all fairness to recreational boaters, Channel 16, dualism has inadvertently contributed to Channel 16 misuse. Designed as a dual-purpose frequency, its originators cleverly designed a means in which a marine radio could be used as a hailing device between mariners and as an emergency carrier. This provides the user the advantage of receiving and sending calls while maintaining a watchful ear out for those in distress. Indeed, ingenious.

Then along came recreational boaters. Those who conceived this marvelous maritime innovation decades ago never imagined the locust-like invasion of Channel 16 by recreational boaters. Whereas commercial users of Channel 16 numbered in the hundreds on Lake Michigan and across the Great Lakes, recreational marine radio operators number in the thousands, all hailing on and listening to Channel 16, and often hailing more than listening. And whereas commercial mariners use proper discipline in their use of Channel 16, recreational boaters simply willfully use it. It is the worst scenario of a good thing gone bad. What was meant to save lives now threatens to take them, and it seems many recreational radio users couldn't care less.

Channel 16 definitely needed fixing but how. As Coast Guard officials pondered over a solution their concerns mounted. A boater's nightmare would be to call for help over marine radio and not be heard because the mayday is muted in a hail of radio chatter. Todd Leiblam, telecommunications specialist at Coast Guard Group Grand Haven's Communication Center said, "On a busy summer weekend, there is so much radio chatter over

Channel 16 that boaters calling for Coast Guard assistance sometimes can't be heard."

Group Grand Haven, Group Milwaukee and Group Sault St. Marie Communications Centers maintain a 24-hour radio watch over Channel 16. Powerful Coast Guard "Hi-Site" antennas located around Lake Michigan pick up radio calls from the smallest boat to the largest freighter. Few radio calls escape their sensitive ears.

But it was those few possible missed calls that concerned Coast Guard officials. Commander Roger Dubuc said, "I'm scared to death that an urgent call for Coast Guard assistance will go unheard because someone with a more powerful radio will be discussing their fishing plans with another boater. In this situation we will only hear the more powerful radio transmission. With the thousands of recreational boats that access Lake Michigan, many carrying marine radios, Channel 16 needs relief, and Channel 09 is the remedy."

Prompted by Commander Dubuc's concerns, Lieutenant Karl Willis, Operations boss at Group Grand Haven, tasked me in the Spring of 1999 with developing a public outreach program to encourage boaters along Lake Michigan's eastern shore to use VHF-FM Channel 09 rather than Channel 16 as their hailing frequency. I leaped at the opportunity after years of enduring Channel 16 misuse.

During 1987, I wrote an article for the *Manistee News Advocate* addressing radio misuse. The article described how a Station Manistee radio watchstander counted 250 calls made over Channel 16 within a period of two-and-a-half hours. One boater placed 24 calls in less than 20 minutes. "If I heard one more time 'Hey good old buddies how's the fishing out there?' or 'Hey big daddy what's you hooking?' I was going to leap out the window," said the radio watchstander.

One charter boat captain expressed his views about callers who repeatedly overuse Channel 16 as a hailing frequency: "During my years fishing in Manistee waters, I've yet to catch a fish with my radio. Experienced captains just don't pull up lines and fly off to a reported fishing hole. Hell, a good fisherman knows where the fish are without using the radio. I want that radio aboard in case

I need help. It ain't no toy, it could save my life," said the charter boat captain.

To reduce the heavy load on Channel 16, the Coast Guard, with the approval of the Federal Communications Commission (FCC), assigned VHF-FM Channel 09 as a calling frequency between recreational boaters on Lake Michigan effective May 1, 1999. The FCC regulations permit non-commercial vessels such as recreational boats and private stations such as marinas to maintain a watch on Channel 09 VHF-FM for call and reply purposes. Using Channel 09 as a calling frequency promised to greatly reduce Channel 16's heavy load.

So effective was the outreach program that at times while underway aboard a Coast Guard boat I thought the radio was malfunctioning because Channel 16 was so quiet. In order for Channel 09 program to continue to work on Lake Michigan, boaters must subscribe to the following Channel 09 guidelines.

Channel 09, Q & A

Is using Channel 09 as a hailing frequency new?

No, using Channel 09 as a hailing frequency between recreational boaters began in Boston Harbor in 1991. And in one year reduced radio traffic over Channel 16 by nearly 50 percent. Today, the use of Channel 09 has spread across the northeastern United States. Coast Guard officials in the region hailed recreational boaters for clearing up Channel 16. The same positive results occurred on Lake Michigan.

Will the Coast Guard monitor Channel 09?

Since Channel 09 will act as a hailing frequency between recreational boaters only, the Coast Guard will not monitor the channel. Vessels requesting Coast Guard assistance should do so over Channel 16.

Over what Channel will the Coast Guard broadcast Marine Advisories?

Although the Coast Guard will not monitor 09, it will broadcast marine advisories and safety information over Channel 09 and Channel 16.

How should recreational boaters contact Commercial vessels?

Commercial vessels, freighters, and pilot boats should continue to use Channel 16 as a hailing frequency. Recreational vessels should use Channel 16 when hailing these vessels.

Has the Federal Communications Commission (FCC) approved 09?

Not only has the FCC permitted Channel 09 as a nationwide secondary calling Channel on VHF marine radio, it highly encourages its use, especially since it greatly reduces congestion on Channel 16.

What areas will Channel 09 cover?

Coast Guard Group Grand Haven, Group Milwaukee, and Group Sault Ste Marie are involved in the Channel 09 program, which includes all of Lake Michigan and its connecting navigable rivers and lakes.

Why is using Channel 09 as a hailing frequency important?

The reason for using Channel 09 as a primary hailing frequency between recreational boaters is it greatly reduces hailing radio traffic on Channel 16. Its success, however, depends on recreational boaters understanding Channel 16's primary role. It is their main link to the Coast Guard and other rescue agencies. In short, Channel 16 is the boater's equivalent of 911. It should be reserved for emergencies.

Channel 09 works well on Lake Michigan since it is totally under U.S. jurisdiction, but the other Great Lakes are shared with Canada, which apparently has equipment challenges with the Channel 09 program. Canada has the high site radio antennas to transmit and receive Channel 16 radio traffic, but the antenna sites are not equipped to hail or receive 09 radio traffic. And thus Channel 16 remains the main hailing frequency on the other Great Lakes.

As we move onto the next ignorant issue I'm not sure whether you should come aboard for this session unless the captain can assure your safety. Don't be surprised either if the captain turns out to be a family member ill-equipped to do so. After reading what's to follow, I feel confident you will be capable of deciding for yourself whether the captain is jeopardizing your safety.

PASSENGER JEOPARDY

How many people who get underway on boats consider if the operator has a clue as to what they are doing. I don't believe many passengers even give it a thought. So I ask who is more ignorant the person who blindly places their fate over to a boater's care, or the captain who jeopardizes his passengers by not caring at all whether he or she lacks the most basic boating skills.

Such ignorance can be so perverse that it can even override a father's instinct to protect his kin. Captain Rick Hopper of the *Lake Express* expressed this view about fathers while I was riding on the bridge of the *Lake Express* on my way to Milwaukee in October of 2004. Captain Hopper said, "Fathers will go to extreme measures to protect the family, yet place them aboard a recreational boat and they will throw caution to the wind."

The captain's statement brought to mind an interview I conducted several months earlier with Coast Guardsman Jason Grimm of Motor Lifeboat Station St. Ignace. In August, he responded to a rescue operation in the Straits of Mackinac. A father along with his wife and son departed the De Tour Passage enroute Mackinac Island, located 41-one miles west of the passage. Fog set in during the voyage and the father ended up running his powerboat onto the Northeast corner of Bois Blanc Island, located just south of Mackinac Island. The Coast Guard 47-foot motor lifeboat could not access the grounded boat due to shallow water. A salvage company ended up freeing the boat. There were no injuries to the people aboard.

The grounded powerboat did not carry radar or a GPS. The route the wayward father followed in fog is one of the heaviest trafficked commercial shipping lanes on the Great Lakes. Would the same father drive an automobile with his family aboard down a major trucking route with a blanket draped over the windshield? Absurd, not really, he did just that but with a boat. Already the book has touched on a number of cases involving passenger jeopardy and there will be more to follow; however, let me share some real dusers of passenger jeopardy. Nuts would better suit.

ON WATCH: Lake Michigan's Eastern Shore, August, 22, 2001. I spent an afternoon aboard Station Muskegon's 25-foot inflatable rescue craft on a law enforcement patrol. My running mates were Officer In Charge Chief Hinken, Petty Officer Jason Bernard, and Greg Patten, a veteran agent, Michigan Department of Natural Resources (DNR). While eastbound on Muskegon Lake, we spotted a 32-foot trawler heading outbound towards the Muskegon Channel. The boat had no registration numbers on the hull or name on the stern. Within moments, we were alongside the trawler with our blue light flashing. Chief Hinken and Petty Officer Bernard boarded the trawler. I maintained station alongside with the DNR agent.

During the inspection, the boarding team discovered that the new boat, on its maiden voyage, carried only four life jackets for the seven people aboard, lacked the proper number of fire extinguishers, and carried no registration at all. Lake Michigan weather called for three to-five foot seas. Chief Hinken terminated the voyage due to a lack of life jackets and fire extinguishers and directed the captain to return to his moorings. The DNR agent also cited him a registration violation.

Several days later three fishermen sat disabled and adrift aboard an 18-foot Bayliner off Muskegon, Lake Michigan. Oil loss had led the engine to overheat and shut down. The three men aboard began paddling for shore, but around 11 a.m. the wind and seas picked up, pushing the boat further off shore. Around 11:30 a.m. they dropped anchor in 200 feet of water, but only carried 150 feet of anchor line, which was nothing more than water-skiing rope. The anchor did, however, slow their drift. By late afternoon they had drifted to Grand Haven where they watched a Coast Guard helicopter pass overhead. But since no one had yet reported the boaters overdue, the Coast Guard aircrew flew on.

The boat carried no visual distress signals, no radio, and no cell phone. Past Grand Haven, they decided to pull the anchor aboard and paddle for shore. They paddled continuously in vain while further drifting south. At one point, seas reportedly reached 10 feet and winds 25 to 30 knots. Exhausted from paddling, they dropped anchored again at 11 p.m. to nap. Then at 11:50 p.m. they again started to paddle. Finally, at 12:50 a.m. a Coast Guard aircrew spotted them. Loved ones had reported them overdue at 5:25 p.m. A Coast Guard boat crew out of Holland transferred them off their boat and towed the boat into Holland. In all, they had drifted nearly 23 miles over 15 hours. When the Coast Guard crew found them, no one was wearing life jackets. They reported that at 11:00 a.m. they passed within 100 yards of a yacht; they waved their oars but apparently went unnoticed by the yacht's crew.

I strongly suggested that the captain enroll in a boating safety course. I wonder if the two fellows aboard would go out with him again. I'm sure the passengers in the following passenger jeopardy story will avoid a certain captain. In fact, after what he put them through they might avoid boating altogether.

ON WATCH: South Haven, Michigan, September 30, 2001, 4:30 p.m. Group Grand Haven's radio operator received a Mayday call over Channel 16 from a boater reporting he was "stuck" between South Haven and the Palisades, which are located around four miles south of South Haven Harbor. However, the vessel calling provided a latitude, which placed it north of South Haven. The transmission then ended. Attempts by Coast Guard Group Grand Haven to call the vessel went unanswered.

Now what? We have a vessel reportedly "stuck" approximately four miles south of South Haven Harbor, but the operator provides a latitude (no longitude) that places it north of the harbor. Also, does "stuck" mean the boat ran aground?

A Good Samaritan aboard the vessel *Bugs Tug* responded to the Mayday call. The tug's captain volunteered to search the waters south of South Haven; he reported back "negative sightings."

He then proceeded to the latitude position provided by the distressed vessel, which took him north of South Haven Harbor. He again reported "negative sightings."

Meanwhile, further attempts to hail the boater went unanswered. Then, at 6:07 p.m., one hour and 21 minutes after the first call, Group received another call from the operator of the vessel in distress stating his motor had stopped. End transmission. Group called him back, but he failed to respond. Fifteen minutes later the boater again contacted Group and reported he was now off South Haven. Again attempts to establish radio contact failed.

Group radio directed the Auxiliary vessel *Whilelm Buam* to launch and check the South Haven harbor entrance, and to call the distressed boater. The *Baum's* radio calls went unanswered. The *Baum's* captain, Jim Bradley, later told me the situation was very confusing. The boater would occasionally call, followed by a long silence. Adding to the confusion was the fact two different voices made the calls, leading searchers to believe perhaps more than one vessel was involved.

At 6:30 p.m. Group Grand Haven received another call from the vessel stating they were south of the Palisades Power Plant. The group radioman asked the operator if he had a GPS aboard and if so would he provide his latitude and longitude, which he finally did after the radiomen instructed him on how to read the GPS. The coordinates placed the boat eight nautical miles northwest of South Haven, and approximately 12 miles north of the Palisades. Obviously this boater didn't have clue as to his location.

With night approaching, Group launched the Coast Guard helicopter from Muskegon. Meanwhile, a Coast Guard 21-foot rescue boat raced north from Station Saint Joseph. At 7:20 p.m., two hours and 43 minutes hours after the original call to the Coast Guard, the helicopter located the boater eight nautical miles northwest of South Haven Harbor. The St. Joe rescue boat arrived on scene shortly afterward and towed the 15-foot, tri-hull boat and its four occupants into South Haven.

BOAT SMART BRIEF: Later, I discussed the case with the Coast Guard coxswain of the 21-foot inflatable rescue boat. He said the 30-year-old male operator had decided, along with three 16-year-old girls—one was his sister—to head offshore to wave jump since the water near shore was too calm. He told the Coast Guard boat crew his boat had developed engine problems and when he removed the engine's cover several parts fell into the lake.

He told the coxswain he had jumped into the lake several times with a line and attempted to swim to shore pulling the boat behind him. Unbelievably, he was eight miles off shore near the shipping lanes. He said he had fired off several flares, but no one responded. No one had reported flare sightings to the Coast Guard. When the coxswain asked him about hypothermia, he said, "What's that?" The coxswain noticed signs of hypothermia and provided the operator a survival suit. The air temperature was 60 degrees and the water temperature 51 degrees. With nighttime falling upon the four occupants dressed in only skimpy summer attire, adrift eight miles off shore near a major shipping lane, and clueless as to their location, things might have turned ugly.

After listening to the coxswain's account, I inquired if the operator was under the influence of alcohol or drugs. "No," said the coxswain.

Later when I told this story to Terry Jungle, Executive Director, Michigan Sheriff's Association, he said, "He was under the influence all right—the influence of stupidity." Jungle continued, "If these boaters want to be the author of their own demise, that's their choice; unfortunately their actions often harm other people." With over 28 years in law enforcement, a career he began as a marine deputy, Jungle is a staunch advocate of mandatory boating education. Is it any wonder?

Cases of boaters taking innocent passengers for "rides" and putting them in harm's way number in the thousands according to Coast Guard *Boating Statistics*. Between 1986 and 2005, the Coast Guard engaged in 137,843 search and rescue cases across the Great Lakes, affecting nearly 300,000 people. Granted, not all these cases involved boaters, but the number of people assisted versus the total number of cases clearly indicates that many of the search and rescue cases involved more than one person. It's a safe bet that those multi-person cases involved boats or in rare cases aircraft.

Yes aircraft.

On April 25, 2005, a single-engine Piper Archer inbound to Milwaukee's Mitchell field crashed landed into Lake Michigan after running out of fuel. The 17-year-old pilot climbed on top of the aircraft and called 911 on a cell phone. By the time the Coast Guard reached the location of aircraft approximately ten miles east of Milwaukee, the aircraft had sank. The water temperature was 41 degrees. A 15-hour search failed to find a trace of the aircraft.

Several days later a commercial diver located the aircraft in 160 feet of water. Laying alongside the aircraft on the lake floor was the cell phone. The young pilot remains missing. Although the story involved aircraft; once it reached the lake it makes little difference whether it's boat or aircraft, especially if it sinks. Pilots should pay heed to the message this tragic accidents sends: carry life jackets and survival raft when flying over a major body of water. Coast Guard aircrews do.

Let's move on to another form of mind-boggling ignorance: boaters' inability to determine their location on the water. Every boating season across the Great Lakes the Coast Guard receives calls for help from lost babes upon the waters. The most vexing calls involve lost boaters equipped with Global Positioning Satellite devices that can pinpoint their position, yet the person calling can't read the device.

Boat Smart Anchor Points

How to avoid passenger jeopardy

↪ Passengers should insist that the captain point out the location of safety equipment, especially life jackets. Are there enough aboard for the passengers.

↪ Test a life jacket before getting underway to become familiar with its use.

↪ Does the captain have a throwable flotation device aboard and where is it located.

↪ Where are the visual distress signals and how are they deployed.

↪ If there's a marine radio aboard request instruction on its use and how do you call the Coast Guard.

↪ Did the captain check the weather forecast.

↪ What recovery procedures does the captain have should someone fall overboard.

↪ What plan does the captain have to recover someone from the water.

↪ Does someone aboard besides the captain know how to operate the boat. If not, insist that the captain provide instruction.

↪ Is there an anchor aboard and where is it located.

↪ Should the captain send someone up to the bow, make sure they are wearing a life jacket, especially while docking the boat.

↪ If there is alcohol aboard is there a designated driver.

↪ If operating at night, are all required navigation lights burning brightly.

↪ Did the captain advise loved ones of this boating plans and expected arrival time back home. This also applies to the passenger. Let loved ones know the name of the boat and whether it carries a marine radio or cell phone. Leave numbers.

↪ While requesting this information should the captain brush it off as non essential, get the hell off the boat.

↪ Bottom line, take care of yourself. It may be the captain's boat, but it's your life. Be in command.

ELECTRONIC IGNORANCE

When Global Positioning Satellite (GPS) navigation first hit the maritime market, only commercial shipping, aviation and military units could afford the high-priced hardware. Today, GPS devices are affordable to most recreational boaters, with some units costing as little as $99. While the cost curve may have dropped dramatically for GPS units, the learning curve for some boaters appears to be lagging far behind.

The following Boat Smart story finds rescuers needlessly wasting time while depleting resources searching for a GPS illiterate boaters.

ON WATCH: Lake Michigan, July 20, 2002. Sean Eaton, a Group Grand Haven Duty Officer, told me of a recent case where a boater called the Rescue Coordination Center on his cell phone requesting Coast Guard assistance. The boater said he was carrying a GPS, but didn't know how to use it. Dealing with boaters unfamiliar with their GPS devices is not an uncommon event for the Coast Guard rescue responders.

Bob Walters, a Group duty officer, told me of a recent case that drove him to his wit's end. A boater called Group Grand Haven, reporting he was lost. Reportedly they had set out from a Chicago marina for New Buffalo, Michigan, on a track that would take him on an easterly course. Walters estimated the distance was around 42 miles.

However, the boater said he had been underway for three hours at a speed of 17 mph. Walters, a navigational specialist, quickly figured that at a speed of 17 mph over three hours on an easterly course would place the boater on land nine miles east of New Buffalo. This was highly unlikely unless he had a hybrid car/boat. So where was he?

The boater could, at least, provide latitude and longitude off his GPS. Walters plotted the coordinates, which placed the boater off South Haven, Michigan, some 33 miles north of New Buffalo, where he had run out of gas. Although the boater could read the GPS's latitude and longitude, he did not have charts aboard. Charts provide GPS coordinates and the means to determine a boat's position and the presence of nearby hazards. That's, of course, if boaters can read the GPS or charts.

BOAT SMART BRIEF: For those not familiar with latitude and longitude displays on a GPS screen, the top row of numbers displays the latitude and the bottom row the longitude. These geographical coordinates are what guide smart bombs to desired targets. So precise are satellite-supplied geographical coordinates, they could hit the "L" on my computer keyboard. Of course, that's if the user knows how to read the devices, which apparently some boaters find difficult to do. Or could it be that they don't understand the basic concept of latitude and longitude? Walters said, "I asked one boater to give me his latitude and

longitude and he came back and asked, 'Is that the top or bottom numbers?'"

Lines of latitude run east and west; lines of longitude, north and south. These lines cross at ninety-degree angles at points called a geographical positions (GP). That's how satellite-fed GPS coordinates pinpoint your location, or can guide you to a desired destination or waypoint.

The inability to read north and south coordinates on a GPS is one thing, but to confuse latitude and longitude for something else reveals GPS illiteracy at its worst. Walters relates, "I asked one boater to provide his latitude and longitude; he instead provided the distance and compass bearing to the waypoint." In another case, Walters said a boater provided only the latitude number and then asked if Walters needed any other numbers.

The great seagoing navigators of old are probably spinning in their graves—and well they should. GPS navigation represents the most profound advancement in maritime navigation since the Englishman John Harrison perfected the seagoing chronometer in 1735. His precision timepiece solved the problem of keeping accurate time at sea, which is essential to measuring the westward movement of celestial bodies in relation to the earth's 24-hour rotation. This allows calculation of longitude essential to making a accurate star fix.

Even with the chronometer, celestial-based position-fixes involved lengthy and tedious mathematical calculations that would challenge an MIT math whiz. Even then after a lengthily calculation old-timers would miss the mark. Modern methods and computers have made celestial navigation fool proof, well, almost. Imagine if one of those seagoing old-time mathematicians could experience the wonders of GPS navigation. He, no doubt, would be in awe. A pinpoint position-fix automatically provided on the screen of a hand-held device—truly a miracle. That many modern-day GPS users can't even read the screen would find old timers in even greater awe.

Perhaps the folks who write the instructions for GPS's devices are actually old-time navigators reborn and taking revenge on boaters for their disregard for this navigational wonder. But even with easy-to-follow instructions, key usage

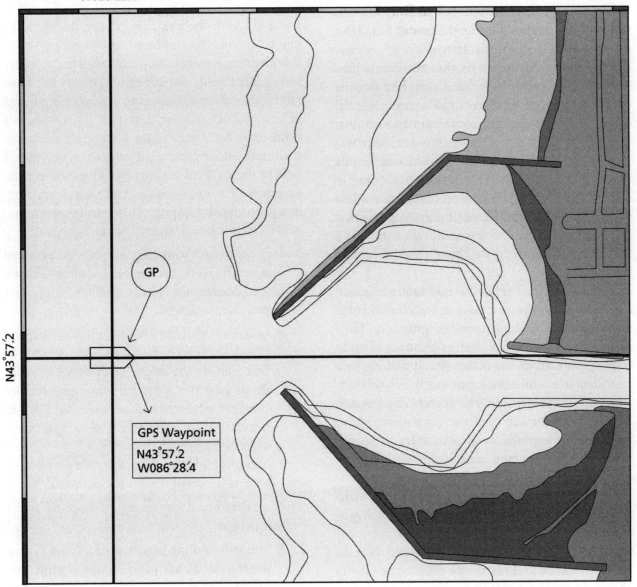

W086°28′.4

N43°57′.2

GP

GPS Waypoint
N43°57′.2
W086°28′.4

GPS devices provide boaters the means to instantly provide latitude and longitude to rescue responders, which can lead to a timely rescue.

and data entry can differ greatly between sets. Whenever I encounter different GPS devices, I seek out instruction on basic key operations and data entries such as entering waypoints, calling up waypoints, and the man overboard function. And then I write down the instructions. I keep it simple, and believe me simplicity has served me well with GPS devices.

Also, I have discovered an important rule about GPS skills: if you don't use, you lose. So I would, at least once a week, run through basic GPS entries like entering waypoints, and calling up waypoints

to make sure the GPS range and bearing to these waypoints were reading true. A common error, however, regarding waypoint readings is that boaters when requesting assistance are providing rescue responders the coordinates for a waypoint rather than the coordinates for their current position.

Jim Farris, Station Manistee's Executive Officer told me that on July 14, 2005, he received an assistance call from the operator of a 37-foot power boat. The boat's port shaft packing had parted severing a raw-water intake hose. The boat was taking on water and he needed immediate assistance. He provided the Coast Guard his GP coordinates. When the coasties plotted them on a chart it placed the boat on the pier at Frankfort some 25 miles to the north. After some radio airway GPS instruction from Farris, the captain provided revised GPS coordinates that placed him directly off Manistee Harbor. His confusion regarding the GPS readings ate up precious time while his boat was taking on water. Fortunately the boat was nearby and the *Manistee* crew was able to rapidly respond and stabilize the situation. According to Coast Guard rescue responders boaters misreading waypoint coordinates for their current position is not uncommon. In this case, failing to provide a current position could well have cost the captain his boat.

When you consider how far maritime navigation has come and yet to see it set back as such could only stem from the smoldering soil of ignorance. How simple can it get. It's no longer the case of making the calculation, but rather simply making sure the calculator is functioning properly. For this old-time seagoing navigator, it's a modern day wonder. The means to identify one's current position with a latitude and longitude, a course to steer to a desired position, and expected arrival time—what more could an enlightened boater wish for?

Apparently for some boaters rather that wishing upon a celestial star they prefer worshiping at the altar of ignorance. I didn't believe these accounts of GPS ignorance could be topped. Not so. A senior search and rescue coordinator at Group Milwaukee told me that he has heard boaters state they were carrying a GPS, but they didn't want to turn it on in fear it might break. However, it's all right to needlessly deplete rescue resources for the sake of a GPS. Now that's ignorance. No, I do not make up these lame stories.

Granted, my rescue cohorts might be somewhat jaded, an infliction certainly not intended, but rather be it a disgruntled byproduct of the afloat buffoonery they must deal with 24-7. I asked a search and rescue coordinator at Group Milwaukee his solution to boater ignorance, and he said, "Drain the lake." Boating education would go a long way in squaring boaters away, that and laying down the law.

LAYING DOWN THE LAW

I would like to believe that education offers the key to solving the ignorant issues addressed in this chapter; however, there comes a point where law enforcement, not education, offers the most effective counter measures to abate certain forms of ignorant behavior on the water. This especially holds true for operating a watercraft while intoxicated, under controlled substance, or drugs. I believe the states of Indiana and Florida offer fine examples of a no-nonsense approach to cracking down on drunk boating. Other states would do well to follow suit. Indiana law reads:

1. It is unlawful for owners of boats or personal watercraft (PWC) to operate or allow anyone else to operate their boat or PWC while that person is intoxicated.

   - Indiana law defines intoxication as having a blood alcohol level of 0.08% or greater, or being under the influence of alcohol and/or drugs such that a person's thoughts and actions are impaired and he or she has a loss of normal control of faculties to such an extent as to cause danger to others.
   - You may also be arrested if your blood alcohol level is less than 0.08% but over 0.05%.

2. If arrested and convicted of boating while intoxicated:

   - You will face the penalties of a Class C misdemeanor. In addition, if this is your first offense or the first in 10 years, you may lose all your driving privileges (*motor boat and motor vehicle*) for at least 90 days and up to two years.
   - If you are convicted a second time within five years, you may be fined and jailed, and lose the privilege to operate a *motor vehicle*, boat or PWC for at least 180 days and up to two years. More severe penalties exist for additional convictions.

3. A person boating while intoxicated who causes the death or serious injury of another person will, upon conviction, be guilty of a felony.

4. By operating a boat or PWC on Indiana waters, you have consented to be tested for alcohol or

drugs if requested by a law enforcement official. If you refuse to be tested, you will be subject to arrest and punishment consistent with the penalties described above and lose your privilege to operate a vessel for at least one year.

No doubt, the real teeth in the law is linking a boating under the influence conviction to a person's motor vehicle record, and should a convicted drunk boater cause the death or serious injury to a person, he or she will be charged with a felony. Many states have in place laws that fine a boater for operating under the influence of alcohol and repeat offenders may even lose their boating privileges, but tracking the violation trail can be difficult. For instance in the State of Michigan when a person renews their boating registration, even though he or she has been found guilty of operating a boat while intoxicated, the citation will not show up on the boater's registration record. Not even if the person failed to appear in court, and that includes all boating citations.

Now, should a duly appointed officer of the law stop a motor vehicle and during a routine liens and warrant check find the operator had failed to appear in court, that individual is going in. However, if a person keeps clean and avoids a motor vehicle stop, boating violations will go undetected including a boating under the influence (BUI) conviction. Not so in Indiana: a BUI conviction will show up during an automobile license renewal as it will during a boat registration renewal.

Linking BUI citations to an individual's automobile driving record gives the law a real bite. After all, driving a recreational boat is an option; driving an automobile a necessity. Losing the latter, now

that would hurt. It sure would give me cause to pause before indulging in afloat libations.

Florida law calls for mandatory sentencing if a drunk boater kills or causes serious bodily injury to another person. Sentencing guidelines mandate five years in state prison and a fine of up to $5,000. By operating on Florida water-ways, you are deemed to have given consent to be tested for alcohol or be arrested for operating under the influence. Refusal to submit to a test may be used against you in a court of law: Good for you, Florida.

There is nothing good about the SOBs who broadcast false Maydays, I would stop nothing short of keelhauling. In the Dutch navy of old, delinquents were tied to a yard-arm with weights on their feet, and dragged by a rope under the keel of a ship, in one side out the other. The ordeal often proved fatal as barnacles along the hull inflicted razor like wounds.

For me, no punishment is too harsh for these reckless keelhaul losers that make false Mayday calls. These fools endanger rescue responders, they deplete life-saving resources, and they endanger homeland security. Federal prosecutors in recent years have grown more aggressive regarding false Mayday convictions. As they built their portfolios based on convictions, hopefully jail time and monetary fines will increase while time to prosecute hoax cases decreases. Run them through, as they say. I urge prosecutors and judges to give these cases top priority and show no mercy on these wolf-crying reprobates.

Let's move on now to Chapter 7, and life jacket denial a sure one-way ticket to the bottom.

Life Jacket Denial

I WILL DO NEARLY ANYTHING TO PERSUADE PEOPLE TO WEAR LIFE JACKETS. I would even go so far as to crash Grand Haven's annual Coast Guard Festival parade by running along the parade route in emperor fashion wearing only a life jacket. Yes, I would do that to draw attention to the life-saving device.

Naked or not, I will not go out on a small boat without wearing a life jacket. I couldn't care less whether it's flat calm, ten feet from shore, or one-hundred degrees. Why? I've spilled enough tears as a rescue responder and Boat Smart columnist dealing with needless drownings due to life jacket denial. I want not and will not allow my loved ones to spill tears over me because I needlessly drowned all for the want of life jacket. Boaters that scoff at wearing life jackets belong in the same denial pot as those folks who refuse to wear safety belts in automobiles. At least in a fatal car crash the next of kin, for whatever solace it might offer, has a body to validate final closure.

When a person slips beneath the waves for evermore there will be final closure as well as the lake seals all traces of its victim leaving behind only remorse and grief for loved ones to ponder. A good friend of mine, Richard Brauer lost his older brother, Chuck, who went overboard late at night off a 26-foot sloop near Sturgeon Bay on September 24, 1985. Sturgeon Bay Coast Guard recovered the sailboat a day later after it had washed onto rocks six miles north of the entrance to Sturgeon Bay. His brother's body, however, was never recovered. Nor has Richard recovered from the loss that has haunted him for years. Richard said, "I can be walking down the street and see someone with Chuck's mannerism and I think of the son-of-a-gun. How I wish he had worn a life jacket."

What I find sad about the incident even in rough weather, Richard's brother had failed to wear a life jacket. "Chuck was an excellent sailor, and knew better," said Richard. A Coast Guard helicopter pilot, who conducted the search, told Richard he estimated the seas were 12 feet high. A failure to wear a life jacket in such conditions has puzzled me for years. You would think he would have known better. To prevent these tragedies do we legislate mandatory wearing of life jackets? Hardly. I'm realistic enough to concede that a legislative proposal to mandate the wearing of life jackets would most likely fizzle away in some obscure legislative committee, if it ever got that far.

Perhaps legislators should enact a law that requires a life jacket be worn under certain conditions such as in heavy weather or by solo sailors. But even then I realize the chances of that happening are remote. The marine environment being the seductive creature it is lends not to rational thinking—legislators included. She often works her deadly will in the beguiling ways of an alluring form much like the Venus Flytrap seduces its victims. How can one legislate against that?

A VENUS FLYTRAP

The Venus Flytrap is an "insectivorous bog plant native to the Carolinas. It sprouts spiny-edged leaves divided in halves that snap shut when sensitive hairs on their inner surface are touched.

The carnivorous Venus flytrap digests insects to obtain nutrients. Traps can remain closed for a week or two. Then the trap reopens, exposing the victim's dried out shell. Lake Michigan as with most waters, after devouring its prey, also traps the victim for a while; however, when once released it's far more unsightly.

What led me to the Venus Flytrap analogy were the number of boaters dying in benign conditions. I mulled over Coast Guard's *Boating Statistics*, especially fatalities, and noticed that year after year most fatalities occurred, not during nasty weather, but on "nice days." That isn't to say that hostile conditions didn't reap their share of victims. Still, nearly 83-percent of recreational boating fatalities, according to *Boating Statistics*, occurred during mild weather. A major portion of these fatalities involved drownings and in many of those cases the victim was not wearing a life jacket.

That Lake Michigan and surrounding waters lay claim to so many victims in similar fashion carried me to the conclusion that many water buffs view the Lake as an innocuous body of water, as an insect might view the Venus Flytrap. I believe the flytrap syndrome explains why boaters elect not to wear life jackets; they simply fail to see a need for them. After all, what could go wrong on a beautiful boating day? And too, most people can swim, so why the need for a life jacket? It's just a manner of climbing back onto the boat.

This affinity for water begins at a very young age. Look at children near water: they gravitate towards it like it is a liquid magic. Its spell lured me as a child, and still does, for I experience exhilaration when near it, when on it, and when in it. It's the reason, besides my beautiful soul mate, I uprooted from California and moved to Michigan, and now live within yards of Lake Michigan. I couldn't imagine now residing anywhere without a body of water within close reach. And with my affinity for water, if not for my Coast Guard affiliation, I too could be a flytrap victim all but for the lack of a life jacket.

ALL BUT FOR THE LACK OF A LIFE JACKET

According to Coast Guard recreational *Boating Statistics*, approximately eight out of every ten victims in fatal boating accidents were not wearing life jackets. Over the years *Boating Statistics* consistently show that approximately 62 percent of the boaters that died could have been saved had they worn a life jacket. Based on that norm, if you take the 47,273 reported recreational boaters who have perished over the last 43 years, that comes to approximately 30,000 boaters that died simply because they failed to wear a life jacket.

Life jacket denial echoes across the entire spectrum of recreational boating from novice boater to the most experienced sailor. The following life jacket denial story was committed not only by an experienced sailor but committed under adverse conditions that would find even the most inexperienced boater reaching for a life jacket.

CASE FILE: Mackinac to Chicago Race, Lake Michigan, 1994. Ike Stephenson crewman aboard the sailboat *Experience*, at first, thought it was a whistle. "No way," he mused, not in the middle of Lake Michigan, late at night, amidst a passing squall." He inhaled the heavy marine air, and turned his eyes to seaward and peered into the black void.

Others aboard the 39-foot racing yacht, *Experience*, heard the whistle and assumed it was an engine alarm. During the 2200 watch change the crew had planned to fire up the auxiliary diesel to charge the batteries. "I thought it was the squealing alarm you hear when you turn the key switch to turn on the engine," said Ike.

Then came the cry of "man in the water." Standing near the helm at the boat's stern, Ike watched two horseshoe buoys with strobe lights hit the water and quickly float off in the boat's boiling wake. Ike's eyes ran over the deck and quickly accounted for all nine crewmen aboard. There were no other boats in the area; their position placed them 25 miles northeast of Racine, Wisconsin. How did the person in the water get there, thought Ike.

It was a fleeting thought as Ike and his mates responded to the "man in the water" alarm. The captain ordered the crew to drop the sails and clear all lines from the water. Helmsman Michael Consideine, pointed the sailboat into a stiff breeze, lines slapped against the aluminum mask, sails flapped in the wind as crewmen struggled to haul them on deck away from the boat's prop. The engine roared to life, snuffing out deck racket as crewmen quickly secured the sails and turned eyes to seaward while inhaling the unfamiliar odor of diesel fumes on open waters.

"I'm not sure who spotted him first, but I'll never forget the adrenalin surge as we bore down on the man." The heaving sail boat pitched and rocked dangerously near a head that bobbed and weaved in the tormented sea. "We had to get this guy aboard, he wasn't wearing a life jacket and his dark clothing made it almost impossible for us to see him," said Ike.

Ike and several mates groped at the elusive target heaving about near the hull; finally they yanked him aboard, thrilled by the rescue, until he asked, "Did you get my buddy?"

Again the captain sounded the alarm; again eyes peered into the blackness. The captain steered the boat towards the flashing strobes attached to the horse shore ring they had earlier thrown overboard. Miraculously, they spotted the second man who was also wearing dark clothing and no life jacket. "We missed him on the first pass, but he grabbed a flashlight from a crewman as he passed down the side. The light provided a lighted target to steer for," said Ike. Within moments, Ike and his mates yanked the second man aboard.

Both had been washed overboard off *Nitemare*, a 40-foot racing boat, which was knocked down in 35-knot winds generated by a squall that had attacked the racing fleet. Why the two crewmen failed to wear life jackets at night under storm conditions is almost as mind boggling as a person leaping from an aircraft without a parachute. One of the guys was a former navy seal. If ever the claim for the existence of guardian angles need validation the *Nightmare*

crew would be that evidence. By all accounts the two crewmen should have perished if not for?

It's devastating enough to witness a drowning, but its even more devastating when a boater drowns and there is no witness, no account, no trace to allow closure for the next of kin. The following Boat Smart story, "We Will Never Know What Really Happened," should be read by every boater who runs solo.

ON WATCH: White Lake, Michigan, August 21, 2000. Perhaps the most painful aspect of a missing boater is that loved ones will never know what really happened. Perhaps even more painful for loved ones is the life jacket question—would the person have been saved had he or she worn a life jacket? It is a question that can haunt loved ones across a lifetime.

Boaters foolish enough to go out on Lake Michigan alone without wearing a life jacket take an awful risk of drowning should they fall overboard. And should they go overboard and their boat drifts off or motors away, their fate is for certain sealed. Especially if the incident occurs well offshore. Even with nearby boaters around, the chances of survival are slim, perhaps made even slimmer by the age and health of the person, and whether nearby boaters saw the person fall.

Over the last year, I know of three overboard cases on Lake Michigan—I was involved in two of the searches—that claimed five lives. One involved a father and his two young daughters. In all three cases, the victims were separated from their boat and were not wearing life jackets. The most recent case occurred several weeks ago off White Lake, Michigan. A fisherman, age 59, aboard a 20-foot Hydro Sport fishing craft disappeared without a trace.

The boat was last seen by a fisherman around 10:30 a.m. on Monday, August 21, 2000 approximately five to seven miles off White Lake. The weather at the time called for 10-knot winds, four-foot seas with air and water temperatures at 68 degrees.

White Lake

The Coast Guard began searching the area on Tuesday afternoon after the fisherman's daughter expressed concern about her father's whereabouts. By Wednesday afternoon, the search had expanded all the way across the lake to Milwaukee and involved Coast Guard helicopters, surface rescue units, a 140-foot icebreaking tug, a four-engine C-130 Canadian aircraft, and Coast Guard C-130. What had searchers baffled was that the search, conducted under ideal conditions, did not provide a single clue. A brief but violent storm struck the area Tuesday afternoon, but even if the vessel had fallen prey to the storm, according to the boat manufacturer, the vessel was made to withstand heavy seas. If the vessel did capsize, it was designed to stay afloat with a large portion of the vessel remaining out of the water.

Family members reported that the captain was an experienced and cautious boater in excellent health with a well-equipped boat, but he did not like wearing a life jacket.

So where was the boat? The question was answered Thursday afternoon when authorities in Milwaukee located the boat beached just north of Milwaukee harbor. Its electric kicker motor was still engaged with two down riggers set trailing 200-feet of line; all four life jackets that it normally carried were aboard. The distance from its last reported position off White Lake to Milwaukee was 70 nautical miles. Coast Guard air and surface units continued their search off White Lake for the captain until Friday when the search was suspended. In fact, I ran that final search. In all, the search consumed about 1,100 man-hours, covered over 1,000 square miles, and shut down boat crews at stations in Ludington, Muskegon, Grand Haven and Air Station Muskegon because of fatigue. That heavy strain on the rescue system, however, pales in comparison to the strain placed on loved ones regarding the missing captain.

So what happened? We will never really know except for the clues the boat offered. That his trolling kicker motor was still engaged and his down riggers set suggests that he could have been landing a fish when he fell overboard. There is one factor, however, that seems certain: he was not wearing a life jacket.

Believe me, my heart goes out to the family. Those who read my column regularly know how I feel about wearing life jackets, especially on small boats, and especially if a boater is alone. Understandably, some boaters find life jackets uncomfortable and even intrusive.

To those who scoff at life jackets, especially those who find them intrusive, I suggest they check out inflatable life jackets or upper body mesh Type III life vests; both are user-friendly. What a great gift for a boater from a loved one who seeks insurance against being haunted by the "What happened?" curse. Boat smart, and don't become an unanswered question. Wear a life jacket. If not for yourself, do it for your loved ones.

Several weeks later after the fisherman fell overboard off White Lake, Coast Guard Group Grand Haven boat crews were involved in two search and rescue cases over the Labor Day weekend that involved three boating fatalities (drownings). In both cases, the victims were separated from their boat and were not wearing life jackets.

BOAT SMART BRIEF: Not to point fingers at fisherman, but all these cases involved fisherman. Perhaps some fishermen view it as a macho thing not to wear a life jacket. A fellow chief told me of a 12-year-old boy who bragged to him that his father didn't wear a life jacket, his grandfather didn't wear a life jacket, and that he wasn't going to wear a life jacket. And a Coast Guard auxiliarist told me that fishermen in response to his offer to conduct a vessel safety check, have told him: "I don't need one. I'm a fisherman, not a boater." As if Lake Michigan gives a hoot.

Notwithstanding the macho inference, fishermen hit the water in spring through fall, and some even in winter, when water temperatures plunge, and there are few boaters on the water to assist should a fisherman fall overboard. A good friend and retired Coast Guard chief, John Taylor, an avid fisherman, simply will not fish alone on Lake Michigan. Why? He's retrieved enough water-bloated cadavers who did.

The following Boat Smart story, tells its own sad story of two fishermen who failed to wear life jackets and drowned.

A Coast Guard boat crew at Station Holland, MI. model several user-friendly life jackets: an all-weather float coat, an upper-body mesh lightweight type III, and an inflatable life jacket.

ON WATCH: Coast Guard Station Ludington, Michigan September 30, 1996. I listened to the Coast Guard radio working frequency, VHF-FM Channel 23, at Station Ludington on Monday morning, and knew the radio traffic between rescue units on Spring Lake and Group Grand Haven Operations Center was serious. The disjointed information was forming a pattern, and it suggested fatalities.

Reportedly, a boat, with two fishermen aboard, was last seen around midnight on September 28, anchored in eight to ten feet of water on the Grand River near Spring Lake. Morning twilight found it capsized and empty, still anchored from bow and stern. Not good. Rescue responders traced and matched the boat owner's van and trailer parked at a nearby boat launch. The information was growing more ominous, and my gut feeling told me while listening to the rescue unit's radio traffic

that somewhere, someone would not be coming home. And I suspected why.

I did not seek divine providence for the answer but instead predictable human behavior. On a peaceful river, under an inviting September moon, two adult men went overboard off an 18-foot boat. I knew before I picked up the phone to call Chief Miller, assistance operations boss at Group Grand Haven, that they were not wearing life jackets.

They weren't.

Coast Guard folks go about rescue work like most rescue professionals, with a focus on the rescue at hand. At times this may appear to the outside eye as indifferent and even callous behavior. It is not: mix emotion and mission, and expect mission breakdown.

But then there are the moments long after the rescue that creep into the head, especially now as I write. What can be learned from two deaths that devastated two families. Often it's the little things that boaters overlook or fail to recognize until it's too late. In your mind's eye, imagine a boat rotating on a pole running down its center line; it will rotate left and right as you shift weight from side to side. It doesn't take a rocket scientist to understand where those off center are headed, especially if one has fallen overboard and the other is trying to drag him aboard.

But this isn't about anchoring, this is about seduction. Two gentlemen seduced by a serene late September evening on a gentle river flanked by the security of nearby banks. No, this is not about anchoring nor divine providence, this is about human frailty. And the best defense against boater frailty is a life jacket.

Two men with a combined age of 141 years didn't wear them. What do you think they would say if they could get back just a second or two of those last moments? "If only…" Boat Smart, wear a life jacket. Only dead men don't.

CASE FILE: Losing a grandpa can be painful enough but to lose a child, all for the want of a life jacket, can be unbearable. On Sunday, August 15, 1999, Harry Bull, 39, and his two daughters Maddie, seven, and Lexie, five, set out on an over night sail from Monroe Harbor, Chicago, aboard their father's 26-foot sail boat. Twenty-four hours later, family members grew concerned when the sailing trio failed to report home. The Coast Guard launched a massive search. On Tuesday evening the empty 26-foot fiberglass sailboat was found about 30 miles northeast of Waukegan with its swimming ladder extended into the water and two towels draped over the rail. The jib sail was down and lying across the port bow and the main sail was secured to the boom.

The search continued, and on Wednesday afternoon a Coast Guard Auxiliary boat found Bull's body clad in swimming trunks, and a Coast Guard helicopter found the body of Maddie, also wearing a swim suit, about a quarter-mile away. Neither wore life jackets. The distance from the bodies to where the boat was recovered was about 20 miles. Lexie, 5, remains missing. How they ended up in the water remains a mystery, but one thing is for certain: they were not wearing life jackets. Coast Guard officials discovered five life jackets aboard—two child sized ones on deck.

While visiting our District Headquarters on November 18, 2004, I met Lieutenant Commander Dawn Richards, who was the Search Mission Co-ordinator that day at Coast Guard headquarters in Cleveland. She spoke several times with Pam Bull, the wife of the missing captain. The wife had expressed hope that her family would be located; after all, the name of the sailing vessel was *Semper Spero*-Latin for "Always Hope," which could well have been the case had they worn life jackets. Commander Richards, a veteran Coast Guard pilot, believes the older girl might have fallen overboard and the father dove in to retrieve her. The younger one, now alone on the boat, may have soon followed. That the father and seven-year-old Maddlie were found close together indicates that they entered the water almost simultaneously. That the boat's outboard motor was in the water and its tanks empty suggest that the boat was motoring along when they went overboard; it also explains why searchers located the boat 20 miles from where they located the father and daughter.

Whether the father and his daughters would have survived had they worn life jackets we will never know, but the odds of survival would've been much higher had they. As it was they could tread water for only so long before gravity took hold.

Enough said about these fatalities, for they cut deep into my heart when I revisit them, especially stories involving young children. Let's review some life jacket stories that offered life-saving dividends.

The following Boat Smart story finds a young couple stranded in Lake Michigan ten miles off Chicago at night.

CASE FILE: Lake Michigan, July, 2002. Of the many fatalities I've reported over the years, the most agonizing to me are the ones that find a boater overboard in a vast reach of water with nowhere to go but down because he or she lacked personal floatation.

Desperate open water struggles are not that uncommon: what is uncommon are the few who survive to tell their story. Nancy Mariani and Todd Verhalen, both of Chicago, recently beat the odds and feel divinely blessed. On July 21, 2002 they were separated from their 16-foot Hobie Cat on Lake Michigan, ten miles off Wilmette Harbor, Chicago.

"We were having a great day of sailing and around ten miles out we decided to swim to cool off from the heat," said Mariani. "I entered the water and didn't think much of it until the boat began slowly drifting away." Mariani figures she was twenty feet from the boat when she began struggling in the choppy seas. She cried out for help.

Todd Verhalen, her sailing mate, sensed her danger. He hastened to bring the Hobie about but realized that Nancy needed immediate help. He grabbed two life jackets and dove into the lake. As they struggled into the life jackets, they watched the Hobie Cat sail off. It eventually reached St. Joseph, Michigan, some fifty-three miles away.

Alone and adrift 10 miles offshore, the Chicago skyline a distant ridge, and with night approaching, what were they to do? "We kept stroking towards Chicago, feeling a profound confidence that we would prevail," said Nancy. At times the couple experienced an energy burst, then bouts with sleepiness, but they kept stroking onward. To the south, the Chicago skyline sparkled above the lake, offering an encouraging beacon.

"At times the water grew chilly and other times lightning flashed above the horizon, but we kept moving towards shore," said Nancy. Some fifteen hours after the couple entered the water, the crew of the fishing boat *Snow Goose* spotted them in early morning light clinging to a sail buoy two miles from shore. They pulled them to safety.

Were they lucky? You bet! But they were also the beneficiaries of favorable circumstances: the water temperature hovered in the low 70s, the skyline of Chicago offered a guiding beacon, they were young and vital, they possessed a strong will to live, they shared strong beliefs in a greater power, and foremost, they wore life jackets. "Without life jackets, we could not have survived," said Nancy.

The next Boat Smart story reveals the life-saving value of life jackets in cold water.

ON WATCH: Grand Haven, September 21, 1999, 5:20 p.m. The Group Grand Haven Command Center directed the Station Grand Haven boat crew to launch. An observer on shore reported a wind surfer experiencing difficulty north of the Grand Haven Pier.

Boatswain Mate Second Class Chris LaCroix and his crew aboard the 47-foot Motor Life Boat (MLB) broke the pier heads within minutes and began searching. Mind you, they were searching for a wind surfer as reported. Sailboards provide a reasonable target to locate because of the sail, an advantage enhanced by the MLB's flying bridge, which offers a vantage point 14-feet above the water. From that height, the probability of locating the sailboard seemed high.

But they found nothing.

LaCroix cell-phoned the reporting party, who then directed the MLB to the location he last saw the sailboard. Still they found nothing.

The MLB continued a series of searches parallel to the shore line with a half-mile distance between tracks. Remember, they were searching for a sailboard; they are nearly unsinkable. So where was it, or was it a sailboat at all? Frustration began to gnaw at the Coast Guard crew. They had already run a number of legs parallel to shore. The Group Duty Officer directed them to conduct one final near-shore leg. Bingo! About a mile south of the pier head they spotted a person in the water about 100 yards off shore in eight feet of water.

That was the good news, but then came the bad—he was not alone. When his small sailboat, not sailboard, sank around a mile north of the Grand Haven pier heads, he swam for help. He said his friend aboard, a poor swimmer, had drifted away from the boat. Now the hunt narrowed down to a person in the water who, according to his buddy, was wearing a green life jacket, not an easy target for the eye to find amongst the Lake's green and blue hues.

What's more, 10 to15 knot winds along with two-foot seas had carried the person along in the 59 degree water for over two hours. The good

A Coast Guard boarding team makes an afloat inspection of a recreational boat. Foremost on the boarding officer's mind is whether the boat is carrying enough life jackets for people aboard. If not, the officer will terminate the voyage and escort the boat to a safe mooring where a citation will be issued.

news: the atmospheric conditions offered unlimited visibility. Still, the probability of detection was slim with a search area of about five square miles with dusk approaching.

LaCroix and the crew proceeded to the area where the boat reportedly went down and planned another series of parallel searches with a smaller track spacing between legs. A small search object such as person in the water demands narrower search legs. Although this increases the probability of detection, it also increases the number of search legs to run—not good with nightfall approaching.

Around a mile south of the Grand Haven pier head and two miles away from where the sailboat reportedly went down, Coast Guardsman Jason Grimm spotted the second person drifting in a stupor. "When we hauled him aboard he was rigid.

His eyes possessed that thousand-yard stare," said Grimm. Within minutes, they were back at Station Grand Haven where paramedics raced the two survivors to the hospital. The second person, a male, 25, was in critical condition suffering from severe hypothermia. with a body temperature of 85 degrees, up three degrees from when the CG crew snatched him from the Lake.

"Had not the survivors worn life jackets they would have perished in the cold water," said Grimm.

Boaters certainly can provide Grimm and his mates a fighting chance to successfully execute life-saving search and rescue missions by wearing life jackets. It's your choice.

The next good-news life jacket story illustrates the positive influence of a woman regarding her husband and life jackets.

ON WATCH: Muskegon Lake, August 20, 1998. The telephone caller reported a person in the water at the east end of Muskegon Lake near the entrance to the Conservation Club Marina. Coast Guard Group Grand Haven ordered Muskegon Coast Guard to launch, and within minutes our 21-foot rigid-hull inflatable arrived at the reported location.

The bottom of a boat greeted us. I first felt dread, then elation, as we cruised up to a nearby boat and found the capsized boat's single male occupant alive and wet, but well.

So, what happened? First off, what didn't happen? The man, 63, did not drown. Why? Because he wore a life jacket. Some 35 minutes after his boat sank, a person on shore saw him floundering and called the Coast Guard. Moments later a nearby boater plucked him from the water. Lucky? Perhaps. Wise? You bet, at least regarding the life jacket. Ironically, he had made a pledge to his wife just months earlier that he would wear a life jacket while boating.

Later, on shore, he vowed again his renewed faith in life jackets. Well he should; one saved his life. That said, let's look at why he capsized.

BOAT SMART BRIEF: He began fishing around 7 a.m. at the east end of Muskegon Lake aboard his 1998 17-foot Crestliner. Around 10:15, after catching a batch of fish, he decided to pull anchor. Moreover, 15-knot winds and one to two foot seas had turned a pleasant outing into an uneasy setting. Earlier, during calmer weather he had set two anchors: one off the bow, the other off the stern. For whatever reason, he decided to first pull the bow anchor.

The wind and sea quickly swung the stern into the elements. Here began his woes. The anchor had snagged on an underwater slab, and as he pulled up the anchor with a hand crank, the stern of the boat dipped under the waves, which quickly poured over the stern. Wisely, he cut the anchor line and scrambled to the bow in order to raise the stern—a prudent move, until he decided to raise the motor. To do so, which he later admitted was a boneheaded decision, he moved toward the boat's center console and engine throttles. That weight

shift offered the advantage to the seas, and the boat sank in seconds. In all, it took less than five minutes for the lake to swallow its prize.

Wind and seas slowly carried him away from the boat into shallow water near the lake's east end. Here, he could stand, head above the water. The entrance to the Conservation Club Marina lay within a hundred yards or less. To reach it required swimming across a 10-foot-deep channel. He removed his life jacket and set out, but soon realized that sea, wind and fatigue would outmatch him. Wisely, he donned his life jacket, but its buoyancy would not allow him to cross the channel.

A man on shore watching the ordeal called the Coast Guard. Soon after the call, a boater plucked him from the water. We arrived shortly thereafter. On shore we all breathed easier. That he survived made the loss of his boat seem like small stuff. Besides, later that day Sea Tow provided assistance and recovered everything except seat cushions and, to the captain's dismay, his lost catch. There would be more fish to catch, for the ordeal would not dampen his love for fishing. But next time, he would be a little more cautious and certainly wiser. And thanks to the vow he made to his wife, there will be a next time.

BOAT SMART BRIEF: Let's review the three life jacket life-saving stories. The young couple that survived overnight in Lake Michigan off Chicago, had the male grabbing the life jacket as he dove into the Lake to assist his sailing mate. The need for a life jacket apparently didn't occur to him until faced with a crisis. He had sailed ten miles out into the lake and probably would have sailed back to shore without ever having considered wearing a life jacket. I believe this case represents a prime example of how boaters fail to associate danger with a seemingly benign environment. I wonder if the next time they go out sailing, they will wear life jackets. It would be difficult to imagine that they wouldn't.

In the second rescue, those two sailors deserve a thumbs up. Had they not worn life jackets, both would have died. The one the Coast Guard crew rescued out in the lake, according to his buddy, was a poor swimmer. Here is an example of someone who apparently associated danger with the marine environment and took appropriate measures, although I doubt you will find him sailing on Lake Michigan again, at least not in late September.

As for the last case, this one I find rather amusing. Apparently the man's impetus for him wearing a life jacket came not from the dangers of the marine environment but from his wife and her insistence that he wear one. God bless her instincts! I wish more male boaters would listen to their mates, and apparently some do. A friend of mine told me she warned her husband that if he failed to wear his life jacket while boating alone, she wouldn't remove her life jacket when he came trolling into their bedroom waters. He now wears a life jacket.

The next good-news life jacket story, which I love to tell, not only reveals the life-saving value of flotation devices, but also it reveals the power of listening to one's inner voice be it a guardian angel or whomever. Whatever it may be, it saved a man's life.

CASE FILE: White Lake, Michigan, June 14, 2003. Jerry Calabro, age 62, had just launched his recently purchased 14-foot boat at White Lake's Municipal Marina for an early evening test run. "I was around a mile from the marina when I realized there wasn't a life jacket aboard. I almost blew it off, but something told me to return to the marina."

With a life jacket on board, he was soon back on the water. "I normally don't wear a life jacket, but again something told me to put it on." As he neared the open waters of White Lake, a boat wake slammed into his portside, spilling him overboard. Mr. Calabro floundered in the cold lake for 30 minutes. A passing boater aboard a 30-foot power boat spotted his empty 14-foot boat and moments later he saw Mr. Calabro, waving a hand, barely detectable in the evening twilight.

"I was so cold, my legs were numb. The folks that saved me were real nice, a young couple with two kids." Calabro stressed, however, that the life jacket was the real lifesaver and without it he would have drowned long before help arrived: "That life jacket saved my life."

He told me he had failed to attach the boat seat to the boat. When the wake struck the boat, the seat tipped, toppling him overboard.

Good news life jacket stories come to me in varied forms and occasionally reveal a new insight into the value of life jackets that I hadn't considered before.

ON WATCH: Lake Michigan, July 25, 2004. Coast Guardsman, Jay Douglas, Station Muskegon, responded to an open water rescue involving three adult males in their fifties, whose 21-foot boat rapidly sank after a series of waves washed over the stern. "Good Sams" aboard a nearby boat plucked them from the water; all were wearing life jackets. One of the survivors wore an oxygen support system. "Without that life jacket, the man's oxygen support system would have failed and he would have been in dire straits," said Douglas.

Lesson learned: a physically handicapped person *must* wear a life jacket. Imagine being in a leg or arm cast, worse yet being in a wheel chair and ending up in the water without a life jacket. I would rather not.

The reasons for wearing a life jacket are many and none more valid than murky water, an insidious danger that even experienced boaters ignore. That is until a tool falls overboard into the murk never to be seen again. I wonder if they read the telltale sign the lost tool passed: would they too disappear if they fell into the murk and would they be seen again? Good question.

MURKY WATER A SUBTLE DANGER

Many of the river channels that feed into Lake Michigan flow from streams and rivers that reach miles into the interior. Bank sediment, tannins leached from plants, silt and other organic matter brew dark, murky water that looks like diluted mud. This sedimentary conglomeration is readily apparent from the air, particularly at river channel mouths that feed into Lake Michigan. The murky water transforms the lake's transparent hues into an opaque sheen.

Many river channels, inland lakes and marina basins lie shrouded in this river brew, hiding from the eye what lies immediately below.

ON WATCH: South Haven, Michigan, August 2001. Several years ago, I helped a couple moor their 45-foot cabin cruiser alongside a finger pier at South Haven's municipal marina. A man stood at the helm while his female passenger stood on the bow to handle the forward line. She was not wearing a life jacket. As the boat eased into the slip, it brushed against a piling. The women shuffled her feet to maintain her balance. With bow side rails extending just two feet above the deck, I doubt the rails could have prevented her from pitching overboard nor could she have grabbed them, not at knee height.

After they secured the boat, I approached her in uniform and pointed out how she nearly stumbled overboard. I told her should she fall and be knocked unconscious, she would sink to the bottom and it would be impossible to locate her in the murky water. It would be difficult locating her in four feet of water, let alone in the seven feet at her moorings.

She looked at me and said, "You know, I never thought of that. Thanks"

"Few do," I replied.

A week or so later I approached another couple making dock under the same circumstances, except their boat was much larger. I offered the same life jacket advice. The woman threw me a disdainful look as if to say "Who do you think you are talking to?" She then brushed me off as if I were a meddling public servant, beneath her pedigree. As for her rude response, I mused, "Have it your way, Queen Pollyanna." It also brought to mind my dad's advice: "Son, don't cast your pearls before swine, especially arrogant swine." Apparently, advice well given.

When I advise boaters to wear a life jacket while mooring a boat, they tend to treat my advice as if

Murky water offers a subtle danger that many boaters overlook. The best defense against murky water is to wear a life jacket.

it were safety overkill, that is until I share a murky water story or two. Eva Seng, of Seng's marina, Manistee Lake, watched a couple approach their moorings in a 34-foot power boat. Forty feet from the dock, the male operator backed hard down, pitching his female mate overboard. Several weeks later he repeated the stunt pitching her into the drink again. Eva said, "After that second pitch she wore a life jacket. It's usually the woman who handles the bow line while the male drives the boat. He starts barking out orders, and you can feel the tension in the air." I told Eva, when "Captain Bly" launches into a tirade, it's more reason than ever to wear a life jacket especially in murky water.

The following Boat Smart story, tells of a young lad's last hope of being rescued sealed by murky water.

ON WATCH: Muskegon Coast Guard Station, Thursday, June 18, 1998, 5:47 p.m. We had just moored the Coast Guard small boat at Station Muskegon and were entering the station building when the phone rang. The Coast Guard Operations Center at Group Grand Haven had received a call that a boy had gone under the water at Harbour Towne Marina, Muskegon Lake. We immediately launched and in less than three minutes reached the reported position of the victim at the entrance to Harbour Towne Marina.

Those at the scene told us that a male, age 19, was swimming at the channel mouth with several friends when he experienced a cramp and went under. A boater in the area heard calls for help and raced to a nearby fuel dock where the attendant notified the Coast Guard and 911. The original call came in at 5:46 p.m., and by 5:50 p.m. the Coast Guard, Muskegon police and fire department were on scene. That's less than four minutes from the original call. By anyone's standards in the rescue business, that is quick.

I note this rapid response time not to boast. I mention it because even with the quickest rescue response teams available, it's sometimes not quick enough. At 6:06 p.m., Muskegon fire department divers recovered the victim and began resuscitation; at 7:00 p.m. they pronounced the victim dead at Muskegon's Hackley Hospital.

WATER-WISE BRIEF: What could have been done? Could anyone or anything have saved the young man? Perhaps. His swimming mates dove under to assist him, but murky water obscured their vision. However, there were a number of factors working in his favor.

The air temperature hovered in the low 80s, the water temperature was 74 degrees, the seas calm, and the distance between the harbor mouth jetties, where the lad was attempting to swim across, was only one hundred feet. According to the depth finder on the Coast Guard boat, the depth there was less than 10 feet. He stood at six and two inches, placing his head less than four feet from the surface. We were the first rescue responders on scene, and all we could do was probe the mud-like water with an expandable aluminum boat hook.

As the Coast Guard's on scene commander I maintained a professional countenance, but inside my emotions told another story. Somewhere a mother's and a father's life would soon be emotionally blitzed, and in a way, so would mine. Over the years these tragedies reap their emotional toll. It's one reason I write the column, to release the frustration of dealing with needless calamities. There's a lesson here that speaks to us all, and we should listen very closely: we are not fish, nor are we amphibious. We are solely land creatures. When we are over our head in water, only two things can happen: we float or we sink. A life jacket certainly offers wonderful life insurance, but when you're 19 years old, life jackets and adventure seldom mix. The sad thing was that several hundred feet north of the jetty lay a designated swimming area that offered safe water. But then again, these are tangible things.

The challenge is to get water goers to recognize the intangibles that lure them into danger. That false sense of security a warm inviting day offers. We are land creatures and should never forget, even bathtubs can be life-threatening to our gill-less bodies.

My heart goes out to the parents of the young man more than I can express in this space, but I'm sure they would agree that if just one of us is saved by learning of this tragic loss then perhaps this story would be told less often, until there are no more sad drowning stories to be told.

That case painfully revisits me now because I can see the hysterical despair in the eyes of those on shore frantically attempting to tell us what happened and where to look. Our boat was stationed directly over the body, but at the moment we did not know that. Who would, in that murky water? A horrible feeling of hopelessness carried across the air. I wanted to scream. From the time the divers hit the water until the time they recovered the body, fifteen minutes had passed. It took them that long to find a body in an area no larger than a standard-sized living room.

The following Boat Smart story reveals just how difficult it can be for divers to find a body in murky water. The story also illustrates the false security offered by nearby shores.

CASE FILE: Manistee Lake, Tuesday, September 21, 1994. Few events in a boater's life bring greater pleasure than the purchase of a new fishing boat. It's common for fishermen while on the water to fantasize about the boat of their dreams and the much-anticipated day of purchase. For a Manistee man, the dream turned into nightmare only hours after he took possession of his dream boat.

John Majchrzak, 56, had just purchased his new 14-foot Sea Nymph. An unusually warm afternoon in late September found him heading for Manistee Lake to try out his new boat. According to an article in the *Manistee News Advocate*, he stopped by his brother's home. "John just stopped by ten minutes before this happened to show us his new boat," said his brother, Joe Majchrzak. "I never would have thought buying that boat would result in this."

After leaving his brother's house, John and his son drove to a small boat ramp located on Manistee Lake's western shore. According to Manistee Sheriff Ed Haik, the man was testing out his new fishing boat, driving it at different speeds near the Ninth Street boat launch, when the accident occurred.

Just after he had dropped his son off on shore, Majchrzak reportedly took off across the lake at a high rate of speed. When he turned to head back to the dock, the boat flipped over within 200 yards of shore. Nick Mungie, 14, and two friends happened to be at the Ninth Street boat ramp when Majchrzak was thrown from his boat. Jack Woodworth, 12, and Peter Wittlief, 14, said they watched the man gun his outboard motor and then try to turn abruptly at a high speed. The boat flipped over once and landed upright in the water.

"He was waving like this and looking right at us," said Woodworth demonstrating with his arms in the air. "He said 'help' four times, and went under."

Mungie responded to his call for help, dove into the lake and swam about two-hundred yards to Majchrzak's boat, but Majchrzak had gone under by the time Mungie got there. "I tried to get to him," Mungie said. "I took a breath and went down twenty feet and I couldn't see him at all." Mungie said he noticed a life jacket inside the boat when he climbed aboard. Manistee Public Safety Director, Bob Hornkohl, said the man apparently wasn't wearing a life jacket. According to the victim's brother, "He was an excellent swimmer. He could swim this lake back and forth."

After nearly 20 hours of diving in the murky waters of Manistee Lake, police recovered the body at 2:02 p.m. Thursday in 42-feet of water. "He was in a lot closer to shore than the witness indicated," said Haik. An autopsy later revealed that drowning was the official cause of death.

I later discussed the rescue with one of the sheriff divers. He told me that below ten feet he could barely see his own outreached hand. Haik added, " Divers could be a foot from him and not see him."

BOAT SMART BRIEF: That the victim's brother claimed the deceased was an excellent swimmer suggests that Majchrzak may have been stunned or knocked out when the boat flipped. Had Majchrzak been wearing a life jacket, the teenager who made a valiant effort to reach him may have succeeded in rescuing him. People who believe they can leap in and rescue someone who sinks in murky waters have a better chance of hand-catching a fly in a darkened room. It causes the hair on my back to bristle when I see parents allowing their kids to swim without life jackets off the stern of anchored boat in murky water regardless of how shallow it might be. They might just as well allow them to play on a busy freeway. At least there, in the event of a mishap, they can recover the body.

This chapter has addressed the alluring conditions that seduces people into a sense of false security, and why they fail to wear life jackets. Now lets set sail for the waters of fairyland boating where boaters assume all is well. We'll soon discover all is not well, so batten down the hatches, store all loose gear, and hold on.

Naïve Assumptions

AS WE ENTER INTO THE MERCURIAL WATERS OF RECREATIONAL BOATING, let's heave to for a moment for a quick mission brief. Make no doubt about it, the recreational waters we are about to enter can be as hazardous as barrier reef-infested waters of the great oceans, and in many ways recreational waters can be far more dangerous. Barrier reefs by agitating the sea around them can announce their presence to wayward sailors. Other visual aids like charts and reference points on land can also aid sailors in determining a barrier reef's location.

Recreational boaters, however, have morphed into a new form of barrier reef that lies totally hidden from the eye and is impossible to detect for it exist in the mind only. And unlike a barrier reef's charted location, this new form of reef moves about propelled by a carefree mindset, void of concern, and fueled by denial. Any old or new sailor worth his or her salt will tell you to presuppose one's well being on the water can spell disaster.

As we ease into recreational waters, keep a sharp lookout for an array of elusive and deadly mental reef barriers ridden with recreational boating wreckage and the bones of careless boaters.

First, some telling numbers.

RECREATIONAL MISHAPS ALARMING

Between 1986 and 2005, the Coast Guard has conducted 137,843 search and rescue cases involving over 292,800 people across the Great Lakes.

Nearly all of those cases involved recreational activity. Those are Coast Guard cases only, and do not include rescue cases conducted by marine sheriff's boat crews, by state conservation officers, commercial towing services, commercial captains, marinas assisting their clients, or boaters simply helping other boaters known affectionately in the marine world as "Good Sams."

It's difficult to determine the number of rescues Good Sams have made across the Great Lakes. Coast Guardsman Larry Hall of Station Ludington, however, made an interesting observation. On July 4, 2004, he observed 15 different cases of Good Sams towing fellow boaters into Ludington Harbor. Who knows then what the exact Good Sam count might be, but I suspect it's huge. Add up all the rescues that occurred over the 20-year period between 1986 and 2005: Good Sam boaters assisted, those assisted by other rescue agencies, and the 300,000 people the Coast Guard assisted, and the bottom line could well total over a million recreational people who required assistance on the water.

Then on top of those figures tally in Canadian recreational rescue cases and people assisted across the four Great Lakes the U.S. shares with it northern neighbor and the million people assisted over the 20-year period could well be understated. The challenge, however, is not validating the exact number of recreational boaters assisted—as enormous as it might be—but explaining why so many boaters required help while engaged in a seemingly innocuous pastime. And therein could lie the heart of the problem: a naïve assumption that recreational boating is nothing more than an aquatic theme park adventure with fairyland expectations where harm and mishap seldom visit. Nothing could be further from the truth.

GIANT AQUATIC PARK

Of the seven factors that provide Lake Michigan and other bodies of water the opportunity to devour their wounded, none could be more insidious than boaters making naïve assumptions. For such a mindset fails to even recognize the potential for danger. I liken it to a Pollyanna mindset, similar to the blindly optimistic child heroine created by

In the fabled Land of Oz, the Wicked Witch's means of aerial transportation was a broom. For boaters of Oz, it appears to be personal watercraft.

early twentieth century American writer Eleanor Porter. Such naiveté could well be attributed to many Lake Michigan recreational boaters and water buffs with their child like illusions of Lake Michigan. Many behave as if it were nothing more than a giant aquatic theme park.

Although after years of witnessing bizarre boating behavior, I'm more inclined to view such behavior as being more reminiscent of Oz-land characters. A reporter once asked Judy Garland where is the land of Oz. The film star of the 1939 box office smash, the *Wizard of Oz* said: "It's not a place you can get to by a train or boat." I don't know about trains, but boaters often do visit the Oz-land theme park. But unlike the Oz fables originated in the year 1900 by American writer Frank Baum, wherein his fictional characters seldom died—except for the Wicked Witches—far too many do die in the aquatic fairyland of recreational boating.

Why? Because some boaters seem unable to understand that a serene environment that appears fairy-book like, could be in fact the Wicked Witches' brew. The following concoction of stories reveals that whether it be witches' brew or Pollyanna lemonade far too many boaters seem to be under a spell when it comes to their own safety.

ON WATCH: Traverse County, Michigan, Spring 2002. Dave Gummere, is a member of the Coast Guard Auxiliarist in the Twin Bay Flotilla, Traverse City, Michigan. Dave lives on Karlin Road near Buckley, Michigan. It's a popular route to Highway 37 for boaters heading to Traverse City or the Leelanau peninsula. He watches a steady stream of vehicles hauling boats starting in early May and continuing through the summer months. "I hear cars trailing boats with their bearings squealing. I see boats sitting cockeyed on trailers and gear flying off boats, like life jackets. I found one life jacket in its original plastic wrap. I pick up boat lines, fenders, life rings, rain coats. If they are that mindless about towing their boats and stowing their gear, how mindless are they on the water?" said Gummere. I later spoke with Gummere in the spring of 2004, and he said: "I'm looking forward

to collecting a new batch of road-side goodies. Mid summer, I can hold a large garage sale featuring marine supplies."

Gummere shares my opinion that this heedlessness stems from a fairyland-like mindset that fails to even recognize a need for safety equipment. This free-and-easy mentality reveals itself during Coast Guard auxiliary courtesy vessel safety checks (VSC) on recreational boats. VSCs on average, yield a 33-percent failure rate, mostly due to a lack of safety equipment. Coast Guard Auxilarist Frieda Herman told me while conducting a vessel safety check at a Manistee marina in 2003, a woman called her husband on a cell phone twice seeking the location of safety equipment on the boat. That's after she had not once but twice rummaged through the boat looking for it.

Boater's lacking safety equipment is a common on-going event. Frieda told me that by the end of August 2004 of the 286 recreational boats the Manistee flotilla inspected 41 percent had failed due to lack of safety equipment. While inspecting an 18-foot boat the operator told her that he wasn't even aware the safety items were required. "At least he had enough life jackets aboard for his wife and three kids," said Frieda.

That was a good day for Coast Guard safety inspectors. Coast Guardsman Jay Douglas advised me that of the 365 vessels inspections on recreational boats that Station Muskegon boarding teams conducted during the 2004 boating season, they sent 65 boats back to the docks because they lacked enough life jackets, carried defunct fire extinguishers, or lacked proper navigation lights. But then who cares in the fairyland waters of recreational boating?

Jay Douglas certainly cares. When he inspected an 11-foot boat in May with seven people aboard—two adults four children and an infant—he was shocked when he discovered only two life jackets amongst them. The two adults together packed over four-hundred pounds; add the weight of the five children and the human cargo far exceeded the weight capacity of the tiny boat. "Scary? You bet, said Douglas. "They had been on Lake Michigan for over four hours with water temperatures in the mid-forties."

Frieda Herman of Station Manistee conducts a Vessel Safety Check (VSC) on a recreational boat. Volunteer Life Savers conduct thousands of VSCs nationwide. I urge boaters to take advantage of this invaluable free service. Search on the web for "*vessel safety check web site.*"

Here's yet another fairyland boating story. Coast Guard boarding officer Emily Roulbal of Motor Lifeboat Station, Two Rivers, Wisconsin, told me she and her boat crew inspected an 18-foot power boat at a local Two Rivers' marina. The boat had just come off Lake Michigan. During the inspection she discovered no flares, no sound producing device, and no boat registration aboard. Lack of flares, alone, could draw a hefty fine.

Acting in the spirit of the law, Roulbal provided the operator an opportunity to correct the infractions on the spot, if he purchased the items at a nearby marine supply store, which he did. She then issued him a written warning for failure to carry a current boating registration certificate. It was a win-win situation for all, until a short time later Roulbal encountered the clerk who sold the boater the items and discovered he had returned them. She detailed the scam in a supplement to the original boarding report and sent it off to the Coast Guard officials responsible for levying fines. Needless to say, someone was in for a nasty surprise.

But what greater surprise would there be than for this fairyland boater to reach for his flares

Two Rivers

during an emergency only to find a return sale slip. But then life-threatening emergencies don't occur in fairyland boating. Oh, how pretty to think so! During the 2004 boating season, I'm aware of 22 boating fatalities. And in the spring of 2005, word reached me of 16 more boating fatalities; the young boating season had just pulled away from the dock. All these cases shared a common thread—all could have been prevented. I often wonder how many other boaters have barely escaped making the final down payment if not for a mere nuance in fate.

Let me take a moment here to clarify the difference between what I perceive to be ignorant verses naïve behavior by boaters. Often when I discuss a boating mishaps with people there's a tendency to contribute the activity to ignorance and some of it is, but a great deal more mishaps stem from naïve assumptions. There is a distinct difference between the two. Roget's Thesaurus does not list naïveté' and ignorance as synonyms and they aren't. The reason I make the distinction between ignorant behavior as addressed in Chapter Four and the naïve behavior addressed in this chapter is that ignorant behavior for the most part can be checked by law enforcement, naïveté by education. The later is far more challenging because it's totally up to the boater to invest in his or her safety. But even more challenging is getting the person to even recognize the need for safety including safety equipment. And apparently for many boaters that isn't an imperative, worse yet one that isn't even considered. Take the guy who cashed in new flares for a refund, no more than twenty bucks at most. He apparently considered a few bucks more valuable than flares; however, when socked with a hefty fine he might decry his ignorance for being so naïve.

But what greater surprise would there be than for this near-sighted fairyland boater to reach for his flares during an emergency only to find a return sale slip. The fact that he is assuming he won't need the flares is but one of many assumptions fairyland boaters make. Following are list of ten dangerous assumptions recreational boaters often make that can lead to serious mishaps and the final down payment.

TEN DANGEROUS ASSUMPTIONS BOATERS MAKE

1. We assume that the boat is seaworthy and fire safe.
2. We assume that in a boating emergency we will have ample time to respond.
3. We assume that safety equipment will be readily available and easy to deploy.
4. We assume we can simply climb back aboard if we go overboard.
5. We assume we can swim back to a boat.
6. We assume the engine throttles are disengaged.
7. We assume paddle craft are harmless.
8. We assume that a safety harness is a lifeline.
9. We assume that autopilot means freedom to go about our ways.
10. We assume that rescuers are at our immediate beck and call.

1. We assume that the boat is seaworthy and fire safe.

The practice of jumping into a boat and taking off without a pre-underway check of equipment and engine spaces has blindsided countless boaters. Failure to check something as obvious as a boat plug can quickly turn a boating day into a swim-for-your-life day.

CASE FILES: Ludington Harbor, June 2003. Three men set out in a small boat from Loomis Street boat launch, located near the mouth of Ludington Harbor. After breaking the pier heads into Lake Michigan, the operator noticed the boat filling with water. The three occupants frantically began bailing out water but soon realized they couldn't keep up with the water intake. They called the Coast Guard and headed for a nearby beach where they beached the boat. The Coast Guard crew arrived and soon discovered that the operator had failed to insert the boat plug.

While attending a Great Lakes captain's conference in Traverse City, a married couple who own and operate Star of Saugatuck boat cruises, told me their moorings are located adjacent to a public boat launch in Saugatuck, Michigan. One day, as they watched a man prepare to launch his boat, his daughter begged for her father's attention, but he shooed her off despite her repeated outcries. As he prepared to back the boat down into the water, he paused as he finally gave in to her pleas. And well he did, her waving hand held the boat plug he had failed to insert.

"Oh, Daddy!"

Boat plug oversights may seem naïve, but boaters commit similar naïve oversights that are a lot more subtle, and with far swifter and more serious repercussions than the intake of water from an unplugged through-hull fitting. The most dangerous of naïve assumptions involve a boat's engine compartment. The following Boat Smart story reveals just how quickly calamity can strike below decks without warning.

CASE FILE: Arcadia Lake, Michigan, August 1, 2003. A 23-foot power boat with four people aboard caught fire at Arcadia's Veterans Memorial Marina shortly after departing the fuel dock and exploded. The blast blew out the cabin windows, propelled a cooler and other gear into the lake, and blew the eyeglasses off a woman standing near the engine hatch.

Arcadia

According to Ron Stoops, an Arcadia Township volunteer fire fighter, the fuel vent line had deteriorated, dripping fuel into the bilges. When the operator attempted to restart the boat a third time it blew. The operator knocked down flames welling from the fuel tank with a fire extinguisher. "If not for that fire extinguisher it could've been a disaster," said Mr. Stoops. Remarkably, only two of the four people aboard suffered minor burns.

A Holland man was not as lucky.

ON WATCH: Lake Macatawa, Holland, Michigan, July 24, 2004. Shortly after departing a local marina, a 27-foot wooden boat with two males and a dog aboard exploded. The explosion shook nearby homes along the lakeshore. The blast stunned the men. One of the males gained consciousness, grabbed his dog and jumped into the lake. The other male, 52, perished in the inferno that sent boiling black smoke skyward over the morning calm. "The fire was so hot I couldn't near the boat," said Coast Guardsman Jason Bernard, who responded to the incident with Station Holland's 25-foot inflatable rescue boat. The owner, a 59-year-old male, and his dog were rescued. He was treated for minor burns and later released from the hospital.

According to Chief Stein of Station Holland, they had a full tank of gas on board and the owner recently had repairs made on the carburetor. A follow-up investigation determined that a metal gas line leading to the carburetor had cracked, sending fuel into the engine spaces, which set off the explosion. The fuel tanks of the vintage 1959 wooden boat were located under the captain seats in the steering station.

BOAT SMART BRIEF: Regarding the Arcadia boat fire, Mr. Stoops, who owns Acadia Marina and later repaired the fuel line, offered the following advice. He stressed the surest defense against boat fires is preventive maintenance. He suggests that boaters check fuel lines, hose clamps around fuel fittings, and the fuel fill system for leaks and deterioration. Engine vibration and jarring can work fuel line clamps loose so check fuel lines and connections frequently and especially after a hard day on the water. Wiping a dry cloth over these areas will pickup the odor of gasoline.

An item that I found boaters often over looked was checking hose connections for engine ventilation discharge hoses. During vessel inspections I would occasionally discover a ventilation discharge hose that had separated from the thru-hull fitting. I advise boaters that, after turning on their engine blowers, they place a hand over the outside exhaust port to feel for air discharge. Hearing the blower is one thing; feeling air discharging, another.

Before starting the motor, a prudent boater will open the engine hatches and check for fuel in the bilges, and apply the surest of fuel vapor sensors—the snoot.

A massive explosion claimed a boater's life. The fire source was a leak from a fuel line in the engine compartment.

PHOTO BY JIM KRANSBERGER

Several weeks later after the Arcadia boat fire, I happened to be visiting Station Frankfort when the crew responded to a fire at a local marina. Here's an excerpt from a Boat Smart story I wrote regarding that fire, with valuable lessons learned.

ON WATCH: Frankfort, Michigan, August 23, 2003. Saturday mid-afternoon. An urgent boat fire call over VHF-FM Channel 10 from the Frankfort Municipal Marina cut short my conversation with Coast Guardsman Kevin Cook. Within minutes, a Coast Guard 30-foot rescue boat arrived at the marina to find a 34-foot Tiara powerboat engulfed in flames.

On shore, fire fighters scrambled to put together enough fire hoses to flood the inferno. Concerns over a possible fuel tank explosion troubled fire fighters. Police, sheriff officers and Coast Guard personnel cordoned off the area as a large crowd gathered. Firefighters beat down flames that threatened to spread to nearby vessels. The heat curled fishing poles standing in rod holders on the stern of a fishing boat moored adjacent to the Tiara.

While I was assisting officials to cordon off the area near the fire, a woman standing nearby on a knoll caught my attention. She was writhing in anguish with hands pressed against her cheeks, praying out loud that no one was on the boat. I suspected she had a personal connection with the boat, but there was little I could do to abate her fears.

Fortunately, her fears proved to be nothing more. In her anguish, however, lay a message: if someone were in the forward cabin of that boat, could that person have escaped through an overhead hatch? When we arrived on scene, flames and boiling black smoke consumed the entire stern of the 34-foot Tiara. No one forward of the cockpit had a chance escaping from the forward cabin. Their only hope of exiting the burning boat would be through a forward overhead deck hatch, if it worked. And that could be a big if.

The cause of the fire remains under investigation, but fire officials suspect an electrical malfunction near the battery housing may have sparked the fire.

BOAT SMART BRIEF: For whatever reasons, and there are many, overhead hatches may not open. Boaters should not assume that they work and should frequently check these escape hatches to assure that they open easily. Also, familiarize crew members on their use. During a fast-spreading boat fire, a quick escape could be your only defense against highly toxic fumes generated by the petroleum-based materials so common to pleasure boat interiors.

The foremost defense against fire is a smoke alarm system that will announce a fire in the mak-ing, whether in the bilges or above deck. Boaters should check alarm systems often; boat vibrations and motion may cause a malfunction.

Boat Smart: keep it cool before it turns hot.

A hot issue that many boaters consider cool and fire free are boats with diesel engines. Much ado has been made over gasoline fumes in engine spaces and explosions, but little is said regarding diesel fires because few occur. That is, at least, from diesel fumes collecting in engine spaces. Boaters who operate diesel engines shouldn't assume then they are immune to boat fires. During the summer of 2001, an outburst of boat fires erupted along Lake Michigan's eastern shore over a seven-week period. Coast Guard crews responded to eight boat fires, including a 47-foot diesel powered motor boat off White Lake, Michigan. The blaze forced two people into the water. Both were rescued.

It's unusual for diesel fuel to ignite, since it has a flash point between 125 and 185 degrees Fahrenheit. However, fuel spray or mist from a ruptured fuel line will flash if it contacts an exposed hot exhaust manifold. That may have occurred in this case, but we will never know since the boat sank.

Firefighters beat down a fire that broke out at a Frankfort, Michigan marina. Investigators suspect an electrical short near the battery housing sparked the blaze that gutted the 34-foot power boat.

It's standard operating procedure (SOP) for Coast Guard boat engineers aboard the Coast Guard's 47-foot motor lifeboats to make engine rounds on the hour, as it is on all standard Coast Guard boats and cutters. Several years ago while transiting the heavily trafficked shipping lanes near California's Santa Barbara passage aboard an 82-foot patrol boat a routine engine round snuffed a serious fire in the making. The engineer, while making the 8:00 p.m. engine rounds, discovered diesel fuel spurting out from a ruptured pressurized fuel line that fed one of two Cummins 800 horsepower diesel engines. He called the bridge and requested an immediate shut down of the engines.

Wouldn't you know, bearing down on the helpless cutter was a southbound freighter. We energized two all-round red lights on the mast, signifying a vessel not under command, and followed up with a security call over Channel 16 announcing our casualty. The freighter immediately changed course while the engineer repaired the ruptured line. Ship board SOPs followed. Rules of the Road observed. Disaster averted.

BOAT SMART BRIEF: I discussed the fuel line rupture aboard the 82-foot patrol boat with Chief Steve Brown, chief engineering officer, Station Manistee. The station's primary rescue boat is a 47-foot motor lifeboat that carries twin Detroit diesel, 435 horespower engines. Pressurized fuel lines carry number two diesel fuel to the cylinders; under load a pin hole leak will spray fuel, which will ignite if in contact with a high heat source like a hot manifold. Although manifolds should be covered with thermal "blankets," they, however, offered their own fire hazard should they become saturated with diesel fuel and ignite. Chief Brown said, "It's standard operating procedure for Coast Guard boat engineers to make an engine round every half hour aboard Coast Guard standard boats." After my experience aboard the 82-foot patrol boat, I approve that message.

During 2003 and 2005, the Coast Guard responded to 383 boat fires across the Great Lakes, most of which involved recreational boats. A fire during the spring of 2003 claimed a 48-year-old man.

He perished in the early morning hours in a fire aboard a 28-foot Thompson power boat at a Ludington marina. Investigators suspect that he fell asleep and a lighted cigar sparked the fire. Several boats moored at adjacent slips were damaged.

Don't assume your alarm system is working. Test it often.

Another area boaters often overlook regarding engine compartments is water in the hold. How many boaters regularly check below-deck items like engine cooling water intake and discharge hoses? The following Boat Smart story shows what can happen when a boater neglects to make repairs to a cooling water discharge system.

ON WATCH: Muskegon, Lake Michigan, July 5, 2003. Coast Guardsman Jason Jones and his crew responded to a report of a 25-foot Four Winns twin-screw power boat taking on water two miles north of the Muskegon pier head. "When we arrived on scene, six of the seven people aboard were wearing life jackets, including a 16-month old infant. They were five minutes away from going swimming," said Jones.

The Coast Guard crew removed two children, the infant and the mother. "We pumped out around four-hundred gallons of water," said Jones, who escorted the boat to Great Lakes Marina in Muskegon Lake.

The boat captain later told me he had failed to replace self-bailing drain hoses in the engine space. When the passengers shifted to the starboard side, their weight, coupled with the weight of a 30-gallon water tank, dipped the drain port below the water line, allowing water to enter the engine space, which shorted the batteries, disabling the bilge pump.

Bilge pump failures can and do sink boats, as the following story shows.

ON WATCH: July 6, 2003, Holland, Michigan. As Ken Korhorn prepared to launch his 34-foot Regal power boat, he discussed with a friend whether they should take two boats. Although the Regal could easily accommodate his 13 guests, the captains decided to take two boats. Five guests got underway aboard a 22-foot Sea Ray, nine aboard the 34-foot Regal. Taking two boats would prove to be a blessing.

The boats departed Grand Haven and headed south along the shoreline towards Holland, Michigan. Off Holland they stopped to swim. As the boats idly drifted, warm temperatures lured the carefree group into the 70-degree water.

Unbeknownst to Mr. Korhorn, lake water had been seeping in below deck. Upon entering the cabin, he stepped into knee-deep water. "It took fifteen minutes from the time I detected the water to when it sank," said Kornhorn.

He directed everyone to don life jackets. As the stern squatted lower and lower, he moved several guests to the bow to counterbalance the stern squat. The Sea Ray attempted to tow the floundering boat, but under strain the tow line parted. As the Regal began its 50-foot plunge to the lake bottom, the entire party had scrambled aboard the 22-foot Sea Ray. A Coast Guard rescue boat from Station Holland and an Ottawa County sheriff marine boat safely transferred the people from the Sea Ray onto rescue boats.

Korhorn suspects that a newly rebuilt bilge pump had failed along with the alarm. Normally, it would have pumped water overboard; instead the water accumulated and sank the boat. Korhorn believes the water came from a crack along the top-side seam near the port quarter. The weight of the swimmers at the stern forced the fractured seam below the water line, allowing the intake of water.

BOAT SMART BRIEF: To get the scoop on how to prevent unwanted water from entering engine spaces and areas below decks I went to my go-to guy retired Coast Guard Chief, John Taylor. Chief Taylor's served as a boat engineer at a number of Coast Guard units. One of those units he served at was the Coast Guard's Marine Safety Office in Toledo, Ohio. There, he performed numerous engineering inspections on commercial vessels. In addition, Chief Taylor has served as a boat engineer aboard a range of Coast Guard vessels. He's one of the most capable engineers I have served with. Chief Taylor is also an avid recreational boater and fisherman.

Chief Taylor has provided some boat smart Anchor-Points that will help prevent unwanted intake of water below decks. See sidebar.

Should a boater overlook or ignore Chief Taylor's advice I suggest they first review the next assumption that addresses how quickly boats sink.

Boat Smart Anchor Points

How to Prevent Unwanted Water Intake

- Close seacocks when leaving the boat for an extended period of time.
- Inspect watertight gasket seals around deck hatches that lead to engine spaces. Dirt and wear can compromise water tight integrity. Run water over the deck and then check the spaces below for leakage.
- Check raw water intake hoses and bait well connectors. Plug bait wells when underway. Occasionally check the water feed lines to the bait wells for kinks and hose separation at connection joints. If a line separates, the bait well bilge will discharge water into the boat below deck.
- All hose connector clamps should be double-clamped and Coast Guard approved for marine use.
- Inspect cockpit drains and transom drain tubes for watertightness. The discharge thru-hull ports allow deck water to escape through cockpit drains at the stern. Make sure the flappers that prevent water from entering these discharge ports are in good working order. What goes out can also come in. Scuppers should be four inches about the water line. Excessive weight at the stern can lower the scupper ports to water level.
- When underway, occasionally check spaces below deck for possible intake of water. This is a safety procedure Chief Taylor stresses.
- Should any of these devices fail, grab a bucket. A boat captain once asked Coast Guardsman, Mitch Muehlhausen, what was the best way to dewater a boat. "A scared man and a bucket," he replied.

2. We assume that in a boating emergency we will have ample time to respond.

It's unbelievable how quickly recreational boats sink, even in the most benign conditions. And unless a person has experienced first-hand a boat sinking, I suspect their conception of a sinking boat is based on movies like *Titanic*, which in real life took nearly two hours to go down. In the movie it seemed even longer as human drama upstaged the event.

That ain't the way it happens in the real world of small boats. I've known recreational boats to sink in seconds. Perhaps the quickest plunge I know of was told to me by a friend who said his cousin hit a wave while driving a fast boat on Sandusky Bay, Lake Erie. The boat went airborne, ejecting him from the boat. He hit the water, went under, and quickly resurfaced, buoyed by his life jacket. He looked all around. No boat. It had already gone to Davy Jones.

I told this story to Joe Marion, the executive officer at Coast Guard Station Ludington, and he told me that while running as first mate aboard a fishing charter boat on Lake Huron, he watched two fishermen approach off the starboard side in a 16-foot boat. A four-foot wave rolled over the stern, the bow shot skyward, and within seconds the boat sank, leaving the two fishermen floating in the lake.

Jeff Seng of Seng's Marina in Manistee described a similar bow up stern down sinking on Manistee Lake that dumped the operator into the lake in seconds. The boat operator moments after launching the 16-foot aluminum boat from a launch ramp, engaged the throttle of the outboard engine to go forward. No response. The boat by now had drifted several hundred feet off shore. The operator engaged the throttle in reverse to return to the ramp. It engaged all right as did the lake as water streamed over the transom rocketing the bow skyward propelled by the operator's 290-pound bulk at the stern. He made it to shore, his boat to the bottom. For two boaters in the following story, there was no returning to shore.

Patrick Lafreniere, a deckhand on the Car Ferry *Badger*, said he and the crew watched a small outboard boat with two men aboard beating across Pere Marquette Lake in Ludington, Michigan.

It was November of 1989 and the small inland lake, home port to the *Badger*, was white-crested with waves. Lafreniere said, "I watched the boat crest a wave, then dip out of sight, then reappear, then dip again. But this one time it failed to reappear," said Lafreniere. The boat flipped in a heartbeat, and two men aboard drowned. They were not wearing life jackets.

Some boaters are more fortunate. They can at least announce their plight before the boat sinks.

I received a distress call over Channel 16 from a boater claiming he was going down. I asked for his position. He replied, "I can't give one, I'm in the water." End transmission. The caller had just purchased a brand-new 19-foot Thompson power boat and was beating out into Lake Michigan on its maiden voyage. Around four miles west of Manistee, the operator throttled back and turned the stern into the seas to set up fishing lines to troll. However, as the boat had pounded into three-foot seas on the way out, the boat's engine mounts had separated from the hull, creating a gash athwartships. Lake water now streamed in through the gash, and the boat sank in moments. Later the captain told me he quickly swam away from the 19-foot boat, fearing it would suck him under. Sound like the movies?

Shortly after that case I responded to another "quick sinker" involving a 16-foot boat that sank three nautical miles west of Manistee Harbor in 68 feet of water. The two men aboard were rescued by a nearby boater.

"My brother and I were landing a fish," said Frank Maddens. "The next thing we knew the boat was filling up with water."

His brother, Jack Maddens, later told me that they were both standing near the stern trying to land the fish. "Just as we tossed our catch into the boat it began taking on water. There was nothing we could do. It went down fast," said Maddens.

In the brothers' haste to pull the fish aboard, their combined weight dipped the stern below the surface. *The Manistee News Advocate* ran my story front page with the headline: "Big Fish Sinks Boat." Chalk one up for the underdog.

Here's a quick-sinker story that bodes well for two squared away well prepared boaters. Oh, how I love these stories.

Escanaba

On September 11, 2003, two adult males aboard a 20-foot Patriot boat began taking on water while transiting Little Bay De Noc en route to Escanaba, Michigan. The owner, Zack Boudreau, told the Coast Guard the boat sank in 20 seconds. He did not hit an underwater object. The owner did report water gushing up from the floor of the boat at the base of the pedestal seat. He believes a major catastrophic hull failure in that area caused the sinking. Both men aboard were wearing life jackets.

While in the water he called the Coast Guard over Channel 16 with a hand held radio, and then fired off a flare, attracting the attention of several nearby boaters, who also heard the distress call over Channel 16 and came to the rescue. Nice story, squared-away boaters, sweet ending.

BOAT SMART BRIEF: Notice all the above rapid boat sinkings involved small boats. Except the 20-foot Patriot, which suffered a catastrophic hull failure, all the other boats were swamped. Most swampings result from water riding over the stern. Combine the weight of the operator, passengers and an outboard engine, then add a following sea—watch out! Under these conditions I plead with boaters to don a life jacket and expect to make a rapid call to the Coast Guard should they be swamped and lose battery and radio power. Don't wait, either. Immediately call the Coast Guard.

A prompt call to the Coast Guard saved two brothers whose boat swamped north of Ludington Harbor on June 8, 2005. The brothers while trolling in the waters near Big Sable Point snagged a fish net with the boats downriggers. The downriggers pulled the 17-foot Crestliner's stern downward; water spilled over. The owner, Joe Fronteiera, told a *Ludington News* reporter: "The water was coming in good and we couldn't get it to stop," he said, adding that even the two pumps on board couldn't stop the influx of water. "There was nothing we could do."

Yes, nothing could have be done regarding the flooding, but they did do things that saved their lives: They donned life jackets and immediately called Ludington Coast Guard. Within ten minutes, a Coast Guard 30-foot rescue boat reached the brothers. Crewmen pulled the men from the 59-degree water.

Unfortunately many boaters assume that in an emergency they will be prepared and that their safety equipment will save them. Maybe so, maybe not.

3. We assume that safety equipment will be readily available and ready to deploy.

I often encountered boaters fumbling around the boat looking for safety equipment while conducting a Coast Guard boarding on their vessel. Now, if boaters are that neglectful regarding the location of safety equipment during an inspection, where will their naïve assumptions leave them in an emergency?

In the following Boat Smart story, a boater offers his opinion on the importance of having safety equipment, in particular life jackets, readily available when calamity strikes.

CASE FILE: Lake Michigan, August 2000. Within a heartbeat the three fishermen were in the water, clinging to their swamped 22-foot fiberglass boat two miles off White Lake entrance in Lake Michigan. Fortunately the fiberglass boat didn't sink, although it did roll over, trapping life jackets and other safety equipment inside the overturned hull.

A nearby boater spotted the floundering trio and plucked them from the lake. Lucky. Absolutely. Several miles off shore, three foot seas, safety equipment including life jackets trapped in the capsized hull, 60-degree water—not a pretty picture, possibly made a lot less pretty had not the Good Sam assisted.

Later at Station Muskegon I spoke with the captain as he retrived items our rescue crew had picked out of the water. The captain said he was trolling in two to three foot seas when a large wave crashed over the stern. Smaller waves then crawled over the transom and within seconds the boat swamped, yawed and capsized. None of the fishermen were wearing a life jacket.

I asked the captain what lessons, if any, he learned from the ordeal. "Having the life jackets readily at hand and flares," he said. "We would've had to dive under to reach the life jackets and the flares if help had not arrived."

He told me he almost took his wife along. "Oh my goodness," I thought, "Your boating days would have ended, or least, your boating days without wearing a life jacket."

It's bad enough stumbling about a boat looking for life jackets or other emergency equipment, but even worse is turning into a stumblebum while deploying the safety device. That is, of course, if the device can be located. During routine Coast Guard vessel inspections, I would occasionally request that someone aboard demonstrate how to put on a common Type II life jacket. The U-shaped life jacket slips over the neck. The devise is secured to the body by drawing a strap around one's back and hooking it together in the front with a snap hook. Normally, I would request that youngsters perform the drill in order to spare the adults the embarrassment should they fail. Sounds simple, donning a life jacket as such. For some, indeed, it was, but considering the number of times the kids failed the drill, it proved to be anything but simple. The parents, however, received the message, a real-life lesson that accomplished far more than my preaching could hope to convey.

I know of others who also promote the life jacket creed through creative means. Sergeant Bill Halliday, of the Racine County Sheriff Water Patrol, conducts a drill during safe-boating classes where he selects three students from the class. One person wears a life jacket, another person has one readily available, and a third person, however, has to locate the jacket hidden somewhere in the room. The students have thirty seconds to don their life jackets.

For the first two persons it's no sweat. It's the third person, who must locate and don the jacket, that nearly always fails the drill. Sergeant Halliday understands first-hand the importance of having a life jacket readily available.

CASE FILE: Racine, Wisconsin, April 29, 2001, Halliday responded to a boating emergency on Lake Michigan. A 33-year-old man and his dog drowned after their 22-foot boat struck a reef in two to three foot seas off Wind Point, near Racine, Wisconsin. The reef tore a hole in the boat; it filled with water and rolled over. The man and his female passenger attempted to swim to the nearby shore. He drowned, along with his dog. The Racine County Sheriff's Water Patrol boat rescued the woman. The air temperature had reached the 70s; however, water temperature hovered in the low 50s. Halliday told me that while inspecting the boat he discovered life jackets jammed into a forward cuddy cabin, sealed inside a Teflon container.

Flares are another safety item that can bring on a fumblebum state. Even if a boater locates the flare does he or she know how to use them? Emergencies are not the time to be reading instructions. While struggling to read the instructions throw in a bouncing boat, worse still a sinking boat, or worse yet an injured boater in the water struggling to fire off a flare for the first time—well, you get the picture.

I discussed the high stress factor that normally accompanies a real flare situation with Frank Amodeo, an executive at Orion, a major manufacturer of visual distress signals. He told me he has instructed couples on the proper use of distress flares in a classroom environment. When they become comfortable with the device, Amodeo has them face the class to demonstrate their new-founded knowledge. "They often become flustered and fail the drill, said Amodeo. If facing friendly people flustered them, imagine the fluster level during an actual crisis. You needn't have to imagine—read on.

ON WATCH FILES: Grand Haven, Lake Michigan, Summer 2000. A Grand Haven Coast Guard boat crew responded to a vessel in distress. The coxswain directed the captain to fire off a flare to mark his location; he did—right into the cabin's overhead canopy. The flare ricocheted onto the deck and hissed around his feet. The coxswain aboard the rescue boat told me he could hear over the marine radio a female hollering about leaping overboard. Fortunately she didn't, however, the captain gave the Coast Guard crew hell for not instructing him on how to fire off the flare and the guy was a doctor. Oh my!

In another flare misfire case, Carol Greve of Manistee told me that while out on a fishing trip on Lake Michigan, the 30-foot power boat she was aboard began sinking. She believes the weight of people fishing off the stern forced the stern downward, allowing lake water through the open scuppers. The steady water intake seeped through worn gasket seals around the deck engine hatches. "When we realized the boat was sinking, the affair turned into a three-ring circus," said Greve. "The captain was hollering Maydays over the radio, while the rest of us scrambled to put on life jackets. The captain grabbed a flare gun and tucked it under his armpit. When he grabbed the gun to fire it, he discharged a round into my husband." Greve's husband stands over six feet two inches and weighted 350 pounds. The projectile spun him around. He escaped serious injury. The Coast Guard arrived on scene, removed the people, dewatered the boat and then towed it to port.

Knowing how to properly discharge a flare, especially during an emergency can produce life-saving results. A fellow Coast Guard Chief told me about a case at Ludington where a drunk boater slammed into the harbor breakwater at night. He was killed instantly. His seriously injured wife directed a crewman to the flares, which he fired off. Chief Reed spotted the flare a mile away and responded. "She was in bad shape, with a broken arm and shoulder, and ruptured spleen. Had we not responded in a timely manner and transported her to shore and awaiting medical personnel, she would have died," said Reed.

Let's move on to the next deadly assumption.

4. We assume we can simply climb back aboard if we go overboard.

Over the years, I've conducted dozens of open water "reentry drills" with small recreational boats and Coast Guard vessels. I've used lines, swimming platforms, ladders, motor shaft fins, hoists, and a host of other tricks to climb back aboard. It's seldom simple, even with a ladder, which can offer its own array of challenges. I've even conducted recovery drills in four to six foot seas while looking up at a heaving boat, my head bobbing precariously alongside. In rough seas the boat seems gigantic, and attempting to grab onto the gunwale as it heaves up and down can be exhausting.

By the way, when I conducted these drills, I wore a life jacket and a crash helmet. Lake Michigan's hurried wave action can make quick work of a skull, particularly around the stern area with a heaving engine shaft and prop, or a swimming platform. I've conducted drills in rough seas where I've avoided the stern and elected to struggle aboard alongside the boat rather than take my chances astern. During one drill it took me 24 minutes to climb aboard the side of a 24-foot power boat with four feet of freeboard. This is serious business, climbing back onto a boat.

As homo sapiens we use our legs to walk, run, and climb, but when we are over our heads in water, this is impossible. Water is like an oppressive form of gravity that draws people under. Unless they possess fins and gills, or a life jacket, they are doomed by the laws of physics. The following story was told to me by a boater who experienced first-hand the challenge of retrieving a person from the water. Besides illustrating how difficult it can be to retrieve a person in the water, the story also reveals how easily this could have ended up in the Coast Guard's recreational fatality data base. I wonder how many other overboard cases have barely escaped the computer.

CASE FILES: South Haven, Michigan, July 23, 2000. Tim Israel told me that while inbound into South Haven Harbor aboard his 40-foot power boat, he and his crewman, Jerry Roach, spotted a 30-foot sailboat around a quarter of a mile off the pier heads. The sailboat was trailing a life ring a 100-yards or so off the stern. "We saw two people in the water directly behind the stern," said Israel. "They were clinging to the stern ladder and couldn't climb aboard."

Two ladies standing at the stern watched helplessly. "The man could not climb up the ladder despite the efforts of the second man to boost him up," said Israel, who gingerly approached the smaller sailboat with his steel-hulled power yacht. His passenger, Jerry Roach, grabbed a life ring and jumped into the water.

He later told a *South Haven Tribune* reporter, "The man was out of it. His eyes were bloodshot. You could see red on his forehead where the boom had hit him. I could see that his legs were purplish from the amount of time he had been in the cold water."

Roach climbed aboard the sailboat and between the skipper boosting him up and Roach's topside efforts, they hauled him up the ladder; Roach estimated he weighted around 250 pounds. He figured that the man, whom he believed to be in his mid-sixties, was in the water around half an hour: "The man had no strength. He pleaded for me not to let go of him." Once he was aboard, the sailboat proceeded to the Coast Guard station in Grand Haven where they dropped him off. He reportedly was doing well after the ordeal.

The man's wife summed it up well when she said, "It is serious on Lake Michigan. When accidents happen, they happen so quickly." True; however, overboard accidents can strike boaters in any waters as the following stories reveal. Unlike the previous overboard story, the victims did not fare as well—they died. Wayne Smith, an old friend and fellow Coastie who I served with aboard Coast Guard Cutter *Point Bridge*, in Marina del Rey, California, told me the following overboard stories. Wayne is also an avid rag sailor, having owned a sailboat throughout his adult life.

The first incident involved a "Cal 28" sloop. According to Wayne, the 28-foot sloop experienced a man overboard emergency while sailing to Catalina Island, although in this case it was a woman. Three crew members aboard executed a successful recovery maneuver; however, once they had the woman alongside, they could not haul her 200 pound bulk aboard. In desperation, the crew tied a line around her, snugged her up against the hull, and set sail for Catalina Island. She died en route. Wayne suspects she died from drowning or hypothermia, but then fright is not out of the question.

On April 20, 2005, a 46-year-old male while engaged in a sailboat race off Marina del Rey fell overboard off a 24-foot sailboat. The three-man crew executed a successful recovery pickup, but they could not haul the man aboard even after one of the crewman jumped into the water to assist.

A Los Angeles County Sheriff's Harbor Patrol boat responded and the officers aboard retrieved the man from the water. He was pronounced dead a short time later. Authorities determined the initial cause of death to be drowning.

I discussed these cases with a fellow chief, Steve Brown. He told me while serving at Station Sturgeon Bay, Wisconsin, the crew responded to a Mayday from a woman aboard a sailboat. According to Chief Brown, her husband heaved the boat to and went for a swim. After his swim, he could not climb aboard much as he tried. He climbed onto a small platform on the stern as his wife set sail for Sturgeon Bay, partially dragging his large body though the water. She hailed the Coast Guard over Channel 16 and provided her position. The Coast Guard crew arrived and assisted her husband onto the boat.

If these overboard stories have failed to convince those who assume if they fall overboard they can simply climb back aboard, I suppose then they also assume they can simply swim back to a boat. On then to our next naïve assumption.

5. We assume we can swim back to a boat.

Coast Guard *Boating Statistics* reveal that "departure from a vessel" will result in an 88 percent probability that the event will be fatal. This statistic not only includes boats that sink, but boaters who voluntarily separate from their boats and are unable to get back aboard. I believe, based on my own data, that most boat separation fatalities stem from voluntary separation. In over 400 boat smart columns, I've yet to write about a boater who died as a result of a boat sinking. On the other hand, I've written many stories of boaters whose boat sank but were rescued because they fired off a Mayday marking their location. Then, they took appropriate measures to survive awaiting rescue.

As far as voluntary boat separation, during the 2005 boating season alone, I know of 10 boating fatalities in the western region of the Great Lakes that involved people separating from their boats and drowning. In all these cases, the vessels involved did not experience a causality. For whatever reasons, people entered the water and could not get back to the boat or if they did, they couldn't re-board.

The looped line method along the side of the boat is a safe way to reenter a boat away from the stern in heavy seas. Also the looped line over the side provides the PIW a means to stay alongside the boat by holding onto the line. Make sure the person assisting is wearing a life jacket.

The looped line over the side also works well on small outboard boats; however, the person assisting should stay low in the boat to prevent going overboard while assisting the PIW aboard. By the way, what's wrong with this picture? The guy assisting the PIW is not wearing a *life jacket*.

The rentry ladders on many boats do not extend deep enough into the water to allow a person to step onto the bottom rung. A line looped over the stern, as illustrated, allows the PIW the opportunity to place a foot in the rung and pull upward to reenter the boat.

The rate of drift of a boat on open water has captured my interest over the years. I've experienced boat drift both in the water and from a boat, and even in a light breeze a boat can clip along, especially aluminum boats. Even fiberglass boats can outpace a good swimmer to leeward in a breeze. When you have the opportunity, place your boat on an open body of water when the wind is at play. Mark your position with a GPS, and watch as the seconds on the latitude and longitude readout quickly change. Or just mark a reference point on shore, and watch how your position soon changes in relation to that object.

On a boat, the drift might not seem too readily apparent, but from the water it can seem like the boat is forever out of reach. Sad are the cases where a person goes overboard from a drifting boat and those aboard don't know how to start the engine. All they can do is watch as the person in the water struggles to survive. Several boaters in the following stories stood frozen in horror as they watched loved ones slip beneath the waves.

ON WATCH CASES: Kenosha, Wisconsin, 2002. Chief Ellison, Officer in Charge, Station Kenosha told me about a case his crew responded to involving a 28-foot power boat adrift on Lake Michigan. A man and his brother went for a swim leaving the man's children behind on the boat. The boat slowly drifted away from the swimmers. The man realizing the gravity of the situation swam back to the drifting boat propelled by a burst of adrenalin. His brother followed but couldn't reach the drifting boat. He drowned as his nephews watched. No one could do a thing to save him: the kids couldn't operate the boat and their father could do nothing while in the water. A real-time nightmare too often played out upon the water.

In another case that year off Michigan City, a father, after towing his girls behind a boat on a tube, leaped into the water to assist them. He managed to get them back aboard, but too tired to retrieve himself, he drowned before his daughter's eyes as the boat drifted off. The girls lay adrift aboard their father's boat for two hours when finally their screams caught the attention of a passing boater. And they call it "recreational boating."

In the following Boat Smart story a solo boater elected to swim back to his boat after going overboard. As the boat drifted farther and farther away he would've been better off swimming to a nearby beach.

ON WATCH: Station Muskegon, September 19, 2000. I was laying down blacktop at Station Muskegon when Group Grand Haven's operations center called. A boater had reported that a boat with just a dog aboard was adrift about a mile north of Muskegon's north pier head. I immediately launched our 25-foot inflatable, work coveralls and all. Being a dog man myself, I knew that no man leaves his dog aboard a boat on Lake Michigan. Unless.

Within minutes, my engineer and I arrived alongside a 16-foot Centerline with a chocolate Labrador aboard. The boater who made the call to the Coast Guard lay alongside the 16-foot Centerline in forty-two feet of water, approximately 1500 yards off the beach at Muskegon State Park. After directing the assisting boater to set an anchor on the drifting boat, we began a search of the area. About 150 yards south of the boat we spotted a pair of Reebok tennis shoes and a pack of Marlboro Light cigarettes. We marked the coordinates with our Global Position System (GPS), scooped up the shoes, and continued our search of the area.

Nothing. We then requested assistance from Coast Guard Air and the Muskegon Sheriff Marine Patrol.

This was not good. A boat adrift with a dog, shoes in the water, and a brand of cigarette that matched the same pack laying on the floor of the boat. Too bad the dog couldn't speak. But the chocolate lab, Spirit, did provide a clue as to his owner—his dog tags.

A telephone number on the tags led to the dog's master, a 36-year-old male. The Coast Guard called the number and according to the man's wife her husband had launched early that morning from a Muskegon Lake boat ramp. This was later confirmed by the boat ramp attendant. Also, a boater in the area of the search advised us that he had seen the boat on the lake around 9:30 a.m. with the dog and an adult male.

That the boat was so close to the shoe led us to believe that the operator was somewhere near that location. By now, the Coast Guard helicopter was overhead searching, along with my surface craft and a Muskegon County Sheriff's boat. The weather was ideal for searching, with clear skies, unlimited visibility, seven to ten knot winds, one-foot seas, air temperature near 70, and a water temperature around 65 degrees, although it felt colder than that.

While conducting the search, I kept thinking, "What may have happened that put the 36-year-old in the water? And why did he remove his shoes? Did he accidentally fall in and then remove his shoes to swim to the boat, which was drifting away, pushed by the wind and seas?" It wouldn't take much to push along the 16-foot aluminum-hulled boat. Reportedly he was a good swimmer. Oh, how often have I heard that fatal proclamation!

By day's end the Coast Guard helicopter had flown a series of searches; two Coast Guard surface vessels had combed the search area, racking up 17 hours before nightfall. In addition, two Sheriff Marine boats performed searches, and a dive team from the Muskegon Fire Department also took part in the hunt. Add to that a steady flow of vessel traffic through the search area. All failed to come up with a find. What's more, and very discouraging news, the wife and a close fishing friend of the missing boater told the Coast Guard that he never wore a life jacket.

What I find disturbing about the case was that the dog, Spirit, apparently had been trained to stay aboard, no doubt with his safety in mind, yet when it came down to it, who had a better chance of surviving in water? Perhaps Spirit's master should have considered his own safety and vulnerability as well. A month later the fisherman's body washed up onto a beach several miles north of Muskegon. Let's move on to another boat separation case that faired no better.

ON WATCH: Green Bay, Wisconsin, July 25, 2003. Len Van Denack, a Coast Guard auxiliary member, told me about a "boat separation" case that he responded to in lower Green Bay. A man in his early 20's set out aboard a 12-foot boat powered by a 15-horsepower engine. He was accompanied by two jet skiers. A short distance into the bay, he stopped the boat to enjoy the day. His buddies on the personal watercraft took off. Around a half hour later they returned to find an empty boat bobbing in three to four foot seas.

Van Denack believes the man went for a swim or fell overboard. There was one sandal in the boat and another floating in the water. Also, a life jacket was on the floor of the boat. The air temperature hovered in the upper seventies, as did the warm water. Did he attempt to swim back to the boat while being carried away by four foot seas and a stiff breeze? Perhaps. One thing we do know: he was not wearing a life jacket. About a week later a lookout aboard a freighter spotted the victim's body near the northwest shore of Green Bay, some 20 miles from where he went overboard.

On July 24, 2005 in Calumet Harbor, Chicago a 38-year-old mother drowned as her kids watched in horror from a 32-foot powerboat. She had gone for a swim and as the boat drifted away from her those aboard could not start the engine to return to her. She drowned as those aboard looked on.

On August 12, 2005, a 26-foot powerboat was found adrift on Lake Huron approximately 11 miles northeast of Mackinac Island. The unoccupied boat was idling in neutral. The Coast Guard launched a massive sea and air search along with the Michigan State Police, Mackinac County Sheriff Department, Cheboygan County Sheriff Department and the Coast Guard Auxiliary. Authorities called off the search after failing to find the occupants of the boat, a 35 year-old female and a 34 year-old male. Reportedly the last person to talk with them was a family member who they had contacted via cell phone to advise they would be arriving at Mackinac Island that afternoon.

On August 24, 2005 divers from the Michigan State Police Underwater Recovery Unit recovered the body of a white female. Authorities determined that it was that of the 35-year-old female who was aboard the adrift boat. As to how and why did they became separated from the boat it is not clear. Did they go swimming and the boat drift off? Perhaps, since the engine was in idle. There is one thing for certain—neither were wearing life jackets. Nor did they have a tether line with a floatation device attached that would have allowed them to stay in touch with the boat.

Not all overboard boat separation incidents end in the final journey. They do occur but far less often than those that don't. A Coastie I served with, Joe Stepanovich, told me that while he was serving at Station Frankfort a woman showed up at the station dripping wet. She claimed to have swum to shore for help. She told Joe her boyfriend's boat had broken down around two miles off shore. Joe looked her in the eye and said, "Madame, please don't take me wrong and I don't mean to be a wise ass, but you are a rare sight to behold. You're the first person I've encountered who did what you did that didn't end up a corpse."

Yes, people do survive boat separations and some can even be humorous as in the following boat separation story.

CASE FILE: Leland, Michigan, Mike Grosvenor captains the *Mishe Mokwa*, a transport boat that ferries passengers and supplies between North and South Manitou Islands and Leland Harbor. During a run I made with him to North Manitou Island, he told me a humorous boat separation story. A man, while sailing naked with his wife off Leelanau, Lake Michigan, fell overboard. The sailboat, operating on auto pilot, continued on its way with his wife below decks, unaware of her husband's nude departure. The boat soon ran aground onto a nearby beach. Meanwhile, the overboard sailor had swum to shore where he commandeered a beach towel from a young man.

Leland

Rescue responders located the boat, pulled it off the beach and reunited the husband with his wife. While crossing over from the marine sheriff's rescue boat to his sailboat, the husband's towel fell away as a gathering of local town folks, looked on. "What I found amusing about the story is that he remained in town that night with much of the town's folks aware of his ordeal," said Grosvenor.

"That could be so," I told the captain, "but a lot of folks probably didn't recognize him with his clothes on."

BOAT SMART BRIEF: The surest way to keep in touch with a boat is to stay in touch. Should a boat drift away a simple tether line running between a person in the water and the boat offers a life-saving link. A rescue heaving line is my linkage of choice. I will shout it from the highest mast: next to life jackets, a rescue heaving line is the most important safety flotation device a boater can carry. The type Coast Guard rescue boats carry is a 70-foot, 3/8-inch braided synthetic line with a floatation ball at the end. It's an absolute must, whether it be for a 60-foot yacht or a 16-foot outboard. It's easy to stow, it's easy to toss for distance, it's easy to retrieve, and it *floats*.

Life rings or a Type IV throwable device with a tether line attached also offer an effective means to link a PIW to the boat. I just prefer the rescue heaving line because of its ease of use. The rescue heaving line definitely can play a huge safety role in the next deadly assumption—propeller strikes.

6. We assume that the engine throttles are disengaged.

There is no more horrifying mishap on the water than a propeller strike. A whirling blade strike can cause severe bleeding that can claim a life in seconds and there is little that can be done to stop the blood loss. What can be done, however, is to make absolutely sure the propeller is not engaged with a person in the water (PIW) near the stern.

Only in a dire emergency wherein immediate assistance must be rendered to a person in the water should a boater engage an engine throttle(s). Even then such a dangerous maneuver would most likely be more hazardous to the PIW than the emergency at hand. However, most propeller strikes have little to do with a desperate need to recover a PIW. Instead propeller strikes stem from good-old operator error as the following propeller strike cases tragically portray.

ON WATCH FILES: Holland, Michigan, Spring 1988. Retired Coast Guard Chief John Taylor describes a prop strike incident he responded

A crewmen tosses a rescue heaving line to a PIW. He can then pull the PIW to the boat without having to maneuver the boat near the PIW thus avoiding prop strike.

to while serving at Station Holland. A Coast Guard 44-foot motor lifeboat was crossing Lake Macatawa outbound to Lake Michigan with Coast Guardsman Taylor aboard. A small pleasure craft approached the Coast Guard boat. The people aboard were hollering that a person had been struck by a boat propeller.

"With a minute or two we were alongside a 21-foot powerboat with a man floating face down. The water around him was blood red," said Taylor, who along with a crewman jumped into the water to assist the man. "He was sliced open from the buttocks to his neck like a diced orange peel. I held his head above the water while my mate administered open mouth breathing. We could see air bubbles gurgling from the wound in his back," said Taylor.

The boat had three people aboard: the man's wife, his 10-year-old son, and a male friend. The Coast Guard crew lifted the lifeless victim onto the Coast Guard boat and transported him to shore. "The utter anguish of the wife and son as they looked on haunts me still. I felt horrible for them," said Taylor.

Commander Anthony Popiel, Commander Group Grand Haven, told me of an overboard incident he witnessed during the 1996 Chicago air show. He watched a man in his mid-forties standing on the stern of a 30-foot powerboat at anchor off Chicago Harbor. The man dove into the lake. For whatever reason, the captain engaged the throttles, slicing the man's calf with the propeller.

Commander Popiel said, "I was aboard a Coast Guard 41-foot rescue boat directly astern of the boat. Several Coasties aboard leaped into the water to assist the man. He bled to death before the crewmen could get him to our boat. He was only 30 feet away," said Commander Popiel.

On June 28, 2004, near a Michigan, City beach a 28 year-old male backed down a 34-foot powerboat onto his ten-year-old niece after she jumped off the stern. She died from propeller strike moments later, despite the valiant first-responder efforts of off-duty Coast Guardsman Troy Wile. He happened to be with his girlfriend on a nearby beach. Wile said, "The prop struck her leg first, then pulled her torso into the prop. She was dead before we reached shore." The girl's mother witnessed this gruesome nightmare while standing at the stern.

The following propeller strike fatality occurred on Lake Erie on August 27, 2004. Several teenage boys were swimming off the beach at Westside Park located near the entrance to Cleveland Harbor. While hanging onto a log, the teens called out to a nearby boater for assistance. The operator of a 28-foot cabin cruiser heard their calls and responded. One of the swimmers climbed aboard the cruiser. The other teen while climbing aboard was struck by the propeller, which pulled him beneath the surface. He drowned after losing a substantial amount of blood. A Coast Guard crew from Station Cleveland Harbor responded; however, the teen died before they could free him from the propeller, which had locked up on his thigh bone.

The most threatening aspect of a propeller strike is that it can bleed out a life in minutes if not seconds.

BOAT SMART BRIEF: Coast Guard Boating Statistics show that during 2003 and 2004, propeller strikes claimed the lives of 63 people. I would much rather swim in great white shark infested waters than swim near the spinning propeller of a recreational boat. Far more people in the U.S. were killed by propeller strikes in 2004 alone than from great white sharks since 1916: In U.S. coastal waters between the years 1916 and 2004, great whites claimed only ten lives.

The major difference between a shark attack and prop strike is that one is random, and the other is totally controllable and absolutely preventable. Notice that in all these cases, there was no dire need to remove people from the water. Pickup could have been handled in a slow and deliberate manner.

In the case of the teen who was caught up in the propeller, I was told by Coast Guardsman Scott Leahy, Second in Command, Station Cleveland Harbor, that at the time of the accident there were four people standing at the stern of the boat.

Could the boat operator see the person in the water? I doubt it, not only due to the height of stern above the water, but because those standing at the stern probably blocked his view of the PIW.

The inability to see a PIW from the helm might also explain the Chicago propeller strike. Perhaps the operator throttled ahead to provide swimming room for his buddy, but failed to first check where his friend was in the water. But, whether the operator could see his buddy in the water or not, he knew for certain he was near the stern. That alone is reason enough to clear the throttles, shut down the motor and step away from the helm.

As for the 10-year-old child prop strike, Coast Guardsman Troy Wile told me that he believes the uncle had gone forward to set the anchor and on returning to the helm started the motor in order to back down to set the anchor. He further believes two other youngsters aboard had jumped off the bow and that the uncle may have thought his niece had too. Also, reportedly, the neutral safety switch was malfunctioning. The neutral safety switch prevents the engine from starting if the boat gears are in engaged. In the captain's case when he started the boat and if the throttles were in reverse, the boat blades would engage. This would be like an automobile ignition turning over in the drive mode.

As for the propeller strike case that Chief Taylor responded to, he told me that the crew had lengthy discussions on the incident. They came to the conclusion that the operator, while backing down to pick up the man in the water, had inadvertently pushed down the throttles rather than placing them in neutral. With the throttles, in reverse he backed over the man in the water. That the wounds extended from the neck to the buttocks indicates the boat rode down on the man in the water. Chief Taylor strongly advises: "Turn off the motor when recovering someone from the water."

In all of these tragedies, it appears the operators lost account, or were confused as to the location of those in the water. Or the operator was unfamiliar with boat. That is reason enough not to even look at the throttles, let alone engage them with a PIW near the boat.

I have performed numerous open-water recovery drills with persons in the water. My standard operating procedure was to step away from the helm and throttles while assisting the PIW. Often I would shut down the engine. I didn't even like maneuvering the boat with a person off the bow. I preferred approaching the PIW at a slow rate of speed, then bringing the throttles to neutral and coast up to the PIW, keeping them at a safe distance off the bow.

The Coast Guard calls this the indirect approach. By tossing the PIW a rescue heaving line I could easily pull the PIW to the boat. Let me stress it again: a rescue heaving line is a critical safety item that all boaters should have aboard, including man-powered craft like canoes and kayaks. It's also useful for beach-goers assisting a swimmer in distress.

Another safety issue worthy of repeating: never, never assume where the PIW *might* be: leave the throttle and find out for sure the PIW's location. Then toss them a rescue heaving line, life ring or Type IV throwable with a tether line attached. Unless there are poltergeists aboard, the throttles will remain in neutral just as they should. Also some advice to those in the water: do not approach the stern of a boat until absolutely assured the operator has either placed the throttles in neutral or has shut down the motor. And do not take the word of a crewman—get confirmation directly from the boat operator. Miscommunications could result in a missing limb or worse yet.

So far, we have discussed propeller strikes regarding stationary boats, but propeller strikes also occur off moving boats, and they can be just as deadly. For those who have been approached by Coast Guard personnel, DNR agents, or marine deputies regarding bow riders, please understand they have the boater's safety utmost in mind. I've been one of those marine officials who have approached boaters with bow riders, and I have seen the disgruntlement in boaters' eyes when directed to correct the hazardous situation. I would much rather see disgruntlement in eyes than mournful tears generated by a propeller strike. Coast Guardsman Scott Leahy told me he responded to an emergency off Cape Charles, Virginia. Two teenage girls while bow riding aboard a 18-foot power boat popped off the bow after the boat jumped a wave. The propeller instantly killed one girl; the other died from severe bleeding moments later after rescuers transported her to shore.

Leland marine deputy Bruce Garland advises that should a person fall overboard, turn the bow towards the direction that the person fell. This will kick the stern away from the PIW. Garland described a case where a person fell off a boat in Lake Leelanau. When the operator approached the PIW with the seas on his stern, he turned the helm hard over away from the PIW, which threw the stern towards the PIW, striking him in the rump with the propeller. Talk about a pain in the ass. It required fifty stitches to sew up the wound, but at least the fellow lived.

George Miller, Director of Flight Operations, County Rescue Services, Green Bay, e-mailed me about an emergency MEDIVAC he flew in late August 2005 near Iron Mountain, Michigan. According to Miller, a young female along with friends were riding along on the front of a pontoon boat. The young lady slipped and fell between the pontoons and was struck by the boat's propeller. The propeller sliced off her right breast and prop entered her right lung; it then continued down her right side inflicting severe deep gashes. On top of that dirty water had entered the wounds. She survived thanks to the quick response from those aboard the boat who rushed her to a nearby hospital. "She will survive her injuries but she will never forget how she received them nor will her friends," wrote Miller. Hopefully those who read this won't either. Please!

I've had enough of these stories. They sicken me because every one was absolutely avoidable, but maybe not in the land of fairyland boating.

The next assumption perhaps is the most insidious of all assumptions because by its very nature it appears harmless. After all, what dangers could a small paddle craft incur?

7. We assume that paddle craft are harmless.

I once approached the owner of a kayak store and asked him if he offered instructions for first-time kayakers on particular safety advice. "They don't need that stuff," he said. I almost knocked him on his brains, I was that offended by his self-serving let nothing stand in the way of a purchase mentality. Instead I walked away fuming.

It's ironic, so many fume and fret over personal water craft (PWC) and the dangers of that sport. Yet, over a recent ten year period Coast Guard recreational *Boating Statistics* show that nearly 30 percent more kayakers and canoeists have died than PWC operators. And in recent years, across the Northeast a staggering 50 percent of recreational boating fatalities have been in canoes and kayaks. The Coast Guard's Accident Report Database for 2004 reported a noteworthy increase in the number of reported fatalities involving canoes and kayaks. These small craft are extremely vulnerable to the marine environment, and are the least economically prohibitive to buy. Not a promising combination for the unenlightened boater.

In the following Boat Smart story, "Kayaking not for the untrained," it becomes readily apparent why boating education is so important for paddle-craft operators.

CASE FILE: Lake Michigan, Manistee, Michigan, September 2001. It seemed like a grand idea for Shannon Shull to celebrate her friend's 40th birthday with a kayak trip on Lake Michigan.

The ill-planned Lake Michigan adventure nearly turned fatal. Ironically, the women launched their Kayaks from Johnson's Funeral home located along the Manistee River Channel. Both nearly returned to Johnson's in a hearse. What a way to celebrate a birthday.

The mild September afternoon sun had lifted the air temperature into the 70s, with the water temperature around 60 degrees and a warm inviting wind fanning across the waters. The half-mile paddle out to Lake Michigan went without concern for the novice kayakers even though small craft advisories were in effect. Shannon had recently purchased the kayaks and frequently used them, but she had no formal training. Her friend had no experience at all.

As they neared the Manistee River mouth, all hell broke loose. The south breakwater that extends 1900 feet out into Lake Michigan offered a lee for the paddling duo, but as they neared the harbor mouth they lost the lee. Breaking waves poured over them, blocking their view of the nearby 55-foot high North Pier head light as they plunged in and out of the trough. Wind and waves swept them north.

When they attempted to return to the harbor Shull's friend capsized. Fortunately she wore a life jacket. She struggled to re-entered the kayak, which she did, only to capsize again. After 40 minutes of struggling she re-entered the kayak exhausted. All the while, the wind drove them north, further away from the harbor. On shore, beach strollers appeared as tiny figurines moving along the water line. The ladies carried no flares or other means of attracting attention. They wore only bathing suits and life jackets.

Shull, a former lifeguard, paddled towards shore and prayed they didn't capsize. Two hours after breaking the harbor mouth the lake dumped them on the beach. Lucky? You bet. Had the wind shifted, had night fallen, had it turned cold as it often does in mid-September, they might have returned to Johnson's in boxes. One thing is certain, with their limited kayak experience they did not belong on the lake. I would like to quote my friend, Vicky, an experienced scuba diver: "arrogance and ignorance kill." Shannon agrees.

Shannon Shull after several years of training now kayaks on Lake Michigan with confidence. Shannon's life jacket carries a strobe light, whistle, flares, knife and signal mirror.

Would Shull do it again? You bet. Since that experience Shull has spent hundreds of hours kayaking, attended kayak training camps, and refined her skills with her husband, Jay, also an experienced kayaker. Jay experienced a similar kayak mishap that inspired him to pursue training. In fact, the couple met during a training camp. Today, both feel confident that they can handle most situations, and they know which ones to avoid.

Safe boating simply boils down to training and awareness. And, because you're well-trained and experienced on one watercraft, doesn't mean you qualify on others. Shannon and Jay provided me a lesson in basic kayaking 101. I approached the lesson as if I had never been on a boat, which soon became apparent. With Shannon and Jay nearby providing instructions, I grew comfortable dealing with the kayak's handling features. Should I pursue the sport, I definitely would seek additional training, especially with experienced folks like Shannon and Jay.

The next naïve fairyland assumption is apparently shared by many sailboaters, who naively assume that their tether line and safety harness will save them should they go overboard. Yet, if this were so, then why do many veteran sailors call them "death straps."

8. We assume that a safety harness is a lifeline.

There are sailors who view safety harnesses as lifelines, yet other sailors swear that safety harnesses are actually death straps. The fact is they can be both. So how does one explain the yin and yang of safety harnesses. Easily, for the conflict does not lie with the tether line and safety harness, but in how it is used. The following case files illustrate how a safety harness when used incorrectly can turn the device into a death strap.

CASE FILES: Holland, Michigan, September 20, 2002. A 50-year-old male had departed Holland, Michigan, at 7 p.m. on Friday evening aboard a 38-foot sailboat in a solo race to Michigan City. A shoreline resident discovered the boat with the mainsail up, Saturday morning about a mile south of Holland. Responders found the solo sailor tangled in the jib, secured by a tether and safety harness.

Once again I take a firm stand: I strongly oppose sailors wearing a safety harness that trails enough tether line to dump them in the water still attached to the boat. Safety harnesses are meant to keep you *on* the boat, not drag you through the water. Take this case. What could the captain have done while being dragged through the water while the main sail driving the boat along at eight knots in four-foot seas? The strain on the harness release mechanism may have restricted his ability to release it, especially with nostrils and mouth inhaling water at a rapid rate. As for a knife, I believe being dragged through the water would have prevented its use. Then add darkness, cold water, and body shock— the results speak for themselves.

I believe many sailors assume that if they are attached to a boat with a tether line and safety harness they can simply pull themselves back aboard, or if that fails, simply release themselves from the safety harness. Sailors may speculate endlessly about going overboard, but when you hit that water attached to a tether line, reality, not supposition, takes hold, often ruthlessly. Take my word for it. I've been there, and it's something you don't want to go through unless absolutely trained to do so.

Before I pass on my own experiences of being dragged through the water attached to a tether line, let me share another safety harness fatality that struck down an experienced sailor. During the 1999 San Francisco Bay Area Multihull Association Double-Handed Farallones Race, veteran sailor Harvey Schlasky was thrown from his race boat, dragged behind it, and drowned. The fellow sailing with him was also knocked overboard, but he remained alongside the boat attached to a tether and safety harness. He was able to re-board the boat, but because of a boom failure, he could not reduce sail enough to stop the boat to save his mate.

Apparently the surviving sailor was able to keep his head above the water by grabbing onto a topside fitting on the lee side. If not, his chances of surviving were zero, unless he could have released himself. These maneuvers must be swift; the time crunch can compress to seconds for a person being dragged through the water. I recall years ago reading about a world class sailor tumbling overboard into the Pacific ocean off Washington State while attached to a tether line and a safety harness. Despite his crew's attempts to stop the sailboat and pull him aboard, he drowned, right alongside the boat.

In a more recent safety harness fatality, Erik Reid, 22, reportedly went down with a sailboat while he was attached to it with a safety harness. The accident occurred on February 21, 2004, off the California coast near San Francisco. The sailboat got caught in a storm, floundered off a beach near the Bay entrance, swamped, and sank. A Coast Guard helicopter plucked two crewmen from the water.

I contacted Master Chief Bill Michael at Coast Guard Pacific Area Command Center (PACAREA) regarding the case, and he hooked me up with a search and rescue coordinator at Coast Guard Group San Francisco. She told me that according to Reid's father, his son was attached to the 20-foot sailboat with two safety harnesses.

That they were out in 60-knot winds, in high seas off the entrance to San Francisco Bay, can only arouse wonder. I received an e-mail regarding this case from Master Chief Dave Spadoni at PACAREA, Alameda. I served with "Spud" for two years aboard the cutter *Point Bridge*. The master chief wrote: "When I heard commercial vessels near the Bay entrance passing their concerns about the sailboat, I knew it was a bad situation." Being strapped to a sinking boat indeed is a bad situation, one that I can relate to based on my own personal experiences.

BOAT SMART BRIEF: I have conducted a number of tether-line safety harness drills on Lake Michigan. Some drills I performed in three to four foot seas, others in one to two footers. The drills performed in the three to four foot seas were more realistic in that the possibility of a sailor going overboard would be greater in running seas. I worked the first set of drills with the Manistee Coast Guard auxiliary off a 22-foot power boat with a line trailing around 50 feet off the stern, safely away from the boat's propeller. I began the drill at a slow rate of speed, two knots, to test several shackle release mechanisms and to become familiar with the devices. I chose a snap hook with a U-bolt system that could be quickly released under load.

The fastest speed I reached was four knots and that was being dragged in the direction of the seas. Conditions were far too dangerous to be pulled into a four-foot chop, which would accelerate the intake of water into the mouth and nostrils. Even in following seas, the drag pulled my head below the surface. If I opened my mouth for air, I feared my lungs would fill with water. Surprisingly, my full body floatation suit drove me under. The suit filled with air, which traveled to the legs, creating buoyancy that lifted my legs upward while the tether line attached to my upper body drove my head under. And, at four knots, whether I lay on my back or stomach, my entire body was pulled under the surface. A photo taken by Pamela Cronenwett a Coast Guard auxiliarist aboard a nearby safety observation boat, catches only the bright orange colored sleeve raised above the surface revealing a fist signaling for the drill to stop. My raised arm cutting through the lake chop looked like an orange periscope.

Several days later I traveled to Coast Guard Station Holland, Michigan, determined to experience the harness drill at six knots, a speed more true to life in a real overboard situation. I got underway with Chief Reed and his crew aboard a 25-foot inflatable rescue boat. The seas out in the big lake were around one foot. After several runs, I reached six knots, both while on my back and on my stomach. Both times my entire body was pulled under the surface despite the full body flotation suit. The hydraulic force on my body and the stress exerted on the safety harness totally overwhelmed me, and if not for the quick release system I would have drowned in moments.

The idea of using a knife to cut the tether line seemed futile. It would require tremendous focus to reach for a knife—that is if one were readily available—then draw it up and cut the line while the senses are under brutal siege. Right off the bat when you hit the water, body reflexes will kick in if the water is cold. Cold water will induce instant torso reflex that will cause the mouth to part. Instead of sucking in air one will be sucking in a rush of water, leading to gagging and immediate panic. I liken it to sticking a fully charged garden hose into one's mouth.

I discovered that by flipping on my back, I could shield my eyes and mouth and reduce the intake of water, but the head hood of my flotation suit around my neck filled with water, pulling my head back. With water cascading over my face and into my nostrils, it felt as if someone had shaken up several soda pop bottles and shot them up my nose. It's been my experience that these types of real-time drills are full of surprises.

Hell with this. End of drill. This Navy Seal stuff is too daring for an aging retired Coast Guard Senior Chief trying to prove a safety point. There was, however, a worthwhile message gained from the ordeal—stay on the boat.

CASE FILE: Queen's Cup Race, Lake Michigan, 1986. Jeff Allen, who has sailed in a number of major races on Lake Michigan once experienced an overboard plunge while attached to a safety harness and tether line. During the Queen's Cup Race, Jeff had gone forward on the deck of a 33-foot Tartan sailboat late at night to haul down the spinnaker. The sail went aback and he was knocked overboard.

His six-foot tether line was attached to a jack line that ran aft. The harness line ran down the jack line and Allen found himself being dragged astern at six knots in six- to eight-foot seas. I asked him how long he was in the water. "It seemed like an eternity," said

Allen. "I rolled onto my back. I would have drowned face down had I not. It took three crewmen to haul me aboard. Another minute in the water and I would have been done. I hit the rack after the ordeal and slept. I was physically whipped."

BOAT SMART BRIEF: As stated earlier, these real-time episodes are full of surprises. Allen said the 12-inch high sea boots he was wearing filled with water and acted like a drogue, making it even more difficult for the crew to haul him aboard. Allen said, "Since then, I've cut my sea boots down from twelve to five inches, which I can now remove. The twelve inch boots acted like anchors when filled with water, making them nearly impossible to pull off." Allen was fortunate that were three able crewmen aboard to haul him aboard.

What if there wasn't brute strength available to haul aboard an overboard victim? Then what? I conducted a drill with the Holland boat crew in order to answer the question, but this time I stayed on the boat and used a dummy—besides myself—called Oscar, a mannequin outfitted in a full-body exposure suit with weights that scaled him out at around 100 pounds. We normally use Oscar for overboard recovery drills; this would be his first safety harness drill.

I attached a safety harness around Oscar's upper body. I then attached a three quarter inch double braided nylon tether line to the safety harness and threw him overboard. The tether line's bitter end was attached to the 25-foot rescue boat's towing cage with a carabiner, a connecting device I suspect some naïve sailors might consider to be suitable. Well, the drill proved just how naïve the use of a carabiner would be. Under heavy load I could not slacken the nylon tether line attached to the carabiner in order to release the eye of the tether line. Even if I could open the sleeve, if the line surged, the sleeve closing on my finger could rip it off. Oscar's only chance—cut him free with a knife.

After the failed carabiner drill, we hauled Oscar aboard, and again tossed him overboard. It took 10 seconds from when I pulled a four-inch serrated knife from a sheath on the towing cage to when I cut the line. We performed the drill again. This time I used a small foldout two-inch serrated knife

that I pulled from my pocket, opened, and cut the line in four seconds. Oscar lived.

The Offshore Racing Council's Sailing Special Regulations advise: "Each crew member shall have a safety harness, and safety line not more than six feet long with a snaphook at each end. And a knife shall be provided for each crew member." A tether line with a snaphook is also highly recommended by the council. The Regulations also state that the harness should be fitted with a crotch strap or tight straps, a safety device that I've been told is not commonly used by the sailing community on Lake Michigan. Most captains, however, issue standing orders requiring a crotch strap safety harness to be used when working aloft.

And with good reason. Should a crewman fall from aloft, the body shock when the safety tether line takes load will be distributed over the torso. The danger with using the chest and shoulder safety harness is that the shock will centralize around the upper chest area where the safety tether line attaches to D-rings near the sternum. Ouch! I suspect an injury to the sternum area could also occur if dangling partly submerged, while being pounded about in rough seas off the hull of a sail boat.

Captain Thomas Kelly, Master of the school ship schooner, *Inland Seas*, home ported in Suttons Bay, Michigan, told me about a friend of his who rescued a sailboater suspended over the side while attached to a safety harness. While departing Sturgeon Bay, Wisconsin, his friend came upon a sailboat that appeared to be in trouble. On approaching the floundering craft, he discovered a man hanging over the side attached to a tether line and safety harness. A woman on the sailboat could not haul the man aboard. Bringing his boat alongside, the friend jumped aboard the sailboat, hove to, and hoisted the man onto the deck.

I have been conducting an on-going survey with sailors regarding safety harnesses and tether lines. The feedback is not encouraging. Let me share one such interview. I approached the captain of a sailboat that had just moored at Manistee's City Marina. I introduced myself to the captain and explained the reason for the visit.

He had made an overnight passage from South Manitou Island aboard a 29-foot C & C sloop. He had used a safety harness the night before in heavy weather while hauling down the head sail. "I almost slid over the portside and into the lake," he said. "I grabbed a life line to keep from going overboard." He said he was wearing a safety harness.

The captain produced the life harness and six foot tether line he had used. He had attached the tether line to a jack line that ran fore and aft, center deck. I pointed out that the length of the tether line plus slack in the jack line when taking load would place him in the water for certain. Unless he could quickly release himself he would drown.

And he would have drowned since the safety harness d-rings were attached to a carabineer at the end of the tether line. It's nearly impossible to open the release arm of a carabineer under load. Then I pointed to the gear he was wearing: weather-proof coveralls that resembled chest waders and were tightly secured at the ankles. I pointed out that if he went overboard, his outfit would act as a sea anchor that would pull him beneath the surface.

He took my suggestions well, unlike some sail-boaters who look at me in scorn as if I had proven their safety harness god to be false. Although,

While being dragged through the water a PIW will drown in moments unless he or she can quickly be released from the safety harness. If not for the above snap hook and a U-bolt system, I would have drowned without a quick means to release myself.

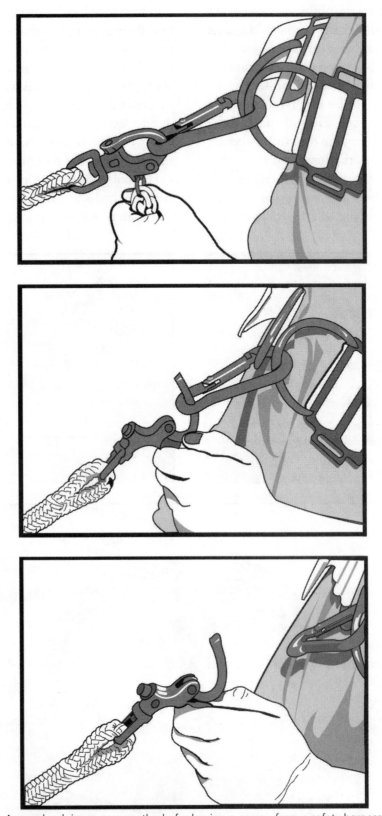

A snap hook is a proven method of releasing a person from a safety harness.

I suspect they felt sheepish for not thinking this issue through. So what would you do if your were being dragged through the water attached to tether line?

If you hesitated with your response, you're dead.

9. We assume that autopilot means freedom to go about our ways.

Autopilots, the self-steering devices found aboard recreational boats, are intended to augment safe navigation, not hinder it. Placing a boat on autopilot and going below decks would be like placing a motor home on cruise control and walking back to the kitchen to make a sandwich. No way, you say! Well that's what I say about recreational boaters who abandon the helm while running on autopilot. As for the following autopilot cases, may I once again make my standard disclaimer—I do not make up these stories. Who could.

CASE FILES: Manistee, Michigan. Jim Mrozik of Manistee told me about two brothers who bought a 34-foot power boat. Reportedly, they had little or no boating experience, which is often the case with new boat owners. They had planned an early morning fishing trip on Lake Michigan. At the last moment one of the brothers bailed out, leaving the other to man the boat by himself. After casting off lines, he backed the power boat into the Manistee River Channel and pointed the bow towards the harbor mouth located around a quarter mile away. He then set the boat on autopilot, left the helm, and walked to the stern to rig fishing lines.

Wham, the boat plowed into a cluster of pilings marking an elbow in the river channel. Mrozik said, "The impact knocked an opening in the hull large enough to fit a bushel basket through the hole. The guy set the boat on autopilot believing it would automatically steer the boat around the bend in the river channel and out into Lake Michigan," No way, I told him. But Mrozikl said he saw firsthand the damaged hull, and he talked with the operator. Unbelievable, but then, maybe not—read on.

Chris Johnson, Leelanau District Ranger, a 20-year veteran for the National Park Service, told about a 26-foot sailboat that ran aground on the northwest side of North Manitou Island near Pt. Hole. The solo occupant was sailing on autopilot when he ran into the island. He stumbled onto the island and was discovered by a hunter who found him wandering down a trail.

Manitou Islands

The marooned captain told Ranger Johnson that when he hit the island he thought he had run onto the mainland. He confessed he had limited sailing experience and that he was below deck when the boat ran aground. He had departed Wisconsin and was heading for Leland Harbor. It took salvagers two weeks to pull the boat off the beach after punching several holes in the hull.

What blows me away about this case is that Leland Harbor sits approximately 12 miles east of where the sailor ran aground, and the track line to Leland Harbor crosses the Manitou passage—one of the more heavily trafficked shipping lanes on the Great Lakes. This novice, doing whatever below decks, thought he had hit the mainland. It's just as well he did run aground onto the island rather than being run down in the Manitou passage. Not necessarily by a commercial boat, but by another autopilot incorrigible merrily whizzing along in the aquatic fairyland.

Captain Mike Grosvenor, owner of the freight and passenger vessel *Mishe Mokwa*, told me of such an encounter with a fairyland autopilot buffoon. Captain Grosvenor's family has been making the Manitou Islands run since 1917 and Captain Grosvenor for over 37 years. The *Mishe Mokwa* is 65 feet in length. The steel-hulled boat weighs 52 tons and would probably demolish a recreational boat in a collision, a catastrophe the good captain barely avoided one day while transiting the Manitou passage.

On that memorable day, Captain Grosvenor remembers the Manitou passage was blanketed in fog. About half way across the passage, he picked up a large contact on radar off his port bow: "The target was quite large, and I thought it was a commercial vessel," said Captain Grosvenor who hailed the vessel on VHF-FM Channel 16.

No response. He then hailed the approaching boat on Channel 13, the ship-to-ship working frequency. No response. The target was rapidly closing with a constant bearing and decreasing range—a collision course for certain. Even though he was the stand-on vessel with a boat approaching from port, Captain Grosvenor wisely elected to follow Inland Rule 8: "If necessary to avoid collision or allow more time to assess the situation, a vessel shall slacken her speed or take all way off by stopping or reversing her means of propulsion." In accordance with Rule 8, he brought the *Mishe Mokwa* down to bear steerage to allow the target to pass ahead. He said, "Out of the fog emerged a 70-foot yacht flying along at twenty knots on autopilot with no one at the helm. The boat passed within yards."

Captain Grosvenor believes that affordable electronics like radar and GPS are offering boaters a false sense of security. He also pointed out that these electronic devices are drawing more recreational boaters out into deep water. The captain of the fairyland boat that nearly ran into the *Mishe Mokwa* was lucky that an experienced captain prevented a collision.

Imagine if Captain Grosvenor instead of being a commercial captain was an another fairyland boater whizzing alone on auto bliss. You needn't image just read on.

CASE FILE: White Lake, Michigan, August 24, 1996. According to the Muskegon County Sheriff's accident report, a collision between two powerboats occurred at 11:44 a.m., a mile or so off the entrance to White Lake Harbor. The collision involved a 34-foot Carver and a 44-foot Sea Ray. The latter boat, according to the report had the autopilot engaged.

Why the operator of the 44-foot Sea Ray chose to engage the autopilot while clipping along near a busy harbor mouth on a Saturday morning with heavy outbound traffic was not addressed in the sheriff's accident report. But then how could you explain it. It was more like a stunt one might find in a Steve Martin movie with the comedian below decks hosting a champagne breakfast. Funny as it might be for a Hollywood script, it was not so funny for the two occupants of the 34-foot Carver

who watched in disbelief as the 44-foot Sea Ray bore down on them. The terrified souls leaped overboard seconds before impact. A nearby boater retrieved the stunned pair from the water.

The following auto-pilot misstep may have resulted in serious injury to 26 college students on an educational science cruise off the waters of Grand Haven, Lake Michigan. It once again validates my belief as to why few mishaps seldom occur between recreational boats and commercial vessels.

CASE FILE: Grand Haven, Lake Michigan, Summer, 2004. Captain Tony Fiore told me he was underway in fog aboard Grand Valley State's research vessel *D.J. Angus* when a fishing charter boat nearly ran into his vessel. At the time of the incident, he said visibility was less than 100 feet at the open-water research station located approximately one nautical mile southwest of the Grand Haven piers.

Following standard operating procedures for a professional captain, Captain Fiore announced over VHF/FM Channel 13 a working frequency between commercial boats, and over Channel 16 that the *Angus* was on station, not making way, conducting research. He then provided the vessel's latitude and longitude and ranges to nearby geographic reference points. Captain Fiore was also sounding the appropriate signals for a power vessel not making way in restricted visibility: at intervals of not more than two minutes he sounded two prolonged blasts in succession with an interval of about two seconds between blasts.

The veteran captain and retired Coast Guard Chief felt confident his fellow commercial captains would pay heed. Still, he kept a close eye on the radar. Captain Fiore said, "At around ten o'clock, I picked up seven contacts on radar moving outbound from the Grand Haven channel. I again announced over Channel 13 and 16 my position to alert the vessels."

Apparently one of the outbound skippers failed to hear the broadcast and headed south. "I watched on radar a target heading towards me on a collision course with a decreasing range and constant bearing. Out of the mist emerged a boat that abruptly stopped within feet of my vessel. I could see the vessel was equipped with radar and a VHF radio antenna," said Captain Fiore. He later discovered that the boat was operated by a charter-boat captain. According to sources, the captain was known to place his boat on auto pilot as he set up fishing rods.

This wayward captain, along with other autopilot delinquents needs to be reminded of Rule 5 of the Inland Rules: "Every vessel shall at all times maintain a proper lookout by sight and hearing as well as by all available means appropriate in the prevailing circumstances and conditions so as to make a full appraisal of the situation and of the risk of collision." The guy was fortunate that Captain Fiore was retired. Had that happened when Captain Fiore was wearing Coast Guard blue, he would've nailed him for Negligent Operation. In fact, with 26 students aboard the *Angus*, Gross Negligent Operation would be more in line. A Gross Negligent conviction is a felony violation subject to stiff fines and jail time.

This final autopilot story makes me wonder do poltergeist skipper these boats, or someone with a death wish who wishes to become a poltergeist. My fellow Chief Don Hefner runs the radio room at Group Grand Haven's operation center. On June 14, 2005, he was in the Group radio room when he heard a large motor vessel hailing a sailboat in the northbound shipping lane. "For five minutes, the motor vessel attempted to contact the sailboat over Channel 13 and 16 with no response," said Chief Hefner. "Finally the motor vessel had to change course to avoid the sailboat."

We both agreed that the sailboat was probably on autopilot and that the captain was below decks: just the spot to be while transiting a major shipping lane. I asked Chief Hefner if this happens often and he said, "Unfortunately this has happened more frequently than my comfort level would prefer."

Let's move on to the next assumption. These autopilot cases get my blood boiling and I suspect yours too. I can't promise the boiling will stop either as we move onto the next naïve assumption that has often found me boiling over.

10. We assume that rescuers are at our immediate beck and call.

While visiting South Manitou Island in August of 2003, Park Ranger Nate Mazurek spoke to me about his concerns regarding recreational boaters who expect authorities to instantly respond to their whims. "Recreational boaters act as if the Coast Guard were a birthright," said Mazurek.

His supervisor, Chris Johnson, described a case where four kayakers departed Glen Harbor in fog, bound for South Manitou Island. Partially across the passage, the group, paddling in a westerly direction, elected to turn north for the island, except for one Kayaker. He continued to head west, in fog, alone, and without a compass. The threesome made it to the island. When the maverick kayaker failed to show, his buddies called 911. Rescue responders, including the Coast Guard, launched an extensive search. In the end, the fourth kayaker paddled his way to the island unharmed. Chalk it up as yet another needless search for a recreational boater charged to tax payers. Are you boiling, yet? If not, let me throw some more logs on the fire.

That they set out for the island, in fog, across a major shipping lane is naïve enough. But then to expect authorities to bail them out after they made a poor choice suggest that their ultimate safety lies not in their hands, but in the hands of rescue responders. Ranger Johnson said, "Nine-One-One has become a real challenge for us: cell phones abound and people feel if they need help, simply call 911. The downside, is that we receive far too many trivial calls that tax resources while diverting them from real emergencies."

Recreational boaters' myriad misadventures and shortcomings suggest that many boaters fail to understand search and rescue's intended purpose. This remarkable rescue response system grew out of necessity, not personal convenience. The early lifesavers would be appalled by how current recreational boaters view search and rescue. But then, who could have imagined that Lake Michigan would transform from an industrial-age waterway into a giant aquatic playground for landlubbers.

The fact is, far too many recreational boaters call the Coast Guard due to needless shortcomings:

running out of gas, dead batteries, adrift in fog, poor navigation, inept radio communications and running aground. All are common repeats that draw on rescue resources. A coastie told me he assisted one boater twice in the same day; both times the boater had run out of gas. These and so many other recreational boating miscues like hoax calls, and needless overdue reports, deplete search and rescue resources.

As needless calls to rescue responders increase, along with legitimate calls that may require a live-saving response, will resources be available to respond with enough seaworthy rescue boats and aircraft, and people trained to handle the challenge? Bear that in mind as we move on to Chapter Nine: Capabilities and Limitations of Rescue Responders.

Rescue Responders Capabilities and Limitations

Y ES, THE COAST GUARD DOES FACE LIMITATIONS, as does its fellow rescue agencies. Careless boating behavior can exasperate those limitations, and thus the capabilities of rescue responders to assist those in real need. This chapter will address these issues like needless overdue reports made by loved ones concerning the whereabouts on the water of family members or friends. Also addressed are frivolous calls the public makes to the Coast Guard regarding perceived dangers to boaters on the water. These calls often lead to extensive searches and needless depletion of limited resources.

This Chapter will also deal with the challenges Cost Guard boat crews encounter conducting near shore rescues.

Although several stories in this chapter might seem a little off course regarding the chapter theme, the stories nonetheless further the Boat Smart Chronicles objective to pass along to boaters critical lessons learned. I'll let you know when I make a slight course change on chapter theme, besides the stories are too interesting to pass by without a look.

Let's begin with a Coast Guard profile and the unique role it plays in the maritime affairs of the nation. I've been associated with this agency for over thirty years and still marvel on how it accomplishes so much with so little. Proud? You bet. Some of the finest folks I know wear or have worn Coast Guard blue.

COAST GUARD—ONE-OF-A-KIND

In 1790, the First Congress authorized funds for the establishment of a Revenue Cutter Service, the forerunner of the United States Coast Guard. Eight years later in 1798, Congress established a Navy Department. Not only is the Coast Guard older than the Navy, it is a unique service in and of itself. Other than national defense and homeland security, the only other element they share is water.

Both services even serve under different agencies. The Navy operates under the Secretary of Defense, the Coast Guard under the Department of Homeland Security. Where the Navy packs awesome fire power, the Coast Guard packs awesome law enforcement power. Several years ago, I stopped a boater in the Muskegon Channel to inspect his vessel. He wanted to know what right I had to come aboard his boat. I advised him by the time I explained that right, I would be through with the safety inspection and he could be on his way.

It was a fair question and if time permitted I would've explained that first off it is not a right but an authority mandated by Congress. Federal laws implicitly state that Coast Guard boarding officers do not require search warrants, a captain's consent to board, or probable cause. Several years ago while working a joint mission with the FBI aboard a Coast Guard cutter off Santa Barbara, California, I quoted to an agent Federal Code, 14 USC 89, which authorizes the Coast Guard to search, seize and arrest those in violation of laws of the United States. That same authority, by the way, applies to recreational boats and federal laws that mandate boaters carry required safety equipment and that their vessels meet prescribed safety standards like proper ventilation in engine spaces and flame arresters for gasoline fueled motors.

The agent couldn't believe that Coast Guard personnel could board, inspect and search a vessel without a search warrant. "If only the FBI could wield such authority," he sighed. Such authority, he noted, makes the Coast Guard the most powerful law enforcement agency in the federal government. Oh, indeed, that authority has been contested in court, but to no avail. And in light of Homeland Security interests, I suspect future legal contentions will end in similar fashion.

Coast Guard authority to enforce federal laws stems from the Posse Comitatus Act passed during the reconstruction era after the Civil War. The act forbid the use of the military to "execute the laws." In effect, Posse Comitatus prohibits direct participation of Department of Defense personnel in civilian law enforcement. The Act does not apply to the Coast Guard since it operates under a civilian department while still maintaining status as one of the five armed military services.

In addition to national defense and homeland security, the Coast Guard carries out a host of other missions that support the nation's maritime economic imperatives. Should the Coast Guard shut down, it would cripple our maritime industry. There would be no central command or agency to regulate and enforce congressional economic mandates that underpin our maritime stability.

What affords the Coast Guard the means to expedite the nation's maritime will are its people. They must be as flexible and diverse in their skills as the manifold missions they are tasked to perform.

What I find so remarkable even after thirty years associated with the service is how they accomplish all this with a total force of only 39,000 active duty members, 8,100 reservists and 35,287 auxiliary volunteers. To put it in perspective: the Coast Guard's active duty force is equal to New York City's entire police force of 39,000 personnel.

New York City looks like a postage stamp compared to the 3.5 million square miles of ocean, and 98,000 miles of coastline the Coast Guard must police and regulate with an armada of 232 cutters, 211 aircraft, and 1,400 small boats. That includes all the maintenance, support, shore facilities and administrative support it takes to facilitate such an enormous endeavor.

On the Great Lakes the Coast Guard has on call 48 surface search and rescue stations with 188 boats and two air stations. Annually they process 7,500 search and rescue cases. The total number of coasties carrying out Great Lakes' missions represents only six percent of the entire New York police department. What allows them to accomplish so much with so little is their fierce commitment to satisfy the nation's pressing maritime needs.

LAKE MICHIGAN COAST GUARD CREWS COMMITTED

The mission demands placed on boat crews have never been greater, nor has the urgency to qualified crewmen and coxswains in light of Homeland Security demands. The Coast Guard is also a public-mission driven service at the willful call of the maritime community. There are no time-outs to regroup and reload. These youngsters must be pressed into service come hell or high water.

The pressures can be intense. Many find themselves far away from home for the first time. For 24 hours a day, they must deal with personalities, whether they care for them or not. It's not like an eight to five job where personality conflicts are left behind at the office. Young Coasties must adjust to a demanding work environment that expects perfection; and they are subject to the Uniform Code of Military Justice (UCMJ), which means one doesn't get fired, one gets discharged, usually dishonorably. A less than honorable discharge can haunt one for a lifetime. I advise young folks that the Coast Guard is a wonderfully benevolent organization, but like a shark it will chew them up if they drift too far into the forbidden waters of the UCMJ.

People occasionally ask me it the Coast Guard would be the right service for their youngster. I frankly advise them that the Coast Guard is not a rehabilitation center for correcting parental malfeasance. The Coast Guard needs squared-away youngsters who can serve their country in a service that annually saves thousands of lives.

When a seaman apprentice fresh out of boot camp reports aboard, station management hands him or her a simple objective: get qualified on the rescue boats. As simple as this sounds, the process can be complex, especially aboard the Coast Guard's space-age, million dollar, 47-foot motor life boat. On a 47-footer a young seaman—or sea woman for the gender sensitive—must master nearly 450

boat tasks, pass an oral board conducted by salty senior petty officers, then undertake an underway check ride demonstrating seamanship skills. Along the qualification journey, which can take three to six months, the trainee must absorb 1,077 pages of the Coast Guard Seamanship Manual, born of years of small boat knowledge and compiled by seasoned chiefs.

Those that qualify may pursue coxswain qualification, which can take up to nine months and many hours of underway training. Then pass another grueling oral board and a boat check ride. In addition to deck tasks, boat engineers, who oversee the engine spaces and auxiliary machinery, must master engineering qualifications and complex onboard computer systems. During the year 2001 Station Manistee's entire crew faced the daunting

A Coast Guard boat crew aboard Station St. Joseph's 47-foot motor lifeboat muscles aboard a crewman during open water recovery drills in Lake Michigan. Coast Guard boat crews are in a perpetual training mode in order to meet ever-present mission demands, in particular law enforcement, search and rescue, and homeland security.

task of qualifying the entire station, 18 members including the commanding officer, aboard their new 47-foot motor life boat. They accomplished this while standing duty to meet the needs of the local maritime community, in particular search and rescue. Boat crews could be up to all hours performing rescues and law enforcement missions and still be required to pursue training the following day.

Michigan winters add to the pressure since boats are laid up. Which means boat crews are pursuing qualifications during the short boating season, which competes with search and rescue and other mission demands. Then on top of that, boat crews and engineers must pursue law enforcement qualifications that can be just as demanding. The process of maintaining boat and law enforcement qualifications finds crews on a endless track. And I won't even address the onerous paperwork that station crews must wade through, often on their so-called off-duty days.

Yet somehow they maintain, and I can boast that during my 23 years associated with Group Grand Haven we have had the finest station managers and crews ever. They are the heart and soul of this service, and I would sail with them anytime, anywhere and in any sea. Let me not forget that without support from Coast Guard Reservists who contribute over 300,000 person hours to Coast Guard missions annually, plus the support from Auxiliarists who themselves contribute over 600,000 operational person hours annually, the Coast Gaurd simply couldn't meet missions demands.

COAST GUARD LAKE MICHIGAN RESOURCES

Lake Michigan has 19 Coast Guard stations and one air station to stand guard over the entire lake. Each station has assigned areas of responsibility along the Lake Michigan shores. Beside covering near shore waters, river channels, and connecting

Coast Guard Station Manistee's 47-foot motor lifeboat pounds out into the open waters of Lake Michigan on a training mission.

lakes, areas of responsibility also extend out to mid-lake. Although stations may have several boats, normally only one duty boat crew stands by to run search and rescue. In short, one boat for one crew. It doesn't require an MIT degree to figure out the strain needless searching can place on these limited resources. Needless searches coupled with bonafide mission demands can lead to crew fatigue and shutdown. During the 2000 season, I placed the Coast Guard search and rescue crew in fatigue status eight times at Station Muskegon due to mission overload.

It's not uncommon for command to stand down boat crews at search and rescue facilities around Lake Michigan due to fatigue. That isn't to say they won't respond if need be, but only to "urgent search and rescue" where those requesting assistance require urgent help. Also, boaters should not expect the Coast Guard to place crews and equipment in harm's way to execute a rescue that reaches beyond the risk envelop. The Coast Guard calls the process, "risk assessment." If it's determined that the rescue at hand is too hazard-

ous to the Coast Guard crew, the Coast Guard will opt to stand off.

I once followed up on a story about a 27-foot sailboat that ran aground south of St. Joseph, Michigan while a Coast Guard crew looked on. I contacted the captain and identified myself and my desire to write a story on his ordeal. He mistook me for a newspaper reporter and began lambasting the Coast Guard crew. He harped on about how the St. Joseph boat crew had failed to assist him and that they were under-trained and lacked the skills to save his boat. Full of his own bloat, he swore he was going to notify Coast Guard high command and his congressman and on he raved.

Finally, though the diatribe I managed to convey that I was a Coast Guard Senior Chief. I stressed that boat crews can't always execute a successful near-shore rescue. He grew even more irate. Hell, he was going to blame the Coast Guard crew, regardless. I knew better than to pursue the point that the grounding stemmed from his own shortcomings. No doubt others have voiced displeasure with Coast Guard near shore rescue

Coast Guard Station St. Joseph, Michigan represents one of 19 Coast Guard Stations located around Lake Michigan. The structure dates back to the nineteenth century and the United States Lifesaving Service.

attempts, so let me set the record straight regarding this issue.

I believe his assumption that modern day rescuers can always perform these dangerous near-shore rescues stems from lingering impressions of United States Life Saving Service feats a century ago. These brave surf warriors executed a number of rescues from shore. Their boats lacked mechanical power, and high seas and gale force winds overwhelmed their oar-driven surfboats. They often deployed Lyle line-throwing guns and Breeches Buoys attached to a block and tackle system to pull stranded sailors ashore. Many of these rescue were attempted in late fall and early winter in heavy surf, frigid waters, and below zero wind chills that gnarled fingers and toes. Their lifesaving rescues were often heralded in local newspapers and carried accolades like "storm warriors" and "soldiers of the surf." An admiring public further embellished these feats, leaving an indelible imprint on future generations and their expectations of future storm warriors.

The disgruntlement over modern-day Coast Guard rescue shortcomings vented by the captain of the 26-foot sail boat is apparently shared by other boaters. The following story, told to me by ferry boat captain Willie Dodge, reveals another unrealistic expectation and unwarranted criticism of Coast Guard rescue responders.

Willie Dodge captains for Shepler Lines, a long-established ferry boat and commercial freight enterprise that transports passengers and supplies across the Straits of Mackinac from Mackinaw City and St. Ignace to Mackinac Island. Several years ago, while making the run in fog from Mackinaw City to the island, he heard a boater over VHF-FM Channel 16 talking with Coast Guard Station St. Ignace. The boater reportedly was lost somewhere in the Straits.

According to Dodge, a 1000-foot motor vessel had just issued a security call that it was nearing Round 1, a junction point that cuts between Mackinac Island and Bois Blanc Island. Once through the narrow island passage, large motor vessels either veer north towards Lake Superior or head east across Lake Huron. The lost boater believed he was near Round 1 and requested

that the Coast Guard locate him on radar and provide a course to steer to avoid the freighter.

In order for the Coast Guard to take such action would require the presence of Vessel Traffic Service (VTS) system that requires numerous radar sites, closed-circuit T.V. sets, several VHF radio sites, and a team of highly trained personnel to monitor vessel traffic. VTS systems, located at major U.S. seaports, operate much like air traffic control systems that coordinate air traffic.

The only component of the VTS system the St. Ignace station had was a radio, which the watchstander used wisely. He contacted the 1000-foot motor vessel and advised the captain of the situation and requested the freighter reduce speed. He then advised the small boat skipper that the Coast Guard could not provide a position or course to steer. The captain's reply: "What the hell am I paying my tax dollars for."

My reply to that: Maybe in the future your tax money will go for a VTS in the Mackinac Straits so that commercial captains needn't be burdened by clueless boaters like you. I talked with a 15-year vet at Shepler, and he suggested that VTS for the Straits could come to pass if recreational boating continues to proliferate along with recreational boaters' less than smart boating behavior.

By the way, I take umbrage with boaters who whine about Coast Guard capabilities when it was their own limitations that drew them into a mishap. Please, don't misread either, Coast Guard rescue responders will attempt near shore rescues. And should rescue attempts fail it often has little to do with a crews' capabilities or limitations but instead to an unruly lake that knows few limitations.

It's time for a story and the one I have for you regards a near-shore rescue that went amuck despite the valiant effort of a Coast Guard 44-foot motor lifeboat crew to save a sailboat in heavy surf near shore.

ON WATCH: Big Point Sable, Lake Michigan, August 12, 1999. Just past noon, Coast Guard Group Grand Haven radio received a Mayday from the captain of the sailboat *Bittersweet* requesting assistance. He reported his position was off Big Point Sable, Lake Michigan. The Coast Guard

Situation Report cited the following weather conditions at the time: wind: 22 kts/330 t, seas 8–12 ft, vis: 8 nm, A/T 68 f, W/T 64 f.

A Coast Guard rescue craft out of Manistee responded to *Bittersweet's* Mayday. When they arrived at Big Point Sable aboard a 28-foot inflatable craft around 1:00 p.m. the crew noted that building seas would prohibit towing the sailboat to a safe harbor. They requested assistance from Station Ludington who soon arrived on scene with a 44-foot motor lifeboat (MLB).

After passing the *Bittersweet* tow over to the 44-foot motor lifeboat crew, the 28-foot inflatable and its crew beat north towards Manistee, but soon found themselves issuing their own Mayday after the rescue craft's bow dove down a wave, scooping up a load of water that exploded across the deck, blasting out the cabin window. The two crewmen stood in knee-high water as they fought to de-water the floundering craft. The Coast Guard coxswain, Jeff George, issued an urgent radio call to the Coast Guard motor lifeboat, now engrossed in assisting the sailboat *Bittersweet*.

With gale-force winds driving the disabled sailboat towards Big Point Sable, Chief Reed ordered the crew to haul in the towing line from the floundering craft, which now carried a coastie sent over to assist the captain. Reed decided that coasties, possibly in the water, took higher precedence than the sailboat. It was a split-second decision the veteran coxswain made without hesitation. Those on the sailboat were afforded the protection of the boat, but if the coasties hit the water, they alone must deal with the high surf and looming rocks and steel abutments that rimmed Big Sable light.

Good fortune prevailed: the crew of the 28-foot inflatable stabilized the boat, allowing Chief Reed to pound back to the *Bittersweet* now on an unrestricted race towards shore. A defining moment in the rescue: either Chief and his crew hook up the sailboat ASAP, or be it a bittersweet ending for the 32-foot sloop.

Let me pause for a minute to stress a point. Although it all seemed so under control, believe me, it was not. Chief Reed faced a relentless violence that bore down on the 20-ton rescue boat and tore at his crew who were strapped to the superstructure with safety harnesses. The elemental assault pushed hard-earned skills to the max. Countless hours of training could possibly produce life-saving dividends. Hands worked throttles and the helm; eyes darted to the sea, back to the sloop; commands barked out above the uproar; bodies jerked and twisted about; diesel engines screamed; the 3/16 inch steel hull shuddered as it blasted through 16-foot waves; lake water cascaded water down on the crew, blurring vision while tearing at nerves. Make one error, and the lake has you by the shackles. It takes tremendous effort to keep focused not only on the crew's survival, but on the survival of the *Bittersweet* crew. Notching up the pressure even further, the sloop was within yards of entering the surf zone and crashing waves.

Fighting through the chaos and a rapidly ticking clock, Chief Reed's crew again worked the tow line over to the sloop. The crewman on the sailboat flopped about on the sloop's bow pulpit like a rag doll in the mouth of a playful canine. The motor lifeboat's depth finder read 15 feet, and within yards loomed a sand bar. The crewman fought to attach the eyes of the towing bridle to the sloop's bow cleats while struggling to stay on the boat. Chief Reed gave the order to haul in the towing line and bridle and directed the young crewman to the stern. The sloop was on its own.

The high surf took little time in dumping the sloop on the beach. Miraculously, the captain and crewman later walked away unharmed. Were they lucky? Beyond words! To understand their good fortune note when the seas settled down the sloop sat so high and dry, you could walk around it without getting wet feet. And yards away from the sloop lay a steel sea wall encompassing the Big Point Sable light. Yes, the captain was lucky, at least that is until he received an $8,500 salvage bill. It took two tugs and special heavy equipment to remove the sloop.

One certainly can't fault the capabilities of Coast Guard crews, they were dealing with elemental madness, but they did face limitations set by an unruly lake, limitations further exasperated by the limited experience of the *Bittersweet's* captain. Let's review boat smart bittersweet lessons definitely learned the hard way.

The sloop *Bittersweet* heads outbound from Muskegon Harbor on a calm uneventful day. In less than 24 hours, its Texas-native captain would encounter seas unlike any he had experienced in Gulf Coast waters.

Coast Guardsmen aboard Station Ludington's 44-foot motor lifeboat take the opportunity in heavy seas to conduct training in Lake Michigan. This is the same motor lifeboat that assisted *Bittersweet*.

BOAT SMART BRIEF: As with most boating mishaps it's the little things. When the captain approached Ludington Harbor, he couldn't read the charted light characteristics of the pier head lights. He had reading glasses aboard, but had stowed them in a forward cabin and feared leaving the helm due to weather conditions. Although equipped with an autopilot, he told me heavy weather prevented its use.

As daylight broke, he struggled to deploy a staysail only but it was torn and proved ineffective. Concerned about mounting, seas he strapped himself to the helm while steering the heavy boat with a tiller that further advanced his fatigue.

As for the mainsail, the rigging atop the mast had separated. This made it impossible to reef As for motoring into the seas, the 13-ton sloop's

36-horsepower diesel engine lacked the power. The sloop carried an anchor, a 16-pound Danforth, but far too light for the conditions and size and weight of the boat. The captain told me he lost his 40-pound Danforth anchor in the Mississippi River near St. Louis. It's doubtful, anyway, the weary 70-year-old captain could've deployed an anchor in those seas.

So as the little things add up, Lake Michigan with willful delight took full advantage and delivered a bittersweet lesson.

In the next story thanks to the capabilities of a very seasoned Coast Guard crew a sailboat captain and his family are alive and in spite of the sailboater's own sailing limitations. The story also involves my old mate, Chief Reed. Boy, does he get around. But again, he was the right guy for the right rescue.

ON WATCH: Saugatuck, Michigan, May 20, 2001. While monitoring VHF-FM Channel 16 at the radio shack in South Haven on Sunday morning, I heard the Coast Guard radio operator at Group Grand Haven try several times to hail a 34-foot sailboat off Saugatuck Harbor. No response.

A 911 operator had contacted the Coast Guard after receiving a cell phone call from a boater off Saugatuck Harbor reporting he was about to go aground driven by high seas. He urgently needed help. Coast Guard Rescue Coordination Center called Station Holland and directed the duty boat crew to make "best possible speed." My heart went out to the Coast Guard boat crew at Holland, facing an eight-mile run to the sailboat's position under those conditions.

As the crew broke the Holland pier heads, a white, wind-swept sea greeted them. The 25-foot rigid hull inflatable blasted sea spray skyward as it plowed south, propelled by following seas. At open throttle, the 25-foot inflatable, as coasties affectionately call the 'rocket,' can reach 42 knots. In those hostile seas, 24 knots was a ball-busting challenge. I've run before the storm with Reed and Beatty the coxswain, and between them they share 40 years of running Coast Guard search and rescue boats. When they told me later that 24-four knots was pushing it I gave them a thumbs up.

Just off the entrance to Holland harbor, Beatty and Reed spotted the floundering sailboat close to the surf line, with an anchor trailing off its stern and seas spilling into the cockpit. The anchor line training off the stern immediately told the Coast Guard crew the experience level of those aboard.

Seas relentlessly drove the sloop, with its anchor dragging, towards the surf line. For the coasties, the anchor line, more than the elemental madness, offered the greatest threat. Snag it with the rescue boat's outboard screws and experience a joint grounding. Haul the anchor aboard, and accelerate the sloop's race to shore. As six to eight-foot seas bolted the stern upward, the anchor line would yank it down, creating a violent seesaw effect that on the down stroke flooded the cockpit. What choices? Deal with the violent seesawing, or the nearby breaking surf. Beatty elected to leave the anchor down.

During Beatty's first approach, seas slammed the Coast Guard boat against the sloop as coasties yanked off the first terrorized soul. She cried out, "Thank you! Thank you!" until Beatty bluntly told her to "shut up," he couldn't hear his crewmen over her adrenalin outbursts. It took four more roller coaster, knee-popping approaches, before Chief Reed, coasties Douglas, and Alexander pulled the remaining crewman onto the inflatable.

This old senior chief couldn't be prouder of that Coast Guard crew. I asked Beatty later if he was nervous. He said, "I was too focused on getting those people off to be nervous."

A 34-foot sloop found its way onto the beach south of South Haven Michigan after a Coast Guard crew rescued four crewmen in eight-foot seas off the harbor entrance at Saugatuck, Michigan.

BOAT SMART BRIEF: I spoke with the Captain, John Thomas, and his daughter, Heather, during salvage operations. The sloop had first run aground off Holland, but Lake Michigan had sucked it off the beach; then the lake after toying with it for a while again drove it aground two miles south of South Haven Harbor. Heather graciously opened her log for me to read. Of the four persons aboard, three had never been on a sailboat. Sea sickness and panic rendered two crew members useless.

The skipper, John Thomas, an ex-navy search and rescue specialist, said his daughter, Heather, performed with "true grit." Conditions forced him to stay at the helm while his daughter staggered about the vomit-smeared deck. She struggled to free the anchor and drag it aft. With seas slamming the sloop about, Thomas feared losing her off the bow, which was a good call. He directed her to drag the anchor aft. Thomas fired off a hand-held flare, but hot ash ran down his arm; he tossed it overboard. He had a flare gun aboard but no 12-guage flare cartridges. Apparently, an electrical short cut out his engine and radio. A crewman made a frantic call to 911; they, in turn hailed the Coast Guard. He could not have made port at Saugatuck under sail, not with that crew.

After I read a segment of Heather's log regarding the ordeal I wondered if something supernatural earmarked the sloop. Sailors, you know, are naturally superstitious. Her log read: "The sloop was struck by lightning and went to the bottom on Memorial weekend a year ago. She went aground on a Memorial weekend a year before that, and this Memorial weekend she ran aground again." Heather further wrote: "I put my arm around my dad's shoulder and said: 'The next time you buy a cursed boat I think a little more research is in order." And, Heather, I might add a little more training.

May I also suggest, next Memorial weekend, plan the family gathering at a bowling alley. Also, you may want to change the sloop's name: *Freudian Sloop*. Could that be what aroused Lake Michigan? Whatever, one thing is for certain, she devours her wounded. Boat Smart, deny her the opportunity.

This final story reveals what a user-friendly Lake Michigan can do when it suddenly turns ugly for boaters floundering near shore. The stories also graphically reveal again the challenges Coast Guard crews face while attempting to assist boaters near shore.

ON WATCH: Coast Guard Station St. Joseph, Michigan, July 4, 2002. The report of a possible drowning off the South Haven pier had Chief Larry Ahlin of Coast Guard Station St. Joseph transferring command of the 47-foot motor lifeboat over to Coast Guardsman Joe Margherome.

The plan was to send the 47-foot motor lifeboat 22 miles north to conduct search patterns off South Haven pier. Meanwhile, Ahlin would wrap up the security patrol for the fireworks show that had just ended at the mouth of St. Joseph Harbor.

Now aboard the station's 23-foot rescue boat, Ahlin figured it would be an uneventful closing to an evening that found little need for rescue resources. So he thought.

Before the fireworks began, the Coast Guard received a call from a 31-foot power boat anchored three-and- half miles south of the harbor, reporting engine problems. The captain elected to drop the anchor and watch the fireworks. Besides, with the harbor mouth secured, there was little the Coast Guard crew could do until the show ended. At the time of the call, the seas were calm but began to build during the fireworks. Oh, how Lake Michigan enjoys setting up boaters.

Soon after the 47-foot motor lifeboat departed for South Haven, Chief Ahlin received a call again from the skipper of a disabled boat reporting that his anchor was dragging. When Chief Ahlin and his crew reached the boat, it was bobbing on its anchor line in nine feet of water, within yards of a sand bar. In order to take the boat in tow, the Coast Guard crew had to de-anchor the boat. Its anchor line was tending off the bow into the seas. Besides taking heavy strain the anchor was also dragging as well.

Chief Ahlin came along the bucking boat with his bow into the waves. Lake water rained down on the crew as the bow slammed into six foot waves. A crew member hooked the anchor line with a skiff hook. Chief Ahlin throttled ahead in the shallow water while the line attached to the anchor line took strain. A simple maneuver, if performed in

Coast Guard small boats offer a quick means to reach people in distress.

calm seas, but the Coast Guard crew was dealing with a rapid, rap-slap wave action with sand bars just yards to leeward. They also had to deal with a seasick family—two adults and two children throwing up over the deck.

Hopefully, the skiff hook attached to the anchor line would ride down the line to the anchor, thus allowing the anchor line to become a tow line. When Chief Ahlin came ahead, the skiff hook eye took strain on the anchor line, and as the boats moved ahead, the anchor took hold and the line tended underneath the disabled boat. Chief Ahlin directed the skipper to bring in the anchor with his automatic windlass, but the strain on the anchor line rendered the windlass useless. He then ordered the skipper to cut the anchor line, but he did not have a knife. All the while, both boats were rapidly drifting back towards the beach with two hundred feet of towline worming about.

Now what? The Coast Guard crew now had to deal with several hundred feet of tow line snaking off the rescue boat's stern while Chief Ahlin backed down on the disabled craft. The staccato wave motion beat into the small rescue boat's bow, forcing it broadside to the sea. If that happened, there was a good chance the tow line would get wrapped in the rescue craft's prop.

Working the throttles and wheel like a drummer in beat, Chief backed down, keeping the bow into the seas not an easy task with a light bow falling off to the wind. Coast Guard auxiliarist David Gould broke off the tow line attached to the anchor. Then Coast Guardsmen Shawn Barnes and Kevin Stryker performed an amazing feat. Again using the skiff hook, they hooked the boat's trailer eye, a U-shaped bolt that is attached to the bow at water's edge. In those sea conditions, it was like threading the eye of a needle while bouncing on trampoline. Even more amazing, the heaving, tossing boats never touched.

While towing the boat out to open water, the crew received another call of a 24-foot powerboat in the surf one-half mile south of the St. Joseph pier. Now in open water, Ahlin ordered the skipper to drop the anchor. Within moments, the Coast Guard crew lay off the disabled boat. Night had fallen and due to darkness, the high surf, and the boat's proximity to shore, the Coast Guard boat crew could do little but standby. Overhead, a Coast Guard helicopter hovered, providing night light to the floundering 24-foot pleasure craft as it washed up onto rocks. Coast Guard personnel and local police assisted the four people aboard off the boat. Although badly shaken, none required medical care. Perhaps a serious underwear change out.

But the night's work wasn't over yet. A 20-foot speed boat came ashore near the 24-footer. This vessel quickly filled with water and swamped before rescuers could respond. The folks aboard walked ashore.

Meanwhile, the 47-foot motor lifeboat's mission ended the eventful night on a tragic note. Two teens had swum from shore out to the South Haven pier head. One of them made it up a ladder; the other was carried away by heavy seas and drowned.

BOAT SMART BRIEF: I could get into the wherefores, but I'm more concerned about the root cause of these events. That recreational boaters so often find themselves in harm's way suggests they simply don't recognize the danger, or they simply ignore the danger, and when danger calls, many are simply unprepared to deal with it. Or they labor under the illusion that the Coast Guard will bail them out. Unfortunately the boaters dumped onto the St. Joe beach learned the hard way that Coast Guard crews and boats do have limitations and that processing successful rescues as with these cases is not always possible. Two boats were wrecked, a life was lost and if not for the Coast Guard crew, there would have been a third boat lost, and possibly lives as well.

A Manistee boat crew rushs an injured mariner to a Coast Guard helicopter. Coast Guard surface and air crews often team up on MEDIVAC emergencies on the water.

That said, the Coast Guard may have saved the wrecked vessels off the St. Joseph beach had there been sufficient boats and crews available to assist. But isn't that common for most rescue agencies whether it be land or sea, the capacity to assist people hinges a great deal on the availability of resource assets and personnel.

The Coast Guard's resource limitations and its capacity to assist mariners fortunately is bolstered, as with other rescue agencies, by volunteers. Thank God for these good folks who often make a difference with a mission outcome. The Coast Guard's volunteer force is known as the Coast Guard Auxiliary. These dedicated souls play a key role in filling Coast Guard resource gaps.

FILLING THE GAPS

The Coast Guard Auxiliary, America's Volunteer Life Savers, play an important role in Coast Guard operations. And if I had my way, I would change its primary name from auxiliary to Volunteer Life Savers or Citizen Patriots. Auxiliary just doesn't cut it, there is nothing secondary about their contributions to the Coast Guard, as the word "auxiliary" suggests. They are to the Coast Guard as "the bench" is to professional sports. Try playing without them.

The Volunteer Life Savers' contributions to the Coast Guard on Lake Michigan are well-documented, and perhaps their most profound contribution is stitching together the gaps in the Coast Guard's far-reaching Lake Michigan search and rescue network. Coast Guard volunteers provide 24-7 coverage in remote areas such as Escanaba, Michigan, located in Little Bay De Noc, tucked away above Green Bay. Bay De Noc is a three-hour boat trip from the nearest Coast Guard search and rescue facility at Sturgeon Bay.

In lower Green Bay, Volunteer Life Savers staff and operate a Coast Guard 28-foot rescue boat, performing most Coast Guard missions except law enforcement. Volunteer Life Savers do, however, support law enforcement missions by standing radio watches and filling search and rescue billets. At Station Wilmette, Chicago Volunteer Life Savers man a 24-foot search and rescue boat. This frees up boat crews so they can focus on law enforcement missions. Due in part to the support they received from their Volunteer Life Savers, Station Wilmette's Midnight Badger law enforcement teams bagged 71 drunk boaters during 2004, more drunk citations than any other Coast Guard station nationwide.

Across the lake in Michigan City, Volunteer Life Saver Ed Ross, age 64, qualified as crewman on the station's 47-foot motor lifeboat (MLB). He met all the boat qualification requirements including passing a physical fitness test required of Coast Guard crewman one-third his age. Ross now fills a crewman billet aboard the MLB, which frees up a qualified law enforcement officer. Chief Paul Decker, Officer in Charge Michigan City said, "We have limited personnel to fill operational billets. When Ed filled the MLB billet it provided that extra body we needed to form a special law enforcement unit that focused strictly on law enforcement and specifically on removing drunk boaters off the water." It sure paid off. During 2004, Station Michigan City crews nabbed 23 drunk boaters.

In Traverse City, Michigan, twin flotillas cover East and West Traverse Bays, providing gap coverage between Coast Guard Stations Frankfort and Charlevoix, Michigan. Further to the south the Coast Guard Auxiliary in South Haven alone has conducted over 1,500 search and rescue cases, assisted over 4,000 boaters, and helped save more than 25 million dollars in property.

What makes the operation at South Haven unique is that the Volunteer Life Savers staff the entire operational from standing radio watches, to providing their own boats, to operational planning. It's just like a Coast Guard Station except for its unique paging system.

The primary search and rescue platform is the 50-foot tug *Wilhemn Baum*. The duty boat crew carries pagers that can simultaneously receive a voice command directing them to the *Baum*. Jim Bradley and Leon Sowell have crewed together for over 28 years. They are as seasoned as any Coast Guard crew on Lake Michigan. The local fire department will page them at any time. I know. I once took park in a rescue with them until 3:00 a.m.

Captain Jim Bradley and his wife Sheral sit on the *Wilhelm Baum's* stern deck. The *Baum's* crew, along with fellow Auxiliary members have assisted South Haven boaters for more than 25 years, conducting over 1,500 search and rescue cases.

These volunteers are not retired either. The citizen lifesavers work out arrangements with their employers that allow them to leave work if paged. Bradley, a licensed electrician, calls his own shots, and Sowell plans his work schedule so he can be available during busy boating days like weekends or holidays.

Leon's wife, Pat, has been a radio watchstander and an Officer of the Day at South Haven for over twenty-eight years, and is one of the most experienced radio watchstander in Coast Guard Group Grand Haven. I asked Pat why she gives so much of her time. She quoted her husband Leon: "The service we perform for others is the rent we pay for the space we occupy here on earth." The Grand Haven crew has certainly paid its rent in full.

Volunteer Life Savers perform another gap support role that definitely helps with operational training. They supply their own boats so boat and air station personnel can achieve training objectives. It's normal during spring to see Coast Guard boat crews actively involved in training on Lake Michigan. If you look closely you most likely will also see a Coast Guard auxiliary boat nearby. And the Volunteer Life Savers have proven to be invaluable in filling operational gaps by supplying crews and boats for safety security zones for major marine events like fireworks and major powerboat races. Look around next time you attend one of these events, you most likely will see a Volunteer Life Saver volunteering his or her time or boat to assure you're safe on the water.

A key way in which they keep people safe on the water is by conducting vessel safety checks on recreational boats. At Manistee, Volunteer Life Savers annually conduct nearly 300 vessel checks a year. During 2004, they scored amongst the top five nationwide in vessel safety checks.

It truly takes a total Coast Guard team effort to meet an ever-increasing demand for assistance on the water as more and more boaters access the Lake Michigan marine environment. The challenge will be to husband limited rescue resources through smarter boating practices by the public. The last thing rescue responders need is to have rescue resources squandered by needless mishaps or, in some cases by personal agendas.

That brings us to a subject that has gnawed at me for years: those who selfishly use rescue resources to search for loved ones or friends. To put it more bluntly self-serving overdue reports made to the Coast Guard by those seeking the whereabouts of wayward boaters and I don't necessarily mean boaters lost upon the waters.

NEEDLESS OVERDUE CALLS DEPLETE RESOURCES

Boat Smart Anchor Points

Volunteer Life Savers Contributions to the Nation 2003

Facilities:

↔ 35,287 Members
↔ 4,899 Operational Boats
↔ 277 Operational Aircraft
↔ 2,682 Operational Radio Stations

Contributions:

↔ Patrol Hours: 755,498
↔ Vessel Safety Checks: 109,462
↔ Marine Dealer Visits: 52,740 providing boating safety material for the public
↔ Commercial Fishing Vessel Exams: 1,344
↔ Boating Safety Classes: 26,005/107,745 graduates

↔ Patrols: 33,022 resulting in 9,798 persons assisted and 353 live saved
↔ Total Contributions Hours: 4,302,791 hours at a total output value of $80.8 million to the nation.

For information on the Coast Guard Auxiliary search the web under Coast Guard Auxiliary. For information on the U.S. Power Squadron search under same.

There are three major distracters that needlessly deplete rescue resources: hoax calls, boaters in distress unable to provide a position, and frivolous overdue reports generated by third parties. Unfounded overdue cases can be costly, especially for Coast Guard aircraft not just in dollars but in precious fuel burn time. Flying about searching for seemingly overdue boaters can find an aircraft in a fuel-critical state if suddenly needed for a real emergency.

The following air rescue story describes how a Coast Guard HH-65 Dolphin helicopter faced a fuel critical situation after being diverted from a frivolous overdue case to assist a 30-foot power boat taking on water on Lake Huron near Mackinac Straits. It's also another example of physical limitations Coast Guard crews face over which they have little control. Had not the boater in the following story been squared away the outcome could have proven disastrous if the pilot had to spent critical fuel time dealing with an inept boater. Bear with me as the story leads away from the chapter theme; however, the valuable lessons learned regarding surface-air rescues must be passed on.

ON WATCH: Mackinac Straits, Lake Huron, September 4, 2002. When Lon Bruck, 65, and his wife Vivian, 61, and their three-year-old Cocker Spaniel, Nick, departed Harrisville, Michigan, midday aboard their 30-foot Bayliner, they had no idea that within hours they would end up in the belly of a Coast Guard HH-65 Dolphin helicopter.

"When we departed Harrisville, southerly winds offered little concern," said Bruck. However, as they headed north on Lake Huron towards Presque Isle, Michigan, the winds shifted to the northwest. By the time the Brucks reached Thunder Bay, the winds funneling through the Straits of Mackinac had whipped surface waters into seven-footers with an occasional eight to ten roaming amongst the mix, reported Bruck.

For the experienced captain, it offered a challenge, but one the 30-foot Bayliner could handle, until. "We began taking on water near Thunder Bay," said Bruck. "I thought it was coming from the engine compartment, but soon discovered water coming from the forward cabin. My poor wife and dog were huddled under the galley table, water swirling around them." As the bow dipped into the seas, the prop rose above the surface; vibrations surged through the hall as the prop zoomed. As the helm grew more sluggish Bruck sensed a disaster in the making.

Bruck fired off a "Mayday" over Channel 16 VHF-FM, the International Hailing and Distress frequency. At 1:30 p.m., Coast Guard Group Sault Ste. Marie picked up the Mayday call along with GPS coordinates Bruck provided. Group Sault directed him and his wife to don life jackets, which they had already done, including one for the dog. Later Bruck said, "Life jackets are more important than that stupid boat. If it goes down, what good is it then?"

Group Sault Radio diverted a Coast Guard helicopter from an overdue case. At the time, the helicopter was 19 miles from the Bayliner. "When I arrived the boat's bow was digging into the seas," said Lieutenant Chuck Webb, the Coast Guard pilot. An island lay two miles away, but Webb scrubbed the option. Attempting to reach it would place the unstable craft broadside to the seas. As if reading the pilot's mind, Bruck requested an airlift.

While hovering over the target, the helicopter's rotor roar stifled radio communications. "It forced us to fly two to three miles away to communicate hoisting instructions," said Webb. "He had lots of fishing gear on the stern." The fishing poles and down riggers posed a serious threat to the aircraft, should the gear get sucked up into the rotor blades or become fouled in the hoist cable.

Even from three miles away, Webb found the communications difficult; "It was frustrating; he didn't understand the need to remove the gear." His copilot, Lieutenant Greg Torgersen, worked the radio with Group Sault and with a nearby freighter, in the event they needed their assistance. Meanwhile, he kept a sharp eye on the fuel gauges as the aircraft guzzled fuel.

Group Sault radio relayed the pilot's concerns to the captain. "He removed the gear except for fishing net. We were reaching a fuel critical point in the mission. We had to go in, net or not," said Webb.

As Webb hovered towards the boat, flight mechanic Louis Bishop began calling out distances. Once over the boat, Webb could not see it. At that point, the flight mechanic directed the pilot with terse left, right, forward, back directions while the pilot maintained a set altitude. Webb held position by using waves as a reference point, while occasionally glancing at his radar altimeter. Dropping a basket onto a heaving five-by-ten foot stern, in seven to ten foot seas, with 30-knot wind gusts buffeting the aircraft, demanded precise communications between the flight mechanic and pilot.

"While watching the basket swigging downward, I glanced over, and saw the fish net. I grabbed it and chucked it overboard," said Bruck. He sent his wife up first along with the dog, who peed all the way up and into the aircraft. What dog wouldn't (and even some humans) while swinging in a wire basket under a deafening rotor blast while being peppered by water pellets?

The husband then followed, although with less commotion. When they landed at the airport in Alpena, Mrs. Bruck fell into shock. Coast Guard rescue swimmer Matt Fetzner, who is also an EMT, treated her until an ambulance arrived. Later, Mr. Bruck said his wife didn't recall being hoisted up.

BOAT SMART BRIEF: Bruck believes the seas snapped loose his bow anchor that was secured to the forward deck. The anchor smashed through a port window on the forward bulkhead. The bilge pump couldn't keep up with the water inflow.

Later, a Coast Guard auxiliary boat out of Alpena attempted to take the boat in tow, but high seas forced them to turn it over to a commercial tow.

Lieutenant Webb had nothing but praise for Mr. Bruck. Lieutenant Webb said, "He did a lot of right things. He didn't panic. He immediately called the Coast Guard when he realized he was in danger. He provided an exact GPS location. They all wore life jackets, including the dog. And he monitored our radio traffic with Group Sault radio, which helped overcome the poor communications between our aircraft and his boat."

To get a feel for this story, I requested Lieutenant Webb hoist me off a 22-foot Coast Guard auxiliary boat on Lake Michigan and airlift me to a nearby airport. There he and his flight crew, Lieutenant Commander Chris Day, and Chief Brian Buck, would brief me on the case. No, I didn't pee while ascending up into the belly of the helicopter, although I could certainly understand the urge.

At the airport, we discussed practical measures people can take when stranded and at odds with the maritime environment and in need of air assistance. The book will address these defensive measures in the next chapter. For now, let's get back on center: frivolous overdue calls to the Coast Guard or 911 that needlessly deplete resources. There is no better example of a frivolous overdue call than the following story.

ON WATCH: Lake Macatawa, Holland, Michigan, Saturday, July 22, 2001, 7:21 p.m. An Ottawa County 911 dispatcher notified Coast Guard Group Grand Haven that a woman had called them about several males operating personal water craft (PWC) who had failed to return to a DNR boat ramp on Lake Macatawa. When the woman notified Ottawa County 911, it was dark, and her newfound friends she had just met that evening had failed to return.

Reportedly, the PWC operators told her to wait at the boat ramp while they retrieved gear from a nearby location but they failed to tell her the location. A DNR officer overheard their conversation and advised the two male operators that they must be off the water an hour before sunset,

which allowed them about 45 minutes to retrieve their gear and get back to the ramp. They advised the DNR officer they would comply.

So, now begins yet another overdue predicament that leads to a serious of unanswered questions void of clues. Where were the mavericks? Were they stranded on Lake Michigan? Did they change their plans? If so, why didn't they return to the boat launch as promised, or at least call? Should the Coast Guard ignore the woman's concerns? After all, it was a balmy, peaceful night. Does the Coast Guard assume they are young and irresponsible? Lots of unanswered questions. However, the Coast Guard knew for certain that the PWC operators had failed to return to the boat ramp. Their truck sat parked in a nearby lot. The Coast Guard launched.

Coast Guard Station Holland's 25-foot inflatable and a Coast Guard Auxiliary vessel conducted a shoreline search along Lake Michigan with a search light. Dozens of personal water craft dotted the shore, but none matched the description of the two overdue craft. Meanwhile, a Coast Guard HH-65 Dolphin helicopter swept the open waters off Holland with its "night sun." On Lake Macatawa, Ottawa marine sheriff deputies searched the lake and local marinas. Two Ottawa patrol cars joined the hunt. The search extended eight miles south to Saugatuck Harbor where marine sheriff deputies combed the harbors and open waters of Kalamazoo Lake. From Station Grand Haven, a 21-foot inflatable steamed south, sweeping the shoreline with its search light.

Nothing.

By 4:00 a.m., the Coast Guard command suspended the search until first light. They bagged the exhausted Holland crew who had exceeded boat crew fatigue standards. After resuming the search at first light, searchers received a break around 10:00 a.m. One of the PWC operators called the Coast Guard after responding to a notification that searchers placed on their windshield. In all, nine rescue resources were deployed, involving twenty personnel and over twenty-five resource hours. All the while, the two lads were spending the night at the waterfront home of a friend.

As for the female who reported the overdue, she had long since gone home.

This was not an overdue case, but a case of a young lady using the system to locate two young men who reportedly offered to provide her a ride home and then stood her up. Sadly, too often self-serving motives are the impetus behind overdue reports, as callers manipulate the Coast Guard and other rescue agencies to track down their domestic strays under the guise of an overdue. Example: one night at Station Manistee, we received a call late Saturday night from a woman reporting that her husband and chums took off to fish during their wedding reception that afternoon and had failed to return.

We made a quick sweep of the marinas along the Manistee river. I've been there and done this before tracking down domestic strays, and bingo! We found his boat moored alongside a bar dock. We knew where that marriage was headed when we found the husband with his buddies drinking in a bar rather than doing whatever with his bride on their honeymoon night. It was headed towards the rocks if not already there.

Please, don't take me wrong. There are legitimate overdue cases. One early evening at Station Manistee, I received a call from a woman concerned about her husband, who had failed to return from a local fishing trip at 3:00 p.m. as promised. She provided a description of the boat and her husband. A feeling of dread swept over me. That afternoon around 1:30 p.m. the station's duty boat crew had responded to a report of a vessel running in circles off Manistee's North Pier. When the crew arrived on scene they discovered an unconscious male slumped over helm. The crew jumped aboard an immediately began rescue breathing and then CPR. But to no avail the man had taken his last fishing trip. I had the mournful task of passing this sad news to the woman. Her husband, age 38, died from a massive heart attack. Welcome to the heartbreaking side of search and rescue.

Let me counter this sad story with a happy-ending overdue case that began with another woman's concern for her husband who also had failed to return from a fishing trip as promised. Beside providing lessons learned it demonstrates just how many resources it can take to process a successful overdue case.

ON WATCH: On August 25, 2003, the Coast Guard received a telephone call from Tricia Young that her husband and a friend, Vern Uricek, had departed early that morning for Rockport, Michigan, to go salmon fishing. According to a message Uricek left on his answering machine, he would be returning home to Gaylord, Michigan, that same day around noon. At 4:00 p.m., Tricia Young called the Coast Guard after the fishermen had failed to show up. Local authorities checked the public boat ramp where the fisherman had launched an 18-foot Sea Ray boat. They located the fisherman's vehicle and boat trailer, but no boat. While local officials checked marinas, Coast Guard surface and air units commenced searching the waters off Rockport, Michigan, which is located 75 miles south of the Mackinac Straits.

The Coast Guard pilot reported the following weather conditions on August 26, 11:21 a.m.: wind speed: 25 knots, wind direction: 350 true, air temp: 64 degrees, water temp: 64 degrees , wave height: eight feet; sky condition: clear.

At 2:21 p.m. of August 26th the aircrew spotted a debris field that included a life vest, seat cushions and two homemade buoys. Lieutenant Commander (LCDR) Seaman, the command pilot of a Coast Guard HH-65 Dolphin helicopter began a search of the immediate area. At 4:03 p.m. the aircrew spotted a man in the water.

LCDR Day, Assistant Operations boss at Coast Guard Traverse air, later told me a swim noodle that the victim was holding onto is what the aircrew first spotted. They hoisted him aboard with the aid of a rescue swimmer, nearly 31 hours after the boat sank.

His fishing mate faired far better: he made it to Middle Island after spending 20 hours in the water. At approximately 4:00 a.m. of the 26th, he crawled up onto the beach and broke into a keeper's lodge used to host island visitors. "My heart was fluttering. I fell onto a cot and dozed in and out of sleep," said Uricek.

After dawn broke, he set out searching for a link with the outside world. There was no one on the island, and he couldn't find a telephone or radio to call for help. "I placed a large stop sign on the beach, spray-painted an S.O.S. on a carpet and laid it out, and then wandered across the island holding an American flag over my head hoping it would attract the Coast Guard aircrew."

It did.

"When the helicopter landed, I asked the air crewman, how was John, expecting the worst. When the crewman told me he was alive and on board, it floored me. I thought I was a goner after spending 20 hours in the lake. That John spent 11 more hours in the water speaks volumes for his will to survive," said Mr. Uricek, who attributes their survival to a fierce determination to live, and to a *life jacket*.

BOAT SMART BRIEF: Bear with me as I deviate a moment from the overdue issue to pass important lessons learned. So how did the fisherman end up in the water? Mr. Uricek told me around 9:00 a.m. they were trolling around seven miles northeast of the Middle Island, into one to two foot seas. A wave broke over the open bow, dumping several gallons of water onto the boat. A second wave followed and within seconds the boat filled with water. "There was nothing we could do. The bilge pump couldn't keep up with the flooding, and when John raised the engine, the boat rolled, and we ended up fighting our way through downriggers and fishing lines to escape." Uricek passed a swimming noodle that had floated free to his buddy and being a capable swimmer set out for Middle Island for help.

Uricek told me that during the night a Coast Guard helicopter passed overhead, flooding him in its night sun, but fluttered away. "Apparently they failed to spot me in the white wind-streaked seas. Since then I've purchased a strobe light for my life jacket, and will never go out again on a boat without wearing it and a life jacket," said Uricek. In all, the Coast Guard deployed one Falcon Jet, a C-130 a four-engine fixed-wing aircraft, two HH-65 helicopters and one 47-foot Motor Life Boat, totaling 33 resources hours. In addition, local rescue agencies provided resources. Cost: thousands of dollars. A life saved: priceless.

Less than two weeks later the Coast Guard would be drawn into another legitimate overdue case.

ON WATCH: Frankfort, Michigan, September 14, 2003. Dennis Formosa had set out from Frankfort, Michigan, aboard a 21-foot Thompson boat to go fishing. He called his boat *"Lucky Lady,"* a name well chosen, as time would tell. After fishing with several of his buddies off the Frankfort pier head on Thursday afternoon, he dropped them off and headed back alone.

Two days later he was expected at a family wedding, but failed to appear. His son, Tony Formosa, called the Frankfort Coast Guard, who in turn called their parent command at Group Grand Haven. All indications suggested an urgent overdue case unfolding. The search and rescue system began steaming.

The only clue provided to the search coordinators at Grand Haven came from the overdue fisherman. While dropping his buddies off mid-day Thursday, he boasted about a hot date he had that night with a redhead who worked at a local tackle shop. The Group Duty Officer, Keith Brown, called the shop. The owner advised the coastie the only redhead that worked in his shop was his wife, and she had departed for Houston, Texas, several days ago.

Oh my! Now what? Launch the resources.

In all, the Coast Guard would deploy rescue boats from four stations in Michigan and Wisconsin, two helicopters from Coast Guard Traverse City Air Station, one Coast Guard 140-foot cutter, a Canadian C-130, an Eagle III helicopter from County Rescue Service in Green Bay, a 48-foot Coast Guard auxiliary vessel, and support resources from local and state public safety agencies.

As air and surface crews combed the expanse of upper Lake Michigan, Dennis Formosa had been drifting northward on Lake Michigan, driven by a stiff southerly winds that arrived shortly after the motor suffered a cracked cylinder head.

On Thursday evening, while drifting east of South Manitou Island, he spotted a northbound freighter. He fired off two flares, but the freighter sounded four blasts and continued on its way without notifying the Coast Guard. He normally carried a cell phone, but unfortunately had left it in his vehicle. "I was getting really nervous out there. I ran out of french fries on Friday and had nothing more to eat. I tied a tee shirt to the mast, but what saved me was my pee bucket."

He told me that the seas kept spilling into the boat, so he tied a line to the handle of the bucket and threw it overboard. The bucket acted as a sea drogue, which placed the boat at a 45-degree angle to the seas, resulting in no further intake of water over the gunwale.

On Sunday afternoon, a Canadian C-130 spotted the drifting boat west of Beaver Island. The crew vectored a Coast Guard Auxiliary vessel to the boat. Coast Guard Auxiliarist Perry Lane, skipper of the 49-foot Carver that made the rescue, told me later that the operator was badly dehydrated and that he had not had a drink of water in three days. Asked why he didn't drink from the lake, he responded, "I'm from the Detroit River area." He also told Lane that he thought he was a goner.

The skipper had good reason to be concerned. Shortly after the auxiliary crew picked him up and transferred him to the 140-foot cutter *Biscayne Bay*, the wind shifted from the south to the north and seas were rapidly building, driven by 35-knot winds. In fact, it became so rough that the cutter could not take the 21-foot boat in tow. It later drifted onto Beaver Island.

BOAT SMART BRIEF: This captain was certainly squared away; earlier in the season he passed a vessel safety check conducted by the Coast Guard Auxiliary. Due to no fault of his own he experienced an engine casualty. He fired off several flares, which a motor vessel ignored, and during the ordeal he wore a life jacket; at least he was wearing one when the auxiliary crew rescued him. That no one missed him until he failed to appear at a wedding Saturday afternoon suggests the lack of a float plan. Had he notified someone of his fishing plans and an expected return time to port on Thursday, the search process would have been activated much sooner. I can't stress enough the importance of a float plan shared with family members or friends, followed up with a confirmation that the voyage has ended.

The last two overdue cases demonstrate the capacity of rescue responders and their resources to effect a successful search and rescue. As evidenced the process can be a very intense with high stakes at play. To degrade this remarkable life-saving process with frivolous overdue reports as with the young lady reporting the overdue PWC operators not only diminishes the capacity of rescue responders, it limits already limited rescue resources from performing bona-fide search and rescue missions.

Hopefully those who make frivolous overdue calls now realize in so doing they are degrading the entire search and rescue system. The entire system also includes other agencies that compliment Coast Guard missions. Now let's move on to see how those agencies boaster the Coast Guard mission capabilities.

Boat Smart Anchor Points

How to avoid needless overdue calls

↬ Most overdue reports stem from poor communications. A boater fails to inform loved ones of changed plans, such as unexpected stay over, unforeseen mechanical problems, prolonged fishing plans, and so on. Boaters should always inform family or friends of their boating plans. This does not mean a casual "we're going boating" notice, but the why, where, and when the boating will take place, and the boat's description and name. If plans change, always update your contact so that if an emergency develops, searchers will have an idea as to your whereabouts. And don't hesitate to call the Coast Guard if you suspect a loved one might be concerned about your whereabouts. A moment's call can prevent hours spent in needless searching.

Understand that Lake Michigan is a vast and complex marine environment with a myriad of bays, outlets, connecting lakes and river channels that hold hundreds of marinas and boat launches. The vague and often clueless callers concerned about the whereabouts of a loved one could make Sherlock Homes scratch his head. It's your call. Make it wisely.

STRONG LAW ENFORCEMENT ACCORD

The capacity of the Coast Guard to carry out search and rescue and law enforcement missions on Lake Michigan would indeed be limited if not for support of fellow response agencies. These agencies make up an intricate part of Lake Michigan's maritime safety net. I've been involved in hundreds of search and rescue cases and law enforcement missions, and nearly always the support of fellow agencies has played a key role. I firmly believe that the Coast Guard's capability to carry out its maritime responsibilities would be severely diminished without these key players.

I suspect many boaters view the various marine agencies that operate on the waters as fragmented entities each serving their own agendas. This erroneous perspective has blind sighted many a boater. Woe be it to the boater who discovers the hard way that to mess with one is to mess with all, and this particularly holds true regarding drunk boaters. The boater in the following story probably wished he had corked the bottle before being corked by the collective strong-arm of the law.

ON WATCH: Coast Guard Group Grand Haven June 13, 2003, 4:03 a.m. The Communications Specialist on watch in the Group Operations Center received a call from 911 that a boat had collided with the Grand Haven North Pier. Within minutes, a Coast Guard 23-foot rescue boat along with a 47-foot motor life boat arrived at the North Pier. There, boat crews discovered an empty 21-foot Bayliner lying alongside the seaward side of the pier.

Meanwhile, the Grand Haven police responded from ashore and apprehended three adult males racing down the pier away from the empty boat. Ottawa County marine deputies soon arrived on scene. The young men told marine sheriff deputies that a fourth person, who was operating

the boat, went overboard and disappeared when the boat struck the pier. They were running for help.

The Coast Guard called in air search and rescue and Ottawa County marine divers. What appeared at first to be a law enforcement issue now found search and rescue at the forefront. However, while questioning the young men, Ottawa marine deputy Sergeant Kevin Allman detected the odor of alcohol. Smelling a rat, he pointed first to the Coast Guard helicopter overhead, then to the Coast Guard rescue boats searching nearby waters, and finally to marine sheriff divers and said, "See that helicopter, those Coast Guard rescue boats, those marine divers, those police units? If that fourth guy you claim went overboard is bogus, you will be billed for the cost of those assets."

Two of the young lads sang out like jail birds, confessing to sergeant Allman that the boat operator concocted the story. A background check revealed the operator was facing a possible third alcoholic conviction. Sergeant Allman read him like an oft-read book. That experience, those street smarts, and instant access to state and local law enforcement data are invaluable to the Coast Guard in its efforts to crack down on impaired boaters around Lake Michigan.

During the 2004 Grand Haven Coast Guard festival, I witnessed firsthand how efficient this law enforcement accord can jell. On departing Station Grand Haven, moments before the fireworks began, I watched a Coast Guard boat crew along with an Ottawa County marine boat crew escort a suspected drunk boater to the Coast Guard moorings. The crews handed the boater over to fellow officers on the dock, who processed the case. The boat crews then returned to the river channel, joining DNR and Coast Guard Auxiliary boats enforcing the fireworks safety zone.

The joint task force had already nabbed four other drunks that evening. If these boaters mistakenly thought that law enforcement units would be too involved in enforcing the fireworks safety zone, they received a sobering rebut. And for boozed up boaters who seek the blackness of night to veil them against the intruding eye of law enforcement, they better open their eyes and look around for the vigilant eye of the Badger could be upon them.

During the 2004 boating season, Coast Guard Group Milwaukee unleashed Operation Midnight Badger. Designated Coast Guard Badger boat crews, with support from local law enforcement agencies, roamed the nighttime waters from Calumet Harbor, Chicago, to Washington Island, Wisconsin. These highly-trained Badger crews can readily spot a besotted boat operator: the strong odor of alcohol, slurred speech, bloodshot eyes, beer cans and the like strewed about on the boat, and repetitive babble. All readily portray a Badger target.

Between 2004 and 2005, Badger crews nailed 336 drunk boaters during late night patrols that often found Badger boat crews ushering in a new day. May this also be the dawn of an aggressive campaign that will continue to track, apprehend and remove drunk boaters off the waters.

Operation Midnight Badger offers a side benefit-homeland security. Since Badger crews randomly stop boaters, those boaters harboring 911 aspirations could be caught in the net. Coast Guard crews have instant access by cell phone or marine radio to intelligence sources, both federal and local, that can produce timely information, whether it be about ma and pa or Bonnie and Clyde.

And should the inquire yield a "high target" item, the Coast Guard has on beckon the support of local law enforcement agencies like the Chicago Police Department's Special Operations Section. This cadre of police officers are made up of "Special Response Teams," including the Marine Unit, that are well-armed, to protect the citizens of Chicagoland.

When I met the Commanding Officer, Chicago's Police Marine Unit, Earl Zuelke Jr., the 38-year veteran, sporting a thick mustache and matching eyebrows, instantly reminded me of Wyatt Erup played by Kurt Russell in the movie Tombstone. Zuelke is what you call a street cop, and in spite of his high ranking title, he is as familiar with the Chicago waterfront as a veteran cop is of the street beat.

Take that experience, blend it with the Illinois Conservation Police and the United States Coast Guard, and what you have is a multi-agency complex that makes up the new "Chicago Marine Safety Station." This inter-agency facility is housed in the renovated old Coast Guard Station at the mouth of the Chicago River, Lake Michigan. There will be no left hand, right hand miscues regarding the joint tasks of promoting public safety and homeland security. Whereas the Coast Guard will benefit from the local knowledge these agencies offer, in turn these agencies will benefit from the open pipeline the Coast Guard has to federal databases and the Coast Guard's firepower. To mess with the Coast Guard is to mess with their military counterparts that are but a call away.

The Chicago Marine Police Unit, as with all municipal marine law enforcement agencies around like Michigan, actively contribute to search and rescue. I've served alongside a lot of these marine deputies, and more than once they have covered my backside.

Up the way from Chicago in Michigan City, Indiana, a Coast Guard alliance has also evolved that has different government agencies—local, state and federal—teaming up to answer the homeland security challenge. Coast Guard boat crews from Station Michigan City frequently team up with FBI agents, Indiana State Police, and local police and paramedics to conduct joint training on Lake Michigan. The training objective is to introduce land-based officers to the tight close-quarter rock-and-roll world of afloat law enforcement.

In September 2003, I rode aboard the *Little Murphy*, a Sea Scott training tug, manned by Coast Guard Auxiliary members attached to Station Michigan City. The drill involved street cops leaping from a Coast Guard small boat onto the stern of the tug and then taking down a hostile crew. I watched the small 23-foot Coast Guard boat approaching at a high rate of speed carrying at the bow a group of officers dressed like SWAT commandos. The Coast Guard coxswain eased up alongside the tug's starboard quarter. Within seconds, officers with weapons drawn scrambled aboard. Seconds later they charged onto the bridge where they manhandled the old senior chief in a fashion reminiscent of my Coast Guard law enforcement training. Thank goodness for that training, or else I might have been in need of a breeches change out. These SWAT guys meant business.

Their transition from street alleys to gangways was quite impressive, and what an asset they would be when the Coast Guard called for backup. That teamwork more than anything impressed me. Each brings specialties to the law enforcement table that they can now share, but it was not always like that, not by a long shot until along came 9/11.

Lastly, let's discuss calls made to the Coast Guard from the public regarding perceived dangers to people on boats or aircraft. These important players can often make the difference as to whether search and rescue is quickly processed or whether it turns into a "Condo Commander" wild goose chase that needlessly depletes search and rescue

A Coast Guard boat carrying a SWAT team made up of law enforcement personnel from the Michigan City area make ready to board the tug *Little Murphy* during law enforcement drills on Lake Michigan.

resources; thus reducing the capacity for rescuers to respond to bona-fide emergencies.

CONDO COMMANDERS

The catchy phrase "Condo Commander," is often heard in Coast Guard search and rescue circles. The title suggests a self-proclaimed commander perched in a beach front condo with beverage in hand, carrying out his duties as guardian of the Inland Seas. With a mere phone call, he can launch rescue boats, whether needed or not. Be that what it may, they can be a royal pain in the butt for search mission coordinators as the following On Watch cases reveal.

ON WATCH CASES: A Condo Commander called the Coast Guard in Michigan City, Indiana, from his waterfront roost and reported 50 aerial flares in the skies over Lake Michigan, which turned out to be red collision lights of aircraft in holding patterns off Chicago's O'Hare International airport. Another Condo Commander called Station Frankfort in early spring reporting a 40-foot-high iceberg in the Manitou Passage, which turned out to be a super structure of a large motor vessel. Coast Guardsman Jim Pierce received a call at Station Calumet, Chicago, from a pilot reporting an aircraft in the water off Meigs Field. It turned out to be his own aircraft's silhouette gliding across the water while inbound to Meigs. Then there's the woman who called Group Milwaukee, reporting seeing a sea dragon off Racine, Wisconsin. Whether the reporting parties were influenced by their favorite beverage one can only imagine, but beverage or not, Lake Michigan can play on the imagination.

To untrained eyes on shore, the water offshore often teases the eye. Small sailboats and wind surfers may appear doomed in the mist of wind-tossed seas. However, in my many years of responding to Condo Commander calls, many have failed to live up to the concerns of the reporting party. That isn't to say reporting sources on shore haven't proven to be lifesavers.

A sure method to help rescue responders to process successful rescue is for the reporting source on shore to keep their eye on the target. The following On Watch story reveals just how important it is for a reporting source on shore to stay vigilant.

ON WATCH: Manistee, Michigan, Lake Michigan, August 1985. A woman called Station Manistee from her home atop a bluff over-looking Lake Michigan. She had watched her 65-year-old husband repeatedly try to re-right his 14-foot Sunfish sailboat. She soon realized from her own sailing experience that he needed help.

She was right. A gusty offshore wind had him Wisconsin-bound. She called. We launched and found him clinging to the boat. Fortunately, he was wearing a life jacket. We pulled him aboard, strapped the sailboat alongside, wrapped him in blankets and beat back to Manistee.

Two years later, the radio watchstander at Manistee piped me to the mess deck. Moments later, a man greeted me with a hand shake, "Do you remember me? I'm Mr. Smith; you saved my life."

"Of course, I remember you," I replied, "But thank your wife, not me. She saved you."

I explained the two factors that prompted an urgent response. One, she kept an eye on her husband as she relayed her concerns over the telephone. Two, she knew from her own sailing experiences that he needed immediate help. But, of utmost importance, she kept her eye on her husband.

Too often, though, we find reporting sources racing off to seek help for what appears to be a boater in distress only to return later to find them nowhere in sight.

Now what?

Imagine the Coast Guard's dilemma. Do they launch boats, aircraft and request help from fellow rescue agencies? Once again, Coast Guard officials find themselves betwixt and between. Did the boat sail or motor away? Did it sink? Or was it a boat at all? One thing is certain: the caller opened Pandora's Box and could have easily closed it had he or she just stayed put and waited a while.

Understandably, the reporting party may not be near a phone, but unless it's an obvious life-threatening emergency, staying put to determine

Small sailcraft offer elusive targets for onshore eyes. Wind gusts can knock down the craft but within minutes they can be up, off and away.

the true nature of the concern is far better than running off half-cocked. Even if the emergency seems life-threatening, it still might not be an immediate do-or-die situation. But even if so, it may preclude a timely response unless rescue responders are nearby. In most cases, it is best to stay put and gather useful information to pass to authorities.

Also, call the Coast Guard, not 911. Coast Guard personnel are trained to ask questions specific to the marine environment, an unfamiliar area for many 911 operators. Besides, the 911 operator will call the Coast Guard anyway. To further complicate manners, the reporting party may fail to provide 911 a call-back number, or provide a wrong number, or lose communication due to a cell-phone dead spot. The importance of maintaining an open line with rescuers can't be understated.

When you call the Coast Guard expect to provide a call-back number. A call back number provides the Coast Guard the opportunity, if need be, to seek additional information. A call-back

number also allows the Coast Guard the opportunity to verify the calling source. Who knows, the call may have originated from a condo commander out on pub crawl about town with a little mischief in mind.

I was involved in a case where the caller provided a call back number but refused to come to the phone after his wife answered it. Earlier he had called 911 reporting a capsized sailboat with people in the water just south of Muskegon Harbor. We immediately responded and within minutes reached the reported position and found nothing, not even after conducting a thorough search. I called the number the reporting party provided to 911. A woman answered. She confirmed her husband had made the call, but he was unavailable— he was in the bathroom. I requested that he return the call, which he didn't. After a prolonged search, command directed us to return to the station.

What did the caller expect the Coast Guard to do? He calls for help, then ignores them. Give the Coast Guard a break! Lake Michigan does not offer street signs, intersections or other land marks that guide land based 911 responders. Instead, it offers a vast undulating body of water brushed by a collage of colors and shifting light patterns that can find small water craft darting to-and-fro. Also the wind can knock down a small sail craft, and in no time the operator can re-right it and sail off.

In 2001, while responding to a reported capsized sailboat near South Haven's North Pier, I watched from a bluff through binoculars as the operator re-righted a small catamaran and within minutes beached it a mile or so north of the harbor. When I received the initial call, I had jumped on my bike and raced to a nearby beach. Although concerned about the boater, I was far more concerned about gathering intelligence to determine whether we needed to respond at all. We didn't.

Bottom line: Keep your eye on the target and stay in touch.

In spite of the enormous marine safety net rescue agencies provide boaters, still there is no greater or more effective rescue resource than an intelligent boater. It's not that I scorn recreational boaters, it's that I scorn the reasons so many needlessly die or compromise their safety with foolish behavior. With that in mind its time to move on to discuss the front-line defenses boaters can take to defend themselves against the marine environment. Batten down the hatches.

Sensible Boating Key to Search and Rescue

THIS CHAPTER WILL ADDRESS PROACTIVE MEASURES BOATERS MUST TAKE TO ASSURE A SAFE AND EXPEDIENT RESCUE. The chapter also offers advice on how boaters can defend themselves against the marine environment while awaiting rescue. Let's begin with the marine radio, the first link between a boater in distress and rescue responders. It can be either a life-saving tool or a pain in the stern.

PAIN IN THE STERN

The marine radio offers an instant connection between those in distress and rescue responders. In the hands of professional sailors, it has proven to be an expedient life-saving tool. In the hands of many recreational boaters; however, it has proven to be a real pain in the stern for rescue responders. It's not uncommon for a recreational boater to call the Coast Guard requesting assistance and then provide a sketchy position, or worse yet, no position at all. What an imbroglio the boater has created, now the Coast Guard must conduct a search—but where.

Please, don't let me hear platitudes like "it's their job." It is totally the boater's job to know their position, and those that pass it on to the Coast Guard should bear the following in mind. The Lake Michigan basin encompasses an immense body of water, extending in length over 330 miles with a maximum width of 118 miles and a surface area of 22,300 square miles. The average recreational boat occupies less than 30 square feet of surface area, a mere speck. If I departed my home in Manistee and drove along major arteries that rim the lake, I would drive 800 miles before I rolled back into my driveway. If I walked around the lake along its shoreline including major bays, harbors, nooks and crannies, I would cover over 3,200 miles. It would take fewer miles for me to walk from San Francisco to New York.

That's a lot of area for Lake Michigan's 19 Coast Guard Stations and the Air Station at Traverse City to guard. Each station has been assigned a certain area of responsibility; altogether they cover the entire Lake Michigan coastline. I addressed this issue in Chapter 7, and it demands to be repeated: although stations may have several boats, standard operating procedure calls for only one duty boat crew for search and rescue—one boat, one crew. It doesn't take a doctorate in resource management to figure out the strain that needless searching can

Traverse Bay is but part of an immense marine environment that defines Lake Michigan.

place on limited resources. Nor does it take a slide rule jockey to work out a solution. The remedy lies with Joe or Josephine boater and proper use of the marine radio to activate an expedient and possibly life-saving rescue. Here's how.

MAKE THE CALL COUNT: I believe many boaters labor under the illusion that when they call the Coast Guard, by some magical means the radio watchstander can determine the caller's location.

How pretty to think so, but it ain't so. The boater is the only one who can provide his or her location on the water. But even if a boater should know his or her location, if it can't be passed over the marine radio in a timely manner during an emergency it benefits no one.

Lieutenant Commander Chris Day, Coast Guard Station Traverse Air, drives home this point while conducting public safety seminars. The veteran Coast Guard aviator conducts a drill he calls "make the call count." Using a hand-held tape recorder, he asks participants to pretend it's a marine radio and they are transmitting a Mayday over Channel 16, the International Hailing and Distress frequency. Commander Day then selects someone from the group to issue a Mayday. Five to seven seconds into the broadcast, he switches off the tape recorder, simulating a dead radio for whatever reasons. Then he plays back the brief segment. Participants are stunned how they wasted precious time communicating frivolous information. "Make the call count," he stresses: "Mayday, Mayday I'm five miles off Betsie Point, end transmission. That's enough information to launch Coast Guard boats and aircraft to process a successful rescue," said Day. The following On

Watch stories show the life-saving value of quickly firing off an effective Mayday.

ON WATCH: Ludington, Michigan, April 12, 2005. Two fishermen whose 35-foot fishing boat sank off Ludington Harbor late at night fired off a Mayday that provided the following information in less than ten seconds: location, number of people aboard and nature of distress. Text-book perfect, and it saved their lives. As he slipped on his anti-exposure suit, one crewman was going down with the boat. But due to the suit's buoyancy he popped to the surface after ascending 20 feet below, according to Mat Herrmann, the Coast Guardsman coxswain who rescued the pair.

It took 22 minutes from the time Group Grand Haven received the Mayday, to the time the Coast Guard Ludington crew aboard a 30-foot rescue boat reached the two fishermen bobbing in 35-degree water in three to four foot seas. Their position placed them approximately five and half nautical miles northwest of Ludington Harbor, the GPS position provided in the Mayday. I spoke with Joe Loverti, the radio operator at Group Grand Haven who intercepted the initial call, and he told me a crewman immediately provided a range and bearing to Ludington Harbor and a latitude and longitude. Within seconds the transmission ended. Moments later he received a second call from the operator, who again passed his location and that the boat was going down. End transmission.

On May 14, 2005, in another spectacular "make the call count" rescue, a Coast Guard boat crew from Station Kenosha, Wisconsin, pulled three fishermen from the waters off Kenosha in early evening after a crewman fired off an urgent Mayday. Both Station Kenosha and Group Milwaukee intercepted the urgent call for help. The caller immediately provided the boat's latitude and longitude, number of people aboard, and that it was rapidly taking on water. Station Kenosha immediately launched a 41-foot rescue boat and 16 minutes later, after pounding through four-foot seas, they reached the three fishermen clinging to their overturned 19-foot aluminum boat in 45-degree water four miles east of Kenosha. From nearby Illinois, a Winthrop Harbor police

helicopter crew also responded to the Channel 16 Mayday and was the first to reach the overturned craft. The copter hovered overhead, awaiting the Coast Guard boat.

BOAT SMART BRIEF: Coast Guardsman Ben Spafford, coxswain aboard the rescue boat said, "These guys did everything right: they immediately provided their location, they wore life jackets, and they fired off a flare." Also, I might add the crewman wisely used Channel 16 and not a cell phone, which alerted the maritime community at large, including the Winthrop Harbor police helicopter. In both Mayday cases, the people in the water (PIW) were wearing life jackets or survival suits; however, the PIWs' flotation devices did not carry night illumination devices like a strobe light or glow stick, a must for nighttime boating. The survival suits did, however, carry reflective material that the search light on the Ludington rescue boat picked up, which lead to the fishermen's rescue. Both cases also reinforced an observation that I have witnessed over 19 years of writing Boat Smart columns and as a Coast Guard rescue responder: boats can sink in a heartbeat and often do.

For me, the most gratifying aspect of the rescue is that the boaters knew how to do the right things. While being interviewed by Fox 6 television, one of the survivors stated he owed his life to the Coast Guard Auxiliary and lessons he learned during a boating safety class sponsored by Flotilla 51, Station Kenosha. How sweet it is when boaters learn to take responsibility for their own safety. Would you be prepared to make the call count? If you boat smart, you would.

Understand that the book's stories are a work in progress and that for every example others like it endlessly fill Coast Guard files. For example, just before sending the book off to the publisher, I spoke with duty officer Mitch Muehlhausen at Group Grand Haven's rescue coordination center. He described a case on September 5, 2005 involving a women's husband who was stung by a bee and went into anaphylactic shock. She frantically placed a call to the Coast Guard but had no clue to her position. "I had to really calm her down," said Coast Guard radioman, Chief Ron Helfer.

"She thought she was off Saugatuck Harbor, but then reported passing a big red lighthouse, which is at the Holland entrance." Fortunately, the crew aboard a Coast Guard rescue boat while outbound Holland Harbor, spotted a 24-foot powerboat at the mouth of the harbor entrance that matched the boat's description. The rescue boat came alongside the 24-foot boat, the crew removed the husband and raced him to awaiting paramedics on shore. It saved his life.

It was absolutely happenchance that saved her husband. The marine environment is full of surprises and perhaps the couple never figured that a bee would find its way onto Lake Michigan. But that isn't the point. The point is that when an emergency arose, the boater was less than prepared to deal with it. That is the case with so many recreational boating mishaps: It's all peaches and cream until the unexpected strikes and then it turns quickly sour and down-right bitter if a person is unable to provide rescue responders a location.

I will give the woman credit; however, she immediately called the Coast Guard after realizing her husband urgently needed help. So, lesson learned: should an emergency arise, whatever you do, don't hesitate to call the Coast Guard for help.

DON'T PROCRASTINATE: The old adage, "He who hesitates is lost," couldn't be more apropos than for boaters who procrastinate calling the Coast Guard regarding safety concerns. My dad used to say: "procrastination is the thief of all time." For boaters in distress, procrastination could steal your life. Boaters would be wise to follow a standing order for Coast Guard shipboard watch officers: if you are in doubt, that is reason enough to call the captain. Don't be timid, either. The Coast Guard welcomes calls. You are not inconveniencing the radio operator. He or she stands fully committed, 24-7, to assist boaters. Radio operators take great pride in doing so, especially in a timely manner. It's a lot easier for the radio operator to gather pertinent information up front rather than later during a frantic time crunch brought on by an emergency.

Boaters should also remember to keep an eye on the battery. Don't wait until the juice drops so low that there's not enough power to transmit a radio call. Dead batteries are not uncommon.

Captain Dan McCormick, who ran a Sea Tow operation out of Muskegon, Michigan, assisted over 500 boaters between 1996 and 2001. Captain McCormick said that 55-percent of his tows involved battery failures. "A lot of boaters over-load their batteries by running an assortment of electronic devices like a GPS, fish finder, radio, electronic charts, and downrigger winches. For whatever reasons should a boater's motor die, many fishermen continue to fish while they workout the mechanical problem. All the while electronic devices are drawing on the battery. With whatever life remaining in the battery they call for help over the radio, resulting in poor or no communications at all," said McCormick.

LOST COMMUNICATIONS: A situation that has baffled me for years is boaters who lose radio communications with the Coast Guard. Most boaters contact the Coast Guard over VHF-FM Channel 16: the distress and calling frequency. Once the Coast Guard determines the boater's location, nature of distress, and number of people aboard, it will request, if it's a non-emergency situation, that the boater switch to Channel 22, the Coast Guard's public working frequency. For whatever reasons, communications with the boater cease. The reasons could be many: the boater's radio is not programmed for channel 22, or the boater doesn't know how to switch from Channel 16 to 22, or the boater has a change of mind, or the boater corrected the problem, or the boater received assistance from another boater, or whatever, communications cease.

Understand that once a boater triggers the Coast Guard rescue response system, it sets off a chain of events that terminates when authorities can determine beyond a reasonable doubt that the calling party is safe or, God forbid, deceased. Thus the only person that can stop the search and rescue process is the boater, one way or the other.

I salute the captain in the following story who did stop the search process before it kicked into gear by placing a single radio call to the Coast Guard in spite of embarrassing circumstances. Out of respect to the commercial captain who made the standup call, I will spare using his name or commercial affiliation. The captain told me that while conducting abandon ship drills on Lake Michigan in August of 2004, he turned command over to a fellow captain for his turn at the abandon ship drill. Heading down to the galley, he awaited the abandon ship announcement over the boat's PA system. While waiting, he heard the Coast Guard broadcasting an urgent PAN-PAN over Channel 16 alerting vessels in the area that people were abandoning ship and making ready the life boats.

The captain found it rather peculiar that while they were conducting an abandon ship drill, there was a real one in the making. Strange, indeed, he thought. He scrambled up to the bridge and asked the captain if he had made the abandon ship announcement. "Yes," he said. My captain friend noticed that the hand-held mouth piece for the marine radio and PA system were laying alongside each other on the console. Oh my, he thought, the captain had broadcasted the abandon ship announcement over Channel 16 not the boat's PA system.

The captain called Coast Guard Group Grand Haven on a cell phone and relayed his suspicions. He requested they play back the broadcast and sure enough it was the voice of his fellow captain. How did the Coast Guard respond—thanks much for the comeback. Nothing further—out.

THIRD PARTY CALLS: It's not uncommon for boaters, after observing a boater in possible distress, to depart the scene and later call the Coast Guard with their concerns, which instantly activates the search and rescue system and requires the Coast Guard to take action. Had the reporting party checked out the situation on scene and then communicated with the Coast Guard, they could spare the rescue system an onerous search. Dealing with such calls is like dealing with gossip: it benefits no one. Help rescue responders by staying on the scene so they will not need to track down the facts with boats, aircraft and personnel. Resources that might be needed to effect a timely rescue elsewhere.

Again it comes down to the location factor and I can't stress enough how important it is to remove the search out of search and rescue. Let's review some navigational tricks that can help pinpoint a boater's location and thus lead to a timely rescue.

NAVIGATION CAN LEAD TO A TIMELY RESCUE

Why does it seem that the longer we do something the easier it becomes, or is it that the longer we do something, we find easier ways to do it. At least, that has been my experience regarding small-boat navigation and knowing my position on the water.

My Coast Guard specialty was navigation, which in time has enlightened me regarding the difference between simple application and textbook theories. I labored under the illusion that if students understood the theory they would better understand its use. Hogwash! Often my theory discourses would confuse students. Finally it dawned on me they neither held my rapture for navigation nor were they benefiting from my intellectual crowing.

I discovered if I taught them a few tangible fundamentals, then provided the opportunity for them to demonstrate them on a chart, and later on the water, they soon mastered the lesson. The most fundamental of all lessons and the one I stressed most was the ability to determine their location on the water. The same holds true for recreational boaters. How does a boater expect to be rescued if he or she doesn't know where to send rescuers?

All the king's men, all the rescue responders, and all the 911 operators can't help you if they can't find you. And they may never find you if time takes its toll, stressing yet again the location factor.

That said, let's go for a boat ride aboard a Coast Guard rescue boat and practice some small-boat navigation that will help lead to a quick rescue. Immediately after firing up the engines, I check my electronics: radar, GPS, depth finder and radio. Of those four, GPS and the radio provide the strongest links to a successful rescue. So, first I make a radio check with my parent command to ensure the radio is online. Recreational boaters can make radio checks with a fellow boater or marina on a non-commercial channel designated to recreational boaters (Channels 68, 69, 70, 71, 72, 78).

If operating on Lake Michigan, radio checks can be made on Channel 09. Be aware, though, that many marine radios transmit at one-watt and at 25 watts. When making a radio check, call on one watt, and when calling for help make sure your radio is set at 25 watts.

Next, I check the GPS, especially my latitude and longitude, to assure it agrees with my geographical position. That's my current location. I then enter a nearby waypoint, like the local lighthouse. From memory, I know the range and bearing to that waypoint; if the GPS range and bearing match, it assures me the GPS is properly tracking.

When all systems check out, including my engine cooling water discharge, throttles and steering, I give the order to cast off lines. While passing alongside the pier head at the harbor mouth, I notice that the GPS coordinates match the known pier head latitude and longitude. This check provides an opportunity to share a nifty trick with the trainee. If the pier head latitude reads 44 degrees 15 minutes north, a mile north the GPS will read 44 degrees 16 minutes north. Each minute of latitude represents one nautical mile.

I'll get back to this concept in a moment, but first this tip: As we pound out into Lake Michigan, I note the direction the seas are running and the wind direction by checking the compass. If both are coming from the west, I know that if I put the seas or wind off the stern, I will be heading east and back to shore. Using this trick in fog will get you back to land even without a compass or GPS.

As we head north, soon we will be abeam of a well known creek. I note the latitude on the GPS, and it reads 44 degrees, 19 minutes north, which places the boat four miles north of the harbor we departed. I pass this information to the crew and advise them to assign it to memory. As we steam further north I direct them to pick out other familiar landmarks on shore and note their distance from our home port using the GPS minute of latitude method and assign them to memory. In the event we lose our electronics, we will know how far we are from port by referencing one of these landmarks.

You can also apply the same method when you're driving along the shoreline. When you're abeam of

a known landmark that can be seen from seaward, simply note its distance from your location to the harbor mouth. I did this for years when assigned to a new search and rescue station, in fact, it's standard operating procedure for boat crews to know their area of operation. If a boater calls for assistance and provides a reference point on shore, crews instantly know how far they must travel to reach the calling party.

Why do coasties go to such an extent both on land and sea to know these landmarks? Because they understand that in search and rescue, location removes "search" from the equation, which equals a timely rescue. So, once again may I stress: how does a boater expect rescuers to find them, if the boater doesn't know his or her location? This is not a game of hide and seek but rather hide and sink.

Let's review some small boat navigation tricks and survival pointers that you can easily bag.

NAV TRICKS YOU CAN BAG

I've performed navigation aboard 378-foot cutters, 82-foot patrol boats, buoy tenders and even vintage World War II cutters before LORAN-C and GPS systems beamed shipboard navigation into the 21st century. I've even navigated by celestial navigation, seeking the moon, sun and stars as my guides when sextants and azimuth circles were as common on the bridge as GPS and satellite-guided radar navigation are today.

Sound impressive? I use to believe so until I began navigating aboard Coast Guard small rescue boats on Lake Michigan, which ranged in length from 44-foot motor life boats to 21-foot inflatables. Small boats lack the working area, navigational instruments and comforts afforded larger cutters. Just unfolding a chart aboard a small inflatable rescue boat is like opening a newspaper in a stiff breeze. Add to that a pitching, sea-sprayed deck and even simple tasks can be overwhelming.

When the Coast Guard assigned me to search and rescue duties on Lake Michigan, I had to adapt the navigational skills I learned aboard large Coast Guard cutters on the high seas to small boat operations, quite an adjustment indeed.

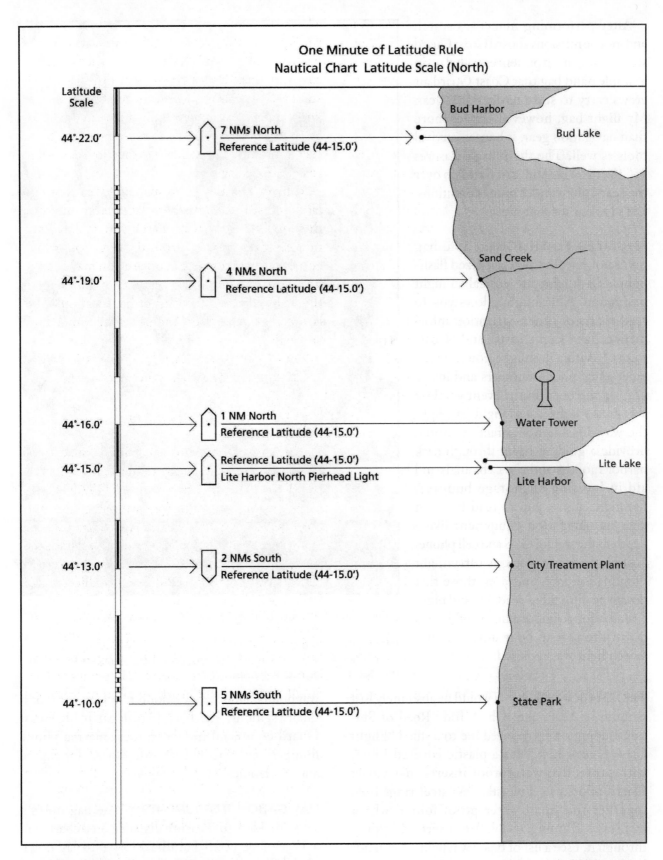

One Minute of Latitude Rule
Nautical Chart Latitude Scale (North)

Latitude Scale

44°-22.0' → 7 NMs North
Reference Latitude (44-15.0') → Bud Harbor / Bud Lake

44°-19.0' → 4 NMs North
Reference Latitude (44-15.0') → Sand Creek

44°-16.0' → 1 NM North
Reference Latitude (44-15.0') → Water Tower

44°-15.0' → Reference Latitude (44-15.0')
Lite Harbor North Pierhead Light → Lite Lake / Lite Harbor

44°-13.0' → 2 NMs South
Reference Latitude (44-15.0') → City Treatment Plant

44°-10.0' → 5 NMs South
Reference Latitude (44-15.0') → State Park

Each minute of latitude represents one nautical mile. The concept provides a nifty method for a boater to determine his or her position to a landmark and a known waypoint reference point.

After performing numerous search and-rescue missions aboard Coast Guard small boats, my experiences ended up in a simple hand bag that Coast Guard air crews carry to store navigational gear. My flight bag, however, carries more than navigation gear, it houses survival tools as well. The flight bag measures 15" W × 11" H. And it has held up over the years, often under brutal conditions. Let's look at its contents.

PEN-SIZED FLASHLIGHT: The bag holds not one, but two pen-sized flashlights. Flashlights are critical to night navigation. A flashlight allows you to read charts or other navigation information like "Light Lists" and "Coast Pilots." With a flashlight, you can read emergency phone numbers and locate gear on the boat. In the event you lose a compass light, a flashlight can light the way. Flashlights attract attention, provide a guiding beam through dark harbor mouths and river channels and aid in locating anchorage buoys. A flashlight allows you to read function keys on navigation equipment like a depth finder, radio, GPS and cell phone. Not all these components carry night illumination keys and even those that do can be difficult to read. I found night illumination so important, I would stand down the rescue boat until a faulty search light was repaired.

A Coast Guard coxswain plots a course on a customized chart he has adapted to a clipboard. On the console sits a "Fight Crew" waterproof folder with plastic inserts containing phone numbers, waypoints, troubleshooting checklists, etc. These and other useful items are stowed in the "Nav Bag" located on the seat.

INFORMATION BOOK: I would be absolutely lost without it. Years ago, Chief Todd Reed of Station Ludington introduced me to a small "Flight Crew Check List." It's a plastic covered folder with protective waterproof inserts that Coast Guard pilots use. Five stainless steel rings hold together the small water-proof folder, which facilitates flipping its plastic inserts. Flipping through it, I see a list of typed waypoints for major landmarks like pier heads and breakwaters; simple GPS instructions for programming and selecting

waypoints; emergency phone numbers for Coast Guard stations, sheriff, and fire department; Coast Guard command numbers; local marina phone numbers, and a troubleshooting insert for engine and electronics.

NAVIGATION INSTRUMENTS: The bag holds a set of dividers to measure distance on a chart, and a Weems & Plath Parallel Plotter to lay down charted course lines. The bag also holds a Weems & Plath nautical slide rule. I also carry my own hand-held GPS as a back up. That's it for navigational instruments.

NAVIGATION CHARTS: Few conditions challenge me more on a small boat than dealing with cumbersome charts. When you unfold one on an open boat even in a light breeze, it's often "Adios chart." Solution: use a legal sized 14" × 8" clipboard, which snuggly fits into the "Nav Bag." Cut the chart down to clipboard size. The clip secures the chart against unruly winds. I can also clip writing paper over the charts to record useful information like waypoints or marine radio traffic. Some boaters prefer waterproof chartbooks which lend well to grease pencils. If possible, always write down information passed over the marine radio or cell phone. Being jerked about on a small boat can quickly numb the memory.

MISCELLANEOUS ITEMS: These are small items offering huge benefits like sunblock. The benefits of sunblock are obvious. Other small but important items include a whistle, a knife, and reading glasses. I carry two sets of these items, one as backup. Let's see what else the bag offers. Light bulbs and fuses and the trouble-shooting guide in the "Flight Crew Information Book" will guide me step by step in replacing parts like fuses and other small boat troubleshooting challenges. Oh, I almost overlooked the GPS instruction book, which I carry in the event the GPS takes on a mind of its own, or I forget how to read its mind.

All this may seem like a lot of stuff, but remember, it's all contained in a small flight bag that validates the old adage: It's not size that matters, but content. Boat Smart—bag your own safety gear, including extra distress flares that can beckon help when all else fails.

LIGHT UP OR PERISH IN DARKNESS

A reader e-mailed me regarding a column I wrote about a disabled boat adrift on Lake Michigan, and how sooner rather than later it will be rescued. The writer begged to differ, pointing out that Fred Ball, while racing in the 2002 Chicago-Mackinac Single-Handed Challenge Race aboard a 50-foot trimaran, capsized in mid-afternoon and lay adrift north of Milwaukee for 11 hours before being rescued at 2:30 a.m. He may have been rescued much sooner if only he had possessed the means to attract help.

Eleven hours adrift on Lake Michigan—that's about half a day. It sounds more like an inconvenience than a life-threatening event, although the accident itself could well have proved fatal. The accident occurred in mid-June with water and air temperatures in the mid-50s. The accident also shows that lessons learned the hard way can even visit veteran sailors.

CASE FILE: According to Fred Ball, around 3:30 p.m. a weather front packing 60-knot winds bore down on him. Releasing the main and jib sheets, he headed down wind; the trimaran surged to 24 knots in seconds. He heard a loud bang; seconds later the stern shot skyward. At 90 degrees vertical to the lake, he leaped as the dagger board whizzed by his head and the boat pitched forward into the sea, bottom side up. Floundering several feet beneath the deck nets, he struggled to the surface where hail chunks rained down on his head.

The fleeting storm soon gave way to sunshine. He crawled onto the over-turned hull. He considered removing his Mustang Survival Suit to dive under the hull to retrieve his survival package, which carried visual distress signals and a radio. However, with a possible torn rotator cuff, he elected to stay put; a wise choice, considering the maze of sails, sheets, and wire shrouds dangling beneath the 50-foot long and 35-foot wide boat.

Ball later told me he had hastily grabbed a spare Mustang suit that lacked survival equipment. Ball since has cut two inverted egress hatches into the starboard and port floats so he can access survival gear if he capsizes again. He hopes never to use them, but then the lake holds many surprises as he woefully discovered.

Ball sat perched on the hull and was rescued 11 hours later by a fellow racer, Carl Karr, who heard his cries for help. He hauled Ball aboard his 45-foot Island Packet sail boat and motored into Milwaukee, aborting the race. Ball told me later he watched several boats pass nearby, but he could not draw their attention.

Had he carried visual distress signals on his person, like an orange smoke flare, hand-held or aerial flare, even a whistle, his chances of being spotted would have, no pun intended, skyrocketed.

Readily available visual distress signals also provide a strong thread of hope that keeps one holding on. After the Coast Guard lost several crewmen overboard at night, all Coast Guard boat crews were required to carry survival vests loaded with day and night attention grabbers. All it takes is one loss. I'm sure that amongst Lake Michigan's close-knit sailing fleet, all it would take is one. Thus far they have been blessed.

During the 2002 Chicago to Mackinac race, the sailing boat *Caliente* capsized in the Straits of Mackinac during a violent downburst. Two crewmen were set adrift in eight to ten foot seas. If not for aerial flares launched from the capsized *Caliente*, the strobe light of a crewman in the water, and the guiding searchlight of the Canadian motor vessel *Algo Marine* leading another racing vessel, the *Kokomo*, to the floundering sailors, their fate would have been sealed by the darkness. Afterward they admitted that had *Kokomo* arrived 15 minutes later it would have been too late.

BOAT SMART BRIEF: A life jacket and night illumination saved these sailors. Reportedly it took 30 minutes from the time *Caliente* capsized to the time they fired off the first SOLAS red parachute flare. That a crewman located the flares in a capsized boat speaks well of the skipper's survival gear management. Obviously this crew had experience, although may I suggest that next time they consider wearing a survival vest with an assortment of signaling devices: hand-held and aerial flares, a whistle, strobe, an illumination stick, and signal mirror. Fred Ball has even added a new hand-held 406 Emergency Position Indicating Radio Beacon (EPIRB) to his personal survival package. The EPIRB alerts the Coast Guard via satellite relay systems of who you are and where you are within a 100-foot radius of the latitude and longitude coordinates, which are transmitted automatically by the EPIRB. Nifty.

One other point regarding visual distress survival gear: always conduct scheduled inspections of safety gear, especially strobe lights. A Columbia River pilot was pitched off the ladder of a freighter off Astoria, Oregon, in storm-tossed seas. When he went to energize his strobe light, guess what? Luckily for him, a Coast Guard air crew spotted him waving a small flash light. Make sure to attach the strobe light to the life jacket with a small nylon line so it can be held above the surface while still remaining attached to the life jacket should the sea snatch it away.

If someone hands you a life jacket with a strobe light attached, test it and I don't care if it's a Coast Guardsman handing you the jacket, test the strobe light. I do. Should I end up overboard bobbing about in a dark void I want to know for certain I can mark my location. That's a certainty I would rather not entrust to someone else who may have tested the strobe because that other one is not in the water with me now but probably home in a warm bed, or bar.

Another safety item you want to check are visual distress signals commonly know as flares. These devices carry a short life, which might shorten yours should they fail, and there's a chance they will fail if the flares are expired.

EXPIRED FLARES COULD BE USELESS

I've read about, talked with, and listened to experts explain why visual distress signals may fail after they exceed their three-year useful life. Such advice made sense; however, staying true to my name, Thomas, I had my doubts. That is until I fired off a number of expired flares.

After conducting a night-time visual distress exercise on Lake Michigan during the summer of 2002, I'm here to testify that expired distress flares often can, indeed, be useless. Coast Guard personnel aboard a 47-foot motor lifeboat and members of the Coast Guard Auxiliary on shore fired off 51 visual distress flares, the same flares carried on recreational boats.

Of the 51 flares we launched, 12 failed. In other words, 23 percent were duds. All the flares, except one, carried expired dates, some dating back to

A Coast Guard survival vest contains the following items: An Emergency Position Indicator Radio Beacon, a strobe light, a signal mirror, aerial flares, a day and night combination hand-held flare, a whistle, and a serrated knife. All items are tethered to the survival vest with small line.

1994. The only currently dated flare that failed carried an expiration date of September 2002, a month before it was due to expire.

Not only do experts advise that expired flares might fail, but burn time, candle power, and altitude reach may be compromised by age as well. That proved to be the case as some flares failed to reach prescribed altitudes, others fizzled out short of their burn time, and a few didn't ignite until far into the night sky.

A flare's expiration date is stamped on the side of the device. Contrary to boater scuttlebutt, the manufacturer does not set the three-year useful life, but rather the Coast Guard, who follows the recommendations of certified independent laboratories. These laboratories demand that manufacturers meet certain standards.

I spoke with Frank Amodeo, an official at Orion Signals, a major manufacturer of visual distress signals. He told me that independent inspectors routinely visit his plant. Inspectors randomly test samples from various production lots. They place the flares into an oven set at 174 degrees Fahrenheit for 24 hours. Then they submerge them under four inches of water for twenty-four hours, then they uncap and submerged them again, with the "ignite button" exposed to water, for an additional five minutes. After that they dry the flares and ignite them using the submerged strikers. Following that, they expose them to high heat humidity in a "jungle room" like environment.

So why do flares expire? According to Amedeo, like camera film or pharmaceuticals, their proper performance relies on the interaction of chemical compounds that can be degraded by the hostile marine environment. According to Amedeo, the U.S. military conducted a test of small-arms primers. A primer is an ignition system on the bullet cap used to fire a bullet or shell; it is similar to aerial 12-guage flare ignition cap. The military study revealed a dramatic increase in the ignition failure rate after three years.

Also, a flare's effectiveness, whether new or old, is influenced by care. Any flare, handheld or aerial, regardless of its age, can be difficult to ignite, or fail to ignite at all, depending on care. It is advisable to check flares for moisture exposure and other negative environmental influences, not just at the season's start, but throughout.

Remember, check your flares to make sure they are current, become familiar with their use, and keep them dry and readily available. In short, Boat Smart. Don't be a dud when it comes to your flares.

Boat Smart Anchor Points

Flare Tips

↪ **INSTRUCTIONS.** Flares are simple to light off if you are familiar with them. I've fired off a number of Coast Guard distress flares even while being heaved about in four to six foot seas; however, I conducted crew training on use before entering the water. And likewise with the commercial flares we tested, we reviewed launch instructions beforehand. Simple, yes, but, imagine fumbling with an unfamiliar explosive on a heaving deck, at night, struggling to read instructions. No thank you. Reading the simple instructions that accompany flares and becoming familiar with their use will lead to safe and productive operation.

↪ **SAFETY.** When launching an aerial flare, turn your head away from the flare. Do not watch it fire off. It may misfire and burn your eyes. When gripping a handheld aerial launcher, do so with your index finder on top of the flare tube and your thumb at the bottom. That will draw your hand upward when you pull the ignition chain. When holding a handheld flare, hold it over the side of the boat and downward to avoid hot ash oozing down the flare onto your hand.

↪ **FAMILIARIZE CREW.** Instruct crewmembers on the flare usage. It can be fun, while refreshing your skills.

↪ **SAVE ONE FOR THE RESCUER.** Do not fire off all your flares at once. Save one for the rescue boat. I recommend boaters carry three aerial and three handheld fares. The aerials can be seen from 16 to 20 miles away, the handheld around five miles. The downside of aerials they burn between 5-10 seconds. The handhelds burn for around two minutes. If rescuers are within five miles, the two-minute hand-held flares will draw their eye.

↪ **FOLLOW-UP** Should you fire off a flare and no longer require assistance, notify authorities immediately to avoid a needless search. Also, you needn't be in a life-threatening situation to fire off a flare. I've found flares to be quite helpful when identifying a distress boat amongst a sea of boats. During the peak of the fishing season on Lake Michigan, the horizon can be dotted with small boat silhouettes and if the boater requesting assistance doesn't carry a GPS, a flare is the next best thing to mark one's position.

↪ **WINTER STORAGE** It's advisable to store your flares in a dry, safe environment during winter. Treat flares like firearms; keep them away from children.

Now let's move on to the next topic: sailboats caught in heavy weather on a lee shore and defensive measures they can take to defend themselves.

SAILBOATS VULNERABLE NEAR A LEE SHORE

Many sailboaters enjoy the best of both worlds: motor and sail. It is a sweet option made even sweeter by the Navigation Rules that require powerboats to give way to sailboats under sail (except when the sailboat is overtaking a power boat). These options, however, can turn bitter for a sailboater when nearing a lee shore in heavy weather.

Many single-hull sailboats carry small, low-power engines. Most sailboats could carry more powerful engines. However, it may not increase speed. A sailboat's speed is a function of its hull shape

When gripping a handheld aerial launcher, do so with your index finder on top of the flare tube and your thumb at the bottom. That will draw the hand holding the flare upward when you pull the ignition chain. If you hold it with your thumb on top you will draw your arm downward and thus fire the flare into the water or into a crewman.

When launching an aerial flare, turn your head away from the flare. Do not watch it fire off. It could misfire and injure your eyes.

When holding a handheld flare, hold it over the side of the boat and downward to avoid hot ash oozing down the flare onto your hand.

and length, not horsepower. Moving through the water, a single-hull sailboat will displace a volume of water equal to the hull weight and its load.

Sailboats, by design, are heavy. The force that the wind exerts on sails must be counter-balanced below the surface, usually in the form of ballast, a heavy mass placed on the bottom of the keel. A sailboat's ballast may be as much as half of the boat's overall weight. To move ahead, it must displace, or move aside, a volume of water equal to its total weight. This is unlike most small power boats that can use their abundant power to create dynamic lift, and actually rise out of the water to skim across the surface. Regardless of how much power the sailboat might have available, it is restricted by displacement forces, having neither the right shape nor the power to plane.

Power limitations can be even greater when a sailboat encounters high seas and strong winds, an environment some sailors prefer. If they didn't, I suspect they would be skippering a cabin cruiser with potted palm trees and similar deck adornments. Even less adventurous sailors may encounter unforeseen heavy seas, and should the engine fail when operating near a lee shore in a blow: watch out!

Hopefully, the sailor possesses the skills to fix the engine casualty. That's not to suggest sailboaters lack mechanical skills or neglect their motors, or that power-boaters are mechanical wizards with finely-tuned motors. Nonsense. What I believe separates power from sail during a mechanical failure is when the incident occurs.

Powerboaters normally experience mechanical problems in mild weather and calm seas. If possible most powerboaters avoid heavy weather; they dislike fishing and cruising in rough seas; and they tend to race back to port when the horizon lights up. I can scarcely blame them. I would run from the storm also. God only knows I ran before enough storms and if provided the option I would've sought a protective harbor.

On the other hand, mechanical mishaps can unexpectedly visit sailboaters in conditions most power boaters avoid. Unlike powerboaters who are often afforded time to handle engine problems in open water and mild conditions, a sailboater may face a rapidly ticking clock in a close-quarter emergency while under siege from the elements.

Hopefully, an experienced sailor would head to open water before winds and sea drive the boat aground. Hopefully too, an experienced sailor would shorten sail and reef the main long before nearing a windward shore. But maybe not.... I would also hope an experienced sailor would test the engine before approaching a lee shore. But not all sailboaters share the same experience level, and even the most experienced sailor can fall prey to a lee shore.

Disabled sailboats have a high drift rate. A drifting sailboat tends to quarter into or ride

A solo sailor ventures out into the vast reaches of Lake Michigan ever vigilant of the inland sea's sudden mood swings. It is before the storm erupts that a sailor should give thought to reefing sail, making ready the anchor, and testing the auxiliary engine.

broadside to the wind. A sailboat heaving in heavy surf with its underbelly, rudder and keel exposed can be stressful enough to watch. But, imagine the stress level of those struggling below deck in a cramped engine space that is difficult to access, even under the best conditions, and absolutely daunting under the worst. And then to be slammed about with tools in hand could overwhelm even the best mechanic.

Even under power, a sailboat may enter sand bars that run nearly the full length of Lake Michigan's eastern shore. Unable to power out of these traps, sand bars could rip off a rudder in a heart beat, as the following On Watch story reveals. The story also shows once again how difficult it can be to execute a near-shore rescue, which in this case required an innovative approach.

ON WATCH: Coast Guard Station Ludington, Michigan, September 25, 1997. At 10:05 p.m. the radio watchstander at Station Ludington intercepted a Mayday call from a sailboater in the waters off Big Sable Point. The captain reported that he had hit a sandbar and lost his rudder.

Station Ludington launched a 21-foot inflatable rescue boat along with a 44-foot motor lifeboat. By the time the crews reached the location, seven nautical miles north of the station, four to five foot seas had carried the sailboat into a steel retaining seawall that rims the 105-foot light. Jay Plyler, coxswain aboard the 21-footer, approached the sailboat with great caution as following seas drove the light inflatable towards the stricken craft. He had elevated the inflatable twin outboards as high as maneuverability would allow to prevent ripping off props in the shallow water. In the end, he literally floated down onto the sailboat, riding hard against the seawall.

When Plyler arrived alongside the sailboat he passed over Shawn Higgins a Coast Guard EMT. Meanwhile from shore, Sgt. Grey Wessendorf of the Mason County Sheriff Department jumped into the lake to assist. But the boat slamming back and forth against the seawall made it too hazardous to approach, which was now tilted on its side. First responder firefighters from nearby Hamlin Township now on scene extended a long ladder to

the boat and removed the captain, who suffered cuts and bruises including a black eye. "These guys probably saved my life," said George Schrink, the 47-year-old captain.

In a more recent near shore sailboat causality, the following On Watch story reveals how little things loom big during a near shore emergency. That a captain neglected to correct an engine mechanical problem—he didn't want to deal with the hassle of crawling into an engine space in rough seas—nearly cost him his life.

ON WATCH: Muskegon, Lake Michigan, July 1, 2005. A beachside resident called Coast Guard Station Muskegon on Friday afternoon reporting a sailboat floundering off the beach north of Muskegon Harbor. Jay Mieras, the reporting source reported a woman on the sailboat was waiving her hands in the air.

Within minutes, the Station Muskegon's 30-foot rescue boat broke the pier head at Muskegon Harbor. Four to five foot seas driven by 20 knot winds greeted the Coast Guard crew as they pounded north towards the sailboat's reported position.

"When we approached the sailboat, I noticed a horseshoe flotation device trailing off the stern attached to a tether line," said Mike Tapp, Executive Officer, Station Muskegon. He added: "This was not good, you had that feeling that someone had gone overboard."

Chief Beatty coxswain aboard the 30-foot rescue boat approached the sailboat. "A female was hollering that her husband had fallen overboard but she didn't know where," said Chief Beatty.

Chief Beatty conducted several quick shoreline searches of the area that yielded negative sightings. The situation was not good: a person in the water and a sailboat being quickly driven towards shore, and its sole operator unable to control the craft.

Now what? Do you look for the husband or do you save the woman and the sailboat? Fortunately the situation resolved itself. A "Good Sam" Jim Homan, 61, had spotted the floundering craft from shore and he and a buddy grabbed a two-person kayak and reached the sailboat just as the Coast Guard finished its second search of the shoreline.

Being an experienced sailor, Homan took control of the sailboat allowing the Coast Guard crew to continue the search.

But where?

Locating a man in seas glazed over by white wind whipped spray did not look promising for the poor soul in the water. Tapp discovered from Homan that the sailboat carried a hand-held GPS. Homan passed the GPS to Tapp. Chief Beatty commenced searching while Trapp worked the handheld device. After two minutes of punching keys and being bounced about he tapped into the track line the sailboat had followed. "I could see where the straight track line ran askew." Tapp figured that is where the man went overboard as his wife began tacking to recover him. Tapp placed a cursor marker where the track line ended and bingo the GPS offer the latitude and longitude of where the man had gone overboard.

Chief Beatty passed the coordinates to a Coast Guard helicopter aircrew who had joined the search. Within minutes, the aircrew spotted the man in the water, wearing a bright international-orange life jacket. Meanwhile Chief Beatty had transferred Tapp and seaman Benjamin Cuddeback over to a Muskegon Sheriff's boat that had pickup the man. Tapp said, "The man was shivering controllable. His lips were blue.

Tapp and seaman Cuddeback removed his wet clothing and applied their own body warmth by direct body-to-body contact with the man as the sheriff boat raced to the Coast Guard moorings and an awaiting ambulance.

BOAT SMART BRIEF: Richard Coan, age 67, was released the following afternoon from Muskegon's Hackley Hospital. His core body temperature when admitted was 86 degrees. There is no doubt that the life jacket saved his life. He had been in the 61 degree water nearly two hours. He later told me the reason he wore the life jacket is because his wife, Robin, insisted on it. God bless her.

He told me he had moved forward on the deck to adjust the main sail and the boom swung over and bumped him backwards and over the handrails. His wife started the engine, but its gears wouldn't engage. Mr. Coan said that when he departed White Lake Harbor, a turnbuckle device on the gear linkage had fallen off and thus he couldn't engage the gears.

After several attempts to recover her husband, the sailboat drifted away. She had tossed over the horseshoe life ring but failed to untie it from the boat. She couldn't luff the main sail to take out the wind because it would require leaving the tiller and going forward to the foot of the mast to release the sail. It's the same reason she didn't call for help over the marine radio, again fearful of leaving the tiller and placing the 35-foot, six-ton Erickson sailboat broadside to the wind and a possible knockdown. In dire straights, she sailed for shore hoping to attract attention, which she did.

Mr. Coan admitted it was the little things that nailed them: when the gear linkage device fell off he should've returned to White Lake and repaired it in calm water. He had recently switched the boom sheets on the main from being controlled from the cockpit area to the foot of the sloop's mast, which required leaving the tiller to luff the main sail. "Had I thought this through, I would not have changed the boom sheets," said Mr. Coan.

As for the life jacket, I advised him to purchase a signal mirror and whistle, a day and night combination flare, and a strobe light. Twice the helicopter had passed nearby but failed to see him in the wind swept sea. Mr. Coan admits that it's the little things that loomed big when the unexpected visited. Thanks to a life jacket the little things didn't add up to the final tally.

In both cases, the sailboat captains found themselves on a lee shore with wind and waves rapidly driving their floundering craft towards shore. The unexpected causalities that visited them provided little room to make corrections including anchoring. It illustrates how important it is to make sure the boat is totally squared when operating near shore. The suddenness of the casualties even denied them the opportunity to run to open water, which is an option most experienced captains will pursue.

It brings to mind my cousin Jimmy's advice: When under siege, run to open water. Jimmy owns a boat maintenance and delivery operation in Santa Barbara, California, that he has run for over

30 years. When he speaks, hardcore sailors listen. I've made a number of yacht deliveries with Jimmy. I recall clipping along in a 48-foot C&C sloop in 10 to12 foot running seas along the California coast south of San Francisco. We discussed pulling into Monterey, but Jimmy decided not to. "I can't understand why sailors attempt to make port in high seas. They should run to open water," he said.

Ike Stevenson, a veteran Lake Michigan sailor, mirrored cousin Jimmy's advice: "A safe port might be nearby, but is it safe getting in there?" Nevertheless, it can be tempting to run to one of Lake Michigan's many ports. For those who do elect to make port in heavy weather, the following precautions should be taken.

- Make ready the anchor. Don't wait. Make sure the anchor system is together and please, no surprises like missing shackles or pins. Many sail boaters, for ballast reasons, stow the anchor in one compartment and the rode in another.
- Start the engine well before nearing port.
- Reef the main or run bare if necessary.
- Don life jackets or survival suits with visual distress signals and strobe lights.
- Call the Coast Guard and advise them of your situation, and notify the Coast Guard when you safely reach port.
- If unfamiliar with the port of entry, consult a navigation chart. At night make sure you understand the light characteristics of aids to navigation on pier heads and seawalls. To confuse them may have you moored sooner than planned. Also, have ready a hand-held search light.

Still, cousin Jimmy's and Ike's Boat Smart advice should be considered foremost: run to open water, for although a safe port might be nearby, it might not be safe getting there. Then there is always the anchor option. Beware, however, anchoring can present its own array of challenges that can test the best. For that reason I will address emergency anchoring in depth, the last defense against an unruly sea.

EMERGENCY ANCHORING CAN TEST THE BEST

Of all the drills I've conducted, anchoring may well be the most true-to-life when performed in heavy weather, and it can be one of the more dangerous. Breaking out a heavy anchor with chain on the bow of a pitching boat invites trouble. Yet I doubt that many recreational boaters view anchoring from a defensive stance or comprehend the dangers involved while setting an anchor in less than pleasant conditions. Experienced Coast Guard coxswains sure do. It's a point coxswains stress during qualification boards for aspiring coxswains. Let's look at a common emergency anchoring scenario presented to want-to-be coxswains before a panel of weathered coasties. The scenario also provides an opportunity to test your anchoring savvy.

A chief on the board will create a scenario like the following and present it to the coxswain break in: "You're steaming along on Lake Michigan around a mile off shore, with visibility less than 100 feet, with heavy vessel traffic in the area, when suddenly you lose all electronics. What would you do?"

"I would bring back throttles and come dead in the water," replies the aspiring coxswain.

"Good! Then what?"

"I would call the station and report the causality, and my position."

"Now, can you do that ? Remember, your electronics are down, including your radio."

"I would use a handheld radio or cell phone."

"Excellent," replied the chief. "Then what?"

The want to be coxswain scratches his head and says, "I would sound the signal for a vessel underway but not making way."

"Okay, what is that sound?"

"Two prolonged blast in intervals of not more than two minutes with an interval of about two seconds between blasts."

"Right again," It's going well for the lad: obviously he's come prepared.

"What else would you do? Oh, before you answer that, how do you know where you are? Remember, you've lost your GPS and radar."

"I tracked my position along a course line on a chart."

"Does your last position place you near hazards?"

"Yes, according to the chart around a mile and half offshore and near rocks."

"So, then what are you going to do?"

The eyes of the six-member board bore in on the lad because they know where the chief's question is heading. The young man hesitated; his eyes sweep the panel searching for a clue. "Well, what else would you do?" asked a senior coxswain, tapping a pencil on a note pad.

The lad scratched his head again. "Set the anchor," he declared.

"Good," replied the chief, "but not good enough. The order to set the anchor should have immediately followed your call to the station. In fact, I would have issued the order before I called the station because of the nearby rocks and onshore winds and seas."

Actually the lad performed quite well, and even though he may think he scored poorly with the board. The important point passed is that he will keep anchoring foremost in mind when facing a close quarter threat. On that point the board members felt reassured.

Most emergency anchoring situations on open water allow enough time and opportunity to take preventive measures; however, that is not always the case in a close-quarter squeeze. The following Boat Smart story "Storm Surprises Coast Guard During Rescue Operation" found the old Senior Chief as squeezed as one can be in a close-quarter anchoring emergency.

ON WATCH: Coast Guard Station Manistee, Michigan, August 4, 1989. While station personnel and guests celebrated the U.S. Coast Guard's 199th birthday on Friday the duty boat crew had little to cheer about as they fought to save their 41-foot rescue boat during a brief but violent storm that hit the town at dusk.

The storm, which blew out windows, disrupted power, and knocked down trees, arrived while the Coast Guard crew was wrapping up a rescue run.

At 9:40 p.m., the station radio watchstander received a distress call from the captain of the *Saber Tooth*, a 20-foot boat stranded with engine trouble two miles west of Manistee harbor. We launched the 41-foot rescue boat.

Around a mile out from Manistee, I glanced at the engine gauges and noticed the starboard engine heat gauge nearing the red zone. I immediately shut down the engine and radioed the station. The engineer checked out the starboard engine but was unable to correct the causality. He secured the engine. Signs of an approaching storm flashed across the horizon. We reached the *Saber Tooth* and took her in tow, hoping to reach port before the storm struck. It would be a tight race; the lightening-charged horizon grew brighter as we lumbered towards the harbor with only the port engine.

A boat with an all-metal deck and a tall aluminum mast provided an inviting target for lightning. As we entered Manistee harbor with the *Saber Tooth* in tow, a band of dark clouds curled towards us, marked by a distant rumble; sheet lightning turned to bolts as we maneuvered the *Saber Tooth* alongside our starboard hip and towed her to the City Marina located approximately one-half mile up the river.

Thunder now rumbled overhead as the air grew deathly still. A break-in coxswain nosed the bow up to a dock; I sprang onto the dock and quickly secured the *Saber Tooth* as the 41-footer maintained position off the dock. Before my crewman and I could scramble back aboard, a downburst roared down the channel at speeds exceeding 70 knots. We watched helplessly as the wind snatched our boat and whisked it away.

Lightening cracked overhead; a bolt zapped into a cluster of trees on the opposite bank, sending sparks skyward. Three-foot white caps churned upriver as the wind grabbed the white caps, spraying the surface white. The lights along the marina walkway flickered, died, then flicked alive. Sailboats healed over, gunwales and lifelines ground against the dock boards; halyards slapped against aluminum masts in a wild frenzy.

I turned my back to the wind to prevent the rage from blowing me off the dock. The marina lights died, shrouding the entire area in darkness. We ran after the boat; lightning flashed, horizontal rain drove me along the river bank, the rain blurring my vision. I reached the Maple Street bridge just as the boat blew through the bridge opening. I bellowed at them to make ready the anchor. The alert crewman on deck not only had the anchor ready, he had managed to lower the 13-foot mast within yards of the bridge. Had he not, the underside of the overpass would have ripped off the mast.

With only the port engine on line, the helmsman dared not engage the engine ahead, fearful it would turn the boat to starboard, exposing it broadside to the gale and the bridge abutment. To keep the boat in mid-channel, he cranked the helm hard over to starboard and backed down, applying power as needed. As the boat's stern swung to starboard, the bow swung to port, which kept the bow mid-channel. When he brought the throttles back, the bow would swing back to starboard and he would repeat the maneuver. All the while the wind drove the boat forward, even while backing down.

Meanwhile we scrambled up a stairway that led to Maple Street. The wind nearly lifted my crewman and me off the bridge. I could barely make out the boat's navigational lights through the driving rain. Lightening flashes lit up the boat's white hull as it approached a second bridge opening partially obstructed by scaffolding. I thanked the Good Lord that the *Saber Tooth* wasn't alongside the Coast Guard boat, because together the boats could not squeeze though the obstructed bridge opening. If the boat safely passed through, another danger lay ahead. A few hundred yards eastward sat a railroad swing bridge with a 10-foot vertical opening between the river and the bottom of the bridge. If the bridge was closed, it could inflict severe damage on the boat and possibly the crew; for certain the cabin would be destroyed. Here I stood watching my boat heading towards hell, truly a defining moment in my Coast Guard career, and I wasn't even on the boat!

I ran across to the opposite bank and scrambled through brush and debris toward the railroad bridge, fearing the worst. A lightning bolt zapped a nearby tree, sending up a hail of sparks. I prayed that the crew had let go the anchor before the

railroad bridge, and if they did, that the anchor held.

Through the railroad bridge lay Manistee Lake and just to the east were shallow marshes. If the bridge was open, the crew still had to let go the anchor in order to prevent the boat from flying across the lake into shallow waters. On that anchor hinged the boat, the crew, and possibly my career. It's ironic too that just several days before, I had conducted anchor drills with that same crew.

Thunder continued to shake the earth, lightening flashed overhead, and then in a flash, it ended. The boiling mass rolled eastward, leaving behind a star-splattered sky. And there, slightly straining on her anchor line, was the Coast Guard boat just east of the open railroad bridge. "Thank you, sweet Lord and a damn fine crew," I thought.

The crew weighed anchor at 12:25 a.m. and limped back to the station. Engineers made repairs to the starboard engine, and the boat was back on line by 3:00 a.m. An hour and half later, we were underway to assist a 39-foot sailboat reported to have run aground some 10 miles north of Manistee. Thanks to an anchor and the skills to use it properly, that run could be made.

Experience and preparation played a key role during that anchor emergency. After the storm struck, the crew had little time to set the anchor. The 41-foot rescue boat normally carries a three-man crew, but in this case only two were aboard: one to handle the helm, the other the anchor, which normally required two crewmen to set. The crewman that handled the anchor burst into action mode. First he lowered the masts; he had to act quickly, the bridge sat just 200 yards ahead of where the wind grabbed them. Then he had to get the anchor ready, which involved dogging open a scuttle hatch with a tee wrench. Then he had to climb down into the forepeak anchor locker, untie the anchor chain secured to an anchor bay, then run the chain up through a deck hawser pipe. Back on deck he had to run the chain through a bull nose fitting at the bow and then haul the chain back to the turtle cabin top where the anchor lay. He then unscrewed the shackle pin and attached the shackle to the anchor eye. Then he had to pay out anchor line onto the deck, but not too much line for should the line worm its way overboard, it could foul in the screw. The helmsman had enough on his hands keeping boat mid-channel without having to deal with a line in the only good screw.

All right or ready stop with the anchor jargon what's the message. First I appreciate that you stayed with me for the jargon carried an important message: emergency anchoring involves preparation and a series of exact steps.

If the crewman had faltered during any of those steps, it could have delayed or doomed the process. What's more, eye-blinding rain driven by 50 to 70 knot winds would amplify any miscue.

Being prepared on board to deal with a close-quarter anchoring emergency can't be overstressed. Some might say, that's a Coast Guard boat, the crew should be trained and prepared. Shouldn't all boaters be prepared? For it matters not to a hostile environment who the players might be. I just want the odds in my favor when I do encounter a close-quarter emergency, and a squared-away boat and crew is my odds maker.

I stood duty as a rescue responder in the twilight years of my career. Even as a Chief, I would make daily boat checks normally performed by junior personnel to ensure that the rescue craft was squared away, including checking shackles on anchor chains. I hate surprises during emergencies. I've addressed this issue with Coast Guardsmen more than once. I told them even though they performed a boat check on day one, do not assume that the boat on day two is still squared away. Such an assumption can lead to a ho-hum boat check.

I served with an honorable chief who dealt with this ho-hum mentality as only a chief can. He would remove items like an anchor shackle pin before the daily boat check. After boat checks, he would pipe the responsible seaman to his office. Chief would go down the check lists with the seaman and stop at the anchor. "I see you checked off the anchor. Did you check to see the shackle pin was attached?

"Yes, chief," replied the seaman, his tone carrying a hint of uncertainty.

"Are you sure?" asked the chief, taking a long drag on his cigar. "Then what the f--- is this?" replied the chief, bathing the lad in choking cigar smoke while holding the pin in his face.

These stories illustrate the importance of a squared away anchor system, and the ability to rapidly deploy it, and why this experienced chief had little patience with a ho-hum boat-check mentality. Nor did I. It's serious business. Although there are many excellent books on the market addressing the mechanics of anchoring, let me quickly cover some key points regarding emergency anchoring procedures that are Coast Guard chief-proven.

The time to consider anchoring is not when the lake has you by the shackles. Again, may I repeat a valuable lesson I learned as an underway officer of the deck aboard Coast Guard cutters: "If in doubt, that is reason enough to call the captain." Call it a shipboard sixth sense, an intuition that familiar patterns seem out of rhythm. A sluggish helm, an unusual sound or no sound at all, a continuous bilge pump light, an unfamiliar odor, a sudden shudder, whatever it may be, these are often telltale sounds of a possible emergency in the making.

It's not just the boat that offers hints of impeding disorder, but the marine environment as well. Unfortunate is the boater who must simultaneously deal with both when nature and boat team up to inflict disorder. Normally, forewarnings, especially regarding foul weather, make their intents known in time to take appropriate action. It's a time that thoughts should turn to anchoring. Hopefully when the moment arrives, the anchor system is in effective working order and the anchor can handle the load. Because, the sole purpose of anchoring is to keep the boat put. How well the boat stays put depends a great deal on anchor type and weight.

Recreational boaters' anchor of choice appears to be the Danforth. Its inventor, R.S. Danforth, designed it for use aboard World War II amphibious landing craft. It proved so effective in holding landing craft off beaches that, following the war, its use adapted well to recreational boats that often operate near shore in shallow water. Flukes shaped like right triangles pivot on an arm allowing the pointed ends of the triangular blades to dig into mud or sand for holding power. Most Coast Guard small craft and even small cutters carry Danforth anchors that can range in weight from two and half pounds to 180 pounds.

Danforth anchors fall under two classifications: Working anchors and storm anchors. Working anchors are designed for anchoring in mild conditions, including overnight stays. For heavy weather, storm anchors are recommended since they weigh more. For example, the suggested anchor weight for a working anchor for a 30-foot boat is 12 pounds, and for a storm anchor, 18 pounds, the latter being nearly 50 percent heavier than a working anchor.

Anchor chain is another weight factor that must be considered. Small lightweight boats under 15 feet should carry 10 feet of 3/16 chain, while a 25-foot boat should carry 15 feet of ¼ inch chain. Length and diameters should increase as boat length increases. The chain acts to hold down the anchor arms so the flukes can dig into the lake floor. Hold it, hold it, enough on details. Let me sum this up by stressing: know your anchoring systems and when and how to use it. And remember emergency anchoring begins dockside.

Simple anchor procedures discussed amongst crewmembers will pay huge dividends when the spray begins to fly. Preparation will allow crewmen to focus on the task at hand rather than how to perform the task when a crisis strikes. I'm nearly lost for words, here, because unless a person has been there, it's difficult to describe the physical upheaval that engulfs a crippled boat and its crew. This isn't some ostentatious survival TV show where a director can holler "cut" when poop hits the rotating oscillator. The only being who can call "cut" when the marine environment begins to devour its wounded is God, and according to proverbs, he helps those who help themselves.

Whether divine wisdom or common sense, the proverb certainly holds true in a close-quarter anchoring emergency, and an effective way of helping oneself is having a pre-anchor game plan.

Two key components of an effective game plan are communications and *life jackets*. Of course, communications won't apply to a solo sailor facing unique challenges. Although when it comes to setting the anchor, the challenges coincide with fully-crewed boats, the most notable challenge is staying aboard the boat. Most anchors are located at the bow, and getting there can be a treacherous journey over narrow side decks. That's if the boat has side decks. Lifelines are normally knee-high above the deck, making them difficult to hold onto unless you crawl. Standing rigging and cabin top grab rails provide greater holding power on a pitching, yawing slippery deck, but still the greatest security of all is a *life jacket*.

Some captains may elect to approach the bow from inside the boat through a forward hatch. Not a bad idea, but beware: water will cascade down hatches. Please, no surprises—make sure the pin that secures the shackle to the anchor ring is moused. If not, the shackle pin could work free when at anchor. Oh, boy!

The crewman should have pliers and a knife readily available: pliers in the event the pin is corroded to the shackle and must be freed so it can be attached to the anchor ring. Of course, with a squared away anchoring system, a finger twist should do. The knife will come in handy in the event a boater has to cut the line due to a fouled anchor that could impede rescuers from taking the boat in tow.

After the crewman makes ready the anchor, communication plays a key role. If the crewman can't hear the captain above the din, hopefully hand signals have been prearranged. Whether by voice or hand, when the captain gives the signal to let go the anchor, the vessel should be heading slowly into the elements if under power, not always an easy task especially for sailboats that tend to fall off when under bare steerage against wind and seas.

Whether the boat is disabled or under power, procedures for letting go the anchor remain the same. Once the captain passes the order to let go the anchor, the crewman should avoid just throwing it overboard, but should pay it out through a chock or bull nose with a half turn around a deck cleat or Samson post. If he does throw it overboard, hopefully the anchor line runs under the life lines and not over them. A wire lifeline could eventually chafe through the rode.

Paying out line allows control over the anchor line and prevents entanglements or a free-running line grabbing a crewman's hand or foot. An 82-foot patrol boat I served aboard experienced an anchor mishap that cost a seaman his foot. A gust of wind had snatched off his hat, and as he reached to grab it he stepped into the bight of the line as it was paying out and it seized his ankle, pulling his foot around a mooring bit and then through a chock, severing off his foot.

The crewman must stay focused and in heavy seas he will be handling an unruly anchor line and a rapid wave action than can jerk, twist and bend the torso about as seas slam into the bow and rain down on the anchor man or woman. Chief Mallory told me when he was serving at Station Marblehead, Ohio he responded to a case involving a woman and an anchor mishap.

The case involved a disabled 47-foot powerboat being driven by winds onto rocks near Sandusky Bay, Lake Erie. The captain had sent his wife forward to set the anchor. Chief Mallory said, "She was standing near the bow with her arm resting on a handrail holding the anchor line palm up. A wave lifted the boat; the anchor chain slacked and when the bow slammed down the anchor took strain. Her forearm resting on the handrail snapped." Chief Mallory a certified EMT added. "When I boarded the boat there was blood everywhere from the open flesh fracture."

For those sail and power boaters, who carry automatic anchor release systems, the ideal of dealing with anchoring off the bow is of little concern. The captain can release a plow anchor off the bow from the helm. No concern that is until the auto anchor device fails—then what? The reasons it may fail are as many as the reasons some assume it will work. Take my word when it comes to heavy weather emergencies all bets are off- have a backup plan in the event it fails.

In all events, should anchoring fail and should near-shore hazards restrict a surface rescue, hope still springs from overhead. And I don't mean divine assistance either, although a prayer or two might be in order. The overhead help I have in mind flutters like an angel and roars like a turbine: these are the helicopters of the Coast Guard's aerial storm warriors.

Coast Guard air crews perform the same feats that made storm warriors of old infamous; removing boat crews off near-shore shipwrecks. But instead of breeches buoys, they use air-lift devices.

Modern day boaters, however, often lack the boating skills that played a huge part in yesteryear's rescues. The following life-saving advice offered by an experienced Coast Guard aircrew will go a long way in getting boaters up to speed on emergency air evacuation procedures.

COAST GUARD AIRCREW OFFERS LIFE-SAVING ADVICE

In the Summer of 2002, a Coast Guard aircrew out of Traverse City, Michigan, airlifted me off a 22-foot recreational boat on Lake Michigan into an HH-65 Dolphin helicopter. We set down at a nearby airport for an interview. For this Senior Chief, it soon developed into shop talk rather than an interview.

The aircrew provided thoughtful insights into the challenges they face assisting boaters and outdoor types who find themselves in need of airborne assistance. Before sharing their thoughts, first let me introduce the aircrew.

The senior member present was Lieutenant Commander Chris Day, an 18-year veteran aviator with the Navy and Coast Guard having spent 11 of those years in the Coast Guard. Lieutenant Chuck Webb flew eight years for the Army and four with the Coast Guard. And the flight mechanic, Chief Brian Buck, is an 18-year Coast Guard veteran. Between them they share nearly 47 years in flight operations, including tours in the Philippines, Korea, Alaska, Florida, San Diego and the Great Lakes. I asked them what advice would they offer an assembly of boaters and outdoor sportsmen regarding air search and rescue. They offered the following boat smart brief.

- **Life Jackets**. The first words out of Chief Buck's mouth were life jackets. The rest of us nodded. "A person in the water wearing a life jacket can be seen from the chest up," said Buck. "Without a life jacket, all you may see is a head." Buck referenced a rescue mission he was involved with in Alaska: "I saw a spot in the water. When we circled back to investigate, it turned out to be a six-man life raft. You can imagine then how difficult it would be spotting a head."

We discussed life jacket colors and the importance of bright colors like international orange, which stands out in water, unlike earth tones such as brown and green that blend with the sea. At night, color is less a factor, but night illumination devices can make a life-saving difference. Any form of night illumination, in fact, regardless of how faint, can be seen with aviation night vision goggles.

- **Night illumination**. Coast Guard aircrews use night vision goggles that can amplify existing light by 40,000 times. The glow from a cigarette will appear as bright as a stop light. A boat's navigational lights can be seen even with a nearly dead battery. The flick from a cigarette lighter will flash like a fully-charged strobe light. A flash light with fresh batteries looks like an airport beacon.

Even without night vision goggles, night illumination devices can catch the eye. Lieutenant Commander Day told of a rescue case on Lake Erie near Cleveland: "A green spinning glow caught my eye from around 500 feet up. It was a boater spinning a green night glow stick on the end of shoe lace." In another case, Day spotted an overdue party in a swamp area. The stranded boater had wrapped a handkerchief soaked in gasoline around an oar and torched it to draw attention. The aircrew vectored Coast Guard boats to the rescue.

Of the stories I've heard regarding airborne eyes picking up surface illumination, the one regarding the woman who fell from a deer stand in a swamp area near Ludington, Michigan illustrates just how well night vision aids can detect the faintest source of light. The woman had fallen from her stand and broken her leg. As night approached, loved ones became concerned as to her whereabouts. The late fall air carried hints of winter and exposure became a concern to rescuers, including the Coast Guard, who along with local rescue responders were combing the swamp lands where she had reportedly hunted.

Overhead a Coast Guard air crew swept the area. "When I first spotted the light with my night vision goggles it caused me to squint my eyes," said the air crewman that was lowered down to investigate the light source. "I spotted the woman lying on the ground alongside a tree. While treating her, I asked for the flash light she had used to beam us. I turned it on and there was no light. I held it up to my palm and could barely detect a faint glow, yet it saved her life," said the air crewman, who urges outdoor types pursuing nighttime sporting adventures to carry night illumination and to check batteries.

- **Location**. Next to stressing life jackets, the aircrew stressed location. "If you make a five to ten second distress call, make it count by providing your location. Search is the first part of search and rescue and it's the hardest part," said Day. The moment they fire up the helicopter, it begins guzzling up rescue time. To spend needless time searching for a boater and then, to at last locate him or her, only to run short of fuel and not be able to assist would be a tragedy, especially if it's a life-threatening situation. Coast Guard aviators are good, but they do face limitations, mainly fuel burn time.

Providing an accurate location not only applies to boaters but other outdoor sportsmen as well. A hand-held GPS, cell phone, or marine radio, are safety equipment all outdoor recreational buffs should consider. A densely-wooded area can seal off the eye from those flying above, which can be even more challenging if those being sought are wearing camouflage clothing. "Sometimes all these factors are fighting us, but none greater than the location factor," said Day.

- **Hoisting**. Now that the air crew has located you, they must now haul you aboard. But first, boaters should stow all loose gear that could be sucked up into the rotor blades or foul the hoisting cable. If the boat lacks a radio, the flight mechanic (mec) will send a handheld radio down on a trail line. Instructions between the pilot and boater will expedite the rescue, enhance safety, and reduce hovering time, which guzzles up fuel.

Those below should avoid touching the basket until the flight mechanic grounds the static discharge caused by the rotor blades. The flight mechanic grounds the cable discharge by contacting the basket with water, the boat, or, if over land, the ground. If you grab the basket before it's grounded, believe me, you won't do it again.

In the event that the hoist appears to be too much of a challenge for those being assisted, or if someone is injured, the pilot will send down a rescue swimmer, who is also an EMT. Fortunately, in most cases, the flight crew and those being assisted can execute the hoist; the rescue swimmer is deployed only as a last resort. Remember too, remove all lose items from the boat deck that could be sucked into the helicopter's rotor blades.

- **Splash it up** Lieutenant Commander Day described a technique that Coast Guard rescue swimmers use to draw the eye of aircrews. "While conducting a rescue swimmer drill in West Traverse Bay, I approached the location of the rescue swimmer, who was around 20 feet off the stern of a Coast Guard Auxiliary boat. My altitude was around 50 feet and I knew his approximate location, but choppy water and sun glare obscured him until he began splashing water vertically into the air. He then stood right out," said Day. This is a standard technique that not only rescue swimmers use, it is now part of Coast Guard pilot's open water rescue training. It does, indeed work, as the following case reveals.

In these same waters of Traverse Bay, Lieutenant Webb located a father and his 11-year-old son who caught the pilot's attention after kicking water into the air. Their 18-foot catamaran had capsized in four to six foot seas. Winds carried the sailboat away leaving

Coast Guard air and surface crews often perform hoisting drills. Their primary safety concerns: remove all loose gear from the deck to keep it from being sucked into the rotor blades, and avoid touching the hoisting cable until it has been grounded to avoid static shock. Recreational boaters should follow these same procedures.

the two adrift in the bay. Both were wearing life jackets, which Web believes saved their lives considering they were in the water several hours and the boy had injured his arm. The helicopter made several pass overs near the pair, but four to six foot seas brushed white by wind and illuminated by a late afternoon sun concealed the father and son amongst the mix. That is until the boy began kicking water skyward with his feet while floating on his back, which quickly drew the eye of the aircrew, leading to a successful rescue.

- **Summary**. Chief Buck led off the discussion by stressing life jackets and he ended it by stressing education. "Boater safety courses are important. There are lots of common mistakes that could be avoided if boaters had a clue. Also, carrying basic safety equipment aboard can pay off big," said Buck.

"The Great Lakes can be very unforgiving in late season," said Lieutenant Commander Day. Hopefully by following the advice of these highly skilled and experienced rescue responders, you will avoid becoming one of the Great Lake's unforgiven. This same advice applies to winter sports enthusiasts as well. The following incredible rescue does not involve a boat, but instead snowmobiles, and considering the number of snowmobile fatalities that involve water, the safety messages it carries needs to be aired for water is water regardless of how one may end up in it regardless of the season.

BEWARE STAY OFF UNSTABLE ICE

What are the odds of surviving for two hours after plunging through ice on a snowmobile late at night into 30-degree water with 40-knot artic winds casting a 50-minus wind chill across ice-glazed Green Bay?

It's a long shot not even Vegas would touch, yet a couple did beat these insurmountable odds, thanks to a retired Coast Guard boatswain mate chief's local knowledge of Green Bay, the survivor's fierce will to live, and the gutsy efforts of an Eagle III,

Splashing water distorts the water's surface pattern and can catch the eye of rescue air crews.

helicopter crew at County Rescue Services, Green Bay.

Now the story.

CASE FILE: Green Bay, Wisconsin, January 21, 2004. The Brown County Joint Dispatch Center received a cell-phone call from a male at 9:49 p.m. "My girlfriend…my snowmobile went under the water somewhere by those flashing lights. I'm OK. We have to get out of here."

The 911 call lasted two minutes, and the location the caller provided was sketchy at best: A green light on the left and a red light on the right and a water tower somewhere in Green Bay. End of call…

Brown County 911 contacted Eagle III rescue dispatch and requested air assistance. At 10:10 p.m., George Miller, Eagle III's Director of Operations, senior pilot and a crew chief launched an all-weather IFR rated twin turbo powered EC-135 helicopter.

The Eagle III crew made several sweeps over the waters of lower Green Bay. They determined that poor visibility called for additional equipment, in particular an Ultra 7000 Forward Looking Infrared (FLIR) system capable of detecting temperature differences down to three tenths of a degree Celsius, which can then be converted into a visible picture displayed on an onboard screen on the EC-135's flight console. In the end, however, it would not be the space-age FLIR system that saved the day, but a couple of inflatable life rings that crew chief Shaun Stammes snatched up just before they launched again at 10:45 p.m.

Back in the air, Eagle III headed for Grassey Island on the 911 read provided by Brain Hinckley, a full-time paramedic on duty that night and a retired Coast Guard boatswain mate chief and

A Coast Guard aircrew aboard an HH-65 helicopter airborne over Lake Michigan sets course for Air Station Traverse City after conducting hoisting drills with Station Manistee's 47-foot motor lifeboat.

auxilarist familiar with Green Bay. Miller made several sweeps over the waters near Grassey Island, which is located two miles north of the City of Green Bay adjacent to the shipping canal. On the third sweep, the helicopter's 30 million-candle watt beam picked up a reflection on the south end of Grassy Island. "I dropped low and headed for the island, no larger than the size of a ranch house," said Miller.

The person in the water had crawled onto the island and was standing as the helicopter approached. "The wind force buffeted the aircraft as I held station while my crewman prepared to pull the victim aboard," said Miller. The rotary blades swirled snow about under the intense glow of the night sun. "I held the aircraft several inches off a boulder while using a nearby stone structure as a reference point to maintain station," said Miller. The helicopter did not carry a cable and basket hoisting system.

Emergency medical technician Mike Orlando crouched in the bay, braced his 150-pound frame to haul aboard the human statue stiffly posed in a frozen body cast. The helicopter hovered inches off the ground ready to receive the frozen cargo. "The guy barely had use of his arms and he wrapped them around Mike's neck as he pulled him aboard," said Miller. "When Mike removed the victim's helmet, it was a woman."

How could that be?

During the two-minute cell phone call to 911, the caller reported: "My girlfriend ... my snowmobile went under the water ...." To Miller and his crew that meant the caller was still out in the winter-locked bay. They whisked her back to waiting paramedics who cut her free of the frozen body cast.

Airborne again, the aircrew raced back to Grassey Island. "We figured he had to be somewhere close," said Miller. Near the island the night sun picked up snowmobile tracks, which led them a mile or so north to Longtail light, a large white cylindrical tower bordering the Green Bay shipping channel.

It was now 11:49, two hours since the initial call to 911.

The aircrew couldn't believe the woman had covered over a mile and a half to reach Grassey Island until Shawn Stammes spotted a flickering red light in the water and realized this is where they broke through the ice. Miller dropped down to several feet off the water and saw a man waving a helmet over his head with a red light attached. "He was struggling to keep his head up." The man was near the 35-foot high channel marker, so near, in fact, that Miller had to keep station off the man so the rotor blade wouldn't strike the structure.

Stammes ordered Mike Orlando to heave a self-inflating life ring, but the rotor wash blew it out of reach: "I maneuvered to the right, hoping my rotor wash would push the inflatable towards the man. It didn't." Stammes directed Orlando to throw a second life ring with a line attached. "He hit the guy right in the chest. The guy grabbed the line with wet bare hands. How he held on to the three-quarter-inch line and life ring in a minus 50 degree wind chill accelerated by the rotor blast is a miracle," said Miller.

The veteran pilot gingerly backed the helicopter away from the structure, pulling the man back about 10 feet through ice and creating a narrow corridor in which he could support himself on the ice with his elbows. Miller then inched forward; the man hooked an arm over a skid. Miller slowly hovered backwards dragging the man under Orlando's direction onto solid ice where he lay in a prone position, too weak to stand.

Unable to land on the unstable ice, Miller stationed the helicopter within inches of the man. At one time, Orlando feared the landing skid might crush him under the 7,000 pound aircraft. The heat from the 30-million candle watt night sun melted ice, which the rotor wash whipped up. The rotor spray immediately turn back to ice on the bottom of the aircraft not exposed to the night sun. The entire bay lay blanketed in ice. Worse yet, condensation from body heat and outside air began fogging the cockpit windows. The rotor blade whirling within a few feet of the 35-foot tower notched up the tension. Orlando was dressed in a flight suit only: a 40-knot wind bearing a wind chill of 50 below zero brutalized his exposed flesh, seeping the life

from his hands while coating his legs arms face and upper body in ice.

"Grab and pull his butt into the chopper," said Miller, concerned the spreading condensation would seal off his reference point to the tower. Mike rolled the man's upper body up onto the cabin floor, his hands all but void of feeling. "It was extremely cold," said Orlando. With the snowmobiler's upper body in the helicopter, his legs protruded outside the craft in a frozen, cockeyed distortion. With a Herculean burst, he hauled the 300-pound ice-crusted stiff aboard and dumped him into a jump seat. The man was twice Orlando's weight. How he pulled the frozen bulk up over the skid and into the aircraft, not even Orlando could explain when I spoke with him later.

Within minutes the aircraft was back at its landing port. Paramedics lifted the man from the helicopter frozen in a sitting position. "His body core temperature was 80 degrees," said Miller.

Miller contributes their survival to a fierce will to live, well-insulated foul weather gear and layered underwear, a red strobe light, night illumination material, and a cell phone.

And, I might add, thanks to some nifty flying by George Miller, a veteran Marine helicopter pilot who served two tours in Vietnam, one as a search and rescue pilot, with over 9,000 logged hours on rotary aircraft. "This was the toughest rescue I ever made, and I couldn't have pulled it off without my crew chief, Shaun Stammes, and Mike Orlando," said Miller. That's from a pilot who received three purple hearts, the distinguished Flying Cross, and 34 Combat Air Medals.

On September 16, 2004, Rear Admiral Robert Papp J., Commander Ninth Coast Guard district, along with the Group Milwaukee Commander. S. P. LaRochelle, awarded the Distinguished Public Service Award to Shaun Stamnes, Mike Orlando, and George Miller for their lifesaving rescue.

Coast Guard Warrant Officer Erick Schmidt described a similar ice rescue while stationed at St. Clare Shores, Detroit. A snowmobiler decided to cut across Lake St. Clair. His buddy elected to skirt around the lakeshore to a chosen destination. The shoreline snowmobilier made it; his buddy, however, plunged through the ice. The incident

From left to right: pilot George Miller, survivor Richard Olszewski, Mike Orlando emergency medical technician, and survivor Beth Casa. On the night of January 21, 2004, the flight crew of County Rescue Services, Green Bay, plucked the couple from the icy waters of Green Bay after their snowmobiles plunged in the bay.

occurred at night. The victim managed to crawl up onto the ice. The following morning a Coast Guard aircrew spotted him. "When we reached him, he appeared posed in ice in a crawling position, his hands and knees anchored by ice. Amazingly he was alive. The full-body protective gear and helmet fended off the sub-zero weather," said Schmidt. The man, however, did suffer severe frostbite to his hands and toes.

As we move onto the last and final chapter, I firmly believe that if you have come this far along in the boat smart journey, you are already a great deal more water wise than when we set out together ten chapters ago. Hopefully along the way you have benefited from those who have experienced misfortune in the waters in which we have passed. Believe me, that situational awareness will serve you well as you strive to boat smart. Let's move on now to the final chapter and a historical perspective of this era of less than smart boating.

Boat Smart Anchor Points

Water-Wise Ice Rescue Survival Tips

Drowning is one of the leading causes of water related snowmobile fatalities. During early January 2003 in Northern Michigan within the span of four days six males in separate snowmobile mishaps drowned after plunging through unstable ice. In February and March, warming weather patterns can produce unstable ice across the Great Lakes. Snowmobile operators should pay heed to weather forecast calling for temperatures in the 30s or 40s. The following ice-rescue survival tips could save your life

Coast Guard surface and aircrews team up for ice-rescue drills. Coast Guard helicopters play a vital role in ice rescue since they can access remote areas such as ice floes adrift with stranded sportsmen, or unstable ice too dangerous for surface rescue crews to forge.

↪ Do not operate a snowmobile on ice over water at night. The couple that plunged into Green Bay were not only operating at night upon unstable ice, they were also from Illinois and unfamiliar with Green Bay.

↪ If several snowmobilers are operating on ice, they should not run in tandem, but spread out fore and aft so if one breaks through the ice the other can assist.

↪ Carry a length of nylon line with a small weight on the end. This could be used to assist another person who fell through the ice.

↪ Should an operator break though the ice, do not accelerate: it could carry you further away from ice into open water and out of reach of help or climbing back onto the ice.

↪ Carry two ice awl picks attached together with a line you can wear around your neck. Place the awls in an upper pocket so they don't ride over your neck if you plunge into water. In the water, there's less chance of losing one or both awls if attached to a line. Should you end up in the water, pick with the awls and kick with your feet to pull yourself onto solid ice. Mike Orlando said the woman told him she held onto a slab of ice and kicked to move forward.

↪ Carry a marine radio or cell phone and flares in a water tight plastic bag, also carry a whistle. Wear a life jacket or flotation suit. At night, carry a strobe light. A hand-held GPS in a water-tight bag could prove to be a life saver. Deploy these devices immediately, before hands grow numb.

↪ Place reflective tape on your foul-weather suit. The reason the flight crew spotted the gal was that the seams of her dark-colored foul-weather exposure suit had 1/8 inch thread piping that reflected light from the nightsun. If not for those seams, it's doubtful they would have spotted her. The man was spotted because his helmet carried a flashing red breaker light.

↪ Wear full body protective suit with insulation and thermal underwear. Mike Orlando told me when he cut away the survivor's exposure suit, the inner layer of thermal wear felt sweaty and warm to the touch, even though the man's core body temperature was 80 degrees F.

↪ Beware! Stable ice can turn unstable in hours. Take special note of warming trends in February and March.

↪ And lastly, lay off the alcohol while operating a snowmobile: over the last ten years, 61 percent of Michigan snowmobile fatalities involved alcohol and drugs.

A Historical View of Recreational Boating

IMAGINE FOLKS A HUNDRED YEARS FROM NOW READING THE *BOAT SMART CHRONICLES* and experiencing first-hand stories based on real-life events that occurred a century ago. While researching ninetieth-century archives, I found no records that covered Lake Michigan boating in the format of the *Boat Smart Chronicles*. Those that I did uncover; commercial ship logs, United States Lifesaving Service logs, and logs of shipwrecks and accounts printed in newspapers, reported weather and fires as the cause of most marine mishaps.

LOOKING BACK

But then what other reasons other than physical causes could explain marine mishaps a century ago; that is until the advent of recreational boating. This modern day phenomenon has unleashed a boater impulsiveness that often fails to even recognize prevailing dangers on the water. Those that finally do often seem to ignore them. Interestingly however, those that finally do get aboard the boating education bandwagon become dismayed in retrospect and often become fervent advocates for safe boating.

Instructors who teach boating safety courses for the Coast Guard Auxiliary and U.S. Power Squadron tell me that boaters are aghast at how naive they had been regarding boating safety and their own well being upon the water. Every boater, they proclaim, should take a boating course. Oh, how I like driving home that point during boating safety lectures, taking note to emphasize the treacherous beguiling side of the marine environment and how it seemingly preys on boaters in denial. Especially the many who assume recreational boating mishaps are weather related. I do my best to subvert this erroneous belief. The fact is the marine environment works its ill will most effectively when in the so called "nice day" mode.

A student once approached me after a boating and safety class where I unloaded a bevy of boating nice-day horror stories and said, "You made me scared to death of boating."

I bore into his eyes and said, "Good!"

I believe the shock approach packs value as illustrated: I received a letter from an 87-year-old lady with a photograph of herself wearing a life jacket. She advised me after reading my stories in her local newspaper that she vowed to be a safer boater. Her big challenge, however, was to get her older brother, who often takes her boating, to wear a life jacket. Halleluiah! You are never too old.

Looking forward a hundred years from now, I'm sure Boat Smart readers will readily see the dangers a woman nearly a century old herself finally grasped. What readers may fail to see or understand is why boaters so often failed to pay heed. Perhaps, it's the name "recreational boating." Do we call automobile driving "recreational driving," or flying aircraft "recreational flying." Absolutely not, and yet recreational boating can be a great deal more complex than driving an automobile. Driving on city streets and highways is facilitated by concrete corridors, enforced rules and familiar road signs. Pilots also enjoy a similar structure maintained by the vigilant eye of air controllers and also licensing requirements.

Obviously, legislators believe flying an aircraft demands certain skills and training, as does driving an automobile. Yet there are no such demands placed on the operators of recreational boats. After years of driving automobiles and boats, I can vouch the latter is far more challenging. I suspect a close look at fatalities will reveal more recreational boaters die than automobile operators per time of use. Most people spend more time behind the wheel of a car in a week or two than many boaters spend behind the helm of a boat over an entire boating season. This comparison holds especially true for Great Lakes' boaters, given the region's short boating season.

If you believe I am overstating my point, consider this: when an automobile breaks down, the operator pulls over to the side of the road and awaits help within the safe confines of an automobile with little or no threat from the environment disregarding, of course, the human threat. When a boat breaks down on the water, the operator can only hope that help will be available. Often while waiting for help—if it arrives at all—he or she could be facing deteriorating weather or worse yet, a foundering boat, or both. Most boaters are ill-equipped to handle either dilemma. And boats seldom stand still, unlike disabled automobiles. Boats often become illusive targets for searchers as the disabled craft drifts to and fro under the willful influence of prevailing and potentially overwhelming forces.

The challenge facing this current generation of boaters is to move beyond a recreational narrow mindlessness and view boating as a serious endeavor while enjoying it in a recreational venue. Hopefully, a hundred years from now recreational boaters will have moved beyond a Pollyannaish mind set, a blind optimism that underscores most recreational boating fatalities. Statistics clearly show that most boating fatalities occur in mild weather the so-called "ideal boating day."

Sad fair-weather tales fill this book and have filled my column over the years and they continue to fill the files of the Coast Guard and other rescue agencies. And there appears to be no closure in sight. Oh, how I wish I could encapsulate these boating mishaps and prescribe them to boaters. Maybe in a hundred years this will be possible. And in a hundred years I hope that wearing life jackets is mandatory for all boaters and that maybe more advanced user-friendly life jackets will have evolved. Please, let us not see blue and green and similarly colored life jackets that camouflage a persons' presence in the water—let safety, not style, dictate the color.

With all due respect to life jacket manufactures, some are moving in a safety-foremost direction with light inflatables and upper body Type III mesh life jackets. But we have a long way to go not only to encourage boaters to wear life jackets but also to make them an item they wish to wear. One way or another, something must be done. Annually, nearly 70 percent of all the recreational boating fatalities are due to drowning, and nearly 85 percent of the victims who drowned were not wearing life jackets. I don't need a hundred years of hindsight to decry that woeful figure, but I might need a hundred years to explain it.

Another subject that no doubt will baffle 22nd century readers is how boaters had little or no instruction. I can only imagine what will they think when they look back to the early 21st century and note that the only qualification demanded of recreational boaters was the ability to turn a key or pull a starter cord. What might baffle them even more is that Coast Guard annual *Boating Statistics* revealed that 83 percent of reported boating fatalities occurred on boats where the operator had not received boating safety instruction. So they might ask, why didn't legislators enact mandatory legislation to assure that boaters boat smart?

In all fairness to federal legislators, they did take positive action to improve boating safety with the enactment of the Federal Boat Safety Act of 1971. Part of the act called for the establishment of a National Recreational Boating Safety Program. A major role of the Safety Program was to allocate monies to states to develop and expand their boating education and other water-related safety programs. Another important provision of the act required boaters to carry safety equipment aboard recreational boats. Since the Federal Boat Safety Act was passed in 1971, recreational boating fatalities have been cut in half, reaching an all-time low of 676 fatalities in 2004. That's very encouraging considering registered boats have nearly doubled to 13 million over the period.

Now the downside, although fatalities have dramatically dropped there has been an alarming increase in serious boating injuries—nearly a 170 percent increase since 1971.

The reason for injuries once again can be found in Coast Guard *Boating Statistics*. Over a recent five year period *Boating Statistics* show that collisions with a fixed object, a floating object and another vessel accounted for 43 percent of all boating injuries. The proliferation of small boats offering a barn-full of horse power could be the cause. For $17,000 a person can purchase a new off-the-showroom 17-foot runabout. The boat can carry six persons and houses a 225 horse power motor that packs enough juice to reach serious speeds. Many small lakes now buzz with small fast boats. Many fishermen have told me they don't fish in certain one-time favorite lakes because of the fast boat factor. I wonder how many of these fast boat operators have taken a boating safety course.

Then, of course, we have the modern-day personal water craft (PWC) craze that has spread across the waters like jet-fueled locusts, occasionally leaving broken limbs in its wake. It's interesting to note, marine authorities advise me that they have noticed a noticeable decrease in PWC infractions from the younger age group. Many states now require young operators to carry a certificate indicating they have completed a state approved PWC safety course.

Although boating safety is moving in the right direction, there are issues that beg to be addressed not only regarding the speed factor, but the establishment of mandatory boating education laws. I believe such laws will come to pass; hopefully, this will happen sooner rather than later and hopefully law makers will get it right.

GETTING IT RIGHT

Hopefully legislators will write into law extensive boating safety course requirements and not watered-downed legislation to placate those opposed to mandatory education. I suspect the strongest opposition comes from financial boating interests fearful that mandatory education laws will create economic speed bumps that will slow down consumer spending. After all, let us not place obstacles in the way of a potential boat purchase. Ironically, it was economics that drove legislators to impose mandatory education and licensing requirements on the commercial fleet. I'll address this in a minute.

First let me point out that on one hand legislators impose mandatory education and licensing requirements on one group within the marine community while completely ignoring another. Yet, both commercial and recreational boaters must deal with the same marine environment and its complexities. In fact, the recreational boater is far less equipped to deal with those complexities. So, tell me why is one required to be licensed and not the other?

It's a legitimate question and I believe money has a lot to do with this fatal disparity. Example, if I take a group out on a 25-foot boat and charge these folks, the Code of Federal Regulations requires that I carry a Coast Guard captain's license. Now, if I take the same folks out for gratis, no license is required. Nothing. I could be old or young with little or no experience and I can go out on a boat unrestricted. Apparently then, it is money, not safety, that dictates license requirements either for or against licensing. The commercial people make fat financial targets so they strive to keep safe. Recreational boating financial interests strive to facilitate the sale of recreational boats so they resist mandatory education.

Sadly, the lack of educational requirements has spelled disaster for the recreational fleet. According to Coast Guard recreational *Boating Statistics*, between 1962 and 2005, 47,255 recreational boaters have died in addition to 111,461 injuries requiring serious medical assistance. Coast Guard *Boating Statistics* year after year show that over 80 percent of boating fatalities reveal the operator had no form of boating instruction. These figures cover state-registered boats only and do not include fatalities involving non-registered boats, or fatalities that occur on private waters not under state jurisdiction. These figures no doubt would push the fatality figure higher; but then come on, over 47,000 fatalities alone is totally inexcusable and totally unacceptable. We simply can't wait a hundred years to get this right and for damn sure it will not take care of itself. Especially as more and more clueless boaters access the marine environment.

As aggressive as state marine officials, Coast Guard officials, and officials representing boating and safety campaigns promote safe boating, it's simply not enough. It's like telling kids they should behave, but then they really don't have to, but please trust us: it's best they do.

Give anyone an option like that and maybe they will comply, if it's convenient for them. Tell me how will a man with a boy-like mentality and the zealous owner of a 19-foot runabout speedboat behave. After a long week in the work harness, he is set free on a weekend. Free to go anywhere his impulsive spirit leads him. Understand, for many boaters, recreational boating represents the last of the true frontiers where body and mind can experience few boundaries. So, no one had better dampen that spirit with boating education requirements. After all, it's the natural marine environment's magic draw on a warm alluring summer day. A time when life seems so laid-back and carefree, it simply does not lend well to impositions. And with an eye on the beer cooler, who really cares.

I understand all too well the open range mentality of recreational boaters.

Often as a Coast Guard boarding officer, I interrupted boaters engrossed in the rapture of the marine environment. The Coast Guard crew, armed with side arms and bearing the authority of what some boaters referred to as water Nazis, stirred up uneasiness. We conducted the inspections with grace in spite of the sour climate. Many boaters brooded, silently musing: why me on this special day that is mine in the sun. Oh, how I disliked intruding on boaters and even more the Nazi inference, but I absolutely condoned the mission objective—keeping boaters safe. I passionately still do, and I strongly encourage the Coast Guard, state Department of Natural Resource officers, and county marine sheriff deputies to keep up afloat inspections. Read on and understand due cause for my fervor.

During August of 2004, I was flying spotter for Coast Guard Auxiliary pilot Ben Lautner during a Homeland Security air patrol along the eastern shore of Lake Michigan. I was manning the marine radio and maintaining radio guard with Coast Guard Group Grand Haven. While flying along the shore near Holland, Michigan, I listened to radio traffic between a Coast Guard boarding officer and radio Group Grand Haven. The boarding officer requested permission to terminate a recreational boat; that is, to remove the boat from the water due to unsafe conditions. From 1,500 feet, I could see very little looking eastward towards Lake Macatawa where the termination was unfolding. But what I could see was an absolutely ideal day for flying and perhaps even more ideal for boating—perfect, in fact.

So why the termination?

The following day I called Station Holland and talked with Coast Guardsman Harvey Hyman, the boarding officer, who terminated the voyage. He said, "This 16-foot runabout, packing a 150 horsepower Yamaha inboard motor, had five people aboard. There were no life jackets or fire extinguishers aboard, and as unbelievable as it seems the ages of the children aboard were three, two and an infant. Let me stress, there were no life jackets, none. Unbelievable," said Hyman.

Oh, how I wish it were unbelievable.

A GRIM OUTLOOK

If current trends continue, exemplified by this clueless boater accessing the water with toddlers and an infant and no life jackets, the future holds a grim outlook for recreational boating. Earlier in the book I addressed an incident on the same lake where a boater jumped a wake that dumped his family into the lake. Fortunately the two adults and three children aboard were wearing life jackets and survived with minor injuries. What if the same had happened to the other boater? Imagine, two adults attempting to rescue two toddlers and an infant after they were ejected from a boat and none of them were wearing a life jackets. It's fortuitous for them that random selection missed an opportunity, but there promises to be more than enough opportunities for recreational boaters to be randomly culled out if trends continue.

Coast Guard recreational *Boating Statistics* in the first four years of the 21st century indicated that if current trends continue the lookout looks gloomy in fact downright depressing. Let the figures tell their own doomsday story.

Take the number of fatalities -708- that occurred in the first four years of the 21st century and multiply it by one hundred years. That's 70,800 projected doomed recreational boaters and possibly far more as recreational boating grows in numbers as the U.S. population expands. U.S. Census Bureau's high series projections forecast that the nation will expand by 268 million people by 2050. Take reported boating injuries requiring medical assistance that occurred during that same four-year period and project it over a hundred years and we are looking at 1.5 million recreational boaters facing possible injures requiring medical treatment. And the financial losses based on current trends are staggering—four billion dollars projected in property damage, and the figure does not include inflation or population increases, or an increase in recreational boats.

If you believe I'm a gloom-and-doom prophet, I urge you to re-read the book, for unless I made up these stories, which I did not, tell me, what's to stop this on-going saga of boating mishaps and mischief and its subsequent costly and deadly fallout?

Recreational boating losses will surely escalate if U.S. Census population projections hold true. Project that same doom-and-gloom figure for commercial boating industry and expect skies to darken with legal vultures flapping about, eager to lay their litigant-fangs into commercial fat-cash cows. No doubt, regulators would shut down the industry. In spite of how lawyers might decry this accusation, I ask, "What have lawyers done to apply the same pressure to prevent recreational boating mishaps?" Little, if nothing: there's little money to be had. After all, what financial legal target is there when a recreational boater dies due to his or her own shortcomings, which is the leading cause of most recreational boating fatalities?

By the way, let me set the record straight regarding commercial captains.

In spite of the legal intimidation factor, commercial captains by instinct and tradition valiantly uphold the safety of their passengers, and because of that and in spite of legal predators the commercial fleet enjoys a near accident-free record. On the other hand, recreational boaters benefit neither from legal intimidation, maritime traditions, or economic imperatives that drive the commercial fleet. Recreational boating is an option, a sport-like activity people pursue out of choice, not economic necessity. In short, they can take it or leave it?

I suspect some in the boating industry fear boaters will leave it if obstacles like boating education become law. I totally disagree with this conjecture. The fact that nearly 13 million registered boaters and countless other water enthusiasts pursue our waterways validates a passion for marine activities. Mandatory boating education will not abate that passion but actually enhance interest as water-goers become more comfortable and confident as they engage the marine environment.

Mandatory boating laws certainly didn't dampen boating enthusiasm in the state of Connecticut. When Connecticut imposed mandatory boating education for all ages in 1997, the number of registered recreational boats was 98,494. In

2004 it had climbed to 111,991 registered boats. I can image certain interest groups were opposed to mandatory boating education in Connecticut as some are currently in other states. I've already bemoaned why certain interests oppose mandatory boating education so let me now plead with them to reconsider their position because it's the *right* thing to do. Especially considering the limited time boaters spend on the water, in particular the Great Lakes.

Don't be mislead, either, by states that claim to have mandatory boating education laws on the books. Many do carry laws; however, these laws address only a limited segment of the boating population, in particular personal watercraft (PWC). Even PWC mandatory education laws can be misleading since the mandatory law targets a younger age group and not all PWC operators. As I stated earlier: marine sheriff deputies who enforce these laws say they have seen a noticeable decrease in violations in the young age group which is subject to mandatory boating education laws. It's the older folks who didn't take a PWC safety course that are committing the violations, including those who rent PWCs. Obviously what worked for the younger people will also work for the older folks. So, to get this right mandatory boating education must include the entire spectrum of recreational boating and the State of Connecticut has taken that initiative. Other states might do well to follow their lead.

CONNECTICUT ON THE CUTTING EDGE

In Connecticut there are approximately 113,000 registered vessels that navigate Long Island Sound and the state's hundreds of rivers, streams, lakes, and ponds. The State has one of the most aggressive and stringent mandatory boating education and certification programs in the nation.

As of October 1,1997, all Connecticut boaters are required to carry a Safe Boating Certificate to legally operate a recreational boat in the State of Connecticut. This includes all boats with motors and sailboats over 19.5 feet in length. In addition, anyone operating a Personal Watercraft in the State must have a Certificate of Personal Watercraft Operation (CPWO) regardless of age. The CPWO allows an operator to drive both motorized vessels and personal watercraft. Connecticut boating officials refer to the program as "Certification" and stress it is *not* a "license."

To obtain a Safe Boating Certificate a boater must complete a state approved eight-hour Safe Boating Course offered by a number of sources, such as community colleges, adult education programs, parks and recreation centers. Volunteer instructors teach all courses. The course and materials are free. There are also a number of commercial vendors who offer State approved courses for a fee.

Connecticut's Department of Environmental Protection, Licensing and Revenue Department's one-time $25 dollar fee for the Safe Boating Certificate funds the entire education program. Since this department already handles various permits like hunting and fishing endorsements there was no need to create an onerous bureaucracy.

Upon completion of the required course, a proctored examination is administered with a score of 80 percent or better needed to pass and obtain a certificate. In addition, the DEP will accept U.S. Power Squadron or Coast Guard Auxiliary boating courses, the applicant must still pass a proctored examination for certification.

The examination covers a range of boating topics: rules of the road, weather, aids to navigation, boating laws, and others.

Connecticut was also the nation's leader in personal watercraft education. Since mandatory education for PWC's for all *ages* took effect in Connecticut during the mid 90s there has been only one PWC fatality in eight years, and that was in the summer of 2001 when a PWC operator passed between a commercial boat towing another boat; the towing cable severed his upper body. Connecticut attributes this near-perfect record to their mandatory education and certification program.

According to Connecticut's DEP Boating Division, critics of the program feel the course is not comprehensive enough, and that it should require on-the-water training and testing. The

Coast Guard Auxiliary and Power Squadrons feel boaters need more than eight hours of safe boating instruction. Still, politically and practically, an eight hour course is definitely better than nothing, and by no means do I mean to depreciate this outstanding program Connecticut has implemented.

HANDS ON BOATING SAFETY COURSE

Will eight hours be enough to make boaters smart or will it require a few days, several weeks, or months, or is time a factor at all? Absolutely, it's a huge factor not necessarily regarding how much time it takes to convey safe boating information but how much time people are willing to give in order to pursue the information. Therein lies the challenge; developing a short but meaningful boating safety course.

I would develop a safety course that would not only be short—two days at most—it would be "chocked-full" of hands-on training and it would be as simple as tying a figure eight knot. I learned a valuable lesson over the years from training Coast Guard personnel on rescue boats—the simpler the instruction, the quicker the person digests the material.

Seamanship by its very nature is simple, and to bog down the learning process with a lot of jargon and definitions is not necessary. During an emergency who cares whether one knows the definition of a transom but what one needs to know is how to climb back aboard the boat's transom or if you will the boat's back end. I've taught many Coast Guard Auxiliary courses over the years and have learned to separate the wheat from the chaff. Take the aids to navigation (ATON) segment that is part of the thirteen lesson Boating Skills and Seamanship Course. The ATON course material comprises seventeen pages, yet I would convey in ten minutes what boaters absolutely needed to know about aids to navigation to keep safe on the water. Don't misunderstand me, the 13 lesson course is fabulous; however, the length is too long a period to mandate for boaters. Although, I highly encourage boaters to pursue the course if time allows and other fine boating courses the Coast Guard Auxiliary and U.S. Power Squadron offer. So what I suggest is that the essence of the topic be plucked from these courses and other boating materials.

Let me provide an example. The Coast Guard Auxiliary's 17-page aids to navigation section boils down to a simple concept: aids to navigation mark safe water and allow a boater to know where they are on the water. To demonstrate the principle I would take two people from the class and hand them a colored construction board cut-out of an even numbered red nun buoy and odd numbered green can buoy. They stand across from one another and face me holding the cutouts. Their function is to mark the outer boundaries of a safe navigational channel. I then pass between them pretending I was a boat. To my right stands the person holding the red nun buoy, to the left the person with the green can buoy. Remember, "Red Right Returning." That is, when returning from seaward or the lake, keep the red aids to the right and the green to the left. To demonstrate the importance of "Red Right Returning" principle, I place a chair to the left of the person holding the red nun buoy cutout and then demonstrate to the class what happens if I pass the red buoy on its left side. Bang, I run into the chair representing unsafe water.

I have performed the same visual demonstration with lighted aids. I turn off the overhead lights to demonstrate the light characteristic of local aids to navigation lights. This hands-on approach of teaching boating safety material is used by other marine safety instructors as well. These hands-on approaches not only send powerful messages, but people will remember them as they partake in the process. And they take little time to demonstrate. It's been my experience that people remember images and experiences for more than terms. I believe one of the drawbacks of boating safety messages and instruction is that they lean too much on terms and not enough on substance. I learned a valuable lesson about writing Boat Smart columns years ago: don't tell them, show them. It works.

The safety topics I would address, just like the stories in this book, would come from the soil of experience. When I began developing the book material I didn't ask what do people need to know to be safe on the water. I let the hundreds of stories I wrote over the years do that: it became readily apparent where people were running into hazards and why. Not surprisingly, the stories parallel the Coast Guard's annual recreational *Boating Statistics* that address boating mishaps. The provocative report, which I have reference throughout the book, has its fingers on the pulse of recreational boating. The reports reveals the what, where, who, why and how of recreational boating mishaps.

From this rich source of material and that of the book, I would develop a boating safety course that would make boaters aware of common mishaps and how to avoid them. As far as instructors, there's a rich pool of experience already available. Coast Guard Auxiliary, U.S. Power Squadron folks, marine sheriff deputies, marina owners, mechanics, harbor masters, Department of Natural Resource officers, coasties both active and retired, pilots, ship captains, the list of experience goes on and I couldn't imagine any of these fine folks not volunteering their time. A number already are.

I also guarantee this course would be enjoyable in fact I will go so far as to guarantee that boaters who take the course will promote it to friends as a must take course. To me that's the key: inspiring boaters to learn safe boating not because of federal and state mandates, but because of its inherent life-saving value.

I'm sure mandatory boating education will come to pass much as seat belt, air bag, and motorcycle helmet legislation came to pass. These safety measures stemmed from overwhelming evidence that these safety items prevent injury or death. Unfortunately, dealing with a complex marine environment doesn't boil down to a single safety item, it boils down to Smart Boating—that's mandatory.

AUTHOR BIO

Senior Chief Tom Rau retired from the Coast Guard in May 2002 after serving over 27 years on active duty and in the active reserves. A great deal of his active-duty time was spent on Lake Michigan at six different search and rescue facilities along the eastern shore of Lake Michigan. One of his more notable achievements included writing the "Group and Stations Communications Watchstander Qualification Guide" used throughout the Coast Guard to train radio watchstanders in handling boater's calls for assistance. In 1990, Rear Admiral Robert Nelson, Chief Office of Navigation Safety in a letter to Rau wrote; "This guide has provided us a valuable tool to improve our service to the boating public."

Rau has had a great deal of experience with the boating public in search and rescue even in his later years as a Chief. On his retirement Senior Chief Rau received his second Coast Guard Commendation medal with The Operational Distinguishing Device. The award cited that from May 1997 to May 2002, Senior Chief Rau personally conducted 150 search and rescue cases on the water and performed 435 vessel boardings. His most noted contribution, which two Coast Guard Commandants have personally awarded him for, is the Boat Smart column. Rau has been writing safety articles since 1986. Many of the columns are based on actual Coast Guard cases he has played a part in. During the 2001 Coast Guard Festival in Grand Haven, Michigan, Admiral James Loy, then Commandant of the Coast Guard, awarded Senior Chief Rau the prestigious Alex Haley award for the Boat Smart column.

Even though Senior Chief Rau has retired, he remains active with the Coast Guard Auxiliary in Manistee, Michigan. He also holds a Coast Guard 100 gross-ton Master License, coastal waters. Rau continues to write the Boat Smart column with the Coast Guard. The popular column now reaches hundreds of thousands of readers through dozens of newspapers and magazines. Boat Smart is also distributed across the globe via the internet. In addition, Senior Chief Rau's 60-second Boat Smart safety messages have reached millions of radio listeners across the Midwest. For all his efforts, that include over 350,000 published words and hundreds of columns, he has never received a dime. Senior Chief Rau feels that if just one life is spared on the water from this effort, that is more than payment enough.

More of what others are saying...

"The Boat Smart Chronicles,' unlike many books, is not comprised of 'urban legend.' Instead, these stories provide real life examples of the ease in which an enjoyable day on the water can turn into a tragic life altering event! All those who enjoy the Great Lakes must include this book as required reading."

Lt. Earl W. Zuelke Jr. (ret)
Commanding Officer Chicago Police Marine Unit

"In 'The Boat Smart Chronicles' Tom Rau tells stories of wayward boaters so amazing that this book could be called Tom Rau's Believe-It-or-Not. Sadly, the stories are true. All hands on deck to read 'The Boat Smart Chronicles' before another boating season begins."

Steve Begnoche
Managing editor, Ludington Daily News

"Few books have ever told the story of the Inland Seas as such. This written compilation of honest, life-saving observations represents two decades in the making by a true sailor-turned-author. Senior Chief Tom Rau's stories will make you think, but foremost they could save your life. This book is that important."

David L. Barber
Managing Editor, Manistee New Advocate

"Boaters and landlubbers alike will truly enjoy the many stories of rescues with valuable lessons learned. A wonderful book from a man who knows what he's talking about."

Jim Shepard
Past Commander Grand Rapids United States Power Squadron
2003 Winner of the Charles F. Chapman Award for Excellence in Teaching

"Senior Chief Rau's words take you right into the heart of the storm. That he has been there so many times himself more than validates his message. This book is for real and if wise enough to follow its wisdom your safety on the water is all but guaranteed."

Donna Hallin
Division Captain 9th Central District, Division 20, U.S. Coast Guard Auxiliary

"The book not only offers life-saving advice for today's boater but for future generations of boaters and water enthusiasts. It is truly a timeless American classic much like Richard Dana's 'Two Years Before the Mast.' An absolute must read boater or not."

Paul Layendecker
Stations Manager, The Radio Stations of Southwest Michigan
Producer, Boat Smart radio messages

"Wow, can all these stories be true? You bet. As a former Coast Guard Motor Lifeboat Surfman, I know all to well about less than smart boating behavior. This book should be mandatory reading for every new boat owner before they're thrown the keys. I urge all boaters to read this book so as not to become yet another tragic 'Boat Smart' story."

Chief Boatswain Mate Anthony W. Fiore Jr., USCG (ret)
Fleet Captain Annis Water Resources Institute-Grand Valley State University